The Flight of
The Arctic Fox

The Flight of The Arctic Fox

Published by The Conrad Press in the United Kingdom 2021

Tel: +44(0)1227 472 874
www.theconradpress.com
info@theconradpress.com

ISBN 978-1-914913-00-6

Printed and bound in Great Britain by Clays Ltd, Elcograf S.p.A

Typesetting by The Book Typesetters,
www.thebooktypesetters.com

Cover Design by Terence Bannon
www.terrybannon.com

Viscount Illustration by Nick Webb, Classic-Airlines.com

The Conrad Press logo was designed by Maria Priestley.

The Flight of
The Arctic Fox

The true story of all those on board flight
BE142, who died in a tragic mid-air collision
over Italy.

Rory O'Grady

Dedicated to all those who died on BE142 over
Nettuno, Italy on October 22 1958

'sé ŗá mo ḃuaṙċa
It is the reason of my sorrow

To Christine,
I do hope you enjoy it.
Rory O'Grady.

By the same author

Stonecutters Bridge, Gateway to Hong Kong's Port
Bonham Media, Hong Kong 2010

The Passionate Imperialists
The Conrad Press, United Kingdom 2018

Contents

List of Plates

Fig 73. Memorial service at Nettuno 2018 with representatives of the Bannon, Bevan, Fogaty, Marshallsay, and O'Grady families.

All photos from the Bannon family collection unless otherwise stated

Maps

1958 Timeline

1958 Timeline January–June

January 1st: Harold Macmillan was Prime Minister
At the time of his death in 1986 aged 92, he was the
longest-lived Prime Minister in British history.

January 31st: First American satellite launched
Explorer 1 followed Sputnik 1 and 2, the first two Soviet
Union satellites launched in 1957.

February 6th: BEA Munich Air Crash
On the plane was the Manchester United
football team, along with supporters
and journalists.

March 24th: Elvis Presley drafted into the US Army
He received his discharge in1964.

March 26th: Best picture The Bridge on The River Kwai
The film directed by David Lean garnered seven
Academy Awards as well as three Golden Globe Awards
and four BAFTAs.

March 27th: Nikita Khrushchev Premier of Soviet Union
The Supreme Soviet voted unanimously to make First Secretary
Khrushchev Chairman of the Council of Ministers thus
recognising him as the undisputed leader of the USSR.

April 1st: Dwight D. Eisenhower was US President
"Ike" Eisenhower was a five-star general responsible for
planning and supervising the invasions
of North Africa and Normandy in World War Two.

April 17th: Brussels World Fair
Expo 58 was the first major World Expo.

**May 18th: USAF Starfighter F-104A set a world
speed record of 1,404.19 mph**
It was the first aircraft to hold simultaneous official
world records for speed, altitude and time-to-climb.

June 10th: UK's first parking meters
An hour of parking cost 6 old pence.

June 29th: Brazil won the World Cup
Brazil defeated host Sweden 5-2 to win
its first World Cup.

1958 Timeline July–December

July 26th: Prince Charles created Prince of Wales
He was invested by the Queen at Caernarfon Castle
at ten years of age.

**August 9th: Central African Airways
Vickers Viscount air crash in Libya**
Crashed east of Benghazi on approach to Benina Airport.

August 29th: The Notting Hill Riots
A series of racially motivated riots took place in Notting Hill,
England, between 29 August and 5 September 1958.

September 1st: The Cod Wars
The wars were a series of confrontations between the United
Kingdom and Iceland about fishing rights in the North
Atlantic.

October 4th: BOAC Comets cross the Atlantic
Two De Havilland Comets departed London and New York,
completing the first trans-Atlantic jet passenger service.

October 9th: Death of Pope Pius XII

**October 18th: First video game
Tennis for Two.** One of the first developed.

**October 22nd: BEA Vickers Viscount in mid-air collision
over Nettuno, Italy**

October 28th: Pope John XXIII elected
Angelo Giuseppe Roncalli Patriarch of Venice
succeeded Pope Pius XII.

November: Women sit in the House of Lords
The first women in the House of Lords took their seats forty
years after women were granted the right to stand as MPs in
the House of Commons.

December 21st: de Gaulle elected President of France
Justice Minister, Michel Debré became Prime Minister.

December 29th: Che Guevara Revolution
The Battle of Santa Clara was a series of events in late
December 1958 that led to the capture of the Cuban city.

Preface

On Wednesday October 22 1958, just before midday, flight BE142 was in the last twenty minutes of its flight from London to Naples, and about to descend from 23,500ft. to make its approach to the airport. My brother, Terry O'Grady, was one of the flight attendants on board the British European Airways (BEA) Vickers Viscount and he would have just started the initial preparations for landing. There were only thirty-one passengers and crew on board. It had been a relaxing journey and he was looking forward to an enjoyable visit to Malta, the final destination of BE142 that day. He would see his uncle and family for a day at the beach, swimming, eating and having fun.

The Vickers Viscount flying to Malta on that fateful day was named the *Sir Leopold McClintock*. That illustrious Victorian explorer was nicknamed *The Arctic Fox* after his famous expedition in search of Sir John Franklin, who died trying to find a route through the North West Passage in 1847.

Nobody knows what happened inside that plane in the last few moments but at 11.50, as it passed over the little medieval fishing village of Nettuno, an Italian Sabre jet fighter plunged from the clear blue skies above at 400mph, sliced off the Viscount's cockpit and exploded. The chances of that accident were one in a million. Given a few more seconds it would have been just another near miss. It is a day I have never forgotten, and can never forget.

Everyone dreads the knock on the front door to be told that a loved one has been involved in a serious accident. For some strange reason if that accident is an air crash, happening thousands of feet above the ground, the imagination goes into overdrive and the trauma feels that much worse.

I was eight years old on that fateful day, living in Bournemouth, Dorset. I had just returned from school at about four-thirty, and after tea my younger brother Sean, elder sister Rosemary, and myself, were sat down by my father and told of the accident over Italy, and that my twenty-two-year-old brother, Terry, was on board. Tears poured down my father's cheeks as he said Terry would not be coming home. We sat in shock and bewilderment, not just from the devastating news of the accident, but at seeing our disciplined, military father who we thought invincible, crying with such sorrow for the first time.

My father had been given the news a few hours earlier by a visibly nervous policeman, followed shortly afterwards by a visit from a young reporter from the local newspaper, the Bournemouth *Evening Echo*, requesting details and a photograph of Terry to go in the first edition the following day.

To make matters worse, my parents' marriage had been struggling. My mother, Molly, had stormed out of the house the previous day after another bad-tempered and heated argument with my father, as they struggled through the dying stages of the marriage, and we had no idea where she was. The day after the crash she was passing a newsvendor stall in the centre of Bournemouth and saw a banner headline on the hoarding, *Local boy killed in Air Crash*. She picked up the

Bournemouth *Evening Echo*, saw the picture of Terry, and collapsed. That is how she learnt of the death of her eldest son.

We were back at school two days later. It seems unthinkable now, but it was thought important that normality should be resumed as soon as possible. Some children of the victims on board the plane were sent back to school the following day. There was no such thing as counselling in schools in those days. If you were lucky you had an understanding teacher, but for most, the difficult task fell to a caring relative or the leader of your church, which was still attended regularly by the majority of people.

A large, emotional funeral was held in a packed St Peter's Church in central Bournemouth a few weeks later, and no children were allowed to attend. It was considered far too upsetting for them.

Grief was considered a private matter, and it was important not to upset others around you. It was only thirteen years since the end of World War Two and many families were still mourning the loss of loved ones during that conflict. It was considered inappropriate to inflict further sadness upon them. This bottling-up of emotions resulted in many mental and physical problems within the families over the following decades, mostly painfully endured with stoicism and the famous British stiff upper lip.

Life carried on, and for the next ten years my mother took my brother and I to the cemetery on the anniversary of his death to place flowers at Terry's grave, and if the weather was good, to have a picnic. Terry's photo always sat in the corner of the living room but he was rarely talked about. It was just too painful. My mother never recovered from the trauma, with a series of mental and physical problems leading to an early death in 1980.

Children are amazingly resilient. My brother and I absorbed these shocks, and somehow did reasonably well at school, lived rich and fulfilling lives and enjoyed successful careers. Over the years the memories of that awful time when I was little, faded, but were never forgotten, just filed away waiting to be rediscovered.

In September 2018 I received a phone call from my cousin Russell Kilmister, saying that Terry Bannon, the son of the radio officer on the plane, wished to contact me, to invite me to a 60th commemoration service in Italy. I was absolutely stunned and intrigued as the memories came pouring back.

The following month, my sister and I travelled to Nettuno and joined the ceremony with members from four other families, local dignitaries and the Commandant of the army base where the plane came down. It was a very moving commemoration service around the engraved granite memorial, which Terry had designed and had built by a local stonemason. After a good lunch I had a long talk to Terry.

He is a memorable character, an imposing figure, clean shaven, with a shock of white hair, full of ideas, a mischievous sense of humour, and mocking his seventy-odd years. He is as Irish as they come, stories gushing out, and passionate about whatever he is doing. In 2004 he decided he wanted to erect a memorial at the crash site, and started by walking into the Italian embassy in Dublin to see if it was possible. It was, and after travelling to Italy and gaining consent, he started his long search for other families. The memorial was completed in 2005 and a service was held, attended by the Mayor of Nettuno, army representatives, local townspeople, and Terry and his family. By 2018 Terry had accrued a substantial amount of information about the crash, and after talking to him, I realised how little I knew about it for all those years, and that what I had been told was full of errors.

During the course of that afternoon I talked with all the families to hear their story. Each was totally different, but as we were all children in 1958, we shared many similar emotions. We realised that the stories of all those on board had never been told, and I knew then that we needed to find as many relatives as possible, hear their stories and recollections of their loved ones, and write a book to honour their memory.

This would not have been possible even ten years previously in 2010. Thanks to the ever-increasing amount of information that is now available on the internet, we have been able to research and detail the lives of every person on the plane. We set up a group of researchers, including one in Australia, and dug through mountains of information on sites like Ancestry.com, census returns, service records, registers of births, marriages and deaths, passenger lists and followed our hunches. We contacted intrigued relatives all round the world, who then contributed to their story from their own memories and archives, often proving our original assumptions about their relatives completely wrong.

By 2020 we had found two widows and one widower still alive. There were brothers, sisters, nephews, nieces, grandchildren and great-nephews and nieces found all over the British Isles, Ireland, Italy, Malta, America, the West Indies, South Africa, and several in Canada and Australia.

We studied in detail the Inquiry Report issued by the Italian Republic Ministry of Defence in 1959 and found the verdict mystifying. After a lengthy deliberation it had concluded that the crash was '*Fatalità,*' translated as '*An Act of God.*' Various recommendations were put forward but there was no mention of the major communication problems that were occurring in Italy between military and civil Air Traffic Control (ATC) centres.

By the end of this journey it was the stories of those on board that shone through. For such a small number of random people, the diversity of the lives that these thirty-one souls on board BE142 had led is amazing. It is the contribution of the families that have turned this book from just another story of a tragedy with a meaningless list of names into an uplifting celebration of their relatives' lives. The stories can now be told to the younger members of the family who were not even born in 1958.

A few of the families have still not been found, but we will continue to search. Hopefully, they will hear about this book and we can include their contributions in the next edition, and maybe they will be able to attend the next gathering in Nettuno to celebrate the lives of their long-lost relatives. I also hope that if any of the Italian pilots are still alive that we can hear their stories, and those too can be included.

I.

FATALITÀ

I t is not known for sure how many passengers will travel on a flight until the plane doors are shut. There are last-minute cancellations and unexpected changes to people's schedules. Sometimes even those that have checked in do not show up, activating the standby list. There can be a medical problem with a crew member and a colleague stands in. This was certainly the case on flight BE142. Crew members Terry O'Grady and James Bannon were both asked to fly at short notice. A number of passengers made last-minute decisions to travel or changed their itineraries, including Charles and Diana Cubitt, who delayed their honeymoon by twenty-four hours after their wedding the previous day.

The thirty-one people on board came from all walks of life, with a wide variety of tales to tell. Amongst the passengers there was a well-known fashion model, accompanied by two press reporters and a photographer on their way to cover a story in Naples, various businessmen flying out to meetings, several military personnel, an American heiress and her British husband starting their honeymoon, a Canadian couple on their way to get married in Italy, and a few wealthy people travelling to the Mediterranean to take a holiday in the late summer sun.

The five crew members were a highly experienced team.

Captain Frank Foster was a senior captain with BEA, an ex-RAF pilot with nineteen years flying experience, twelve years with BEA, an international gold medallist at the gliding World Championships in 1956, and was an expert in aviation safety.

First Officer Geoffrey Wright trained with the Royal Air Force, had flown jet fighters in civil conflict in Yemen, and had been with BEA one year. He had been married for two and a half years to his childhood sweetheart.

Radio Officer James Bannon from Dublin had joined the RAF in 1935. He was an experienced navigator, saw action in Singapore during World War Two, and was planning to leave BEA to start a new chapter in his life.

Rosemary Bevan had worked as a flight attendant for BEA for nine years, had travelled extensively and after this flight was going on a long sightseeing holiday in Europe, to the places she had flown to but never seen.

Terry O'Grady had been a flight attendant with BEA for a year, but was within a month of achieving his ambition, to gain his pilot's licence.

There was one group of four passengers travelling to Naples together to cover a potentially scintillating scoop for the *Daily Sketch.*

Fashion model Jane Buckingham was on her way to a showdown meeting with her playboy prince boyfriend in Naples. Features writer Paddy Watson was there to look after Jane and to write the scoop with freelance reporter Lee Benson. Highly regarded photographer Brian Fogaty would capture the event as it unfolded.

There were three couples on board the plane that day.

Charles Cubitt and his American heiress wife Diana who had only been married a day.

William and Margaret Buchan were successful farmers from Gloucestershire looking forward to a well-earned holiday in Capri.

Mary Mathieson was probably a Canadian spy, and flying with fellow Canadian Robert Allan to Naples, then travelling on to Rome to get married.

Several friends and colleagues were flying together.

Lady Jenny Weir and Frances Miller were flying to Naples then taking a ferry to holiday on Capri.

Colston Luxton and Robert Bruce were friends and both worked at BEA, taking the opportunity to travel together, although with different final destinations.

John Prince and Reuben Silburn were colleagues at BP and on their way to Libya for important oil concession negotiations.

The remaining passengers were travelling alone.

John Booth was flying to Malta to discuss a new construction contract with the brewery company in Valletta.

Robert Chalmers had just started his National Service. He was the youngest person on board the flight, just nineteen years old, and on his way to visit his family in Valletta for a few days before being posted to Cyprus.

Arnold Davies was an hotelier living in Devon, and off on a holiday to Naples.

Richard Golden was a young Irishman in the Fleet Air Arm

and had been posted to Malta. He had proposed to his girlfriend the night before catching the plane.

George Kimble was a popular senior sales manager for BEA on his way to Malta for a sales conference.

Sheila Lane was a dedicated nursing sister in the Queen Alexandra's Royal Naval Nursing Service, serving at RNH Bighi in Malta.

Mary Vassallo La Rosa had just received hospital treatment in London and was heading home to Hamrun, Malta.

Garth Marshallsay was a young air traffic controller completing his National Service in Malta before starting a new life as a novitiate priest.

John Vella had recently undergone successful treatment for throat cancer at the Royal Marsden Hospital and was returning home to his adored family in Qrendi, Malta.

Lastly, Eveline Yuille, was a young nurse working at Worthing Hospital and looking forward to her first visit to Italy.

These thirty-one people would never have imagined what lay before them as they made their way to the airport early that October morning,

By half past seven that day the sun had risen, and Captain Frank Foster and his First Officer Geoff Wright were carrying out the final exterior checks of the plane, on the fuselage and engines. It was Frank's responsibility to sign these off and he took it very seriously, as he did with all safety matters. He was meticulous. It had been mild and frost-free for the last few days so there was no danger of ice on the wings.

This was often on Frank's mind after the tragic BEA air-crash at Munich on February 6 that year in which two crew members and twenty-one passengers lost their lives, including eight players of the Manchester United football team, affectionately known as 'The Busby Babes'. The captain of the flight, James Thain, was one of BEA's most senior and experienced pilots, and Frank Foster knew him well. The tragedy and ongoing appeal continued to receive a lot of publicity.

On February 6 1958 flight BE609, piloted by Captain James Thain, was returning from Yugoslavia where Manchester United had just knocked out Red Star Belgrade in a quarter-final of the European Cup. The flight from Belgrade was heading for Manchester and had stopped at Munich Airport to refuel. Captain Thain was anxious to stay on schedule, and despite the deteriorating weather with snow forecast, considered that as the runway was over a mile long, he could still safely reach take-off velocity if they departed straight away. At 15.03 the plane taxied slowly down the runway. It quickly gained speed but never reached the take-off velocity needed for lift-off. The wheels had hit a heavy build-up of slush, the plane slowed, skidded off the end of the runway and crashed through a fence, crossed a road and hit a house before bursting into flames.

Later that evening the first British newspaper photographer flew in from London. He was Brian Fogaty, working for the *Daily Sketch,* and would be a passenger on BE142 eight months later.

At the subsequent inquiry the West German airport authorities blamed Captain Thain for not checking and clearing ice from the wings. He vehemently denied this saying that the checks were carried out, and that there was no ice at that time, and put the blame firmly on the airport authorities for allowing deep slush to build up at the far end of the runway. The inquiry panel concluded in favour of the airport authority.

By October 1958 an appeal was ongoing but the arguments as to the cause of the fatal crash would continue for another eleven long years. It was not until 1969 that Captain Thain was finally exonerated by a British inquiry ordered by the Prime Minister, Harold Wilson. Meanwhile, James Thain was sacked from BEA, and he and his family suffered terrible persecution while he fought to clear his name. He never flew again and died of a heart attack in 1975 aged fifty-three. Senior airline captains had a grim saying, 'If the accident doesn't kill you, the inquiry will.'

Just after eight o'clock Jane Buckingham, Paddy Watson, Lee Benson and Brian Fogaty were the last passengers to board, and only just made it before the doors were slammed shut and locked. They were greeted by the flight attendant, and their coats taken and hung in a closet near the front exit opposite the pantry, and ushered to their seats.

In the cockpit the pilots were filling in the last-minute details on the Load Sheets, finalising the amount of fuel required from London to Naples. The last few items of heavy luggage were stowed away in the baggage hold, including a large diplomatic bag. The flight attendants walked slowly up the aisle checking that hand-luggage was safely stowed under the seats – only hats and umbrellas were allowed in the small, open luggage racks at that time – and everyone's safety belts were checked. There were ten rows of seats, with three seats on one side of the aisle and two on the other. With only twenty-six passengers on board, just over half full, the pre-flight checks took less than five minutes. Terry O'Grady returned to his seat near the front exit and buckled his safety belt, and Rosie Bevan checked the one toilet at the rear of the plane, and sat in her usual seat adjacent to the rear exit.

Captain Frank Foster radioed air traffic control (ATC) confirming that they were ready to leave and at 08.41 the Viscount pulled out of the parking bay and taxied to the top end of the runway. The four Rolls Royce Dart engines roared into action and within a matter of seconds accelerated the aeroplane down the runway to maximum take-off speed. At full thrust the nose gently lifted into the clear blue sky.

It was a beautiful, sunny October morning and the plane quickly climbed to its cruising height of 22,500ft. turning south towards northern France. Geoff Wright sat to the right of Frank Foster, and James Bannon sat in the corner with his back to Geoff. They were all ex-RAF men, an experienced crew entirely confident in each other's skills and abilities, and quickly fell into an easy routine.

As soon as they reached cruising height, the captain introduced himself and his crew on the radio after a welcome to all those on board, and ran through the route, the weather they could expect during the three-hour flight, and the estimated time of arrival in Naples of 12.10 GMT. He apologised for the slight delay in taking off, but hoped to make up the sixteen minutes with favourable weather and winds. That would be his last communication with the passengers.

Within half an hour, a freshly cooked breakfast was

produced from the small pantry adjacent to the front exit and was being served by the flight attendants. The plates, cups and saucers were all porcelain, the cutlery was silver, and the fruit juice was served in glasses, all neatly arranged on a wooden tray with a napkin, and carefully placed on the flip-down table in front of the passenger.

As there were only ten rows, everyone was in the same class, but the front rows were favoured with a little more attention, including Lady Jenny Weir and her friend Frances Miller, and the happy newlyweds, Charles and Diana Cubitt.

After breakfast was cleared, the passengers settled down to chatting, reading or dozing. There was no in-flight entertainment in 1958, and passengers paid more interest in the scenery below them and their fellow travellers. For those passengers flying for the first time the experience was exhilarating.

By 10.30 they had travelled down the eastern side of France, across the western part of Switzerland just east of Geneva, and had entered Italy. Throughout the flight the weather had remained fine and they had made good progress with an estimated speed of 300mph. As they entered Milan air space, Captain Foster asked James Bannon to radio Milan ATC to request clearance to climb to 23,500ft. which was granted. They were heading towards Rome, which was always busy, and at that height there would be less traffic before starting their descent towards Naples.

At 11.11 James radioed Rome ATC confirming their position and that they would stay at 23,500ft. flying towards Naples. They were cleared by Rome to continue to Naples via the Ostia and Ponza air beacons.

Jane Buckingham was sitting next to the *Daily Sketch* features writer Paddy Watson, and behind them were freelance reporter Lee Benson and photographer Brian Fogaty. It is likely that they had enjoyed a couple of cocktails and the conversation focused on how to maximise the publicity created by the showdown between Jane, the glamorous model, and her playboy boyfriend Prince Shiv. They needed to agree their strategy for the confrontation with the prince when they arrived in Naples. It was just over an hour before they were due to land, and while Jane was getting nervous, the seasoned reporters were looking forward to the fireworks ahead.

At 10.45 twenty-eight-year-old Captain Giovanni Savorelli took off from the military airbase at Pratica di Mare near Pomezia, approximately twenty miles north-west of Anzio, on a routine flying exercise. He was leading a formation of four F-86E Sabre jets, including his own, on a group tactical training exercise in the eastern part of Area Number 15 specifically reserved for the 4th Air Brigade for NATO training. The area was prohibited to civil aircraft.

The other three Italian pilots were younger than him and less experienced, and had been looking forward to this morning's exercise. They were Vittorio Carone, Giorgio Giannotti and Siro Sari.

The American-built Sabre was a well-tried and tested swept-wing jet used by the United States Air Force since 1948. It was capable of a maximum speed of 675mph, and had excelled in the bitter and bloody Korean War from 1950–53. Improvements had been made to the flight control system since the war, increasing its manoeuvrability at high speed.

After approximately an hour of exercises the four pilots started the last phase of the training flight. This was to be a complex manoeuvre called the *Chandelle* which results in the plane turning 180 degrees to go back on its original course. At 25,000ft. the four planes formed a single line configuration called Indian file, about 150ft. apart. They dipped down to 20,000ft. before climbing on a 320-degree right-hand turn back up to 25,000ft. A final steep dive vertically downwards to 20,000ft. would complete the sequence, when they would level out and fly on a horizontal path in the direction from which they had come. A complex manoeuvre like this at high speed required total concentration from all the pilots.

Captain Savorelli led the formation of jets to start the manoeuvre, unaware that flight BE142 was less than ten miles ahead of them and approaching rapidly.

At 11.44 the weather was fine, with clear skies, perfect visibility for over ten miles and little wind. The sun was almost at its zenith. The Viscount reached the Ostia beacon, and Captain Frank Foster sent his last message to Rome ATC, '*142 Roger. Checking over Ostia flight level 23.5. Estimating Ponza 57.*' Rome confirmed they should reach Ponza beacon by 11.57. The two flight attendants would have been starting initial preparations for landing, with an estimated arrival time at Naples of 12.17, only seven minutes later than scheduled.

Just before 11.50, Captain Giovanni Savorelli turned into the final, fatal dive, accelerating to 400mph, and seconds later hit the Viscount at an angle of approximately twenty degrees from the vertical. The left wing of the Sabre struck the nose of the Viscount, slicing open the top of the cockpit and disintegrating the wing of the Sabre. The right wing of the Sabre struck two of the propellers of the Viscount, detaching one of the engines. Within a tenth of a second the fuel tank in the wing of the Sabre exploded, blowing the wing off the Viscount.

The crew of the Viscount had no idea that the Sabre was approaching from directly above them. All those on board would have lost consciousness immediately from the violent decompression caused by the initial impact and nearly all died instantaneously in the massive mid-air explosion.

The remains of the fuselage of the stricken Viscount spiralled slowly down to earth, scattering its contents like confetti over a wide area before it plunged into a field in the middle of a military base near the small town of Nettuno, a few miles from Anzio.

Miraculously, Captain Savorelli was catapulted out of the cockpit of the jet by the force of the impact, as his F-86E disintegrated around him. In the vertical dive he never saw the Viscount, so had no time to eject himself from his seat. The ejector seat cartridge was later found still in place. His emergency parachute had somehow opened and he floated down to land in a tree close to the main debris, seriously injured. His ejector seat landed close by.

When he came round in the hospital he remembered nothing of the catastrophic collision.

The pilots in the three Sabres following Captain Savorelli

desperately swerved to avoid the extensive debris and smoke swirling in all directions. From their witness statements given later that day at the military airbase, it was clear that for the three young men the incident had been like a nightmare unfolding before their very eyes.

Pilot Siro Sari was number two in the formation and witnessed the collision. '...*I suddenly saw a multi-engine plane collide with the plane of my leader. The impact produced an enormous flame. Due to the collision happening so fast, and I was such a short distance away* (approximately 150ft.), *I could not avoid flying straight into the cloud of smoke and debris. My plane was not responding correctly to my commands...*'

He struggled to keep control and flew back to the Pratica di Mare airbase, circling round the control tower so they could visually check if his badly damaged plane was fit to land. He was severely shocked.

Pilot Giorgio Giannotti was number three in the formation. He was 300ft. behind the leader and did not see the collision so clearly. '...*For an instant I saw the shape of a multi-engine plane, and straight after, smoke and debris. I sensed a collision between my leader and the plane, and instinctively pulled right to avoid pieces of the plane...I communicated what happened to the tower and once I had obtained the positions of No2 and No4, I circled the zone and noticed a parachute opening at 10,000 feet...I circled around the floating parachute and could also see pieces of the plane in the same area (*on the ground*). After I saw the parachute land on a tree in the zone south of Tre Cancelli, I noted the position of the multi-engine plane wreckage. I radioed back their positions and thereafter flew back to the base.*'

Pilot Vittorio Carone was number four in the formation. He was 450ft. behind Captain Savorelli at about 24,000ft. when the collision occurred. As he was diving down he saw an enormous flame corresponding to the trajectory of his leader, and sensed there had been a collision with a plane. '...*I moved immediately to my right and started to circle over the spot... noting the wreckage from the planes. Later I saw a parachute, and watched it descend. I had the impression that it was being pushed by the wind away from the land towards the sea. I saw plane No3 had also seen the parachute and was now following it. I therefore went to take a closer look at the condition of plane No2 which was damaged and having some trouble. I landed at 13.10 (12.10 GMT) about ten minutes after the collision.*'

Captain Savorelli was transferred to Rome and was in hospital for many months. In March 1959 he was able to make a statement for the inquiry. It concluded, '... *I now entered the area reserved for the 4th Air Brigade east of Terracina, and as we were five minutes away from the base (I remember checking the clock and saw that it was 12.45 [11.45GMT]). I ordered the team to move into a single file in order to use the remaining time for the diving phase of the manoeuvre. From this moment I cannot recall anything else. My next memory is in Nettuno hospital, with no recollection of what had happened.*'

The explosion was also witnessed by some staff at the Pratica di Mare airbase, and two passing aircraft, one military and the other an *Alitalia* passenger plane, who reported seeing black smoke near Anzio. Repeated transmissions were sent by Rome ATC to BE142 until 12.04 but there was no reply.

All air rescue services in the area were alerted.

2.

THE CREW

The Captain
FRANK FOSTER

F rank Foster's greatest passion in life was flying. If he wasn't flying commercial airliners he was gliding or preparing for the next gliding competition. He was a world class glider pilot, winning a gold medal in the 1956 World Glider Championships in Saint-Yan in France.

It was probable that gliding that was on his mind when he left his home early on the morning of Wednesday October 22 1958, and drove to London Airport to captain flight BE142 to Naples and Malta.

Frank was born on March 29 1919 in Steyning, a small town in West Sussex close to Ditchling, where he spent his childhood. It was an idyllic rural setting, living with his parents Edmond and Grace and his younger sister, Edna.

Ditchling, just north of Brighton in the shadow of the South Downs, is a perfect spot for gliding. The Southdown Gliding Club was established in 1930 but dates back to 1909 when sixteen-year-old Gordon England flew a short distance in a machine made from wood and string from Amberley Mount, near Storrington, and is one of the oldest gliding clubs in Britain.

Frank's father was a carpenter in Ditchling, at that time an important centre of the Arts and Crafts movement. A large artistic community had moved there under Eric Gill, with painters, sculptors, weavers, printers, carpenters and silversmiths creating some of the most beautiful pieces of practical art of the time. From an early age Frank was fascinated by the variety of strange flying machines he saw swooping across the Downs and over Ditchling Beacon. He had been told of the International Gliding Competition that had been held at nearby Itford Hill sponsored by the *Daily Mail* newspaper in 1922, when a world record of 3hr 21min was set by Frenchman Alexis Maneyrol to stay aloft in his Peyret tandem monoplane.

In 1930 a group of enthusiastic amateurs formed the Southdown Gliding Club. As a teenager Frank helped move the planes and equipment, all the time watching and learning. In 1936 a dinner and ball was held to raise money for a new club house, attended by the Mayor of Brighton and Hove, and Gordon England. He was invited to take a flight in the club's two-seater glider which had been positioned at the end of the ballroom! The event was a great success. Southdown membership increased, races expanded with other clubs, and competitive flights commenced across the English Channel to France.

In 1938 the club was flying from Wilmington near Eastbourne, and teenage Frank was taking his first flying lessons. He was an eager pupil and by the end of the year he had gained his pilot's licence. He had also gained an admirer, a local eighteen-year-old girl from Shoreham-by-Sea, Helen

Patricia Humphrey (always called Pat). An attractive, vibrant girl, Pat was also keen on gliding and the two met whenever they could.

This idyll came to an end in September 1939 with the outbreak of World War Two. Frank was twenty years old and keen to join the Royal Air Force to fly. He wasn't interested in being a hero, just in staying alive, and applied to train as an instructor. After passing an assessment test in 1940, Frank was sent to Brize Norton Flying Training School (FTS) where he earned his wings, and then to RAF College FTS Cranwell for a Flying Instructor's course, which included mastering the art of aerobatics. He finished his training at FTS Cranfield.

The casualty rate for pilots during the Battle of Britain in the summer of 1940 was very high and left the RAF short of qualified fliers. An intensive recruitment campaign was launched to train pilots from the Commonwealth. Frank was first sent to an Elementary Flying Training School (EFTS) in Southern Rhodesia (now Zimbabwe) to begin their instruction. The trainee pilots were given fifty hours of basic aviation instruction on a simple trainer plane like a Tiger Moth. Those who showed promise went to advanced training at a Service Flying Training School, on fighter and multi-engined aircraft.

Frank grew a fashionable moustache to hide his youth, as many of his students were his age or younger. Conversations recorded after the war with some of these pilots in *Flight* magazine remembered him as a fine instructor.

In 1941 Frank was transferred to South Africa, to No.6 Training School in Potchefstroom in the Transvaal flying Tiger Moths. A group photograph shows him sitting in the

middle of his pilots and South African officers, eve.
wearing shorts and sporting fine tans, looking seriously into
the camera. In 1942 he was posted to 21 Air School at
Kimberley where he was stationed for nearly two years.

The war turned in the Allies' favour, and Frank was briefly
sent to RAF Aqir in Palestine. In 1944 the situation in
Palestine had begun to deteriorate, with sabotage carried out
by Jewish terrorists waging a violent campaign for the
foundation of a new Jewish state. The RAF brought in
Lancasters and Halifaxes, and established the Glider Pilot
Regiment equipped with Horsa gliders. Later that year Frank
was sent to 37 Squadron at Foggia in southern Italy, flying in
Vickers Wellington bombers for Transport Command.

While Frank had been abroad with the RAF, Pat had been
working as a catering manager, and they had kept up frequent
correspondence. As soon as Frank arrived back in England he
proposed to her, and they were married on June 21 1945 at
St Margaret's Church in Ditchling.

Frank looked impeccable in his RAF uniform, and Pat
looked exquisite, dressed in a heavy, white-crepe wedding
dress with a Limerick-lace veil, and a stunning pearl necklace.
She held a beautiful bouquet of lilies and red and pink roses,
and smiled radiantly. Frank's sister, Edna, and Freda Spence
were her bridesmaids, and Pat was given away by her brother.
The reception was held in Ditchling and Frank and Pat spent
a blissful honeymoon at a hideaway in the New Forest in
Hampshire.

Frank was demobbed from the RAF a few months later and
on December 12 1945, he joined the *British Overseas Airways
Corporation* (BOAC). This was a British state airline formed

in 1939 with the amalgamation of *Imperial Airways* and *British Airways Ltd.*

BOAC had continued civil operations during the war, but by 1945 its aircraft were out-of-date. The corporation was locked in difficult negotiations with the American company Lockheed to buy their Constellations, which were pressurised, for which there was no British equivalent. The size and design of these planes would enable BOAC to fly new Australia and trans-Atlantic routes.

Frank joined BOAC as a First Officer in 1946 and by the end of the year he was already promoted to Captain. A further celebration that year was the birth of Pat and Frank's daughter, Carol.

British European Airways (BEA) was originally a division of BOAC but on August 1 1946 it became a crown corporation in its own right, first operating out of Northolt and Croydon, and then in 1950 moved to the new London Airport.

In 1946 BEA began flying to Europe, North Africa and the Middle East. Frank was seconded to BEA soon after it started operating and flew Dakotas to Madrid and Athens via Marseille and Rome. He was also flying Vickers Vikings and Elizabethans. These were piston engine airliners, faster than Dakotas but just as noisy. There was no such thing as comfort in those early days – the concept of luxury travel was some way off!

Frank and Pat's priority was to find a house to live in. Frank had a full flying schedule so he needed to be close to Northolt and the new London Airport. It also needed to be within easy reach of a gliding club, so the London Gliding Club (LGC) based near Dunstable would be perfect, and they looked for a property in north London. The problem was that during the war years it had been very difficult to save, but now that Frank had a permanent job he could get a small mortgage from the bank, enough to buy a plot of land and build his own house. This would also ensure he had enough money each month to keep gliding.

He found a small piece of land on the outskirts of Chalfont St Peter, ideally located between Northolt and Dunstable, and drew up plans for a house. While the house was being built, the family lived at Hedgerley, near Farnham Common. Pat looked after Carol full-time, with Frank travelling frequently, and in his spare time he worked on the house. Pat found the pressures of adjusting to motherhood difficult, but the outlet for them both was gliding. By 1947 Frank had become chief flying instructor at Southdown and he taught Pat to fly, and that year they also joined the LGC in Dunstable.

The LGC had been inaugurated in 1930 and it used Ivinghoe Beacon as a launch site. On September 12 the famous Austrian glider pilot, Robert Kronfeld was giving demonstration flights, and Edward, the Prince of Wales decided to pay a visit. Crowds flocked to see them and blocked all the surrounding roads. The police were overwhelmed, and the club had to move to its present location on Dunstable Downs, taking their fans with them.

During the war the LGC ceased its gliding activities and was used as a small prisoner of war camp. It was handed back in 1946 and the enthusiastic amateurs returned, constructed a new clubhouse, and gradually installed all the equipment required to launch and maintain a fleet of gliders.

In 1939, a young pilot called Geoffrey Stephenson was the first to glide across the English Channel from Dunstable to France. Frank and Pat joined the club at a time when some hugely talented pilots were members, including Geoffrey, with whom Frank became great friends.

In 1947 Frank entered the National Gliding Championships held at Bramcote in Nottinghamshire as a member of the LGC team in a *Slingsby Gull*, and they came twenty-first out of twenty-six. In 1948 the World Championships were held at Samedan in Switzerland, the first since the end of the war. Ten nations entered thirty-seven pilots, with Britain entering five, captained by Mrs Ann Douglas (later Welch).

Frank finished fourth out of twenty-nine in the 1950 National Championships flying a *Rhonsbussard*. He flew as often as he could, honing his skills and techniques. Pat supported him whenever she could, driving, winching and hauling the glider into position. Carol had also been involved at an early age – even as a baby she was used as a counterbalance on the wing! Every flight was different depending what the weather had in store, and the pilots never stopped learning.

In 1951 he came fifth out of thirty-four, again in a *Rhonsbussard*, which was one of the worst performing gliders in the competition so an excellent result, and contributed to him being chosen for the Great Britain team in the World Championships in Madrid in 1952. Geoffrey Stephenson and Frank were part of the five, British single-seater entries chosen to fly in the new British-designed and manufactured *Slingsby Sky* sailplane, which had been unveiled at the Festival Exhibition on the London South Bank in 1951. For the first time the planes had built-in anti-icing and oxygen equipment, and walkie-talkie sets. They could at last communicate with their ground crews.

Frank did well in the practice, getting up to 17,000ft. in a thunderstorm, but on the first day of the contest disaster struck when he was caught by a violent wind shear only 150ft. before landing, and hit a telegraph pole. The plane was badly damaged but luckily, Frank escaped serious injury. The team wasn't placed but Philip Wills took first prize, in a *Slingsby*. Hanna Reitsch, a German pilot, was the first woman to compete.

In 1950 BEA transferred to a new terminal building at London Airport, the Queens Building, opened by Her Majesty Queen Elizabeth. Frank completed the house in 1953 and the family were able to move into *Upwind* in Ellis Avenue. Life was more comfortable, and at last they were seeing rewards for all their hard work.

Until 1950 Frank was still flying the noisy Vickers Vikings and Elizabethans. In 1953 the first order of Vickers Viscounts arrived. They were turboprops, much quieter, with considerably less vibration, much to the delight and comfort of the crews and passengers – no more holding onto your drink after it was served! For the next two years Frank concentrated on training himself and his crews on this impressive new aeroplane that would dominate his life for the next five years, but still found time to compete in the Camphill Nationals coming third out of thirty-four.

Frank missed out on a place in the 1954 World Championships held in England at Camphill, Great

Hucklow in Derbyshire, but all the family attended as support crew living in a bell-tent for two weeks. The competition was opened by Lord Brabazon of Tara on July 22, who welcomed the nineteen different nationalities in five languages. Heavy rain rolled in constantly from the Atlantic Ocean and Philip Wills was lucky to come second in his *Skyplane 2*. A new instrument was introduced at this championship, the Cook compass, which had all the advantages of a gyro-compass but could be used in blind flying.

At Dunstable Frank met fellow pilot, Nick Goodhart and the two men soon realised they would make a good team. Nick was a Royal Navy officer, the same age as Frank, who finished his career as a Rear-Admiral. Over several months they spent many hours of practice in the air in the *Slingsby T-42B Eagle*, and it paid off. Nick and Frank were selected for the British team in the two-seater class for the World Championships in Saint-Yan, France that summer, which would run from June 29 to July 13 1956. Nick was the P1 pilot in the front and Frank was the P2 pilot behind.

Saint-Yan is halfway down France, 35 miles north-east of Vichy in the Bourgoyne region. Some competitors, including Nick, arrived by their own planes but most of the British team, managed by Ann Welch, drove through France towing the gliders and equipment in sturdily built Standard Vanguard cars provided by the Standard Motor Company. Sixty-three competitors came from twenty-nine nations including the USA, Poland, Hungary, Czechoslovakia and Japan. The majority of the British party arrived on June 24 along with most of the other teams, except the Polish, who nearly missed the entire event when they were detained at their own border!

Around 500 pilots, mechanics, meteorologists, managers, family and friends converged on a temporary village of marquees and chalets. All the competing nations' flags waved from flag poles in the breeze. Rows of bell-tents were erected by the French army to accommodate the pilots and support teams over the next two weeks. The French organisation was superb and the competitors were warmly welcomed to Burgundy.

During the first few days, the crews busied themselves with preparations for the competition, familiarising themselves with the local and regional maps, analysing the weather briefings and studying the complex and ever-changing air masses over France. There was initial disappointment that the area around Saint-Yan was so lush and green, which was bad for the air thermals needed to lift the gliders, but they need not have worried. An exciting fortnight of racing lay ahead. The following pages are descriptions of that competition from magazine reports and film commentary made at the time. It illustrates just how skillful these pilots were at flying in the most challenging conditions.

The opening ceremony on Friday June 29 was led by Monsieur Duveau, the Under Secretary of State for Merchant Marine, with much flag-raising, and national anthems. Speeches were made and there was an impressive fly-past by the French aerobatic team, *The Sky Blazers* – a team composed of four F-86E Sabre jets, the same type of jet that Frank would tragically encounter two years later.

The competition started the following day with a free-distance race. A squadron of French *Stampe* biplanes lined up and towed the gliders to an altitude of 2,000ft. Within an hour they had all been released into the skies above Saint-Yan. The wind was blowing from the south-west driving the gliders north-east towards the Swiss frontier some 230 miles away. To achieve a greater distance you had to take a northerly bearing, which the winner took, achieving a total of 268 miles. Many gliders landed before 75 miles, but Frank and Nick traversed Dijon managing 122 miles, placing them in eighth position. It was a slow start for them, but a good test for the new Pye radios they used to communicate with their back-up team led by Ann Welch. Within hours of landing they were picked up and returned to Saint-Yan.

Many pilots took nearly twenty-four hours to return to base camp, so the start of the second race, a goal-race to St Etienne 62 miles south, was delayed until 14.30. Within two hours they flew into an advancing, large thunderstorm and the pilots tried to manoeuvre to get up inside it to catch the turbulent thermals. An Argentinian pilot rose to 26,000ft. At that height all the instruments freeze up, and the pilots needed oxygen. Continuous flashes of lightning and rolls of thunder cascaded around them. Several times Frank and Nick found themselves flying blind, but were surprised, relieved and delighted when they emerged out near St Etienne, moving them into third place.

Two days later the third race started. This was on a fixed bearing south to Cuers, near Toulon on the Mediterranean coast, a distance of 262 miles. A mistral wind had started blowing from the north at 35 knots, welcomed by many of the pilots, and anticipated nervously by others. They crossed the Rhone valley with a series of ridge-hopping manoeuvres, catching the thermals, but the currents fluctuated wildly and it required a great deal of skill to keep the glider flying. At one point Frank and Nick rose an exhilarating 3,000ft. in five minutes, and reached a maximum height of 8,800ft. They were rewarded with a magnificent view over the snow-clad Alps lit by a dazzling red, setting sun. Although none of the two-seaters made it to all the way to Cuers, Frank and Nick had flown enough miles to move them up into first place.

The fourth race was a triangular route from Saint-Yan, south-west to La Palisse, south-east to Roanne and finally north back to Saint-Yan, a total of about 75 miles. To their great disappointment, the wind had dropped and many pilots huddled around the same thermals, struggling to get round. Frank and Nick slipped back to third place.

The fifth race was another free-distance. This time the wind was blowing from the west at 23 knots up to 2,000ft, where it switched to a northerly direction, blowing many gliders towards Switzerland, only 95 miles away. Others took the more challenging route of heading south towards Avignon, and they flew the furthest. Frank and Nick flew to Switzerland, out of a col in the Jura Mountains, which follow the France-Switzerland border, across Lake Geneva and returned into French territory clocking up 111 miles, enough to regain first place in their class, with two more races to go.

The next couple of days were much-welcomed rest days, and everyone took the opportunity to relax. The French fired up barbeques and provided some entertainment which revived the bodies, spirits and determination of pilots, and restored the exhausted back-up teams.

Race six was declared a no-contest as there were only minimal thermals, but as the distant, dark clouds began to mass, the prospects looked good for race seven, a goal-race to Moulins, 34 miles west-north-west of Saint-Yan, and back. Frank and Nick flew up the Loire Valley then rose inside the approaching, towering cumulonimbus cloud. Ann Welch listened to the blow by blow account in awe as she stood by the Saint-Yan radio mast. Frank and Nick's glider was sucked up by the powerful swirling vortex from the bottom anvil of this massive storm to 17,000ft, then plummeted down 10,000ft. to 7,000ft. to arrive at Moulins. The two pilots returned to Saint-Yan exhilarated, having flown a distance of 63 miles, enough to retain first place with just the final race to come.

At 2am on the morning of the last race, Frank and his team were awoken by a raging northerly gale that had them rushing out of their tents to lash down the trailers. By sunrise the wind had abated a little, but the forecast indicated that the mistral was still blowing at 40 knots on the ground and an incredible 70 knots at higher levels. The final goal-race would be one that many would never forget.

This was a 188-mile race south-east to St Auban, near Nice. On take-off the mistral was still blowing cold, maritime air from the north. The pilots had to get below the base of the cloud, lift rapidly into it, through turbulence, and descend into the next valley to start again. When they reached the Alps near Mont Ventoux, the sky cleared, and powerful thermal waves generated 70mph winds above the summit, enabling the pilots to reach speeds of a breathtaking 80mph. The fastest average speed was 40.7mph. Frank and Nick climbed to 14,000ft, battled with turbulence and hit speeds over 70mph. They flew a distance of 100 miles, coming in second, but with enough points to win the two-seater title outright.

One of the American pilots, Bill Ivans, from California, wasn't quite so lucky. He hit turbulence under a base cloud and was forced down a narrow mountain valley. A down draught caught him, and he went into a high-speed stall, crash landing in a small field. His *Olympia* craft was badly smashed and Bill damaged a vertebrae. Luckily, a Swedish pilot had witnessed what happened and landed nearby. He helped Bill out of the cockpit, and a military helicopter flew him to an American base in Germany. Despite the crash, Bill still came fifth in the tournament!

After a much-needed day's rest the closing ceremony was held on July 13 to bring an end to the 1956 Championship. Even that day had drama – a thunderstorm struck halfway through the proceedings and the awards ceremony was completed inside the marquee. The winner of the single-seater class was an outstanding American pilot, Paul McCready, who was over 1,000 points ahead of Spain and Poland, and had broken many records during the competition.

Frank and Nick stood proudly on the podium to receive their award as winners of the two-seater class, with the British national anthem playing in the background. They won with 3,828 points, nearly 700 points ahead of the excellent Yugoslavia and Argentina teams. Frank was surrounded by warmth and friendship, and was congratulated by some of the best pilots in the world. It was the greatest day of his life.

The closing ceremonies were followed by a riotous party, and a release of all the stress and tension they had undergone in the previous fourteen days. Six lambs were barbequed and copious amounts of food and local wine were produced as the celebrations and singing, (especially from the American team) continued late into the night. The bonhomie that united the pilots from all the competing nationalities was an acknowledgement of the talents that had been used to overcome the many challenges that Mother Nature had thrown at them. The gliding fraternity was a close-knit, international community where friends were made for life.

The following day was July 14, Bastille Day, and further celebrations continued in the Sporting Club in Vichy, where the Mayor and city officials congratulated the crews and supporters on a fantastic competition. There was another grand dinner, and a firework display brought a spectacular end to the fortnight, with everyone looking forward to the next tournament, due to be held in Poland in 1958.

Frank did not make it to the 1958 championship, but he remained one of Britain's best glider pilots. He returned to Chalfont St Peter, life reverted to normal and he resumed his job, flying all over Europe and to the Middle East with BEA on a busy and expanding schedule.

He was now one of BEA's most senior and experienced captains. He was an air safety expert, and ironically, was a member of a committee set up to study ways of avoiding mid-air collisions in crowded airways. There was concern that the development of air traffic control equipment and systems had not kept pace with the increase in air traffic.

On June 23 1957 Frank found time to set a British speed record round a 100km. triangle from Dunstable averaging 48mph. At around this time, Pat was starting to experience bouts of depression which sometimes required periods in hospital, so Carol was sent to boarding school.

When Frank arrived at London Airport on October 22, he parked the car and headed over to the plane to carry out the usual pre-flight checks with Geoff Wright, his First Officer. Shortly before take-off he was asked to go to his manager's office. A military attaché from the Admiralty in London was waiting for him and handed him a highly confidential package with instructions that it was not to be let out of his sight until he reached Malta. There it was to be given to another naval military attaché from the Malta naval base. Frank took off to Naples with the package by his side in the cockpit.

On the day of the crash Pat was alone at home in Chalfont St Peter and Carol was away at boarding school. On hearing the news, Pat was completely traumatised, and collapsed. She was rushed to hospital for treatment.

Carol was eleven years old when she was told the news by her headmistress, who took the decision to confine Carol to school, and refused to allow her to attend the funeral. She was also not allowed to return home, and was later told that she would stay with her grandparents for the Christmas holidays. Pat was eventually discharged from hospital and returned home, but she never fully recovered from the tragedy.

There were many mourners at Frank's funeral, but only a few from the family. Carol never forgave the headmistress for refusing her the opportunity to say goodbye to her father. At that time it was not unusual for children to be treated that way, in the mistaken understanding that it was somehow best for the child.

There was a moving obituary from Nick Goodhart which included: *'Frank was a well-loved personality who will be sadly missed by many. Flying was in his blood, for apart from his deep interest in his work as a senior BEA captain, he devoted much of his spare time to gliding...it is perhaps fitting to remember that he died as he lived – in the air.'*

A Frank Foster Memorial Fund was established by the British Gliding Association and The Frank Foster Boomerang Trophy is still awarded in his name every year. There is also an annual trophy awarded by the London Gliding Club in Dunstable.

Despite all that happened, Carol continued gliding at Dunstable and a few years later went solo there. Later she moved to the RAF gliding club at Bicester, and qualified as an instructor. She emigrated to South Africa, married, and continued gliding with the Johannesburg club, eventually becoming the Club Secretary. Carol is still an enthusiastic member of the South African gliding community to this day.

Her father's passion for flying continues.

The First Officer
GEOFFREY WRIGHT

Flight BE142 was scheduled to take off at 08.25 on the morning of October 22 1958. It was an early flight but the airport was not far from his house in Cranford, west London, and Geoff Wright wanted to arrive in plenty of time for the all-important pre-flight checks. He was flying as First Officer with Captain Frank Foster, one of the most senior pilots in BEA, and very safety conscious.

Geoffrey Brian Wright, (always called Geoff) was born on September 10 1933 in Boxted, a small village about five miles from Colchester, Essex, fourteen months after his brother, Stuart.

His father, Gordon Whiles Wright was born in 1909 in Lambeth, London, and had started work as a groom and coachman in the 1920s at a large house in Essex. One of his jobs was to drive the family to the town each week, which he did, generally too fast! He married May Davis in the summer of 1931. In the 1930s he took up commercial gardening and worked in the fruit orchards near Colchester until the end of a beautiful summer in 1939.

With the announcement of World War Two on September 1 1939, Gordon signed up for the Royal Army Service Corps and because of his expertise working with horses, he was assigned to the 1st Mountain Regiment. It was a unit that had been specially created to work alongside the infantry brigade in mountain warfare. Working in rugged, hostile terrain, inaccessible to motorised vehicles, horses and mules were indispensable as pack animals, carrying large amounts of ammunition and supplies, and were trained by specialist muleteers. Eventually all the regular mounted regiments stationed in Britain, other than the Household Cavalry, were motorised and the animals were gradually replaced with armoured cars.

Gordon underwent arduous training in the mountains of Scotland and Wales to prepare for the Allied invasion of Italy. The build-up to the assault began with *Operation Husky*, the invasion of Sicily in July 1943 designed to take back the island from Fascist Italy and Nazi Germany. Six weeks later the Allies launched their three-pronged assault on Italy. The Mule Corps in Italy had the manpower of more than five divisions, and over 30,000 mules working to keeping the supply chains open across the Apennine Mountains of Italy. As the Allies advanced further across the mountain range, mules were bought from locals as they progressed. The slow-moving, lighter animals were too easy to spot by the enemy, so they preferred to use those of a dark colour. The lighter animals were camouflaged by spraying them with potassium permanganate! One dramatic record left by Sergeant J. Tuvey of the 85th Mountain Regiment recounted a trek over the mountains to Ripiano in 1944, which gives a feel of the challenges they faced.

'The train consisted of forty mules, twenty Italian muleteers, five British soldiers and myself. We loaded the animals with mortar bombs, machine gun ammunition, rations, wireless spares, and most important of all, rum!...We started about 14.15 with great heavy clouds overhead...far in front we saw other mule trains crawling like ants over the mountains. The going was

very hard in the mud, nobody spoke, and all you could hear was the jangling of the harnesses and the squelching of the mud. It was just about dark when suddenly there was a short whistle and a crump and we realised the first mule train was being well and truly stonked... The shelling didn't last long and after a few minutes we started forward bending into the rain, the darkness as black as ink so you only just see the mule in front...At the top of the ridge I fell over dead bodies of both German and American soldiers, then the mud got thicker and deeper and it reached up to my thighs. A hundred mules and men were feet deep in mud in a horrible tangled mess. Mules were lying everywhere kicking and shooting their loads. Finally, after what seemed an age, still with the fear of being shelled, we pulled out the men from the mud, assembled the mules and got going again towards Ripiano. I still had the rum!'

It was a long, hard campaign, with Gordon promoted to Sergeant and mentioned in dispatches for distinguished service.

Aged only six and seven, Geoff and Stuart were evacuated to Cornwall soon after war was declared, and they spent the entire conflict billeted with a family in the relative safety of the West Country. Being away from their parents, it was a difficult and traumatic experience for many children, often separated from their siblings, and although there were many who enjoyed the experience, not all the foster families welcomed the city kids, some of whom had never been to the countryside or ever seen a farm animal in their lives. The children missed their families and were often homesick, despite visits from their mothers during the school holidays. Geoff and Stuart had the advantage of being together, sharing their new experiences and supporting each other. They attended the local primary school and quickly adapted to their new life, playing in the fields in summer and picking fruit in the autumn. After six long years their father returned from Italy and the family was finally reunited at home in south London.

The years immediately after the war were harsh. The conflict had shattered the economy and destroyed much of the infrastructure of the country. While the bombed-out cities were slowly rebuilt, the population endured a shortage of food and many of the basics of living. The rationing of food, fuel and clothing lasted until the early 1950s, work was scarce and money was tight, and Gordon often had to move around to find work. Many children lost parents in the war and became orphans.

Gordon and May wanted to add a daughter to their family and in 1946 they adopted a young girl called Molly, whose parents had been killed in the war. Like so many children, she had been through a traumatic time and found it difficult to adjust and settle with her new family. The boys were glad to be back in London and returned to school in Balham, where they progressed well in their studies. They were both lean and fit and enjoyed sport, especially swimming. Every weekend they would spend hours in the heavily-chlorinated, blue-tinted water of the public baths in Streatham, diving, racing, playing games and showing off to any girls interested. It was here in 1948 that they first met eleven-year-old Pamela Holland, (always known as Pam) who later went on to play a significant part in both their lives.

In 1946, Winston Churchill, who had led the country

through the war, declared that *'an Iron Curtain has descended across the continent.'* The Cold War that followed was a time of ideological struggle between capitalist United States of America and communist USSR. When the Soviet Union developed its first atomic bomb in 1949, the world was thrown into fear of a global nuclear catastrophe. The Korean War started in 1950 when North Korea, supported by the Soviet Union and China, swept into South Korea heading for Seoul. It was the beginning of a conflict that sucked in many countries from the United Nations. The threat from the east accelerated the development of faster, more sophisticated jet aeroplanes which, in Britain, included the formation of a V-bomber nuclear force consisting of 180 Vulcan, Victor and Valiant bombers, aircraft that required 2,000-yard-long runways. The world was a dangerous place and Britain needed a new generation of pilots.

The appetite for young men to join the armed forces however was waning. The training in flying and aeronautical engineering took two years and there was a drop-out rate of up to fifty per cent. To attract more applicants the RAF introduced an eight-year short service training commission.

Geoff and Stuart were both bright and competitive, excelled at school and passed their final exams with top grades. Both boys had developed a keen interest in flying, and applied together to train as pilots at the RAF College Cranwell. They passed the rigorous selection process that tested candidates both mentally and physically, and were accepted for entry on the same day, December 19 1951.

The college was founded on November 1 1919, eighteen months after the formation of the Royal Air Force to train officers and aircrew. Training initially took place in old naval huts, but after lobbying by Sir Samuel Hoare, the present day neo-classical College Hall was built. The foundation stone was laid in 1929 and it was officially opened in October 1934 by the Prince of Wales. During the war the college was re-designated as the RAF College Flying Training School, (which Frank Foster attended in 1940) and it returned to its former function in 1947.

The brothers would have been picked up from the small railway station at Cranwell by a single-decker bus to take them to the college. The first glimpse of the college is impressive, with a 240-metre colonnaded façade. Striding through the impressive iron gates they may have seen training jets circling overhead, setting their pulses racing. The following day they would have been measured up for their blue cadet uniforms, with the distinctive white bands around their hats and white flashings on their lapels. These had to be kept well pressed, along with perfectly-buffed boots and shoes and polished buttons and buckles. You had to see your reflection clearly in the peaks of the hats. Strict discipline was instilled from the outset, along with a short but intense period of basic training on the parade ground. In addition each cadet would take an oath to the Queen and country.

The next two years for 'the Wright Brothers,' as they were quickly christened, were an intense period of learning and testing. They attended lectures on the basics of flight and advanced to studying all aspects of flying and aeronautical engineering. They were allocated individual tutors who oversaw their learning and who could also assess the strengths and weaknesses of their students. Leadership qualities were looked for but it was just as important to have a balance of skills within the teams. Flying experience started early in the first year in piston-driven Provosts or Chipmunks. In the second year the young pilots were allocated to a group called a 'wing,' which they stayed with for the duration of the course, and they gained further flying experience on different types of jets. An important, nervous day came when they were allowed to do their first solo flight, just one circuit of the aerodrome.

The men were encouraged to participate in a wide range of sports and were sent on courses in the mountains of Scotland and Wales to test their survival, leadership and team-building skills. A monthly, formal dinner in the mess, attended by senior officers, developed and tested their social and political skills. The final year was dominated by intense periods of flying, including their first taste of aerobatics, which tested their flying skills to the limit.

Their academic studies now included military history and strategy, taught by lecturers from the RAF, the Royal Navy and the Army, the civil service and universities. Training at Cranwell was tough and only the very best succeeded. Inevitably some did not last the course, but Geoff and Stuart came through with flying colours. Many of the young graduates became friends for life.

They received their commissions in 1954 in front of a large crowd of guests and proud families with much marching and pageantry, and an inspiring speech from a dignitary warning of the continuing dangers of the Cold War.

On June 2 1953 the historic coronation of the young Queen Elizabeth II took place in Westminster Abbey,

London. To celebrate the occasion, the RAF organised a massive review at its base in Odiham, Hampshire, attended by thousands of dignitaries. It was the largest display of military air power ever seen. Over 300 aircraft were assembled for a royal inspection by HM The Queen and HRH the Duke of Edinburgh, followed by the greatest fly-past ever seen in RAF history.

A helicopter led the display towing the RAF ensign, and was followed by 650 planes, including eighty Gloster Meteor jets, twenty-nine Vampire jet fighters, Venom fighter-bombers, sixty Sabre jets (flown by Royal Canadian Air Force pilots), delta-winged Gloster Javelins, and a two of the latest V-bombers, the Victor and the sinister and distinctively-shaped Vulcan bomber. The amazing spectacle was shown on *Pathé News,* and there is no doubt that Geoff and Stuart were either eagerly watching on television, or may even have been there on that momentous day. On graduation from Cranwell, Geoff and Stuart were allocated to different squadrons, both flying Gloster Meteors.

After World War Two, Britain's influence over global matters began to wane. By the mid-1950s the British Empire was disintegrating and many of its colonies were keen to accelerate their independence. India had raised its new flag on August 15 1947. From 1948 to 1960 Chinese communists infiltrated Malaya and a state of emergency was declared to fight the insurgents. In 1952 the Mau Mau rebellion in Kenya lasted eight bloody years and inspired other African countries to push for their own independence. Local freedom organisations emerged to actively fight against their colonial administrators, with riots, civil destruction and frequent assassinations.

The tiny port of Aden was a Crown Colony on the tip of Yemen and became sucked into anti-Jewish protests after the creation of Israel in 1948. Riots swept through the colony fanned by migrants who had infiltrated from Yemen bringing subversive political ideas. In 1948 a new Yemeni imam repudiated a 1934 treaty with the UK and started supplying arms to rebellious protesting tribes.

In 1954 there were a series of disturbances in the tribal area of Wadi Hatib. The tribesmen were bombed by the RAF but hostilities increased again in the spring of 1955. In July Fort Robat was abandoned and the insurgents levelled it. The RAF base at Khormaksar became the busiest station in the RAF. Geoff's squadron was sent out to Aden and he experienced his first tour of action. For six months the insurgents were bombed frequently, but they were fighting a well-organised guerrilla war and the area became too difficult for the RAF to defend.

At the end of his tour of duty Geoff returned to the UK and he visited the family in London. There he met Pamela again, who was now nineteen years old and had developed into a beautiful young woman. She was bowled over by the tall, dashing, handsome, moustached, young pilot with tales of derring-do and danger. Their romance blossomed and they were married in a joyous celebration at the Church of St Leonard in Wandsworth on May 19 1956.

Although Pam was a young woman, she had learned to

cope with many difficulties in her short life while living in south London. Her father was a musician and was constantly in difficulties both financially and emotionally, causing all sorts of problems for the family. He had died when she was still young. In Geoff she at last found stability and looked forward to sharing a wonderful new life with him.

However, she listened to Geoff's tales of his adventurous time in Aden and was anxious every time he flew a jet fighter and worried about the dangers of being shot down. She knew how much he loved flying, but feared becoming a widow with a young child, and begged Geoff to leave the RAF and pursue his career instead with a civilian airline, where she felt there was less risk.

By coincidence, in 1956 BEA was expanding rapidly, opening up new routes to Europe. It was having difficulty finding experienced pilots to fly its growing fleet of aeroplanes and approached the RAF with a proposal to release some of their short service commission pilots early to join the company. Geoff could see the potential for this exciting new industry and requested an early release to join BEA. It was granted in October 1957.

Pam was overjoyed and they moved to a house in Cranford, West London, located on the busy A4 trunk road but ideal for London Airport. Geoff started intensive training again, this time on Vickers Viscounts. He had to become familiar with a whole new raft of Health and Safety regulations covering the transportation of civilian passengers, and become an expert on the visual checks of the aircraft he would be flying, something that would normally have been done by his mechanics. The world of civil aviation was very different from the military, but because many of his fellow pilots were also ex-RAF, he felt quickly at home.

On the morning of October 22 1958 the final flight checks were completed. Captain Frank Foster signed off the Flight Plan and load sheets, and completed the final fuel calculations ready for the short flight to Naples. With only twenty-six passengers on board, there were no weight issues, indeed, they would save on fuel. Shortly before take-off, Frank was asked to go to the office and returned with a package which he had been instructed to keep in the cockpit, and tucked it behind his seat. They waited for the last of the passengers to board and Geoff noted the interesting collection of passengers they had for the flight. These included the wife of a knighted businessman, a well-known model and an American heiress on her honeymoon. At 08.41, just sixteen minutes later than scheduled, they were given clearance to leave, and flight BE142 headed towards the runway ready to take off.

The previous night, Stuart had woken up in a cold sweat and with a horrible feeling that something was wrong, a fearfulness which he could not explain. The following afternoon, on October 22 the police called at the house in Cranford, but Pam was out. It was a few hours before she was found and told the terrible news, that her husband's flight had been involved in a catastrophic mid-air collision over Italy, and there were no survivors.

The funeral was held in South London a few weeks later. Surrounded by a profusion of flowers and bouquets, Gordon and May comforted a heartbroken Pam, and Stuart. Representatives from both the RAF and BEA joined the family and friends to show their respects. In the following traumatic weeks and months, Stuart and Pam supported each other in their overwhelming grief, trying to come to terms with the loss of a loving husband, younger brother and best friend.

In early 1960 they married and had two children, Grahame and Deborah, and enjoyed a long and happy marriage. Stuart gave up flying and moved into Air Traffic Control, travelling to many parts of the world, working in an industry for which both he and his brother had a common love.

The Radio Officer
JAMES BANNON

On October 21 1958, James Bannon, (always known as Jimmy) was at home in Dublin with his wife Harriet (Harry) and their two boys Liam and Terence, getting ready to fly back to London. Feeling slightly under the weather, Jimmy had complained that he had a cold coming on, and if it got worse he would see the BEA doctor.

The previous night he had taken Harry out for a drink at his favourite pub *The Old Stand* in Wicklow Street, where they had been joined by his brother Bill and his wife Monica. The brothers hadn't seen each other for a few years and they enjoyed catching up and exchanging the latest photos. Not a long session, but pleasant nonetheless.

Back at Jimmy's house they had a nightcap and Jimmy mentioned to Bill he was thinking of a change. They discussed the possibility of opening up a small business together in Dublin. Bill and Monica left around midnight hoping to see them again soon.

The next morning Jimmy felt slightly better and made the decision to go. He kissed Harry goodbye and left the house at one o' clock to catch the train to Belfast, connecting with a BEA flight to London, a flight he had done hundreds of times.

When Jimmy was in London he stayed in a comfortable, three-bedroomed flat in Ruislip, Middlesex, which he shared with two BEA pilots. Early on October 22, before dawn, he closed the door with a lot on his mind. There were rumours that BEA was going to start phasing out radio officers, so maybe now was a good time for a change. He had built up a reasonable annuity with BEA and certainly enough for a small business, maybe even enough to buy a small car.

Jimmy was forty-three years old, and his two sons were still at school in Dublin, so he could not afford to be out of work too long. In the taxi on the way to the airport, he wrote a short letter to Harry saying he was feeling much better, and had been asked to stand in for a flight to Malta via Naples. It was an easy run and he would be back in Dublin on Saturday. He posted the letter when he arrived at the airport.

Jimmy was born in Barnsley, Yorkshire on April 5 1915 during World War One. His Irish father, James was trained as a skilled blacksmith and farrier, originally working with an engineering company in Dublin, travelling around farms sorting out any metalwork issues. After falling foul of a union dispute in 1913, James had to move to England and went to Barnsley. He worked as a farrier in the coal mines, which still required horses for the heavy labour of hauling coal in the pits deep underground.

When war broke out in 1914, James volunteered as a sapper in the Royal Engineers. As the mindless slaughter continued in the trenches in Europe, the Army needed more sappers to dig tunnels under the enemy lines, and James was sent to France. In 1916 at Fricourt in the Somme he was injured by an exploding mine and gassed. He received a small disability pension in 1918, but due to the insidious effects of chlorine gas on his lungs he died from pneumonia in 1919. His grave bears a Commonwealth War Graves headstone. Jimmy's mother, Catherine was left to bring up the five children, Jimmy, Bill, May, Ben and Joseph Patrick (Paddy).

These were desperate times. The stress brought on illness and in 1929 Catherine died from cancer, leaving the children orphans. In 2000, Bill's son-in-law, Pat Macken requested the War Graves Commission to have Catherine's name inserted on the headstone, which it duly did. In 2003 the Bannon family travelled to Barnsley and were at last able to lay a wreath for Catherine.

As so often happened in those days, the siblings were split up. Jimmy was still only fourteen, so he was sent with Bill to live with his grandparents Patrick and Kate Breen in Cork Street, Dublin. Brother and sister, Ben and May, were sent to live with a relative in Manchester, and the eldest, Paddy was old enough to be given a passage to Australia, where he was sent to work in forestry.

Patrick Breen was a cooper in the Guinness brewery, so Jimmy was lucky to get a job there as a messenger when he left school at sixteen. These were difficult times and many men were out of work at the beginning of the 1930s depression.

Jimmy was ambitious and three years later in 1935, he saw an opportunity to join the RAF. A new generation of bombers was about to be introduced, including the Vickers Wellington designed by the brilliant Barnes Wallis, later designer of the dam-busting bouncing bomb. Jimmy enlisted in August 1935, initially trained as a gunner, but went on to also train as a radio operator. He had found his true vocation. He loved flying.

A couple of years earlier, Jimmy had met an attractive, eighteen-year-old Irish girl in Dublin called Harriet (always known as Harry) and their love blossomed. In 1939, as war loomed yet again, Jimmy and Harry were married in the Catholic University Church, St Stephen's Green in Dublin, with his brother Bill his best man.

Just before the start of World War Two, Jimmy was sent to Karachi, India, (which became the first capital of Pakistan in 1948) to train gunners in a squadron of old biplanes. He had mixed feelings. He hated to be parted from Harry, but at least in India he felt he had a better chance of surviving the war.

His fortunes changed dramatically when the Japanese bombed Pearl Harbour on December 7 1941. Japanese forces swept across the Pacific and down the Malay Peninsula with Singapore in their sights. In January 1942 Jimmy was with the retreating forces heading to Singapore with the Japanese close behind. He witnessed the cruelty that was being inflicted on the local people, and it left a deep impression on him. Only one week after landing on Singapore Island, the Japanese were attacking the garrison at the airport, forcing it to surrender on February 15 1942. Jimmy's plane was second to last out of Singapore, taking off in a hail of gunfire. One of the pilots was killed and Jimmy took his seat. It would be three years before Singapore was liberated. So much for Jimmy's quiet war.

Jimmy spent the next two years flying high-risk, dangerous bombing missions over Europe. The stress on the pilots was intense and on the rear gunner even more so, as he was the first target for the German fighter planes. It was also very cold, and he managed to acquire a silk parachute from which Harry made a fine pair of long johns for him. In 1943 he was relieved to be posted to RAF Ballyhalbert in Northern Ireland where he flew Sunderlands and Catalinas. Harry was able to join him, and their first son Liam was born on December 31 1944.

In 1945 he was sent to RAF Ross in Scotland, and on January 6 he wrote a very poignant and revealing letter to Paddy and his wife Cath in Australia. He started with warm greetings and looked forward to them all being together again. He wrote late into the night, reflecting on what he had gone through and that '*Wars are the pastimes of maniacs and greedy money grabbers, but unfortunately like measles it spreads and infects every part of the body willy-nilly. Wars wouldn't be serious if they could be confined to professionals like myself, with humanity paying an entrance fee. That entrance fee in the arena of Mars is a fee in blood, its own blood. However, things go on, and I aim to do whatever I can to be on the winning side. I much prefer Herr Schmidt's wife and child to be on the losing side than Harry and Liam. This war isn't a game of God helping whoever loses, but it won't be my fault.*'

Jimmy's experiences in Singapore affected him profoundly and he considered just how lucky he had been to return home safe and sound. He had been promoted to Flight Sergeant in April 1943 and continued in a more upbeat tone, '*I may qualify for a commission, can't say yet, but it looks like my dearest ambition may never be realised. I'm a chap who is positively happy only when flying. I find myself singing with delight, especially if I am safely behind a couple of guns…*'

He hated the separation from Harry and Liam, and phoned Harry at least once a week pining to go home. He could not wait for peace.

On October 22 1946 Jimmy finally got his discharge, and the following year he joined BEA as a radio officer. He was back where he wanted to be. Flying. At that time BEA were flying noisy, propeller-driven Vickers Vikings and Elizabethans. The number of flights was rapidly increasing as Europe slowly recovered from the war, and the airports were expanding.

In 1948, the crisis in Berlin came to a head, and when the Russians cut off the city, the airlift started. BEA was part of the international effort flying food and provisions to the beleaguered city. It was a dangerous time with aircraft often overloaded and there was a fuel shortage. They were harassed by the Russian airforce, and one BEA Viking was brought down after a collision with a Russian fighter. There were no survivors.

On September 1 1948 Jimmy and Harry celebrated the arrival of Terence, a long-awaited brother for Liam. It was a good time for the family as they started to prosper, and looked forward to a bright future.

By 1950 Jimmy needed a base in London, so he teamed up with two BEA pilots to share a large, three-bedroomed apartment in King Edward Road in Ruislip, Middlesex. There he stayed for the next eight years. The flat was ideal for getting to the airport, and Jimmy could return to Dublin every three weeks to be with the family. In the summer holidays they could come over to Ruislip and spend time in London.

The arrangement worked well, and the children enjoyed a happy, stable childhood. They remembered their father's strong, lined, clean-shaven face, hair swept back and parted in the middle. He was a lanky, lean, softly-spoken man, with a good sense of humour, who could be very funny. He always enjoyed singing and playing the piano.

In 1953 BEA introduced the quieter and more comfortable Vickers Viscount, especially welcomed by Jimmy, who'd had to put up with a cramped corner in the cockpit. The routes were being expanded and he was flying to all the capital cities of Europe, plus Cyprus and Bahrain.

In April 1956 Nikita Khrushchev paid a state visit to Britain. A new Viscount 701, registration G-ANHC was chosen to ferry the entourage around the country and Jimmy was one of the crew.

On June 18 1956, an excited and proud Harry made sure Jimmy's uniform was immaculate, and she straightened his tie before he left on a particularly special flight. He had been chosen to be part of the crew for a Royal Tour. That memorable day, HM The Queen and HRH Princess Margaret came aboard the same Viscount G-ANHC and they were flown from London to Stockholm for a royal visit to Sweden under the command of Captain W. Baillie.

Two years later, on that fateful October morning, Harry did not know that Jimmy was going to be flying on that very same plane in which he met his tragic end in the clear blue skies over Nettuno.

On October 22, Harry heard of the crash on the Radio Eireann news at 1.30pm, only an hour and a half after it occurred. She had not yet received Jimmy's letter he had sent from the airport, so was desperately hoping he was not on board. She walked two miles to the two boys' school in Synge Street to take them out and prepare them. She then went to her sister's house nearby and phoned BEA. They confirmed the worst.

On arriving back home at Rathmines with the boys a few hours later, the press were already on the doorstep waiting to ambush them. Insensitive and crass questions were hurled at them as they battled to get back into the house.

After the crash, Jimmy was flown from Rome to London. His brother Bill, two brothers-in-law James Halford and John Lovatt, and Kevin Gibney, an old friend from the war years, met the coffin in London and accompanied his remains to Dublin. He was taken to the Mary Immaculate Catholic Church in Rathmines, in south Dublin for the funeral.

BEA pilots, radio officers, flight attendants, colleagues, friends and family came from afar. Many were in uniform, with six forming a guard of honour outside the church. They later escorted his coffin, three either side, to the grave for the final farewell. It was a day with no religious differences, only their common sorrow for the loss of a good friend and loving father, Jimmy Bannon.

Forty-eight years later, in 2006, Terry Bannon made a pilgrimage to Italy to see the unveiling of a memorial which he had designed and was erected at the crash site in Nettuno. The ceremony was attended by dignitaries from the town, representatives of the military base, local people, some of whom had witnessed the crash, Terry's extended family and Jimmy's brother, Bill.

The Flight Attendant
ROSEMARY BEVAN

Rosemary left her flat in Kensington, London, shortly before sunrise on October 22 1958 looking forward to the flight to Naples and then the short hop to Malta. This would be her final trip before taking a well-earned three months leave.

Rosemary Lucy Bevan (Rosie, as her friends called her), was born in Westminster, London in October 1922. Her mother, Lucy came from a banking family based in Essex. Her father, Major Reginald Bevan had served in the 1st King's Royal Rifle Corps in World War One and had been badly wounded, and was being cared for at home. It was a large, comfortable, detached house near Chelmsford, shared with her sister Veronica, who was five years younger.

At the age of eleven, Rosie was sent to school in London. She was an average scholar and enjoyed English literature and music. She left school at sixteen and completed a secretarial course just before the outbreak of World War Two in September 1939. The family had moved to Kensington earlier that year but they were bombed out of the house during the relentless air raids by the Luftwaffe on London in 1940. Her parents moved again, out of London. Veronica stayed at boarding school at Ascot, and Rosie, like thousands of other young girls joined the Women's Royal Naval Service (WRNS).

She was sent to work at the top-secret establishment at Bletchley Park in Buckinghamshire, where a small army of women were helping the mathematicians and science boffins, including the famous Alan Turing, break the encrypted German codes. This work was crucial to the war effort, but Rosie found it extremely tedious and wanted a change.

1942 was a traumatic year for Rosie. Whilst working at Bletchley her father died and she was very distraught. A friend of the family helped her through this awful time, and after compassionate leave she was posted to Portsmouth to take up a job in the dockyard.

Many women went to work in the factories during the war, taking over the jobs of the men who had been sent to the battlefields. In Portsmouth dockyard, there were 3,000 women working out of a total workforce of 25,000. Despite suffering massive bomb damage from the Blitz, 2,548 ships were refitted or repaired during the war. In the dockyard, women were not employed in the heavy work, but in welding, electric and light machining, which required dexterity and lightness of touch, and always supervised by men.

Despite Rosie's privileged background, she decided to train as a welder, to work on the many damaged ships limping back to port scarred by mines or brutal naval battles. The conditions would have been dirty, noisy and uncomfortable, but the pay as a skilled worker gave her the opportunity to save some money, and become financially independent. Many women enjoyed this part of their lives. They were playing a vital role in the war effort. They took pride in their accomplishments and enjoyed the comradeship at work.

The war in Europe came to a close in 1945, and in 1946 Rosie applied for a job with a European organisation which set up catering facilities for some of the many British regiments stationed in West Germany. The Nazi threat was defeated, but the Cold War had commenced with the USSR. One of Rosie's passions was horse riding and this could be one of the reasons she chose to work with Army regiments stationed on the Rhine. She also wanted to learn to ski and there were resorts in the nearby Alps which would have been easily accessible.

By 1951 Rosie was twenty-nine and ready for a change. She returned to England and applied for a position with BEA as an air hostess, as they were then called. With her experience in catering and travel she was ideally qualified, and readily accepted the offer in this rapidly expanding company. Now she could combine all her interests and be paid for it.

BEA was constantly adding to its flight destinations. In 1952 the company carried one million passengers for the first time, and in 1953 started flying the first turboprop Viscounts. Rosie was flying from London to Paris, Rome, Madrid, Copenhagen, Prague, Athens and as far as Bahrain. It was a hectic schedule but she was visiting places she yearned to see. She adored the Mediterranean.

In June 1956 she was delighted to be one of the crew on the Queens's flight to Stockholm, for the state visit to Sweden. Travelling with the royal party, which included HM The Queen and HRH Princess Margaret, did not overawe Rosie at all, and BEA selected her again the following year for another royal visit to Europe.

By 1958 Rosie was an experienced crew member, reliable and popular with her colleagues. She lived in a comfortable flat in

London she shared with her good friend, Moira. She was attractive, outgoing and good company. She enjoyed the company of men, but she was also a private person who valued solitude, relishing experiencing things on her own, and wanted to hold on to her independence.

Little did Rosie know that as she boarded the Viscount to start cabin preparations on October 22 1958, she would never reach Malta that fateful day.

Her mother received a very moving letter shortly after the crash from a Czech admirer, (possibly a pilot, one of the many that fought alongside the British in special RAF Czech squadrons). He wrote, *'I knew Rosemary best from her letters and they are now a very dear possession to me. She did not speak easily about herself, but she was a gifted writer... I read a description of Prague so full of deep understanding and reactions which can only originate from a noble soul of tender feelings and with comprehension for human suffering... It is my sincerest conviction that Rosemary will never be forgotten and the memory of her will remain for me an additional bond to England, a country which many of us Czechoslovaks learned to love and admire during the last war when we fought with you side by side.*

Also from Rosemary's last letter dated October 19, I would like to quote you another line she wrote: "Peace, perfect peace, with loved ones far away." That is me tonight. Everybody is away and I have no one to consider but myself. Do not ask me where that quotation came from, but I am very fond of it.'

Ironically, that is a line from a beautiful Victorian hymn written by Edward Henry Bickersteth (1825–1906) that was popular at funerals and still brings comfort to many today.

A moving funeral mass was held for Rosie at Brompton Oratory in London in November 1958. So many staff from BEA were there that day that her sister Veronica wondered if there were any staff left to fly the planes from the airport.

Rosie was just thirty-six, and is buried near her father and mother in Fryerning, in Essex.

Fifty years later, her family was able to pay homage to her at the moving 60th commemoration ceremony held in 2018, very near to the crash site in Nettuno.

The Flight Attendant
TERENCE O'GRADY

On October 21 1958 Terry O'Grady was summoned by his landlady to answer the telephone in the hallway of his modest bedsitter in west London. The call was from the BEA office asking him to stand in for a steward, (or flight attendant as they are now called) who had phoned in sick that morning. The flight was BE142 flying to Naples the next day, which would then fly on to Malta. He accepted immediately. The extra money would enable him to complete his flying lessons to get his pilot's licence, and achieve his dream. It would also be a good opportunity to see his uncle Phil and family again, who were living in Malta.

Terence Michael O'Grady was born on December 31 1935 in Bournemouth, an attractive seaside town on the south coast of England, popularised by the Victorians looking for a healthy spa away from the pollution of the smouldering industrial cities. Bournemouth would be important to Terry his whole life. His father Claude, (always known as Pat) was Anglo-Irish and an RAF pilot who had led a most interesting life. He was born before the flight of the Wright brothers and lived long enough to fly in *Concorde*. His mother Evelyn Mary, (always known as Molly) was from a talented Anglo-Welsh family who had travelled widely.

Pat's grandfather was Patrick O'Grady, born in March 1842 in Kilrush, County Clare. This area of south-west Ireland experienced some of the worst horrors of the Irish Potato Famine when a million Irish died of starvation and disease after the potato crop repeatedly failed between 1845 and 1851. Patrick escaped Ireland by joining the British Army as a boy soldier with the 11th Regiment of Foot, and was sent to Exeter in Devon where the regiment was based. He married in his early twenties and served in the Army for over twenty years as a corporal. By 1879 he was widowed and at the age of thirty-seven he met and married Elizabeth Benney, a young widow from Exeter. Patrick retired from the Army and together they ran the Eagle Tavern in the town. Their only son Albert Michael was born there in 1880.

Albert followed in his father's footsteps in the Army, signing up for the King's Own Scottish Borderers (KOSB) at the age of fourteen, initially for twelve years, and served in the Second Boer War in South Africa between 1899 and 1902. When he returned he went to Newry, County Armagh in the north of Ireland, where he met Annabella White, who came from nearby Bessbrook, and they married in 1904. Their first son, George was born in Colchester the following year, and after the regiment was sent to Egypt, Pat was born in 1907 in Cairo as the Army horse-drawn ambulance taking his mother to hospital crossed the bridge over the River Nile.

Pat's family led an itinerant life with the Army in his early childhood, moving every few years, first to the North-West Frontier in India, where his Indian amah taught him Hindi, then to Dublin and finally in 1918, to Edinburgh. Despite the disrupted schooling, Pat did well under the Scottish education curriculum and achieved excellent results. Seventy years later he could still recite American poetry learnt at school. He had high ambitions, declaring at the age of fourteen he wanted to be a pilot or a brain surgeon, much to the consternation of his father, who wanted him to join the Army.

He won a scholarship to RAF Halton in 1921 where he learnt how to build early wooden biplanes and exceeded in all subjects. From there he won a place to RAF College Cranwell in 1925, and once again excelled. A fellow student in his year was a shy but brilliant engineer called Frank Whittle, who was already developing his ideas on the turbine engine which his lecturer said were impossible. There was also an irritating Leading Aircraftsman who was going under the name of Shaw, but everyone knew was T E Lawrence, (Lawrence of Arabia) researching for his next book.

Pat developed into a tall, handsome young man, competitive, a good sportsman, ambitious and popular. He graduated in 1927 and for the next five years was posted to various RAF stations around Britain to gain experience, and he became an expert on armaments.

The RAF was the youngest of the military services, having only been established in 1918, and attracted an interesting cross-section of individuals, from eccentric earls to bright, young, working-class boys, all drawn to it by their fascination of flying. For the RAF it was the men's ability that counted, not which family they came from. These were the days of the magnificent men in their not-very-reliable flying machines, and crashes and deaths were common. Pat crashed five aircraft and obtained some interesting scars to prove it. The young men worked hard and partied harder. It was the Roaring Twenties and people enjoyed a hectic social life before the Great Depression started in 1929. They were heady days.

In 1931 Pat was posted to Egypt to survey and photograph the deserts of the increasingly unstable Middle East from unreliable biplanes in the early days of aerial photography. It was ground-breaking work, and there was always the risk of being shot at while waiting to be rescued, lying in the shade of the wing of your broken-down plane. Despite a heavy schedule, the pilots still managed to squeeze in some sightseeing among the ancient and historical sites in Egypt. (The tomb of Tutankhamun had been discovered nine years earlier in the Valley of the Kings by Howard Carter.) They also made a memorable trip to Jordan to visit the spectacular, 'Rose City' of Petra by camel, the only transport available at that time.

In Cairo they would go sailing on the Suez Canal in the traditional felucca boats, and at one gathering in 1934 Pat met Molly Kilmister, an attractive, vivacious girl with brown, curly hair and hazel eyes, who looked and acted older than her seventeen years. She was born in Ceylon, (now Sri Lanka) when her father Clive was based in Colombo running a tea plantation in the hills above Kandy. By 1934 the family was living in Egypt, where her father worked as a civil engineer building new aerodromes for the RAF. Molly was enchanted by the tall, dashing pilot and the chemistry between them was instant. Pat proposed to Molly under the Great Pyramid of Giza and within a year they were married.

Their first daughter Maureen was born in January 1935, followed by Terry at the end the year. They moved back to England in 1937 and enjoyed two blissful and happy years. The outbreak of World War Two in September 1939 changed everything.

Pat was assigned to training bomb disposal squads in London in 1939. One of his early pupils went on to save St Paul's Cathedral after a bomb hit it and failed to explode. After the momentous Battle of Britain in the summer of 1940, there was a desperate shortage of pilots. Pat was sent to East London in South Africa to take over a new RAF base specialising in training bomber pilots. At the age of thirty-five he was one of the youngest Group Captains in the RAF. Over the next three years, hundreds of young bomber pilots were trained on his base and sent back to England to spearhead the counterattack in Europe, including Molly's young brother, Phil. One in three of them would not survive the war.

During the war, Terry and Maureen lived with their mother and grandmother Bess in Bournemouth, and they were inseparable. Bess came from a Welsh family with a great love of music, especially opera. She had a stunning voice and Molly once heard her sing a Puccini aria with the Bournemouth Municipal Orchestra under its leading conductor Sir Dan Godfrey in the Winter Gardens.

The children attended schools near the centre of the town, and when the air raid sirens sounded they had to run to the safety of the air raid shelters. As Bournemouth was only thirty miles from Southampton docks, the town was subjected to increasing numbers of German bombing raids, culminating on May 23 1943 when the Metropole Hotel took a direct hit and nearly 200 people died, including many Canadian aircrew billeted at the hotel, preparing for the D-Day invasion of France. By the end of the war over 2,200 bombs had been dropped on Bournemouth killing over 350 civilians and damaging 14,000 buildings. The schools continued to struggle along, with many children evacuated to Bournemouth from Southampton, stretching the scarce resources.

After the Normandy landings in 1944, Pat returned to England and was immediately sent to Germany. His job was to liaise with the American army to assist in the setting up of new transport links behind the Allied front lines. As the American army didn't have a rank of Group Captain he was, much to his amusement, made a one-star General!

By the middle of 1945 the family was finally back together at an RAF base near Bournemouth, but the war and long periods of separation had taken a toll on the marriage. For the next ten years Pat was posted around England to command various RAF air bases. These included RAF Finningley near Doncaster, which was preparing to receive nuclear bombers as the Cold War with the USSR escalated. The family became very efficient at moving house, and three more children, Rosemary, Rory and Sean, were born, each in a new town.

Terry attended Wychwood School in Bournemouth until 1949 and enjoyed the arts, especially English literature, languages and drama. He also loved music, and visits to the Winter Gardens to hear the Bournemouth Municipal Orchestra. When the family moved to Doncaster in 1949 Terry spent two interesting years at Doncaster Grammar School, and in 1952 completed his erratic schooling at Maidenhead Grammar School.

At the age of eighteen, he approached his father apprehensively to say he was very interested in theatre and wanted to go to drama school to train as an actor. This was not well received and he was told very firmly that it was impossible to make a living as an actor and that he needed to get 'a proper job.' He was persuaded to consider a career in aviation, and so in 1954 Terry applied to RAF College Cranwell and was accepted. He proudly followed in his father's footsteps. After just one year though, to his intense disappointment, he failed the strict medical examination and had to leave Cranwell. That same year Pat had to take early retirement due to gout and the family moved to Bournemouth, with Terry rejoining the family to consider his future.

During this time, he worked in the gourmet bar of *The Grand Hotel* in the centre of Bournemouth, and considered a hotel management course in Switzerland, but then an advert in the local newspaper caught his eye – BEA was expanding and needed more staff based at London Airport.

The first charter flights were taking passengers to many of the major European cities. Hurn Airport, (now Bournemouth International) had already started flights to Palma, Mallorca. Vickers was building the new turboprop Viscount at Hurn which many airlines around the world had started to buy. The Viscount 701C that Terry flew on his last flight was built in 1954, only a few miles from where he was born.

Terry applied to BEA to train as a steward (with the hearty approval of his father) with the option to transfer to pilot training when he had gained his pilot's licence. With his previous Cranwell training and his experience in catering he was immediately accepted and started work in 1957, based at the rapidly expanding London Airport.

He loved the job from the start. The combination of travelling to destinations all over Europe, and working with other young, like-minded staff suited him perfectly. Many of the BEA pilots were ex-RAF war veterans still only in their thirties but with a lifetime's experience already. New routes opened up to the Middle East and Terry joined the crews to Bahrain and Iraq. In July 1958 he was on the last flight out of Baghdad as the revolutionaries in Iraq overthrew the monarchy and executed King Faisal and his family.

Still in his early twenties, Terry was often the youngest of the crew but he won over the veterans with his infectious enthusiasm and good humour, and made many friends. Life was busy, fun, and exciting. BEA looked a promising future. He was twenty-two years old, a good-looking young man, just over six feet tall, slim, with hazel eyes and straight brown hair swept over to the right with a parting, very much in style at the time. As a young bachelor Terry had no shortage of girlfriends, but he gave hints to our mother of one special girl, a particularly attractive Greek girl from Athens.

Terry set off to the airport early on Wednesday October 22 1958. He arrived in good time, met the other flight attendant, Rosie Bevan, and they started the cabin preparations for the journey to Naples. There were only twenty-six passengers, so it would not be a busy flight. The first passengers started boarding shortly after eight o'clock, and Terry and Rosemary were ready with welcoming smiles as they took their hats and coats and showed them to their seats.

Terry was looking forward to the trip to Malta, and seeing his uncle Phil, an ex-RAF Mosquito pilot, working as a civil engineer on the expansion of the airport at Luqa. It was always a very sociable occasion with picnics and swimming excursions to Tigne beach near Valletta. Phil and his bubbly wife, Patricia and their two young children, Russell and Frances, always looked forward to seeing his smiling face and enjoying his warm personality.

Phil waited at Luqa airport for flight BE142 in vain. After a few hours he was taken into an office by the BEA manager Mr T. Pollock and told the tragic news.

At around the same time, Pat had a knock on the door at the house in Bournemouth and was given the awful news by a nervous policeman. He was followed shortly afterwards by a young reporter from the local newspaper, the Bournemouth *Evening Echo*. He expressed his condolences and asked for some details of Terry and a photograph to go in the first edition the following day.

Molly was not there. The previous day there had been another major argument with Pat and she had stormed out of the house, and nobody knew where she was. Molly had stayed at an hotel that night, and the following day was walking in the centre of Bournemouth, contemplating her future, when she saw a headline on a newspaper vendor's billboard, *Local Boy killed in Air Crash*. She picked up a copy of the newspaper and saw the photo of Terry staring back at her. She let out a desperate, heart-rending wail and collapsed on the pavement. A terrible way to learn of the death of her eldest son. She was taken to hospital for a few days and returned home. At only forty-two years old she turned grey overnight.

Terry's emotional and upsetting funeral was held at St Peter's Church, in the centre of Bournemouth. It was attended by more than 300 people, including representatives of BEA, pilots, radio operators and weeping flight attendants. He was buried close to the grave of Sir Dan Godfrey.

Molly suffered a series of mental and physical illnesses and never fully recovered. She died in 1980. Pat lived a long life and died in 1994, rarely talking about the tragedy, and Maureen kept a photo of Terry by her bedside until she died in 2007.

My mother took my brother and I to Terry's grave every year on the anniversary of the crash for the next ten years. We would always find a red rose sent or placed on his grave by an unknown admirer, thought to be Greek.

3.

THE PASSENGERS

THE GROUP

The Model
EUGENIE KAWAJA / JANE BUCKINGHAM

J ane Buckingham rushed to London Airport on October 22 1958 and arrived with only minutes to spare to catch the 08.25 flight to Naples. She was in a determined and defiant mood. Two days earlier she had been told that the famous Hollywood star, Eva Bartok, who was shooting a film in England, had refused to deny to the press that she was engaged to Prince Shiv, the man who, up to that point she thought loved her.

Jane arrived at the airport with two reporters, Paddy Watson from the *Daily Sketch* and freelance reporter Lee Benson, together with well-known photographer, Brian Fogaty minutes before the doors of the plane were due to slam shut. She wanted a showdown with the prince in Naples, where she knew he was on his way to see his father, and the *Daily Sketch* wanted a sensational story to sell to the scandal-hungry public.

Jane Buckingham was born Eugenie Eleanor May Moore on

October 23 1933 in Holloway in north London. Her father, James Moore came from a large family in Birmingham and moved to London to work as a tailor in central London. Her mother, Gertrude May, (always known as Trudy) was born in Holborn in 1901 and had five siblings. Her family may also have been involved in tailoring as James was the best friend of her brother. He was a handsome and charismatic character and they married in Hendon in 1929.

It was soon apparent to Trudy that James was flawed with a compulsive gambling addiction, which led to serious monetary problems. Two years after Eugenie was born, Trudy fled the home and dropped the name of Moore so she could not be traced by James.

Trudy was an attractive, vivacious woman with thick, brown hair always set in the style of the times with many talents and a zest for life. She had a good singing voice and in her twenties, when a new age of swing music swept in, she sang in the pubs. She could also play the drums well. Eugenie was a beautiful baby, so to make a little extra money, Trudy entered her into a baby beauty contest. She won, and there is an enchanting photo showing Eugenie looking happily and confidently into the camera, even at the tender age of two.

With the outbreak of World War Two, at the age of six Eugenie was evacuated from London. She was sent to live with a family in Wales and it was over six long years before she returned to London. Trudy remained in London throughout the Blitz, continuing to find sporadic work, and visited Eugenie in Wales several times a year.

As the war dragged on she got tired of running for the air raid shelters every time the sirens went off and started to ignore the warnings. One dark night, her street was hit by a bomb and the force of the explosion brought the ceiling down of the room she was sleeping in. She sustained a serious back injury which, despite several operations over the next few years, gave her pain for the rest of her life.

When Eugenie returned from Wales at the age of thirteen, Trudy was no longer looking at a small girl but an emerging, pretty, young woman. Eugenie had also developed a good singing voice, possibly encouraged by her Welsh family, and in 1948 she won a singing contest in London. She left school the following year and took up her first job in Woolworths, swiftly moving on to John Lewis in Oxford Street, where she won the face of the month within the first few months of starting.

She had inherited her mother's good looks and was starting to gain attention. Trudy quickly saw her potential and took her to a photographer to get some publicity shots done. Eugenie was a natural in front of the camera and her photos started to circulate around the model agencies.

At seventeen Eugenie was an attractive, but quite a shy girl with wavy, auburn hair cut in a fierce fringe, looking older than her age. She loved music and dancing and once she started earning a little money, took herself to the music clubs in London's West End, where black musicians like Ray Charles were introducing soul and jazz from the USA, and others were bringing calypso from the West Indies. One of her favourites was the Humphrey Lyttleton Band, who played regularly at 100 Oxford Street.

Eugenie was determined to get into show business and within a few months passed an audition for dancers and singers in small, provincial musicals. It was during this time that a scout from the model agency *Scottys* spotted her and offered her work in commercials and modelling. Trudy enthusiastically encouraged her and the agency suggested it was time to adopt a new name for her modelling career, and Jane Buckingham was born.

It was also around this time that Eugenie had a brief affair with a young French student and became pregnant. Trudy rallied to her side and supported her during the pregnancy. When her baby daughter Rebecca was born in 1952, Trudy looked after her and brought her up as her mother, which was common at that time, so that Jane could continue with her increasingly lucrative modelling and advertising work.

In 1952 London was still recovering from the destruction of World War Two. The streets were grey and drab, food rationing was still in place, rubble-strewn bomb sites were dotted about, exciting and sometimes dangerous playgrounds for children, and rebuilding of the city was slow. Going to the cinema was a popular pastime to escape from the day to day dreariness of everyday life. Hollywood provided the colour and glamour in lavish musicals, shot in exotic locations with beautiful and charismatic actors, films such as 'An American in Paris' and 'Singin' In The Rain.' The glamorous, international film stars were fêted whenever they visited England, and exclusive London nightclubs entertained them and assured them plenty of free publicity. One such nightclub was *The Embassy Club* at 29 Burlington Street, Mayfair, and it was here that Jane had her introduction to how the rich and famous liked to party.

The Embassy Club had a long history, opening in 1870 just as the Belle Époque was about to sweep through Europe, and more liberal entertainment was being tolerated in France. In the 1920s jazz was the popular music of the time. In 1922 a young conductor called Ambrose fronted a famous 7-piece band at the club entertaining enthusiastic revellers. Visiting Hollywood stars loved it. During the 1930s the Duke of Windsor was a regular visitor, seen courting Wallis Simpson. In 1938 the club went into receivership but was quickly bought and refurbished to continue as a bottle party club during the war.

In the 1950s *The Embassy Club* enjoyed a revival, catering for a new wave of young Hollywood film stars and their entourage looking for a fun-filled evening's entertainment in the heart of London's club land. In the dimly-lit, smoke-filled room the latest music pounded out on the club's sound system, Tab Hunter crooning about *Young Love* and Guy Mitchell rocking the house with *Rock-A-Billy*. Young, attractive hostesses floated about in expensive, sexy frocks, filling the punter's glasses, preferably with champagne, chatting to them, complimenting and stroking their egos. The girls weren't paid well but they could make good money on fat tips, and there was always a possibility of finding a rich husband. For a few of them it was a good life, a glittering alternative to the drudgery of a low-paid, dead-end job in a factory or office. For many it was a slippery slope into prostitution, drug, alcohol and physical abuse.

Over the next couple of years Jane worked hard and flourished in her modelling career. She graced the magazines in fashionable luxury clothing and became a well-known face of various major brands, including tonic water and washing powder.

She was now a stunningly-attractive young woman, just over five feet four inches tall, a slim figure, sparkling brown eyes, light-brown hair in a Marilyn Monroe hair style, and a relaxed, magnetic charm that attracted plenty of male admirers. She moved in the demi-monde of wealthy aristocrats and smart social climbers, which led her to *The Stork Club* in Swallow Street near Piccadilly Circus, run by a charismatic villain from the east end of London called Al Burnett.

Burnett originally ran a club called *The Nut House*, popular with jazz musicians during the war, and when the opportunity arose to take over *The Stork Club*, he became known as the 'Nightclub King'. The club lured in the rich and famous looking for a vibrant and exciting night out. Well-off, old-school aristocrats, extravagant business tycoons, well-known politicians, including upcoming minister John Profumo, (who met his downfall in the Christine Keeler scandal in 1963), and visiting, top-of-the-town entertainers and A-list film stars such as Frank Sinatra, Ava Gardner, Kim Novak, Eva Bartok, Bette Davis, Elizabeth Taylor and Peter Sellers were among the many famous guests.

In late 1954, twenty-one-year-old Jane was invited by some friends to a party in Maida Vale and there she met Reginald Kawaja, a young Lebanese who was studying for his bar exams in the Middle Temple. He was bowled over by this beautiful, well-dressed, elegant and softly-spoken, intelligent young woman. He was smitten, and quickly proposed, promising her a wonderful, care-free life in the sunny West Indies, where he was going to establish a legal practice.

Her romantic imagination went into overdrive. She was entranced by the idea of living in a tropical paradise and bringing up her children in a large house by the beach with an army of servants in Caribbean luxury. Jane and Reginald were married in Kensington registry office in April 1955 with just a few friends as witnesses.

They stayed on in London so that Reginald could complete his bar exams, and Jane gave birth to their daughter, Yasmin in Kensington in January 1956. A few months later they flew to Montreal in Canada so that Reginald could complete further exams, and stayed with his father and some of the family. Jane hadn't prepared herself for the extremes of the climate in Montreal, with hot, uncomfortable summers, and cold, snowy winters, making it difficult to get around with a young baby, and she could not wait to feel the warm, West Indian sunshine. They left for St Kitts in January 1957.

St Kitts and Nevis are part of the Leeward Islands chain which curve away from Puerto Rico towards South America. Christopher Columbus sighted the islands in 1493 and the first English settlers arrived there in 1623. The French arrived soon afterwards in 1625, followed by the Spanish in 1629 who expelled the French, but the islands were returned to the British in 1670. Over the next one hundred years, extensive sugar plantations were established and large numbers of African slaves were imported to work on them. In 1834 slavery was outlawed and over 28,000 slaves were freed. As a result over 90% of the approximate 50,000 population are of African descent, 2% European and 1.5% Indian.

The country suffered badly as a result of the depression in the early twentieth century and many people emigrated to America and Britain. St Kitts and Nevis eventually became fully independent in 1983, retaining its place in the British

Commonwealth with Queen Elizabeth its head of state, and at just over 100 square miles, is the smallest sovereign state in the western hemisphere.

They flew to the small airport on St Kitts called Golden Rock, (now the Robert L. Bradshaw International Airport) and walked across to a sleepy immigration shed and into a waiting car to whisk them to their new home and life. Jane had not realised what a culture shock this was going to be.

The house was a large, family mansion shared with many other members of Reginald's family, ruled in the old Lebanese tradition by his father, a very conservative and strict disciplinarian who made all the decisions and demanded obedience from the family.

The island was still dominated by the sugar plantations, where the black workers were living poor and wretched lives. There were plenty of servants in the house and a nanny to look after the baby. Everything was catered for and there was very little for her to do. It quickly became obvious that Jane and her father-in-law were not going to get on, and despite Reginald being very attentive, and some amicable younger cousins eager to welcome her, she felt very despondent.

After three months Jane realised she had made a terrible mistake, could feel the black cloud of depression enveloping her, and looked desperately for a way to escape.

With the help of the sympathetic cousins and a kind aunt she borrowed some money, secretly bought a ticket to London and left on the pretence that she was going home for a check-up. It meant of course she had to make the decision to leave baby Yasmin in St Kitts, but she knew the baby would be well looked after by Reginald, and hoped that she would be able to bring Yasmin to England later. She also regretted the pain she was going to cause to Reginald, who loved her dearly. She had to leave most of her possessions behind, including her modelling portfolio, essential if she was going to relaunch her career.

The plan worked, and Jane arrived back in London in April 1957 elated and desperate to start work. She immediately visited her family in Peckham and linked up with old friends in London. One aspect of her marriage she had especially disliked was her entire reliance on Reginald for money. She valued her independence and was determined to make her own way in life. She was offered a job in the chorus line of *One Way Street*, a musical revue, and took it immediately.

Jane re-established contact with the model agencies, helped out at *The Embassy Club* and was soon being invited to post-show parties and other nightclubs. She was a little wiser now, but in her heart she was still a romantic who looked for stability, strength and love in a shining knight who would give her the life she had always dreamed of.

One weekend in the summer of 1957 she was invited to a house party at a large mansion near Ascot, in Berkshire. These parties were popular at the time, often thrown by the wealthy, hedonistic partying set where guests could let their hair down and leave their inhibitions at the door, a mixed cross-section of society where dashing young trendsetters would mingle with slippery social climbers, up-and-coming actors and actresses and maybe even a Russian spy or two. They were there to mix with the in-crowd, to connect with the useful and influential, occasionally to do business, but mostly to enjoy themselves.

Jane had been invited by Dennis Hamilton, the first husband of Diana Dors, the prominent British film actress playing characters that mirrored her own racy life. Dennis also had a colourful past, that included at least one stretch in prison, and was there as master of ceremonies to supply lavish and bounteous entertainment, including pretty models and attractive, intelligent girls to chat with and flatter their important guests. At this party Jane was introduced to Prince Shiv of Palitana by Dennis, a meeting that would change her life and ultimately lead to her tragic and untimely death.

Prince Shiv was the son of a Maharajah, the 26th Thakor of Palitana (1900–1964) whose family had ruled an ancient, princely state in west India. The present dynasty dates back over 800 years. Palitana was merged into the state of Kathiavar in 1948 after independence and became part of Bombay, (now Mumbai) in November 1956. The ruling family was enormously rich. Twenty-seven-year-old Prince Shiv was given a generous allowance and was not shy in displaying his abundant wealth. He led a playboy life and was often seen in the most expensive restaurants and trendiest nightspots in Europe, and always with a gorgeous girl on his arm.

Jane had met plenty of rich men and was not overawed by this confident young man. He was impressed by this stunningly attractive, well-spoken, much-travelled young woman who was good company.

When Shiv was not in London, Jane was busy modelling for Christian Dior and other top brands and occasionally worked at *The Embassy Club*. On October 1 1958 Jane moved into a small flat in Wyndham Place, Marylebone, sharing with a girlfriend called Jill. On October 20 she received a bombshell. A close friend told her that the beautiful Hollywood actress Eva Bartok had been interviewed by the press and refused to deny that she was engaged to Prince Shiv. Jane was beside herself.

In 1958 Eva Bartok was a famous international actress with a highly-publicised, complex private life, closely followed by the tabloid press. She was born in Budapest, Hungary in 1927, the daughter of a Jewish father and Catholic mother. From the start of the war, Jews were routinely persecuted and subjected to strict limits on their personal and business lives. In early 1944 the Nazis marched into Hungary and over 500,000 Jews were rounded up and deported to the death camp at Auschwitz. At just fifteen years old Eva was forced to marry a Nazi Hungarian officer, Géza Kovács to avoid a similar fate. She endured continuous rape and as soon as the war was over the marriage was annulled on the grounds of 'coercion of a minor'.

In 1946 Eva began her acting career with leading roles in classical plays in the theatre in Budapest. By 1948 the new communist regime under the Soviets was imposing severe censorship on the arts and she knew she had to flee. In 1951 her friend, film producer Alexander Paal offered to marry her in a 'marriage of convenience' to enable her to leave Budapest and live in England, and that same year he cast her in her screen debut in *A Tale of Five Cities*. A year later she divorced Alexander and married a British publicist, Bill Wordsworth, related to the great nineteenth-century poet William Wordsworth, who adored her and finally gave her the stability she craved in her turbulent life.

Eva was being touted as Britain's answer to Sophia Loren, and when Burt Lancaster offered her the part of Consuelo in *The Crimson Pirate*, she jumped at the opportunity. The film was a box-office hit, bringing Eva many new film offers, and she moved up into the Hollywood A-list, but the success and the many months of separation from Bill when she was away filming on location took its toll on her personal life and her marriage came to an end. A much-publicised affair with the 3rd Marquess of Milford Haven, David Mountbatten, the cousin and best man of the Duke of Edinburgh, led to the Marquess being sued for divorce in 1954, with his wife naming Eva as 'the other woman'.

The affair drifted on and off for another few years, much to the concern of the Royal family, but by then she had already met her fourth husband, popular, tall, blond, blue-eyed Austrian actor, Curd Jürgens. He worshipped her and showered her with expensive presents, everything she could dream of, and they married in a blaze of publicity in 1955. She longed to have children but sadly, a car accident in 1933 had resulted in Curd's life-long infertility.

In 1956 Eva went to Hollywood to shoot her first film with Dean Martin, a light, musical-comedy, *Ten Thousand Bedrooms*. It was filmed in Rome and Los Angeles and became another box office success for her. Inevitably she met Frank Sinatra, whose marriage with Ava Gardner had collapsed, and they had a brief and passionate affair. As a result Eva returned to Europe pregnant and in 1957 gave birth to a daughter, Deana. Curd reluctantly divorced her, but did agree to give his surname to Deana.

Despite her tempestuous private life Eva was besieged with

offers of work and in 1958 she was cast in the film *Operation Amsterdam* with Peter Finch, to be shot at Pinewood Studios near London, and Amsterdam. It was another box office hit when released in 1959. It was during this time, at one of the glitzy showbiz parties, that Eva met Prince Shiv, and at that point the lives of both Jane Buckingham and Eva Bartok crossed.

Prince Shiv became infatuated with Eva and by October 1958, after a whirlwind romance during which he regularly visited her in her rented cottage in Kingston, he said he wanted to marry her. Eva was flattered and enjoyed his company but her focus in life was her young daughter. Meanwhile, Jane was completely unaware how fast this relationship had developed. She was in love with Shiv and still harboured romantic notions that the prince would marry her.

Although the two women came from totally different backgrounds, they did have a surprising amount in common, which could possibly account for Prince Shiv being attracted to both of them. They were both beautiful, elegant and complex, had experienced poverty as children, and were ambitious and keen to run their own lives as they saw fit. Their traumatic experiences and not having a father in their early years left them emotionally scarred, and yet they still yearned for love in their lives and constantly looked for it.

Jane would have read all about Eva's life and loves in the tabloids and glossy magazines over the years. Some of the stories would have been true, others would have been fabrications, made up by journalists to feed a gossip-hungry public.

Lee Benson was a freelance reporter that Jane had often met at the clubs as he tried to extract the latest scandal from inebriated customers or girls eager to sell a kiss-and-tell story for a few quid in the early hours of the morning. He had followed the rumours about Prince Shiv, and Eva Bartok's denial of their engagement, and with a nose for a good story, came to see Jane with Paddy Watson, a seasoned reporter from the *Daily Sketch* who would also jump at such a sensational scoop. He told Jane what he had heard and proposed a way she could settle it once and for all.

It had been reported that Shiv was driving from Paris to see his father in Naples, so they could fly to Naples and confront the prince right there. Lee recommended taking experienced freelance photographer Brian Fogaty, who was adept at snapping the perfect photograph in these dramatic situations. Desperate to get Shiv back, Jane agreed. Lee could feel the juicy story was beginning to unfurl.

On the plane Jane sat next to Paddy Watson. Most of the rows had two seats on one side of the aisle and three on the other. Lee Benson sat with Brian Fogaty behind Jane. There was plenty of room with only twenty-six passengers on board. After take-off, they settled down and Jane told Paddy her story. Lee and Brian had known each other for some years and each had different priorities. Brian would have been thinking of the potential of the light and colours in Naples. Lee looked forward to the confrontation and was already sketching out the story in his head – the Prince, the Actress and the Model, the perfect love triangle.

Eugenie lived a full and complex life in her twenty-four years. She was never far from the gossip columns of the popular press, and her death caught the headlines of all the leading newspapers of the day. She was Jane Buckingham, the glamorous model, front page news, and there were photographs of her in every paper.

On October 22 Eva Bartok was besieged by the press in London as she was about to drive to France in a Rolls Royce given to her as a present by Prince Shiv the previous week. When told about the crash, Eva is reported to have said, *'I had never met Jane, but her death is a terrible shock. I am very, very sorry.'* She never did marry Prince Shiv, who could not be contacted as he was driving down through France in his red Thunderbird on his way to Naples. His father confirmed he had heard of Jane but knew no more details.

Reginald Kawaja was in Montreal studying for a further qualification in aviation law on that fateful day, and on being told the news, said that he had neither seen nor spoken to Jane for eighteen months. He stayed in St Kitts with Yasmin, remarried, and built up a very successful business. St Kitts and Nevis has been transformed over the last sixty years into another West Indian tourist paradise, with luxury hotels, expensive beach villas and developments, with the backdrop of beautiful beaches and crystal-clear blue sea.

Trudy and six-year-old Rebecca were at home in Peckham when a neighbour knocked on the window at lunchtime to ask them if they were all right, unaware that they had not heard the news about a BEA plane crashing in Italy. Within an hour, packs of national and international reporters descended on them, demanding statements to print in their papers, without telling them the facts of the crash. They rampaged through the house leaving Trudy hysterical, until a senior *Daily Sketch* representative arrived with Eugenie's friend Jill, and took them away to a hotel until the furore had died down. BEA had failed to tell them in time.

The next day would have been Eugenie's twenty-fifth birthday, and a cake was sitting on the kitchen table waiting for her return. Eugenie's funeral was held at Golders Green crematorium with Trudy, many friends and BEA representatives attending a very emotional service, surrounded by a mountain of bouquets and flowers. Rebecca was not allowed to attend the funeral and was looked after by an aunt.

Eugenie's ashes were kept in an urn for some years at the crematorium and eventually scattered on the rose beds. Trudy never recovered from the trauma and died from cancer in 1978. Rebecca and Yasmin met for the first time in London in 1979 and have remained close ever since.

The Journalist
PATRICIA WATSON

On October 22 1958, Paddy Watson arrived at London Airport excited, and with plenty of time to spare before the plane departed. She had been given the opportunity to write a major story, and to fly to Italy for the first time. Paddy was a reporter and features writer with the *Daily Sketch* and had her own successful weekly column, *What's New*, but this story was different.

Paddy was waiting to meet Jane Buckingham, a well-known London model. They were to travel to Naples on flight BE142 with freelance reporter Lee Benson and photographer Brian Fogaty, where Jane intended to confront her boyfriend, wealthy playboy Prince Shiv, about rumours that he had recently become engaged to famous Hollywood actress Eva Bartok.

Jane had known Shiv for several months and to her, he was the love of her life. She thought he might even marry her. Eva Bartok was shooting a film in London and had met Prince Shiv just the previous week. They appeared to have had a whirlwind romance as in an interview with the press, she would neither confirm nor deny that she was now engaged to him. Lee Benson suggested to Jane that she could get the *Daily Sketch* to pay her fare to Italy. The story could be dynamite – wealthy prince in love triangle with Hollywood actress and famous model, and a real scoop for the *Daily Sketch*. The editor agreed, and Paddy was selected to lead the team.

Patricia Mary Watson, (always known as Paddy) was born on February 15 1932 in Ryton, a small but relatively affluent commuter town six miles west of Newcastle upon Tyne with a population of less than ten thousand. Although surrounded by rich and fertile agricultural land, it was coal that was the main industry.

In 1239, when Henry III decreed that coal could be mined outside the town walls, mining flourished as an industry. As early as 1367 coal was being shipped south to London. The Stargate Pit opened in 1800 and produced coal throughout the Industrial Revolution until its eventual closure in 1961. In 1840 there was a catastrophic methane explosion in which twenty men and eighteen boys lost their lives. A commemorative memorial can be found at Ryton's Holy Cross Church. Fortunes were made in coal and wealthy local industrialists moved away from the choking sprawl of Gateshead and Newcastle and built large mansions in Ryton.

Paddy's father, Joseph Henry Watson was born around 1883 in Sunderland and was a dentist with a successful practice in Ryton. Both his father and grandfather were Master Mariners from Sunderland. During World War One, Joseph served in a dental corps in the British Army and was based in the pretty town of Honfleur, Normandy in north-west France. He returned to County Durham after the war and built a house called St Mary's in Ryton. In 1919 he married Dora Mary Murphy, who came from a respected, Catholic Irish farming family and they had three daughters, Doreen, Olive (Olly) and Patricia (Paddy). A baby boy, Peter Joseph Osmond was born in 1930 but sadly only lived thirteen months.

On Paddy's fourth birthday tragedy hit the family when her mother died. The girls were brought up by their father. Despite their early trauma the girls had a happy childhood and enjoyed a pleasant lifestyle, with staff to help in the house, including a cook and housekeeper. In the garden they had the luxury of a tennis court to play on.

In the 1930s childhood diseases of polio, mumps and whooping cough were far more prevalent than they are today as the vaccines to fight these diseases had not yet been developed. It was common to see young children who had suffered the debilitating effects of polio wearing leg braces. It was not until 1955 that a vaccine was produced in the UK, and a programme of inoculation started in schools, saving thousands of lives. Unfortunately it was too late for Doreen, who contracted polio when she was very young. As a result she did not attend the local school but was educated at home with a tutor, so successfully that she later qualified as a doctor before she was even old enough to practice.

Joseph Henry was an Anglican but carried out Dora's wishes to bring up the children as Catholics. Olly was sent to La Sagesse Roman Catholic School in Newcastle, an independent school for girls between the ages of three to sixteen run by nuns. It is probable that Paddy also attended La Sagesse.

The imposing Gothic-style building was constructed in the early 1800s and acquired by the *Filles de la Sagesse* (the Daughters of Wisdom), who founded the school in 1912. The *Filles de la Sagesse* was a Catholic organisation founded by Louis de Montfort in about 1707 in Poitiers, and its philosophy was 'to acquire heavenly wisdom by imitating the incarnate wisdom of Jesus Christ.' The sisters of the order nursed the poor and sick of the community. They were heavily persecuted during the French Revolution (1789–1799), accused of harbouring 'fanatic priests.' Many of the sisters were brutally murdered and four met their end at the guillotine. Under Napoleon Bonaparte they recovered most of their property and at his request the Daughters of Wisdom left French soil to nurse the wounded soldiers at Antwerp. Numerous medals were bestowed on them by Napoleon, and by every French government since. Spain, Prussia and Belgium have honoured the community of sisters for nursing the wounded or plague-stricken soldiers of those countries, and the Daughters of Wisdom have grown to a multinational organisation.

During World War Two, Newcastle and Jarrow suffered continuous German bombing assaults on the docks, railways and heavy industrial areas. The bombing raids began on July 2 1940 and continued until the end of 1941. Paddy was attending school in Newcastle and would have heard and felt the massive explosions and seen the night skies lit up by fires caused by the relentless bombing and the dropping of incendiary devices.

There would have been many disruptions to her education, and early in 1944 at the age of twelve she was moved to St Leonard's School in St Andrew's, Fife, in Scotland, a far safer place.

Situated within the walls of the medieval priory, St Leonard's was founded by the professors of St Andrew's University and their wives in 1877. For 122 years it educated only girls and it was not until 1999 that boys were admitted. Dame Louisa Lumsden (1840–1935) was the school's first headmistress. A student and tutor at Girton College, Cambridge, she was a pioneer of female education who maintained that *'a girl should receive an education as good as her brother's, if not better.'* She set high academic standards with the emphasis on classics, mathematics and sport. St Leonard's is believed to be the first school in the world to have played women's lacrosse.

Paddy was fun, bright and popular at school. She was a mediocre student, not academically inclined, possibly due to her interrupted education during the war, and not particularly interested in sport. Her sister Olly had joined the Women's Royal Naval Service, the Wrens, and during the war served in the Fleet Air Arm. In 1947 she got married in Ryton and at the happy family wedding Paddy was delighted to be a bridesmaid.

Paddy left school the following year and little is known of what she did for the next nine years. Her father may well have sent her on a secretarial course, where she would have learned the practical skills of shorthand and typing, a necessity in offices in those days, and essential for a budding reporter.

It is quite likely that she worked for a local newspaper as a junior reporter, honing the skills of collating information and turning them into stories. From there, with some practical experience under her belt, she set her sights on a journalistic career in London.

Paddy moved to London in 1957 and applied for a job with the *Daily Sketch*. It is quite likely she was interviewed by the young features editor, twenty-six-year-old David English. He was impressed by this dark-haired, bright, confident, enthusiastic young reporter who had worked her way up from the bottom, reminding him of his own modest start as a journalist only ten years earlier. He offered Paddy a job as a features reporter and she started work in July 1957.

Sir David English, as he later became, went on to become one of the most outstanding editors of his generation. When he died in 1998 an obituary in the *Independent* newspaper described him as *'the greatest and most creative editor seen in Fleet Street since the time of Northcliffe.'* David English was born in Oxford in 1931. At the local grammar school in Bournemouth he was not particularly academic, but he was clever, charming and ambitious. He left school when he was sixteen and started work with a local newspaper, the *Christchurch Times* as a junior reporter. In 1951, after a brief spell at the *News* in Portsmouth, he moved to London and was offered a job as a reporter with the *Daily Mirror*. By 1956 he had moved to the *Daily Sketch* as Features Editor.

Paddy could not have had a better mentor. He supported his staff unequivocally and ensured that they were well recompensed. By all accounts he was a perfectionist and set high standards. Anyone who did not come up to the mark was quickly shown the door. Paddy had exceptional talents, working long hours and hitting difficult deadlines.

She had a close working relationship with David, and he encouraged Paddy to develop her own ideas, and push her creativity. He understood the importance of attracting women readers, and Paddy was soon given her own weekly column, *What's New,* which became a popular feature of the newspaper. She was in a job that she loved and was happy. She was sharing a flat in Hans Crescent in Knightsbridge, just round the corner from Harrods.

An attractive twenty-six-year-old with a beaming smile, Paddy was great fun and enjoying a busy social life in London. She was seeing a young man believed to be called Jack Starr. Her family thought they had recently become engaged.

On October 22, a flustered Jane Buckingham arrived at the BEA desk at the last minute, and met Paddy. They joined Brian Fogaty and Lee Benson, and after checking in, the team ran to the plane. At the top of the mobile stairs they were welcomed aboard by the cheery young flight attendant as the door swung shut behind them. Paddy settled into her seat beside Jane, clipped her safety belt and looked out of the large, oval, panoramic window, excited at what lay ahead. After final preparations the plane took off sixteen minutes late at 08.41.

Paddy's sister Olly and young son Roger had recently returned from living in Iraq, where a revolution was about to erupt. On October 22 they were travelling across the city to London Airport to meet Olly's husband returning home on a flight from Iraq. Roger could not understand why there were pictures of his aunt Paddy on the front pages of all the evening newspapers.

The funeral was held at Stella Catholic Church in Ryton. The grave overflowed with dozens of bouquets of the most beautiful flowers from the many mourners who came. Sir David English attended the funeral visibly upset. He later visited her father at the family house to pay tribute to Paddy, a young woman who had touched many hearts in her short life.

A memorial service was held in St Bride's Church in Fleet Street, London on November 5 1958 for Paddy, Brian Fogaty and Lee Benson, with a moving tribute by Herbert Gunn, the editor of the *Daily Sketch*. A memorial bench to Paddy was placed in the church grounds.

The Photographer
BRIAN FOGATY

Brian Fogaty was in a rush getting to the airport, but he was used to these last-minute changes. It was just before eight o'clock in the morning on October 22 1958, and he was racing to the BEA check-in desk at London Airport to meet Paddy Watson, who had his ticket for flight BE142 to Naples.

He had only been told about this latest assignment the night before, when Paddy, a features reporter for the *Daily Sketch*, rang him. He was supposed to be going to Wembley Stadium to cover the much-anticipated international football match between England and Russia. Instead, Paddy asked him to go to Naples with her to cover a potential headline story of a showdown meeting between well-known model Jane Buckingham and her rich, Indian playboy boyfriend, Prince Shiv of Palitana.

Jane had been approached by a freelance journalist, Lee Benson informing her of the prince's affair with sultry Hollywood actress Eva Bartok, and he had proposed she go to meet the prince in Naples. The *Daily Sketch* would cover all expenses and in return they would require some photographs of the confrontational meeting.

Brian was one of the best in the business, and as a freelance photographer he rarely turned down a job, especially not one in Italy. It should only take a couple of days. He had no idea that by the end of the day, they would be the story.

Brian was born in Lewisham, south London on April 15 1933, the youngest of five children; two sisters, Doris and

Peggy, and two brothers, Denis and Terry, with a fourteen-year gap between the eldest and youngest. Brian's arrival had been a surprise to his father Leonard and mother Amy, as she had a heart condition and had agreed to be sterilised after Terry was born eight years earlier. Her doctor was equally astonished and sent the details to be published in *The Lancet*.

The family lived in a modest, terraced house replicated in streets throughout London. Little is known of Brian's early life, but we do know that he was doted on by his elder sisters, being the baby of the family. When the German bombing blitz on London started in 1940, he was evacuated to the village of Maids Moreton in Buckinghamshire with Doris, and they returned to London a year later.

Terry was interested in photography at an early age and it was he who triggered Brian's curiosity in the art. Brian left school at fifteen and got a job as a photo library assistant for the Associated Press in London. By the age of seventeen he was already trying to sell his own photographs. In 1951 Brian was called up for National Service and opted for the RAF, where he was given the chance to learn more about the technical side of photography. He also learnt to sail, which he thoroughly enjoyed. It brought out his competitive streak and his skill won him several medals.

He returned to London in 1953, a confident and energetic young man, full of ideas of what he wanted to do with his life. Armed with a camera, he would look for celebrities to photograph and sell the pictures to the tabloids on Fleet Street, always hungry for the latest snaps of the stars. He concentrated on London Airport to catch them arriving straight off the plane, giving him the edge over his many competitors. He could snap Hollywood actors coming and going, up-and-coming starlets, glamorous fashion models, politicians and royalty as they swept through the airport.

Every day he scanned the timetables, tracked the movements of celebrities in the gossip columns, and patrolled the airport corridors with his camera, waiting for the right moment to capture that one eye-catching image. As a freelancer he covered a wide range of work, anything from shooting society weddings to local beauty pageants and photographic portfolios for aspiring fashion models. His income was sporadic.

In 1954 he was invited to a beauty competition in London. He was bedazzled by the beautiful, eighteen-year-old winner, Hazel Moreland and by the following year they were married in Greenwich, south London. That year they moved into a little studio apartment in Chelsea enjoying the life of an emerging swinging London.

By 1957 Brian's talents were being recognised nationally, and occasionally he was called up by Shepperton Film Studios in Surrey to take stills of the movie stars for the production company.

The studios were built in the grounds of Littleton Park, which included Littleton House, built by a local nobleman Thomas Wood in the seventeenth century and used as a location in several films produced there. In 1931, Scottish businessman Norman Loudon bought the sixty-acre estate for his new film company, *Sound Film Producing and Recording Studios*, which opened to business the following year. During the war the site was requisitioned by the Government. Part of it was used for storage purposes and another part was converted for the manufacture of Vickers Wellington bombers. In 1945 it was returned to its owners and purchased by British Lion Films under the famous director Sir Alexander Korda, whose productions included the award-winning *The Third Man* made in 1948.

In 1954 the studios went into receivership and the famous Boulting brothers, Roy and John, took them over to make many memorable, popular comedies and dramas. With film-making in full swing the capacity increased enormously, with over a dozen sound stages varying in size from 3,000 to 30,000 square feet. Five were equipped with huge tanks for water and underwater filming. In 1955 *Richard III* was filmed there, starring and directed by Laurence Olivier, who was an expert in striking an elegant, dramatic pose for a publicity shot. In 1957 Charlie Chaplin directed and appeared in his last starring part in *A King in New York*.

As Brian's reputation grew he was recognised by the starlets as they arrived at the airport, who would pose for his eager camera. He was booked for glitzy publicity sessions, which led to invitations to luxury promotion events and the inevitable celebrity parties, which he enjoyed immensely, his camera always at the ready. On one memorable visit the Hollywood star Ava Gardner invited him to lunch. He mixed with the high-flying, jet-setting, hedonistic set, whose lives revolved around fast cars, expensive houses, gin-palace yachts, sumptuous parties and an extravagant, to-die-for lifestyle.

He worked and played hard and his income jumped overnight. He acquired a taste himself for fast sports cars and wrote a couple off, but professionally he was at the top of his game, full of energy, ideas and confidence. There is a photograph of Brian standing waist deep in one of the studio's water tanks wearing waders, clasping his camera and staring intently at his subject, unaware of the conditions he was in, concentrating solely on capturing that one definitive image. He used a specially-adapted high-speed 35mm camera and did not use a flash.

In 1958 Life magazine published photos that Brian took at the musical My Fair Lady, which had opened at Drury Lane with Julie Andrews and Rex Harrison.

In December 1957 Brian became a father with the birth of his first daughter, Sally.

A contemporary of Brian's was Terry O'Neill. Born in Romford, the son of Irish immigrants, he was five years younger than Brian. His first job was in 1953 working in the photographic unit of the British Overseas Airways Corporation (BOAC) at London Airport, which later became part of British Airways. Terry hadn't considered photography as a career when he started work there, but a colleague brought in photographic manuals demonstrating all the different cameras and he quickly became interested. In his memoirs he remembered, '... *It was just interiors of aircraft, planes flying in the sky and taking off – that sort of thing...Back in those days, there were only two types of airport picture: people going up the stairs and people going down the stairs – usually waving.*' Terry would walk around the airport and snap people in relaxed and informal poses.

One day he took a shot on his Agfa camera of a corpulent, well-dressed man in an expensive pin-stripe suit with waistcoat, dozing in the centre of a group of sleeping African chieftains robed in traditional dress waiting for their plane. He was unaware that the man was the Home Secretary, Rab Butler. A passing hack reporter spotted him and offered twenty-five pounds for the film, which he readily accepted. The next week he was working for the *Sunday Dispatch*, one day a week.

Terry developed a unique photographic style of his own, where formalities were ignored and spontaneity was essential. Brian was struck by his impressive, black-and-white photos and in early 1958 sent an invitation to come over and meet him. Brian saw a handsome, self-assured young man, passionate about photography and jazz, and recognized in him a kindred spirit. He offered nineteen-year-old Terry a job assisting him on the *Daily Sketch*, which he jumped at. Terry never looked back and went on to become one of the greatest photographers of the twentieth century, capturing some of the most iconic images of the Swinging Sixties.

At three o'clock on a dreary afternoon of February 6 1958, BEA flight 609 crashed at Munich Airport while attempting to take off in bad weather. The flight was returning from Yugoslavia with the Manchester United team on board, who had just beaten Red Star Belgrade in one of the quarter finals of the European Cup. Twenty-one of the forty-four passengers were killed, including eight players of Manchester United, the 'Busby Babes' as they were nicknamed, three staff and eight journalists. Brian was sent out by the *Daily Sketch* to Munich later that day to record the aftermath. Dramatic photos captured scenes of some of the uninjured players going back into the burning plane and rescuing other passengers. They were already being hailed as heroes.

Brian arrived in Munich that evening, the first British press representative to arrive. By that time all the survivors were in hospital, some with life-threatening injuries. They were being treated on various floors in the hospital. Brian could see problems arising when the rest of the press pack arrived as pressure mounted from the public for information and photos. He met with a Canadian doctor and a professor to work out how the press could get their reports and pictures and limit the intrusion on the injured survivors. As it was getting late the doctors asked for the meeting at nine o'clock the next morning.

Overnight however, a German photographer gained entry to the wards and took some harrowing photos of the unfortunate victims, which he sold around the world. Distressed relatives of the injured arrived the following day flanked by an army of press reporters and photographers. As the press besieged the hospital the tabloids were accused of forcing their way in to interview the injured at their bedside and chasing the distraught relatives to their hotels. It was an explosive situation. It was eventually agreed that nobody was allowed in the wards where the seriously injured were, and that pictures and interviews of the less serious were only allowed with their permission at a designated time. It was an improvement on the initial chaos, but the damage had already been done.

By the time Brian returned to London there was uproar in the media. Letters poured in, mainly to the broadsheets, complaining bitterly of the disgusting behaviour of the 'gutter' press. Their reputation sank to an all-time low as editors, reporters and photographers alike were branded little more than ghoulish, self-seeking vultures. Brian was asked by his editor, Herbert Gunn, to describe exactly what he witnessed to set the record straight. To inflame the situation even further, Herbert Gunn used his report to argue the justification of publishing some of the photos that were under attack. Little did Brian know that eight months later, his family would be the target of the same pack of wolves.

On October 22 Jane Buckingham was the last to arrive at the airport as the tannoy announced final boarding. Brian walked briskly over the tarmac to the waiting Viscount with Paddy, Jane and reporter Lee Benson. They climbed the mobile stairway to the front door to be greeted by the smiling young steward, who took their coats and were quickly shown to their seats. Brian sat next to Lee Benson, with Jane and Paddy in front.

The crew made their final preparations and the plane took off smoothly at 08.41, just sixteen minutes later than scheduled. Within an hour the flight attendants served breakfast. The team discussed their plans for Naples and then dozed for a while, catching up for lost sleep as the plane headed across France towards Italy. Brian would have had his camera near to hand, but it would have been of no use in those last few seconds.

Friends of Brian working for the *Daily Sketch* managed to contact Hazel and tell her the terrible news before she saw it in the evening newspapers. Hazel was two months pregnant.

The family gathered in London, inconsolable at the loss of one of the most popular members of the family. Brian's body was brought back to London and his cremation was held at Croydon Crematorium a few weeks later. His ashes were scattered on the Garden of Remembrance.

On November 5, a memorial service was held in St Bride's Church, Fleet Street, with many friends and representatives of the press gathered to celebrate the short lives of Paddy Watson, Lee Benson and Brian Fogaty, all of whom had left their mark on the world of journalism. Eight months later, in June 1959 Brian's second daughter was born.

The Freelance Journalist
LESLIE KING / LEE BENSON

With just a few minutes to go before the BEA check-in desk shut, Leslie King arrived breathless clutching his passport and a small suitcase. He was booked on the 08.25 flight to Naples with *Daily Sketch* features writer Paddy Watson, respected photographer Brian Fogaty, and successful London model Jane Buckingham. Leslie had managed just a few hours sleep after spending much of the previous night hanging out in his favourite West End nightclubs on the lookout for stories of the indiscretions of the wealthy and famous. As a result he arrived a little dishevelled from lack of sleep.

Leslie King was no ordinary freelance journalist. He specialised in scandal, especially involving well-known actors with connections to Hollywood. He lived in the shadows much of the time, but such was his chameleon-like nature that he could slip effortlessly between the shady underworld of London's nightlife and Kensington's fashionable drawing rooms. This could be a highly dangerous business, and you could not afford to upset the wrong person, and so as a reporter he used an alias, Lee Benson. This was the name he used to book his flight to Naples, and it was to cause some confusion within the next twenty-four hours.

Lee Benson was an enigma. We know that in 1958 he was thirty years old, lived in Cricklewood in north London, and was possibly married to Hetty King, but even that is uncertain. Apart from that, little is known about his personal life. It is thought he was born in London and became a junior reporter in Fleet Street when he left school. This involved making tea, running errands for reporters and editors trying to hit their deadlines on clackety typewriters, or attending minor social functions that the more senior reporters did not want to attend. This was an apprenticeship that involved listening and watching how the more experienced reporters operated, and to survive in Fleet Street you had to learn fast.

In the early 1950s there was no internet, TV was still in its infancy and the wireless (radio) and the newspapers were the main sources of information for the public. These were controlled by a handful of extremely powerful and influential newspaper barons.

The most powerful was Lord Beaverbrook, (Max Aitken 1879–1964), a Canadian of Scottish descent who trained in finance in Halifax, Nova Scotia and by a series of shrewd business deals buying, selling and merging various companies, became a millionaire by the age of thirty. He moved to Britain in 1910, and became involved in politics, winning a seat in the House of Commons later that year. A knighthood followed in 1911. He bought a majority share in the right-wing, populist tabloid, *Daily Express* from its founder, Sir Arthur Pearson in 1916.

In 1931 the newspaper moved from Manchester to Fleet Street into a specially commissioned art-deco building. Beaverbrook built the *Daily Express* into the most powerful mass circulation newspaper in the world. By 1936 the circulation was 2,250,000 per day, (in 2019 it was 302,690) and became a hugely influential tool for the Conservative party in British politics. In 1933 he bought the *Evening Standard*. In 1940 Churchill appointed him Minister of Aircraft Production, and Lord Privy Seal in 1943.

The *Daily Express* was the first newspaper to carry sport, women's features and gossip. It ran an aggressive marketing campaign and by the 1960s it was described by the Duke of Edinburgh as *'full of lies, scandal and imagination.'*

Lord Beaverbrook had strong competitors. Alfred Harmsworth, (later 1st Viscount Northcliffe 1865–1922) and his brother Harold, (later Lord Rothermere 1868–1940) founded the *Daily Mail* in 1896, *Daily Mirror* in 1903, and rescued *The Times* in 1908. After further provincial acquisitions Amalgamated Press became the largest periodical-publishing empire in the world.

Allied Newspapers, established in 1924, was owned by Welsh brothers William and James Berry. William, (later 1st Viscount Camrose 1879–1954) started work as a journalist and purchased the *Sunday Times* in 1915 and the *Financial Times* in 1919. James, (later 1st Viscount Kemsley 1883–1968), a colliery owner, bought the *Daily Sketch* in 1925 and the *Daily Telegraph* in 1928.

Between these three media giants, they dominated the news content of all the major newspapers in the land and directly influenced every aspect of the political landscape.

The *Daily Sketch* was founded in 1909 by Sir Edward Hulton and had a chequered history. It was sold to Lord Rothermere in 1920, who sold it the Berry brothers in 1925. They incorporated it into Allied Newspapers, and it was merged with the *Daily Graphic* in 1946. It was sold back to Lord Rothermere in 1952 who revived the name, the *Daily*

Sketch. It continued to be a Conservative-supporting, populist tabloid competing with the left-wing *Daily Mirror*.

In the 1950s, competition between the tabloids was intense, adopting the American technique of 'yellow journalism' with banner headlines, lurid features and sensationalised news. An essential ingredient was the newspaper diarist, more commonly known as the gossip columnist. They relentlessly pursued the eye-catching philanderings of members of the aristocracy at social parties, balls and weddings, the indiscretions of misbehaving politicians, and the sexual escapades of not-so-well-known celebrities.

Some newspapers had a named columnist and others had a variety of contributors writing under a column name, such as the William Hickey column in the *Daily Express*. All of them needed sources and some had up to nine freelance reporters supplying them with the latest juicy titbits.

In 1958 Simon Ward was the diarist for the *Daily Sketch*, and Lee Benson was his main source. Lee was now a seasoned freelance investigative journalist, well-known around the London's West End as *'Little Mister Whisper.'* Others were not so kind – one American publication called him *'a chronic boudoir-skulker and chronicler of overcrowded love-nests.'*

He had many contacts in all walks of life, and a smooth, fast-talking style that could get him into elegant London drawing rooms, stylish cocktail parties, and the occasional wild, libertine weekend party in country houses tucked away in the Home Counties. In the early hours he would be spotted in the smoke-filled nightclubs in earnest conversation with the young hostesses eager to earn a little extra for a story of the latest indiscretions.

He always knew more than he passed on. The trick was to walk the fine line of throwing in enough tasty morsels to keep the readers hooked and leave them wanting to come back for more. He was always discreet with his sources. He also had to be careful to abide by the strict libel laws in England. He'd had experience of this the previous year.

In 1957, Lee became involved on the periphery in a criminal libel trial in California against an American magazine called *Confidential.* It had been started by entrepreneur Robert Harrison, the son of Russian immigrants brought up in the Bronx. Harrison was based in New York and saw that there was money to be made from exposing the indiscretions of the big film stars in Hollywood. He took muck-raking and gossip-mongering to a new low.

Harrison set up a spy network of hack journalists, call girls, private investigators, and up-and-coming starlets desperate for money. He used the latest surveillance equipment, and when *Confidential* was launched in 1952 it caused a sensation.

Many big stars were caught totally off guard and panic ensued. Some, such as actors Robert Mitcham, Humphrey Bogart and Victor Mature, laughed it off, not caring about scurrilous tittle-tattle. Others were not so amused, including Errol Flynn, Elvis Presley, Clark Gable, Judy Garland, John Wayne and Joan Crawford. Within months of its launch, sales of *Confidential* shot up to four million and Harrison very quickly became one of America's most successful magazine publishers.

Writs for libel flew about like confetti but Harrison ignored them, hiding behind the constitution's First Amendment, knowing they would not pursue their claims as he had all the incriminating photos and tape recordings stashed away in New York. Anyone and everyone was fair game.

The magazine was so successful he decided to expand it to London. He set up a similar network of spies led by a thirty-year-old former subaltern in the Black Watch called Michael Mordaunt-Smith. His chief informant and spymaster was Lee Benson.

Lee worked freelance, tracking visiting stars around the nightclubs and bars of London, sometimes luring them into honey-traps with well-paid party girls and boys. This sleazy, sordid work was lucrative, but he soon realised there was chilling danger attached. When he started receiving serious physical threats from shadowy figures in Hollywood, Lee knew these were not idle, and withdrew his services from *Confidential*.

He retained all the inside information he had gleaned on his *Confidential* assignments and offered the details for sale instead to the *Daily Sketch,* who gladly accepted them. It needed a boost in sales.

In August 1957, in what became known as the Trial of a Hundred Stars, the state of California took *Confidential* to the Supreme Court in Los Angeles on charges of criminal libel. Subpoenas were issued to 117 stars including Frank Sinatra, Dean Martin, and Lana Turner. Michael Mordaunt-Smith flew in from London to confirm the accuracy of the stories, and Lee was on standby in case he was required.

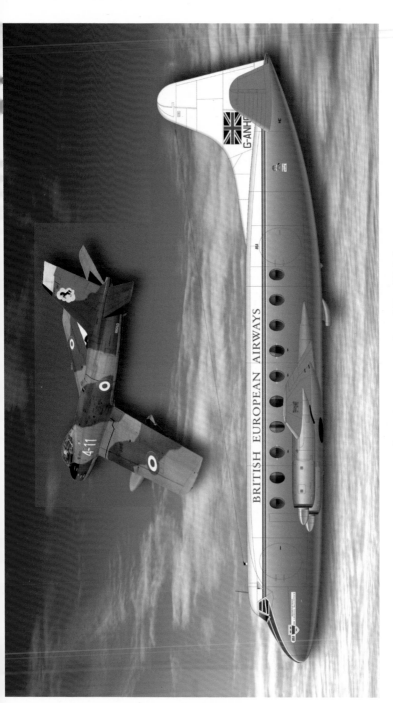

Fig 1. Vickers Viscount 701C and F-86E Sabre jet

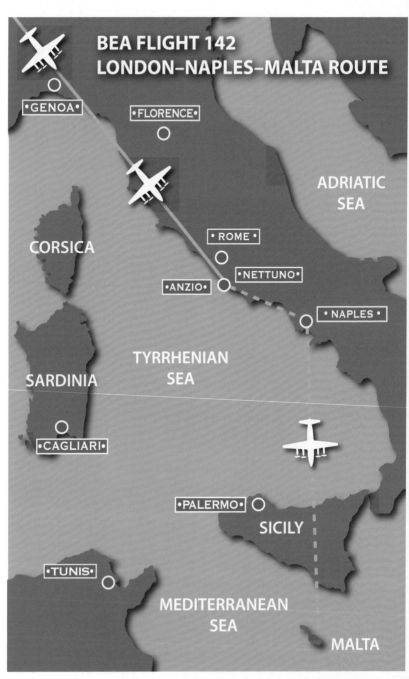

Map 1. Route of Flight BE142 London-Naples-Malta

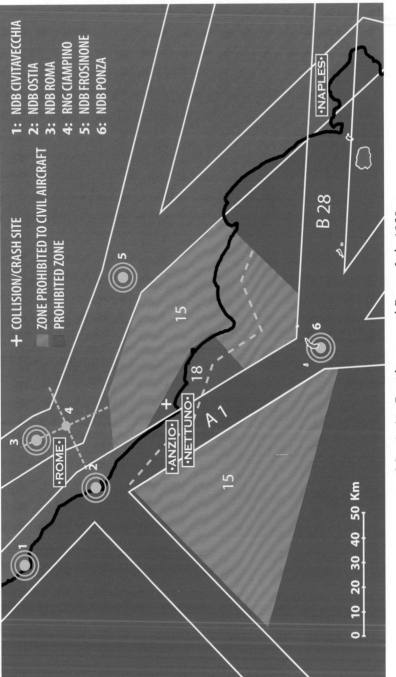

Map 2. Air Corridors around Rome, Italy 1958

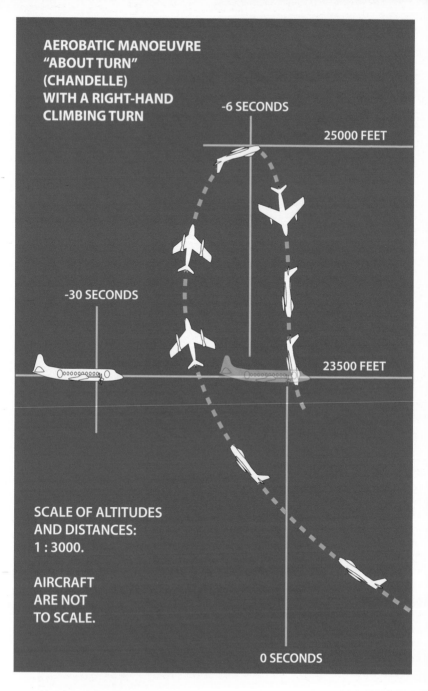

Fig 2. F-86E Jets *Chandelle* manoeuvre

Top Left: Fig 3 and 4. Captain Frank Foster and his wife, Pat 1956
Inset: Fig 5. The Frank Foster Boomerang Trophy
Bottom: Fig 6. The 1952 *Skylark* glider at Lasham

Fig 7. Geoff and Pam Wright's wedding 1956

Fig 8. The Wright brothers

Fig 9 and 10. James Bannon in 1940 and 1958

Figs 11–14. *Clockwise from top:* Terry O'Grady 1958 *"He loved flying"*
Rosie Bevan c. 1952 and Rosie and Terry at London Airport 1958

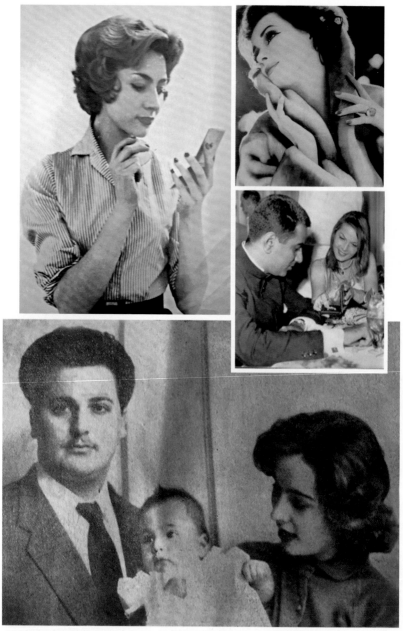

Figs 15–18. *Clockwise from top:* Jane Buckingham, model. London 1957. Jane, London 1958. Prince Shiv and Eva Bartok, London 1958. Reginald Kawaja, Jane and Yasmin 1956

IN MEMORIAM

A Daily Sketch

team :

PATRICIA (PADDY) WATSON
(Staff writer, the Daily Sketch)

BRIAN FOGATY
(Free Lance cameraman)

LEE BENSON
(Free Lance reporter)

ST. BRIDE'S CHURCH, FLEET STREET
Wednesday, 5th November, 1958, at 12.30 p.m.

Conducted by the Rector

THE REV. CYRIL M. ARMITAGE,
M.V.O., M.A.

Figs 19–23.
Clockwise from top:
Brian and Hazel Fogaty
and family at Sally's
Christening, 1957.
Brian Fogaty, 1958,
*"A most talented
photographer"*
Paddy Watson, *"Full of
bubbling energy"* Lee Benson, 1957, *"Little Mister Whisper"*
Inset: Memorial Service Cover, London, November 1958

Miss **Diana Muckerman** to **Mr. Charles D. Cubitt:** *She is the only daughter of the late Mr. L. I. Muckerman, & of Mrs. Byrnece Muckerman, of Park Avenue, New York. He is the son of Major & Mrs. Cyril Cubitt, Edge of the Hill, Crowthorne, Berks.*

Figs 24–26.
Above: Charles and Diana Cubitt 1958
"A top society wedding"
Left: Diana Muckerman, *The Tatler*
October1958, *Below:* St Michael & All
Angels Graveyard, Sandhurst, Surrey

CHARLES DESMOND CUBITT
AND HIS BRIDE
DIANA

WHO DIED TOGETHER IN AN AIR CRASH
OVER NETTUNO ITALY OCTOBER 23RD 1958
OUR LIFE OF LOVE AND

Figs 27–29.
Clockwise from top left:
King Robert the Bruce,
Edinburgh Castle. Robert
Bruce, Edinburgh 1958.
William and Margaret
Buchan *"a devoted and
successful couple"*

Figs 30–33.
Clockwise from top left:
Lady Jenny Weir c. 1956.
Sir Cecil Weir, *"Heartbroken when Jenny died"* RMS *Titanic* 1912.
Frances Miller c. 1956

Figs 34–37.
Clockwise from top left:
John and Joan Prince,
Wedding day 1950.
John Prince, barrister, 1952
HMS *Tartar* "*Lucky Tartar*"
Inset: John and Ellen, 1942

Fig 38. Mary Mathieson's grave in Toronto, Canada

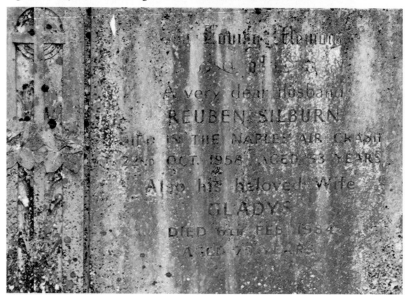

Fig 39. Reuben Silburn's grave in Banstead

Below: Figs 41–42. Robert Chalmers' Presentation in Perth, Scotland, 1958

Above left: Fig 40. John Chalmers above Blackley's, Valletta, c.1930s

Above: Fig 43. HMS *Illustrious* Malta 1942

SHEILA M. LANE
NURSING SISTER Q.A.R.N.N.S
H.M.S. ST ANGELO
22ND OCT. 1958 AGED 31

"I AM THE RESURRECTION
AND THE LIFE:
HE THAT BELIEVETH IN ME,
THOUGH HE WERE DEAD,
YET SHALL HE LIVE."

Left: Fig 44.
Sheila Lane's grave in
Kalkara naval cemetery,
Malta

Above: Fig 45.
The George Cross
awarded to Malta in 1942

Pornographic books and magazines were piled high on the court tables and readings from the magazines were quickly barred after the first sample was read out. Half a million words were submitted, but in the end only Maureen O'Hara and Dorothy Dandridge gave evidence. The jury retired for fifteen days in a luxury hotel to deliberate and could not agree. They were dismissed and the judge declared a mistrial. He wanted a re-trial, much to the horror of the studio bosses, but eventually it was dropped. An out-of-court settlement was negotiated whereby *Confidential* agreed to stop harassing the stars, and all charges would be dropped.

Without its sensational content, sales of *Confidential* dropped dramatically, and a year later Harrison shut it down. He was last seen heading for the Dominican Republic.

The result of this trial in America was to have a significant effect on the quality and veracity of stories being published in Britain. In the fight for circulation dominance, similar 'yellow journalism' tactics were employed, the tabloids became more aggressive, and the libel laws were pushed to the limit.

Lee Benson had been a regular visitor to *The Embassy Club* in Mayfair and knew many of the girls working there, including Jane Buckingham. He knew she was a girlfriend of wealthy playboy Prince Shiv, but also knew that the Prince had been visiting slinky Hollywood actress Eva Bartok at her cottage in Kingston-upon-Thames that she was renting while shooting a film at Pinewood Studies.

Eva Bartok's tumultuous love life was a popular read in the tabloid press, especially after her recent divorce from Curd Jürgens, when she returned from filming in Los Angeles clutching the baby girl born after a brief affair with Frank Sinatra. Around October 20 1958 Lee heard that in a press interview Eva Bartok had not denied that she was engaged to the prince and was about to travel to France.

Lee could smell a potential scoop and quickly formulated a plan. He spoke to Jane, and told her what he had heard. She was distraught and angry, and Lee persuaded her to make a passionate statement to the press, which she did on the evening of October 20. Jane then agreed to fly to Naples with Paddy Watson, a *Daily Sketch* features writer and photographer Brian Fogaty to confront Prince Shiv, who was on his way to see his father. Her pictures would be in all the papers, the *Daily Sketch* would get a scoop and she would win back her prince.

Even though they were all tired, the adrenalin was high and there was a heightened tension in the air when the four of them met at the check-in desk at London Airport on October 22. Jane was being reassured by Paddy, Brian was looking forward to seeing Naples, and Lee was anticipating a cracking good story ahead.

There was no scoop, just the reporting of a terrible tragedy. Lee did hit the headlines the following day. He was put briefly in the spotlight, where he would not have been comfortable.

On November 5 a memorial service was held at St Bride's Church in Fleet Street for Paddy, Brian and Lee, where many friends and journalists gathered to pay their respects. Herbert Gunn, the editor of the *Daily Sketch* paid tribute to him and printed a black-framed article in the paper on October 23 saying, *'He was one of those few journalists who could take tea with a duchess, cocktails with a deb, supper with a prince and still dance with a night-club hostess till dawn.'*

COUPLES

The Bride and Groom
CHARLES and DIANA CUBITT

The marriage of Charles Cubitt and Diana Muckerman on October 21 1958 was one of the most glamourous London society weddings of the year.

The service was held in St James' Roman Catholic Church, Spanish Place in Marylebone, London. It was a magnificent setting. The church was designed by Edward Goldie in early Gothic style and inspired by Salisbury Cathedral and Westminster Abbey, and was opened on Michaelmas Day 1890. The entrance is a copy of the main entrance to Lichfield Cathedral and the arches of the nave are supported by pillars enriched with marble colonettes. The organ, built in 1922 by Alfred Hunter and Sons of Clapham, is considered one of the finest examples of its kind in Britain.

At four o'clock, Mendelssohn's *Wedding March* resounded around the church as the radiant bride glided slowly down the aisle on the arm of her uncle Richard Muckerman, dressed in an exquisite, white satin wedding dress with a beautiful, finely-embroidered veil, sending ripples of delight through the thronged congregation. Charles wore a traditional morning suit, a dark tie decorated with a small, repeated white motif, a grey waistcoat and sported a large white carnation in his buttonhole, looking every inch the dapper gentleman. He turned as Diana entered the church and beamed. She looked stunning.

Diana's American mother Byrnece, and English

grandmother Mary, proudly looked on with tears of joy welling in their eyes. One of the wedding guests, Mrs Endo Stourton said at the time, *'She was truly radiant and bubbling with happiness. Desmond was a very fine man and obviously very much in love with Diana. It was a perfect wedding.'*

As they emerged from the church, a shower of confetti rained down, and cheers went up from a nearby building site. The bride and groom stepped into the gleaming black limousine, Diana glowing with happiness, clutching an exquisite bouquet of flowers that included scented roses, lily of the valley, pink carnations and gypsophilia. They paused for the assembled photographers in a flurry of flashbulbs, and were whisked off to a sumptuous reception at Claridges hotel in Mayfair.

Over 300 guests celebrated in the newly-refurbished, gold-leaf-decorated ballroom. Amongst the guests were peers and peeresses, a sprinkling of millionaires and many friends and relations of the two families. Thousands of red roses had been flown across from America and festooned the tables. The wine flowed freely, verbose speeches and toasts were proposed to the happy couple, from both sides of the Atlantic, followed by music and dancing that lasted late into the night.

Charles and Diana Cubitt left the reception after a few hours to the echoing cheers of the delighted guests with the majority thinking the happy couple were leaving on their honeymoon to Italy. But they had a secret. Diana had suggested to Charles that they delay their departure by one day and spend their first romantic evening in the honeymoon suite of the famous Ritz hotel close by in Mayfair. They could catch the flight to Naples the following morning.

The last of the family members to see them was Charles's nineteen-year-old brother, Gerald. He was to become one of South Africa's leading natural history photographers, and had delayed going to Trinity College, Dublin to be an usher at the wedding.

He saw them in their room at The Ritz that evening when he went to pick up Diana's dog, a little Tibetan shih tzu called *Hardwick*. Diana had just written a poem and was excited about visiting Naples and catching the ferry to the romantic, sun-drenched islands of Ischia and Capri overlooked by Mount Vesuvius.

The Groom
CHARLES CUBITT

C harles Desmond Cubitt (always known as Desmond to the family) was born in Kensington on June 24 1924 into a most interesting and complicated family, that had many curious links to Italy. Some newspapers mistakenly reported that Desmond was part of the building empire founded by the renowned master builder and architect Thomas Cubitt (1788–1855) in 1810. In fact Desmond was descended from Thomas' younger brother Lewis Cubitt (1799–1833), an equally talented civil engineer, responsible for designing both London Bridge and King's Cross railway stations, and many bridges around the world. Lewis was also the younger brother of William Cubitt, who served as Lord Mayor of London in 1860. The Cubitts were an outstanding and prolific family of their generation.

Lewis's grandson was Thomas Cubitt (1870–1947) and Desmond's grandfather. When Thomas was touring Italy in about 1890 he fell in love with a beautiful Italian girl, Fede, from Tuscany who was the only child of Count Adolpho Riccardi of Florence. In order to preserve the aristocratic pedigree of the Riccardi family, one of the conditions of the marriage was that Thomas would bear the title 'Count'. His wife would become Countess Fede Maria Riccardi.

After protracted negotiations within the families the two were married in 1893. In 1905 Thomas was granted a special Royal Warrant by King Edward VII to bear his Italian title and officially became Count Thomas Cubitt-Riccardi.

This however caused a few problems when Italy joined the war against the Allies in 1940, having signed the Tripartite Pact with Germany and Japan. Thomas was on holiday at the *Villa Rosa* in Bordighera at that time, and to his great surprise, (and perhaps to only a few others) was placed under house arrest in his home by the Mussolini regime. This internment lasted for three years.

When Italy capitulated to the Allies in 1943 after the invasion of Sicily, things took a turn for the worse. The Gestapo commandeered the house, and it was time to flee. With the help of the Red Cross, Thomas and Fede escaped and made their way back to England via Switzerland. Thomas decided to stop using his title after that experience.

Thomas and Fede Cubitt had four children, three girls, Vera, Theodora, and Monica, and a boy, Charles Cyril, who was Desmond's father, born in Florence in 1896. Cyril enjoyed an idyllic Edwardian upbringing, which was brought to an abrupt halt in 1914 with the outbreak of World War One.

He distinguished himself as a soldier, serving as a Captain with the Royal Welsh Fusiliers winning the Military Cross in France in 1918. After the war he married Gladys Louise Crake in 1919 and they had five sons. Desmond was the third, born in 1924.

Desmond was sent to Ampleforth College, a leading Catholic boarding school in north Yorkshire run by Benedictine monks which, ironically for Desmond, bore the motto *'God is the Protector'*. Popular with the Catholic aristocracy, it was labelled *'The Catholic Eton'*. At that time the school would have been single sex, strict and God-fearing.

In 1943, at the age of nineteen, with World War Two in its fourth year, Desmond joined the Rifle Brigade as a 2nd Lieutenant, and quickly rose to become a Captain in the Green Jackets. Much to the relief of his father he survived serious injury. Tragically, his elder brother Victor was not so lucky. He died in battle in Italy in 1944 from a stray piece of shrapnel piercing his heart, and is buried in the military cemetery in Assisi in Umbria.

At the end of the war, Desmond returned home and was determined to get away from England, from the pressures of the family, and to travel. His quiet but self-confident and charming personality brought him success in the world of marketing. For the next ten years he travelled extensively, working for various companies, from printers and film makers in Los Angeles to an aluminium manufacturer. He was enjoying this itinerant lifestyle, but at thirty-four years old he was coming under pressure to marry and settle down.

In 1957 he met Diana at a party in London and was immediately smitten by her beauty, sophistication and bubbly personality. In 1958 when Diana said she may have to return to New York, Desmond proposed to her, and to his delight, and the rest of the family, Diana accepted.

The Bride
DIANA CUBITT

D iana Muckerman came from a very different, but no less interesting background. She was born in San Diego, California on August 11 1932, the only daughter of Louis Muckerman and Byrnece MacFadden.

Diana's grandfather, Bernarr MacFadden was born in Missouri in 1868. The American Civil War that ended three years earlier had devastated the south and resulted in great hardship for the people. Bernarr was a sickly, thin child, and determined to get fit.

As a teenager he developed his own exercise and diet regime, gave up meat and white bread, believed in fasting, and ran ten miles every day before breakfast. He moved to St Louis and established a bodybuilding company, published hundreds of books and opened a successful chain of vegetarian shops in the early part of the twentieth century. He became known as the father of American physical culture.

Through his hard work and enterprise he became a millionaire, mixed with Hollywood film stars and politicians, and ran for Governor of New York. He was married four times, and together with his unconventional life and outspoken views on sex, which were far too controversial for the conservative American public, he did not get far in his political ambitions. He died in 1955 at the age of eighty-seven, after refusing medical assistance for a minor illness.

Diana's grandmother was Mary Williamson. She was English and born into a poor family in Keighley, near Bradford, Yorkshire in 1894. She had contracted typhoid when she was younger and took up swimming to recover. By the age of eighteen the family had moved to Halifax and Mary was a working in a carpet factory. She had continued swimming, becoming the local swimming champion, and winning many prizes.

Mary's life changed dramatically in 1913, when Bernarr came to Halifax to judge a contest entitled 'The Most Perfect Specimen of British Womanhood'. Mary entered and was voted the winner. Two months later, twenty-year-old Mary married the forty-seven-year-old millionaire to become his third wife.

During a bizarre one-year tour of England they performed stunts to crowds to show they were the fittest husband and wife in the world. In early 1914 Mary gave birth to their first daughter in Brighton. The following year Bernarr and Mary moved back to New Jersey to start a new life in America. Diana's mother, Byrnece, was born in New York in 1916, the third of six daughters.

By 1932 Mary was tired of the crazy life with Bernarr and they separated. In the divorce petition Bernarr complained that Mary had put on weight and refused to go on the ten-mile walks with him before breakfast!

By the age of sixteen Byrnece was living in St Louis, still the centre of her father's thriving business. There she met a wealthy young businessman Louis Ignacious Muckerman, aged twenty-four, and within a few months they were married.

Tragically, a few months later on March 24 1932, Louis was killed in a car accident in Texas. He was alone in the car when a tyre blew, sending the car careering off the road and down an embankment. Diana was born five months later in San Diego.

Byrnece had gone back to live with her mother Mary, who had separated from Bernarr, and was living in La Jolla, a quiet and affluent coastal suburb of San Diego. Diana spent her childhood there and enjoyed a more traditional schooling.

By the 1930s, films were enormously popular, helping to take people's minds off the economic crisis as the Great Depression deepened, and the busy Hollywood studios were in full production. As a wealthy young widow, Byrnece would have been invited to many money-raising functions, meeting the stars of the day, and started to move in the party circles.

She met a charismatic actor called Georges Metaxa from Bucharest. He had made a variety of films, including *Secrets of a Secretary* with Claudette Colbert (1931) and *Swing Time* with Fred Astaire and Ginger Rogers (1936). In 1936 she married him at the age of twenty. He continued making films in the 1940s but by 1946 the marriage was over and they divorced with no children.

Diana finished her schooling in California and by the age of eighteen, yearned to travel to New York, to move in, what she considered, a more sophisticated set on the east coast. There she mixed with writers, musicians and painters and was known for her enjoyment of a good party.

The 1950s were an exciting time for literature, theatre and music, especially in London, where a new post-war generation of artists were creating radical new works. In 1954, at the age of twenty-two she boarded the *Queen Elizabeth* in New York bound for Southampton and headed for London with the intention to write. She wrote poetry and when asked if she was a writer she replied, *'I am hardly a writer, I have never had anything published, but I write poetry and am trying my hand at a novel.'*

At a party in London in 1957 she met Desmond and she fell for this tall, aristocratic, handsome, worldly businessman who loved her poetry. Diana had already extended and overstayed her visa, but they were blissfully in love and quickly decided to get married.

They announced their engagement in *The Tatler* magazine on October 15 1958, and were married six days later at St James's Church.

On the morning of October 22, Desmond and Diana were warmly welcomed by the crew as they boarded flight BE142. A bottle of champagne awaited them.

At around that time the Muckerman, MacFadden and Cubitt family party were rising and preparing for breakfast in Claridges. It was there, just six hours later, they were told the tragic news about the mid-air collision over Italy.

Desmond's father flew to Rome a few days later to see the British Embassy staff and arrange for Desmond and Diana to be transferred to the funeral directors at Crowthorne in Berkshire. He had now lost two sons in Italy.

The funeral was held in St Michael and All Angels Church, Sandhurst, near Crowthorne, where the Cubitt family plot is situated, and was attended by many of the same people who only weeks earlier had celebrated the young couple's glittering wedding.

The inscription on the grave reads,

In Loving Memory of Charles Desmond Cubitt and his bride Diana
Who died together in an air crash over Nettuno on October 22 1958
'Our Life of Love is God'

The Farmers
WILLIAM and MARGARET BUCHAN

On October 22 1958 William and Margaret Buchan arrived at London Airport in plenty of time for their 08.25 flight to Naples, having stayed in a nearby hotel overnight. It had been a good year for them on the farm, and with the harvest safely gathered in, they were looking forward to their well-earned holiday in Capri and Sicily.

Husband
WILLIAM BUCHAN

William Robert Tullis Buchan was born in the parish of St Nicholas in Warwick on April 28 1897. His parents were both Scots. His father, Robert was born in Cameron, Fife in 1860 and his mother, Jane was born in Sandbank, Argyllshire in 1866. In the mid-1890s they travelled south to Warwickshire, where Robert took up work as a farm bailiff on The Home Farm, Guy's Cliffe, near Warwick.

Warwick is an ancient and historic town, dominated by its medieval castle originally built in 1068 by William the Conqueror shortly after his successful invasion of England. The River Avon runs through it, and when the Grand Union Canal was constructed and the railway built in 1852, the town was connected to Birmingham and other major cities. For centuries Warwick was a thriving market town, and served as a centre for the local area for agricultural produce supplied by the surrounding prosperous farms.

William spent his childhood in Warwick with his two elder sisters, Alexandrina and Alice. It was the ideal place for a young man to learn the pleasures and pitfalls of farming in Edwardian England. On market days he watched the buyers and sellers battle it out for the best deal on their livestock and crops. William also witnessed what happened in the bad years, when disease struck or crops failed, when farmers went bankrupt as they struggled to pay their debts. He saw the anguish suffered by the tenant farmers when his father had to reclaim monies owed to the landowners.

Sometime after World War One, the Buchan family returned to Scotland and William spent ten years farming at Auchterforfar Farm, in Forfar. In 1925, at the age of twenty-eight, William married his first wife, Jane Buchanan, a farmer's daughter, at the Church of Scotland in Culross, Fife. They lived on the farm and raised a family there. William specialised in breeding good quality beef cattle, but in 1938 he decided to diversify and formed the Forfar Potato Company, which thrived when World War Two started in 1939. He also developed the farm into a shooting estate.

Although married to Jane for fifteen years, the marriage faltered when William fell in love with Margaret McVicar, who lived locally in the village of Carmyllie, and was to become his second wife.

Wife
Margaret Buchan

Margaret Lawson McVicar was born in the Free Church manse, Glen Lyon, Perthshire on March 5 1911. Her father, Robert Barr McVicar came from Coupar Angus in Angus and was a minister of the strict Free Church of Scotland. Her mother, Williamina Booth came from Dundee. Margaret's three siblings, Charlotte, Peter and Robert were also born in Glen Lyon.

Summer was an idyllic time for the children. Glen Lyon is the longest enclosed glen in Scotland running for thirty-four miles, and described by Sir Walter Scott as *'the longest, loneliest and loveliest glen in Scotland.'* There were magnificent walks through sunlit wild meadows, surrounded by craggy mountains, snow-capped in winter. Wild animals roamed the land, and there was always the chance of a glimpse of a magnificent red stag. The rivers teemed with fish and were popular with fisherman.

In 1916 the family moved to Dumfries to another Free Church, but in 1919, Margaret's father changed to the more relaxed Church of Scotland and became the minister at Carnoch, Strathconon in Rosshire. They were living in another remote and beautiful area, where Margaret would walk several miles to get to the primary school at Milton. The nearest secondary school was thirty-five miles away, so in term-time Williamina took Margaret and her two brothers to stay at their grandfather's property in Newtyle, so they could attend school in Dundee.

In 1926 the family moved again to Carmyllie in Forfarshire, where Margaret attended Arbroath High School, which was originally a grammar school. She was a bright pupil and at the age of nineteen won a scholarship to St Andrews University in Fife, where she graduated in 1933 with an M.A. (Hons).

Carmyllie was only seven miles from William's farm at Auchterforfar, and the church was the centre of social activities in the area. It is most likely that this is where William and Margaret first met, and their relationship began.

By 1939 Margaret had moved to London, working as a private secretary and was sharing a flat with her brother Peter in Hampstead. He was employed as a draughtsman with an engineering company. Whether she moved to London for employment or to avoid the scandal of a minister's daughter becoming entangled with a married man we shall never know.

In 1940 William asked for a divorce, and Jane refused, with their teenage children supporting her. Jane probably thought he was having a mid-life crisis and a brief fling with a younger woman fourteen years his junior. William though was adamant. He left Scotland and returned to England to manage various farms in Somerset with Margaret. In 1943, Jane realised she had lost her battle for reconciliation and reluctantly agreed to the divorce in the summer. The children remained with her and became estranged from their father. Within three months, William and Margaret married in Bristol.

They made a noticeable couple. At over six-foot-two, William was a tall man. He had a strong, intelligent face, emphasised by his receding hairline. Next to him, Margaret was tiny at just five-foot-two. She was slim and petite, with dark-brown, curly hair, a bright, intelligent face and a ready smile. They were very much in love and determined to make a success of their marriage and new life.

The farm at Auchterforfar and the Forfar Potato Company were sold, and William and Margaret started to look around Gloucestershire for a new farm. It took two years to find the one they wanted. In the meantime they managed a farm in Leicestershire.

They found Lowesmoor Farm in 1945 near the little village of Cherington, between Cirencester and Tetbury. There were over 600 acres of prime arable land and it came with a seven-bedroomed Grade II listed farmhouse, with cottages and outbuildings. Many old properties had paid the price of neglect during World War Two, and little maintenance work had been carried out on the farm for over five years. There was much to be done.

William had a clear idea of how he wanted to develop the farm and with Margaret's enthusiastic support he set about it with vigour. The Cotswolds was fertile and nutritious grazing land, and he introduced some of the best breeds from Scotland to produce top quality beef. He developed new methods for self-feeding the animals. He grew a variety of crops and encouraged the tenants living in the cottages to be involved and work on the farm.

The first few years at Lowesmoor were very challenging as Britain struggled to recover from six years of war. One of the worst winters on record started in January 1947 with heavy snow driven by strong easterly winds creating deep snowdrifts that blocked roads and railways. Even the Isles of Scilly were under eight inches of snow. Coal could not be delivered to power stations, causing massive disruption to energy supplies. Vegetables were frozen into the ground. There were food shortages and rationing was introduced, even more draconian than during the war.

Getting feed to the animals marooned in the fields was impossible. The countryside was gripped by the bitterly cold weather throughout February, and the misery for farmers continued into March, and when the thaw finally came, it caused widespread flooding. 10 to 20% of the cereal and potato crops were lost, sheep farmers lost 25% of their flocks and thousands of cattle starved to death. Anxious friends and relatives sent food parcels from Canada and Australia, and Army engineers were sent into many rural areas to assist. Thousands of Britons emigrated to Australia, and the United States sent millions of dollars in financial assistance to Britain through the Marshall Plan.

William and Margaret battled with all these challenges and over the next ten years built up the farm to one of the best run and most profitable in England. They won awards from the Gloucestershire Root, Fruit and Grain Society for their output, especially of wheat, barley and potatoes.

They led the way in finding methods of increasing the fertility from the land, and increasing yields by the introduction of new machinery. The self-feeding methods they developed for the animals became widely used, and they were popular in the farming community.

They were involved in helping the local villages and Margaret was on the board of the local school. They were both active participants in the local and area branches of the National Union of Farmers.

When they set off for Naples on October 22 1958, a relaxing holiday in the Mediterranean sun was just reward for their hard-earned success at Cherington.

William and Margaret were buried together at a quiet funeral at St Nicholas' Church, Cherington. They had no children, and the inscription on the simple headstone erected by the family gives little away of their interesting lives.

'In Memory of William Robert Tullis Buchan and his wife Margaret Lawson McVicar of Lowesmoor who died in an air accident over Italy on 22 October 1958.'

The Spy and the Executive
MARY MATHIESON and ROBERT ALLAN

Mary stepped out of the cab at London Airport early on October 22 1958 on the arm of her fiancé, Robert Allan in a buoyant and happy mood. A tall, well-dressed, elegant woman with striking red hair, she radiated all the charm and confidence of a woman well-travelled. She had stayed the night before with Robert at his flat in Pont Street, Knightsbridge, where they had spent the evening planning their week in one of Europe's most beautiful cities. Today was a very special day, for they were on their way to Rome to get married.

The Spy
MARY MATHIESON

Mary Elizabeth Mathieson was Canadian, born in Belleville, a thriving city situated on the shores of the Bay of Quinte on the north-eastern edge of Lake Ontario. Her family had lived there for many years. Her father, William ran a dental practice in Belleville and her mother, Lily was one of the first female doctors in Belleville Hospital.

The area around Belleville was originally home to the Mississaugas tribe of Native Americans, one of the Anishinaabe-speaking, First Nations people of Canada. The earliest Europeans to encounter them were French voyageurs in the early 1500s, professional canoe-paddlers who transported furs and other merchandise over long distances in the lake and river systems of northern America. Settlers arrived in the district in the eighteenth century and established Singleton's Creek in 1789. After a visit by Sir Francis Gore, the Lt. Governor of Upper Canada in 1816, the town was renamed Belleville, after his wife Lady Annabella. The waterfront town prospered, with three cloth factories, a paper mill, three tanneries and two breweries providing a rich variety of employment to the local people. In 1856 the Grand Trunk Railway reached Belleville and it became an important rail junction for transporting lumber. By 1865 the town's population had swollen to over 6,000. Electricity, water and telephone systems were installed and although logging died out in the 1870s, many new light industries replaced it, including a thriving cheesemaking industry.

In 1877 Belleville was officially incorporated as a city. With short, hot summers, long, cold winters and the breathtaking spectacle of acres of fiery russet and gold maple trees in autumn, this area of outstanding natural beauty made it one of the most popular places to live in Ontario.

Mary's mother, Lily Faladean Boyington was born in 1885 and came from a family who believed in the value and importance of education. She studied at medical school in Toronto and qualified as a doctor soon after the turn of the century. She worked at the hospital in Belleville where she met William Mathieson, who ran a dental practice. They married in 1908 and later that year their first daughter, Violet was born. Mary Elizabeth followed in 1910 and William Ronald, (always called Ron) was born in 1917.

In 1914 William bought a rural, wooden cottage at Hunters Point overlooking a beautiful little lake north of

Belleville. Every summer the children would take the train from Toronto to Trenton, accompanied by their grandmother, Grandma Boyington, a tiny but strong and feisty woman who struck fear into the hearts of the children if they played too boisterously. From Trenton a ferry boat would transport them to Hunters Point, where the men went fishing and the children spent idyllic summer's days swimming in the clear, cold water, canoeing and exploring all round the lake.

Fresh food was delivered by horse-drawn carriage from the local village and delicious meals were prepared over a blazing wood fire. In the heat of summer, freezing slabs of ice were brought up from the village by boat wrapped in straw, then hoisted out and kept in a crude but effective icehouse.

The children grew up with fond memories of long, hot sunny days, family outings armed with pails to go berry picking, and the sight of elegant ladies dressed in pretty, flowing cotton dresses ambling through the pristine, wild woods to share afternoon tea with their neighbours and catch up on the latest news. In 1947 a road was built around the lake and those halcyon days disappeared.

All the children enjoyed a first-class education in Belleville, and both Violet and Mary went on to study at Trinity College, the University of Toronto in 1928. Violet had been ill the previous year and unable to start, so they took up their places at the same time and graduated together in 1931. Violet went back to Belleville to become a popular High School teacher, while Mary took up a temporary position assisting the curator at the Royal Ontario Museum, Doctor Currelly, while she considered her next move.

Mary had developed into a bright, attractive woman with a natural ability for languages. She was a talented pianist and had a thirst to see the world. She wanted to escape this *'backward colony'* as she called Canada and was eager to explore the cultural cities of Europe and beyond. In the mid-thirties her father died, and her mother Lily, a strong-minded woman still not yet fifty, left her position at the hospital to set up a medical practice in Belleville. Violet lived nearby and was able to support her mother, so Mary decided that this was the time to start travelling.

She sailed to England in 1937 at the age of twenty-seven and did not to return to Belleville for another twenty years. She travelled to London with a friend, Henrietta Ball, but they separated soon after arrival when Henrietta met Dr. Sir Frederick Banting (1891–1941), who she married later that year.

Sir Frederick was an extraordinary man. A Canadian medical scientist, physician, and highly regarded amateur painter, he was a joint winner of the Nobel Prize for Medicine in 1923. He and Charles Best discovered insulin and its purification was a giant step forward in the successful treatment of diabetes. Tragically, he was killed in an air crash in Musgrave Harbour, Newfoundland in February 1941 when both engines of the Lockheed L-14 Super Electra he was travelling in failed.

In 1989 a *'Flame of Hope'* was lit in London, Ontario by HM Queen Elizabeth the Queen Mother as a tribute to him and all the people that have lost their lives to diabetes. When a cure is found for the condition, the flame will be extinguished by the researchers who discover the cure.

Henrietta returned to Canada and trained to become a doctor. She is buried with her husband in Toronto.

For the next two years Mary travelled around Europe, but as the war made its inevitable approach, travel restrictions were imposed. By 1940 Mary was based in London and it is believed by her family that this is when she was recruited as a spy for the Canadian Government.

The Intelligence Service in Canada was first formed in 1864 under the control of the Montreal police commander to protect the Canada-USA border, and to counter the rising threat by the Irish republican Fenians, who were mounting a terrorist campaign for a free Ireland. The service became the Royal Northwest Mounted Police in 1904 and then the Royal Canadian Mounted Police (RCMP) in 1920.

During the 1930s, there were deep concerns about the rise of the Nazi Party in Germany, and new alliances were formed with the British and American security agencies to gather and exchange information about sympathetic right-wing organisations. New government committees were established and Canadians were recruited to work in a variety of intelligence capacities both at home and abroad.

By 1940 Mary may have been aware of fellow Canadian, William Samuel Stephenson, a brilliant man who ran one of the greatest intelligence-gathering organisations in the western world. His friend, novelist Ian Fleming wrote, *'James Bond is a highly romanticised version of a true spy. The real thing is... William Stephenson.'*

Stephenson was born in Winnipeg, Manitoba in 1897. His mother was Icelandic, his father an immigrant from Orkney, in Scotland. After his father died, he was adopted by his Icelandic aunt. In 1916, he enlisted in the Winnipeg Light Infantry to fight in Europe and was sent to England. After recovering from an injury received during a gas attack, he joined the Royal Flying Corps as a pilot, and by the age of twenty had shot down twelve enemy aircraft in his Sopwith Camel, been shot down himself, been captured and had escaped from a prisoner of war camp. He was awarded the Military Cross and the Distinguished Flying Cross in 1918 and returned to Canada a hero.

After several failed ventures he moved back to England, where his astute business acumen began to pay off. Described as a 'brilliant scientist' he patented a system that enabled the transmission of photographs over telephone lines, a process important in the development of television broadcasting. This was the start of many other successful enterprises, including buying the film studios at Shepperton, Middlesex, but it was in the business of developing a network of international contacts that provided valuable industrial intelligence that Stephenson really excelled.

In the mid-1930s he one of a small team who supplied Winston Churchill with reliable information on how Adolph Hitler was building up his armed forces. Churchill used this in some of his speeches during his 'wilderness years' on the backbenches warning Parliament of the rise of Fascism in Germany.

When he became Prime Minister in 1940, Churchill asked Stephenson if he would head up the British Security Coordination (BSC) in New York. Churchill wanted him to coordinate and expand the British intelligence network, and to use it for anti-German propaganda and espionage. Stephenson accepted, and was given the codename *Intrepid.*

Stephenson arrived in New York on June 21 1940 and set up his headquarters at the Rockefeller Centre in Manhattan and called it the British Passport Control Office. It swiftly became the administration centre for special operations, the communications centre between American and British networks, and a propaganda machine to the American media for pro-British and anti-Axis views designed to persuade a reluctant America to come to the aid of a desperate Europe. Thousands of discreet and dedicated people were employed, including hundreds of intelligent, sophisticated and well-travelled Canadian women.

With Mary's credentials she was an ideal candidate, and would have gone to New York for training before moving back to Europe. It was vital to have spies moving in top diplomatic and political circles in the capitals of Europe to gather sensitive information, and women were skillful operators.

One of the most famous agents recruited by Stephenson was Amy Elizabeth Thorpe, an American and the same age as Mary. Born in Minneapolis, her mother was the daughter of a Minnesota state senator, and she was introduced to the Washington social scene at a young age. She met and married Arthur Pack, the second secretary at the British Embassy in Washington in 1936 and the following year they moved to Warsaw, where she started to obtain sensitive information for MI6. On returning to Washington she continued gathering valuable intelligence through romantic relationships with diplomats from Vichy France, Nazi Germany and Fascist Italy.

Her greatest triumph was in 1942 when she obtained codes

from the Vichy French embassy which were of great assistance to the Allied invasion of North Africa. When her husband died in 1945, she married one of her best informers, Charles Brousse, a Vichy French press attaché, and they settled in France. Amy Thorpe's work undoubtedly changed the course of the war and she died in 1963, reputedly one of the most successful spies in history.

After the war Mary worked for the United Nations Relief and Rehabilitation Administration (UNRRA). It was set up in 1943 by forty-four nations to tackle the massive refugee problem that the war had created across Europe. Millions of people were displaced, many starving and stuck in countries thousands of miles from home.

Refugee camps were set up to feed, clothe and provide medical facilities to them and to organise their repatriation. It was an enormous operation and was taken over by the International Refugee Organisation in 1947 when there were still around 643,000 displaced persons.

Mary wrote regularly to the family in Canada, and there was always excitement when the next blue air-mail letter dropped through the letterbox from some far-flung corner of the world telling them of her latest adventures. She travelled constantly, first to China, where her movements were limited due to the ongoing civil war, and then the length of Africa from the Cape to Cairo, passing through countries where British colonial rule was being challenged and the call of independence rising across the continent. Although she had several relationships and was engaged twice, she showed no sign of settling down.

In 1957 Mary was living in Beirut. Back in Belleville, Violet decided that she wanted to visit Paris with her sister-in-law, also called Mary, and wondered if her sister would be able to join them. Mary replied that she would be delighted.

Beirut is one of the oldest cities in the world, having been inhabited for more than 5,000 years. Mary described it in one of her letters as *'the most beautiful city I have ever seen.'* Excavations in the downtown area have unearthed layers of Phoenician, Hellenistic, Roman, Byzantine, Arab, Crusader and Ottoman remains. After World War One and the collapse of the Ottoman Empire, the Middle East was carved up and Lebanon was placed under French mandate with Beirut as its capital.

Lebanon achieved independence in 1943 and after World War Two ended, it became a major tourist destination and a banking haven, especially during the Persian oil boom. It was a fascinating time to be living in Beirut, a prosperous city full of intrigue, surprise, and spies.

In October 1956 President Gamal Nasser nationalised the Suez Canal and this led to an invasion of Egypt by Israel, Great Britain and France. It reopened soon afterwards in 1957 but any influence that Britain and France might have had in the Middle East vanished. In Lebanon a power struggle between the ruling Maronite Christians and the opposing Muslims threatened civil war over the government's refusal to break diplomatic relations with the western aggressors. Tensions ran high.

Mary could see trouble brewing, and Violet's invitation to spend Christmas in Paris would be a timely break.

When the 'two colonials' arrived, as Mary called them, they were delighted to see her waiting for them in the lobby of the modest and comfortable Hotel Mermoz, near the Champs-Élysées, where she was staying. She greeted then warmly, pleased to see them after nearly twenty years. They found her still stunningly attractive, well-dressed and looking every inch the feminine and sophisticated lady. Certainly not the look of a backpacker or refugee worker!

The hotel was ideally situated for the two visitors to enjoy the sights of Paris that Mary recommended, but she did not join them. She knew Paris well and had her own itinerary, but she met up with them in the evenings and listened to their adventures, chuckled over their misunderstandings with their high-school French, their frustrating attempts to get to grips with the Metro, and their perplexities at the eating habits of the local Parisians who rarely ate dinner before 9pm.

It was a relaxing, fun-filled visit, culminating in celebrating New Year's Eve on the Champs-Élysées. They had a late dinner in their favourite restaurant and hugged with other excited diners as the church bells struck midnight to welcome in 1958. Fireworks erupted in a blaze of colour in the night sky and they dashed out into the exuberant crowd. *We headed for the street to join the dancing, singing revellers. A handsome man grabbed Violet and kissed her soundly. 'I came here from America to kiss a lovely French mademoiselle.' Violet giggled and replied, 'and I was looking for a handsome Frenchman!'*

It was a wonderful holiday and Violet and Mary felt sad at seeing Mary standing alone waving them off in the departure lounge at the airport.

Mary had enjoyed seeing them in Paris. It reminded her of her carefree, happy days as a young girl and she decided it was time to revisit Belleville the following summer. She arrived from London in late September and spent two weeks reacquainting herself with the town, and enjoying the reunion with her family and old friends. Her mother Lily was ecstatic, and rushed around preparing the homecoming.

Mary stayed with her brother Ron and his wife Mary in Northglen Road in Toronto and was chauffeured around the city. She was amazed at the changes, now no longer a sleepy, colonial backwater, but a wealthy, modern, cosmopolitan city. Lily also took her for a wildly erratic scenic drive around the Belleville countryside revisiting places they knew as girls, bringing back fond memories of their childhood.

Shortly after arriving, Mary made a surprise announcement. She was going to get married in Rome the following month. This was received with astonishment, especially from a sceptical Violet who knew she had been engaged several times in the past, but never ended up walking down the aisle. Would she really get to the altar this time? Her prospective husband was Robert Allan, a fifty-eight-year-old Canadian from Vancouver, living in London and an executive of a large, multinational British company.

She spent the next few days with Violet preparing for the wedding, shopping in the top department stores in Toronto in search for a trousseau and honeymoon outfits for Italy. The two sisters had a wonderful time and Mary returned to London with a small maple leaf pin that her sister-in-law had given to her just before she left to wear on her wedding day.

Two weeks later, on October 22 the family were listening to the radio in Toronto and heard the news that a BEA Viscount had been involved in a catastrophic mid-air collision over Nettuno on the way to Naples. They were unaware that Mary was on board. A few hours later there was a knock on Lily's door in Belleville. A policeman was standing there to break the terrible news that Mary and her fiancé were on board, and had not survived.

The grief-stricken family were traumatised as Ron liaised with the airline to arrange for Mary to be flown to Toronto and organised the funeral. Mary was buried in St John's Norway Cemetery in Toronto with her father, later to be joined by her mother Lily in 1966, her brother Ron in 1988 and sister Violet in 2006. Another devastated family struck by the tragedy of flight BE142, which affected them for decades.

A few months later Lily received a small package. Inside was the maple leaf pin and a bracelet that Mary was wearing on the plane.

The Executive
ROBERT ALLAN

Robert Allan arrived at London Airport in an ebullient and joyful mood. He was in love with Mary Mathieson, a beautiful, fascinating woman. They had shared a romantic evening together and this morning she stepped out of the taxi on his arm, and they were flying out to Italy. It was October 22 1958 and they were about to board flight BE142 to Naples, and then continue to Rome to get married.

Robert is another enigma, a man who left only a faint footprint of his life for us to follow. We know that he was a Canadian citizen, born in 1900, almost certainly in Vancouver. His father was a marine engineer and he had a younger brother called William. His mother died when he was young and his father remarried Minnie Tait, who died in 1955.

Vancouver frequently ranks as one of the world's most desirable cities to live in. Situated on the coast of British Columbia near to the mouth of the Fraser River, it has a stunning backdrop of rich, coniferous forests and ancient mountains containing extinct volcanos. The North Pacific Ocean currents give Vancouver a temperate climate on the coast with mild, dry summers and wet winters, while snow covers the mountain peaks. The glaciers of the last Ice Age retreated north eight to ten thousand years ago leaving evidence of the First Nation early encampments.

The Spanish were the first Europeans to arrive in 1791 on an exploratory voyage led by Captain José Maria Narváez, followed by a British survey expedition the following year led by Captain George Vancouver. After the Fraser Gold Rush in 1859 the area was settled, lumbering became a major industry and the first sawmills were built.

The population grew and the British incorporated Vancouver as a city in 1886. A few months later a catastrophic fire destroyed most of the town, but on rebuilding, electricity lines, water mains and a tramcar system were speedily installed, and by 1888 the Canadian Pacific Railway had arrived, making Vancouver the western terminus for Canada.

The town expanded rapidly with immigrants from all round the world going to live there, and by 1901 the population was 26,000. It became an important port of call for the ships of the British Empire to pick up vast quantities of timber, minerals, and grain from the prairies.

In 1914, when the call came from Britain to send troops to fight Germany in Europe, many thousands of young Canadians volunteered for the fight, to be sent to the battlefields of France. Having experienced the full horror of war, the few that returned faced a deep economic recession in 1919, which returned in 1923 and hit even deeper in 1929 with the Wall Street Crash. British Columbia was the worst hit province in Canada, and there was massive unemployment.

Robert is thought to have qualified as an electrical engineer in the 1920s and moved to England, where there were more chances of work. In 1939 World War Two broke out and once again, local Canadian militias raised thousands of troops, with battalions arriving in England within four months. Robert was now thirty years old, and with his electrical engineering expertise may well have been involved in the development of new machines for signalling and Radar.

It is possible that he returned to Canada after the war ended, but more likely that he remained in England to join a major industrial conglomerate, *General Electric Company* (GEC) in London.

GEC was founded in 1886 by Gustav Binswanger, (later Gustav Bying) a German-Jewish immigrant who saw the potential of electricity in the home, and started supplying electrical components over the counter. He travelled across Europe looking for the latest products and in 1887 produced the first electrical catalogue of its kind. The following year the company acquired its first factory in Salford, where it manufactured electric bells, telephones and switches.

It expanded into lamp designs and electric lighting, which was so successful that in 1900 GEC was incorporated as a public company, *The General Electric Company (1900) Limited.* The 1900 was dropped three years later, and a purpose-built factory called the Witton Engineering Works was opened near Birmingham.

The company expanded rapidly, setting up agencies all round the world until the outbreak of World War One in 1914. The company's expertise was needed for the development of radios, signal lamps and searchlights, transforming it into a major player. In 1917 it merged its radio valve manufacturing interests with the Marconi Company.

Between the wars the company became a global corporation, expanding into heavy engineering by acquisitions, so that they could then make the claim to supply 'everything electrical'. In the 1920s it was heavily involved in the creation of the UK National Grid. The following year GEC opened its new headquarters in Kingsway, London, calling it Magnet House.

This grand, eight-storey building was designed in Classical style by the architect R. Frank Atkinson, a style popular with the Victorians. On the ground floor it had a large and imposing wooden door with two dominant windows either side, with six major columns, stretching up the next three floors encasing another three large windows with further stub columns. It was topped by an impressive portico looming over Kingsway.

In the next decade their offices were extended either side as the company grew. The façade was made of Portland stone, and two large bronze lamps were fixed above the entrance door, which were made by GEC.

During World War Two, the company became a major supplier of electrical and engineering products to the military, especially communications equipment. In 1940 it made a significant contribution in the development of the cavity magnetron, a specialist oscillator capable of emitting shorter wavelengths. This was a fundamental part of radar sets, and GEC reduced the size to allow it to be more easily installed in night-fighter aircraft and escort ships. After the war the magnetron was further developed to be used in microwave ovens, which now number over a billion in the world.

Robert was working as an executive in Magnet House in the 1950s, when large investments were being poured into heavy engineering and nuclear power. The United Kingdom Atomic Energy Authority was established in 1954, and the first nuclear power station, Calder Hall was opened at Windscale on the Cumbrian coast in 1956. This delivered urgently required commercial energy.

Even more important at that time was that the process also produced weapons-grade plutonium, required for the nuclear weapons that were being built in the increasingly intense Cold War with the USSR. GEC would therefore have been working with the British security agencies, and it is thought this may be where Robert and Mary Mathieson met in 1958, and their lives became entwined. He was intelligent, well-travelled, single and a fellow Canadian. It was a natural attraction.

Robert was living in an expensive, executive flat in Pont Street in London SW1. Mary had stayed with him at the flat on October 21, and that night packed her luggage with her wedding outfit for Rome, and for their honeymoon in Italy.

The following morning, the taxi picked them up and dropped them off at London Airport in plenty of time for their flight. BE142 was running a little late, so whilst waiting they may have chatted with another happy couple on their way to Naples to start their honeymoon. When they were called, Robert climbed the mobile stairs into the Viscount with Mary in front of him, a happy and grateful man looking forward to a special time in Italy.

On the day of the crash, it is thought that Robert's brother, William, was already in Italy. A few days later he went to the hospital mortuary in Rome to identify the couple. Later that week they were flown back to Canada for two desperately sad funerals. It is thought Robert was buried in Vancouver at a small, family funeral.

FRIENDS

The Lady and the Widow
LADY JENNY WEIR AND FRANCES MILLER

The Lady
LADY JENNY WEIR

Early on October 22 1958, Lady Jenny Weir was sitting in her Kensington house in London W8, waiting for a taxi to take her to London Airport. It had been another hectic year, and she was looking forward to a holiday in the Mediterranean sun with her old friend, Frances Miller. Her husband, Sir Cecil Weir was on a business trip to Canada, so it seemed a good time to take a break before the Christmas and New Year festivities in Scotland. The two friends were going to fly to Naples and then take a ferry across the bay to the beautiful island of Capri.

Jenny Paton Maclay was born in Kilmacolm, Renfrewshire in 1894, a small, old, prosperous village sixteen miles west of Glasgow, nestled in the west central Lowlands of Scotland. In the Victorian era the local economy was mostly agricultural, apart from a small weaving factory that produced cotton and linen. This changed when the railway arrived in 1869, and Kilmacolm started to expand as a dormitory town of Glasgow, with large houses and spa hotels. Today it is noted for its golf course and fishing, and a nearby company is still producing top quality leather for the luxury end of the automotive industry.

Jenny was born into a distinguished family. Her father was William Paton Maclay, brother of Joseph Paton Maclay (1857–1951), the first Baron Maclay of Glasgow. One of her cousins, John Scott Maclay (1905–1992) became Secretary of Scotland in 1957 and was elevated to the peerage as Viscount Muirshiel in 1964. The Maclay family was a heady mixture of business and Scottish Liberal politics.

Cecil McAlpine Weir was born in Bridge of Weir, four miles from Kilmacolm in 1890, the youngest of four sons of Isabella and Alexander Cunningham Weir, a prosperous leather and hide merchant in Glasgow. Cecil was educated at Morrison's Academy in Crieff, and then sent to Switzerland and Germany, where he learned French and German, which he spoke fluently all his life. By 1911, at the age of twenty-one, he had completed a business studies course and was made a partner in his father's business, Schrader, Mitchell and Weir.

Cecil knew Jenny from an early age and by 1912 he was completely in love with this beautiful, auburn-haired, blue-eyed Scottish lassie. In 1913 they attended a tennis dance together, and afterwards he wrote a poem to her praising her beauty.

At the outbreak of World War One in 1914, he enlisted with the Cameronians Scottish Rifles and the Tank Brigade with two of Jenny's cousins. Early in 1915, all three were sent to the Dardanelles to fight in the disastrous Gallipoli campaign in Turkey. Cecil was wounded in action and was awarded the Military Cross for his courage. Jenny's cousins were not so lucky. They were killed in action. Cecil returned to Scotland to recuperate from his injuries and was reunited with Jenny. Within a few months they were married.

The following year Cecil and Jenny celebrated the birth of their daughter, Mary. In 1918 they purchased a large, beautiful house in nearby Helensburgh with magnificent views across Gare Loch which they called *White House*. In 1920 their son James was born, to complete the family.

Throughout the 1920s Cecil continued his involvement with Schrader, Mitchell and Weir. He became a governor of the Girl's School Company, that administered several schools in the area. He was a member of the Glasgow Chamber of Commerce, and took an increasing interest in local politics, especially the Scottish Liberal Federation. Jenny had some very powerful connections through the Maclay family, and the *White House* became a centre for hot political debate. Golf and tennis were important pastimes for both Cecil and Jenny.

Cecil was invited to join the board of the British Tabulating Machine Company (BTMC). It was formed in 1902 to sell Herman Hollerith's patented electrical counting machine, manufactured by the US Tabulating Machine Company, (later to become IBM). In 1920, BTMC started manufacturing its own machines – an astute move, considering what lay ahead in the world of computer technology.

The Great Depression struck globally in the early 1930s, and in the United Kingdom it hit Scotland particularly hard. Business and heavy industry collapsed with Glasgow suffering badly. In 1936 Cecil could see the depression and despair that mass unemployment caused, and proposed an idea to the Glasgow Chamber of Commerce – to host an Empire Exhibition in the city, the first since 1911. It was agreed and Cecil formed a committee to oversee the preparations.

He lobbied hard to gain support from local companies, and invited architects to come up with imaginative schemes. His energy and enthusiasm was infectious and within a few months, designs for sixty-two pavilions had been put forward by various Government departments, including Industry, Tourism and the Arts. Money flowed in to support the project.

Glasgow was a large, international port at that time, so there were pavilions showing off the products of the dominions and colonies of Britain including Australia, Canada, South Africa, and West and East Africa. There was an Ireland pavilion, a Scottish pavilion, a Highland village, a concert hall, and an amusement park proposed by a young Billy Butlin. The exhibition covered over one million square feet.

May 3 1938 was chosen as the opening date, and the exhibition was to run for six months. A 170-acre site was selected at Bellahouston Park, a few miles from Glasgow, close to Rangers football ground at Ibrox Park. Work began on July 9 1937, and a foundation stone was laid by King George VI and Queen Elizabeth. Cecil and Jenny rented a house in Paisley Road so that Cecil could be near the site, while Jenny kept everything running smoothly at home.

Construction of the pavilions was completed in an impressive ten months, and the exhibition was opened by the

King, with a spectacular ceremony in Ibrox Park attended by 100,000 people. It was a total success, despite appalling weather that summer, and the Church's insistence that it was not allowed to open on Sundays! The new *Queen Elizabeth* liner was launched on the Clyde on September 27, and the end of the exhibition was marked by another impressive ceremony to close the proceedings.

Its success was due to the vision of Cecil Weir, who showed impressive leadership and organisational skills in procuring and managing the hundreds of talented staff required to complete a massive project in such a short period of time. In 1938 Cecil was awarded a knighthood (KBE) in recognition of his efforts. He had also come to the attention of the mandarins in Whitehall.

By the end of 1938 it was clear that war with Germany was inevitable. Cecil was appointed Civil Defence Commissioner for the Western District of Scotland by the War Office. His job involved overseeing the construction of shelters, and organising food supplies, fire services, hospitals, and the recruitment of staff for Civil Defence. This was in addition to his other role as President of the Glasgow Chamber of Commerce. There was much to do before the first German air raids on Glasgow, which started in July 1940.

During 1941 Cecil was having to spend more time in London. He had been asked by the Board of Trade to help in the transition of various industries to war production. Often the products were completely unrelated, for example a carpet factory converted to the making of parachutes, which involved changes to machinery and retraining of the workforce. There were complex and difficult negotiations with the owners, worried that their livelihoods were at stake. Throughout this time Jenny was based in Helensburgh, raising the family whilst Cecil was commuting between London and Glasgow.

On September 3 1928, Sir Alexander Fleming made his famous discovery of a special mould in his laboratory in St Mary's Hospital in Paddington, London. He called it penicillin. A team of scientists led by Howard Florey and Ernest Boris Chain continued with the research at the Radcliffe Infirmary in Oxford, but it wasn't until 1940 that they found a method of purifying it into a stable form.

By September 1942 the scientists realised they had made a dramatic breakthrough in the treatment of infection, and the drug needed to go into mass production as soon as possible. Within days they approached Sir Andrew Duncan, the Minister of Supply who immediately saw the importance and urgency. He confirmed he knew just the man to get the job done. Cecil was summoned and was requested *'to do everything possible to organise penicillin production on a great scale.'*

A week later, Cecil convened a conference of representatives of all the major chemical and pharmaceutical companies in Britain. He told them there was one single goal and that all details about the research, procurement of materials, and the production techniques must be shared. All agreed enthusiastically and the best brains from ICI, Boots, Glaxo and Burroughs Welcome immediately took up the challenge.

Research went at a breakneck speed across the country. Materials were sourced from all over the world, factories were built at record speed. Within a year, large quantities of penicillin were being produced. Cecil commented, *'How easy is cooperation in wartime!'*

By D-Day in 1944, enough penicillin had been produced to treat all the wounded in the Allied forces. Penicillin saved millions of lives and made a major contribution to winning the war.

In 1944 Cecil was asked to examine the practical problems of demobilising nearly six million men once the war was over. Enormous quantities of clothing would be needed. He oversaw the production of over 100,000 sets per week from the Directorate of Clothing and Textiles. Major retailers turned over their entire production lines to cater for this volume. The operation was another success, and many men returned home to their loved ones a lot better dressed than when they were called up!

Within three months of the D-Day landings at Normandy in June 1944, Cecil was flying across the battlefields of France with government officials to Paris. There they met their Allied counterparts to discuss how to get the destroyed and abandoned factories of France up and running again. By October they had made their recommendations, and missions were set up in Paris and Brussels. By 1946 Cecil had completed similar trips to Belgium, Holland and Germany.

While her husband had been engaged on these six years of continuous public service, Jenny, like many women of her generation, had spent long periods on her own keeping the home going and the family safe, maintaining some sense of normality in those tumultuous times. They kept in close contact by telephone and mail, and Cecil couldn't wait to return to Scotland, to be with Jenny and the family, and to restart his businesses. It was not to be. The government had other plans for him.

By June 1946 Cecil had completed his duties at the Ministry of Supply and was summoned by Sir Arthur Street, the Permanent Secretary of the Duchy of Lancaster. He was one of the most senior civil servants in the country and his department was responsible for German affairs. He asked Cecil to help restore German industry as Economic Advisor to the Allied Control Commission for Germany. It was an enormous task, and extremely important for sustaining peace in Europe. His background and language skills made him ideal for the job.

Cecil returned to Scotland to discuss the implications of this new role with Jenny and the family. Jenny's support and reply was emphatic. *'You might as well say "yes" right away. You will never refuse such an opportunity. If you do you'll be sorry later on.'*

They sold the *White House* in Helensburgh and bought a house in Kensington. From then on London would be their new base.

After two short visits to Berlin, Cecil returned to London and accepted the appointment, with the proviso that Jenny would accompany him to Germany. For the next three years the job would occupy his life seven days a week.

The post carried with it a comfortable official residence, first in Bismarckallee, Berlin, then in Delbrückstrasse, the former residence of Sir William Strang. Jenny turned them into comfortable homes, and acquired a boxer dog called *Dyko,* who energetically welcomed the guests when they arrived. Entertaining both social and business guests was an important function, and Jenny became an expert at helping to organise as many as 250 visitors a month at the house, and showed her remarkable talent for putting guests at their ease.

The new Labour government took power in July 1945 and was keen to make a positive contribution. Cecil was particularly impressed by the new Foreign Secretary, Ernest Bevin, who took a close personal interest in the moral and physical rehabilitation of the German people. He was a great supporter of the Marshall Plan, designed by the USA to help rebuild the infrastructure of Europe's economies with fifteen billion dollars of aid. Bevin was determined that Germany be fully integrated into the rebuilding of a peaceful Europe.

In 1946 the central parts of Berlin were just heaps of rubble. The Reich Chancellery was an empty shell, the great hotels and buildings, crumbling walls and dust. There was a determination by the four allies – Britain, France, USA and USSR, to rebuild the city quickly. Unanimous agreement was needed on every major decision. The three western powers worked well together and made remarkable progress, despite the Soviet obstacles.

At one memorable acrimonious meeting of the Council of Foreign Ministers when the Soviet Foreign Minister Vyaceslav Molotov was speaking, Cecil was seated behind Bevin. He could see Bevin's neck turning red in indignation at the communist diatribe he was hearing. Bevin finally exploded in anger, and responded with a declamatory speech on liberty, worthy of the oratory of Winston Churchill.

By 1947 Cecil had over 7,000 staff under him, and was given some rather memorable transport to travel to meetings. For a while he had the surreal experience of travelling around

Germany in Goering's and Goebbels' special trains that been recovered after the war, and in large black limousines with flashing lights escorted by police riders!

The provision of adequate supplies of food in Germany was a constant problem in the early years after the war. Locally grown food was produced for the German people, but there was a chronic shortage, especially difficult for those working in critical, labour-intensive jobs such as mining.

In 1947, teams of American businessmen were sent to assess the situation. Gradually food rationing was reduced, large-scale agriculture was re-established and vital raw materials for industry flowed back into the rebuilt factories.

On June 20 1948, the new Deutschmark was introduced to create a stable monetary system for Germany. The Soviets objected. Four days later they blocked road, railway, and canal access to the Allied zones in Berlin which lay within Russian-occupied eastern Germany. On June 25 the Soviets stopped supplying food to the civilian population, leaving only about thirty-six days of supplies left in the city. But the Soviets had misjudged the Allies and did not anticipate they would attempt an airlift. The Allied military powers flew in supplies on June 26 led by the RAF, and were quickly joined by many other Commonwealth and American aircraft.

After almost a year, on May 12 1949, the Soviets finally lifted the blockade, by which time the Allies had made 275,000 sorties and delivered around two million tons of supplies. It was an exhilarating time for those living in Berlin, defying the Russians.

Cecil took particular pleasure in the establishment of the

Hanover Trade Fair, bringing back memories of the Empire Exhibition in Glasgow in 1938. It was another huge success and Cecil was pleased to be able to hand the reins over to the German minister, Herr Kübel, to run as an annual event.

The Federal Republic of Germany was established in 1949, a new constitution was inaugurated and the new West German parliament, the Bundestag, was opened. Cecil's last official act in Germany was to attend the opening.

By the time Cecil and Jenny left Berlin there was hardly an MP or distinguished British scientist, soldier, lecturer or writer they had not met, entertained or talked with in Germany. They had made many friends from a number of countries in their three years in Germany, but now it was time for them to return to their home in Thorney Court in Kensington.

Hardly had Cecil picked up the threads of his former life when a telegram arrived from his old wartime friend, Sir Clive Ballieu, asking him to drop in and see him at St James House in London. He made Cecil an offer to take over the Dollar Exports Board, established to help boost trade with the United States and Canada to improve the balance of payments. Cecil discussed the offer with Jenny saying it would be good for his education. Jenny was unimpressed with that viewpoint, but reluctantly agreed, as long as he found more time for the family.

Clement Attlee had been Prime Minister since 1945 and a young Harold Wilson was President of the Board of Trade. Both men confirmed their agreement to Cecil's appointment. By December 1949 Cecil had started the job in London with a small team of twenty staff.

Cecil received invitations from all over the country to speak and, as he put it, *'to sing for my supper.'* The objective was to push British companies to boost exports by removing obstacles to trade, and to support incentives. He made numerous visits to trade fairs in the United States and Canada, from engineering to textiles, motor cars and agriculture. In eighteen months Cecil flew across the Atlantic four times. By June 1951 the balance of payments was looking much healthier and Cecil's job was done.

Over the next few years Cecil and Jenny were at last able to spend more time together. Cecil returned as Chairman of the British Tabulating Machine Company, which had played a crucial part in the development and supply of top-secret machines during the war for the code-breaking teams at Bletchley Park. There was much excitement in new valve-based computers being developed in 1951, which used punched cards for input and output and driving a printer. Later in 1959, BTMC merged with a former rival and became International Computers Limited (ICL), which was eventually taken over by the Japanese company, Fujitsu.

Cecil never really retired. With his enquiring mind and extensive contacts he was always being sought out for his opinions. Jenny had adjusted her life around her successful husband, but Cecil knew and appreciated that her constant support had been a major contributor to his success.

Jenny accompanied Cecil on some of the overseas trips. Their daughter, Mary had married and made her home in Washington DC, so there were trips to America. Their son, James had married an Australian girl, Nancy Latimer, and they had a daughter, Jenny-Marie and a son, Iain, so Jenny and Cecil took the opportunity for an enjoyable visit to Melbourne to see the family whilst Cecil was promoting his latest computer in Sydney. Jenny revelled in her new role as doting grandmother.

When Jenny boarded flight BE142 with Frances Miller at around eight o'clock in the morning on October 22 1958, Cecil was in transit to America, after a trade mission to Canada. It took a day for the authorities to find him and break the terrible news. He returned to England utterly distraught and faced a battery of cameras when he landed at Prestwick Airport on October 24.

Jenny was sixty-four. She was buried at Kilmacolm cemetery, close to where she was born. Cecil died two years later, many said from heartbreak, in Kensington, aged seventy, and was buried alongside his adored wife.

There is a girl of whom I tell
(and I may claim to know her well),
That she's the most delightful maid
On whom my eyes have ever laid.

And this I'd also like to say,
That she has such a charming way,
That when upon her face I gaze
My heart begins to throb apace.

Poem by Cecil to Jenny 1913

The Widow
FRANCES MILLER

At the same time that Lady Jenny Weir was making her way to the airport early on October 22 1958, her good friend, Frances Miller was also setting off by taxi from her apartment in Park Lane, London W1, looking forward to a relaxing holiday in the late summer sun in Capri. Although the two women were from very different backgrounds, they shared a lot in common. They were both late-Victorians, born five years apart in similar small, rural villages. Their husbands had been successful businessmen in their own fields, and they had both travelled extensively. Most of all they enjoyed each other's company.

Frances Amelia Miller (née Turner) was the ninth of ten children. Her father, Charles Turner met her mother, Amelia McCoombe in Bombay (now Mumbai), India, when he was a paymaster in the British Army. Amelia was living there with her Scottish parents, and although she was only fifteen years old and he was eighteen years older, her parents gave them permission to marry. They married in Bombay in 1868, and when they returned to England they lived on a large Army camp in Aldershot, Hampshire. At the age of forty-seven, Charles retired from the Army and the family moved to Church Stretton, an historic market town thirteen miles south of Shrewsbury.

In the early 1800s Church Stretton was a quiet, rural town with a population of about 1,700 and reliant on local agriculture. After the arrival of the railway in 1852, Church

Stretton prospered. Tweed cloth, woollen yarn and blankets were produced in a small way from locally abundant wool. Visitors came to walk upon Long Mynd, whose Precambrian rock formations go back some 570 million years, and the town became popular with the Victorians as a health spa, who called it 'Little Switzerland' because of its ancient geology and the purity of its water.

Frances was born there on February 20 1889, and spent her childhood growing up in this quiet part of Shropshire. Charles drew a small Army pension, but with ten children to support, he needed to supplement his income and worked as a journeyman baker in the surrounding towns.

By 1911 Frances had started work at the Royal Hotel in Kettering, probably recommended by her father. A much larger and more prosperous town than Church Stretton, Kettering was famous for its many boot and shoe manufacturers. The Royal Hotel was an impressive, three-storey, Victorian, red-brick, Jacobean-style building located in the centre of the town. It had gained its Royal status after Queen Victoria stayed there in 1844. It was a popular venue for the business community, especially for those involved with the boot and shoe companies.

It was here that Frances probably met her future husband, Frederick Sidney Miller, (always known as Sidney) who was a director of F. A. Miller & Sons, a successful bootmakers company established by his father.

Sidney was born in 1879 with a mild form of spina bifida, a disease which distorted his spine but did not affect his brain. He was an astute businessman, joining the family firm after finishing school, and quickly learnt every detail of a very competitive business. He was a bright, intelligent man with a strong, interesting face and a determined look. Sidney was able to walk, but his legs were weak and he sometimes needed a cane. He had a passion for snooker and became a renowned local champion. In 1920 he was a finalist in the English Amateur Snooker Championship held at Burroughs Hill in Soho Square, when he was beaten by Arthur Wisdom 356 to 283.

On April 15 1912, Frances heard the terrible news that RMS *Titanic* had sunk off the coast of Newfoundland the previous night after hitting an iceberg. Over 1,500 of the 2,229 passengers had drowned, including her elder brother, Leopold, who was working as a first-class steward. His body was recovered from the sea by a cable repair ship called the SS *Mackay-Bennet*, chartered by the *White Star Line* and he was taken to the nearest port, Halifax, for identification.

His steward's vest and apron were recovered, with a knife, a pencil, six and a half pence and two tickets for rooms 9 and 10. Due to the mortuary at Halifax being overwhelmed by the number of fatalities, he was buried at sea on April 21 1912. He had previously worked on *Titanic*'s sister ship RMS *Olympic,* and had joined *Titanic* at Southampton on April 1. He died on his twenty-eighth birthday, and is still remembered in Church Stretton.

Frances was twenty-five years old when Sidney proposed to her in 1914, and to make their wedding day special, Sidney applied to be married in the magnificent St George's Church,

Hanover Square, Mayfair, in London. The church, with its six great Corinthian columns, was built between 1721 and 1724. The windows were glazed with the finest Flemish glass. Above the altar, an intricately carved Grinling Gibbons reredos frames a striking painting of the Last Supper by William Kent (1684–1748). The great eighteenth-century composer, George Frideric Handel had regularly worshipped there. They married on April 30 1914, a truly happy occasion celebrated by both sides of the family.

The newlyweds returned to Kettering to live in the fashionable Headlands area in a large, six-bedroomed house. The garden had been laid out in classical style, with flower beds lining paved paths dotted with stone statues, and the centrepiece of the garden was an impressive fountain. Sidney's father died in March 1918 and Sidney took over the company as Managing Director. He brought Frances onto the company board, and under Sidney's direction, F. A. Miller & Sons flourished into the 1920s.

Frances had an interest in music and joined the recently formed Kettering Operatic Society as a vocalist. The society was founded early in 1919, and opened on December 16 1919 with a popular comic-opera called *Dorothy,* written in 1886 by Alfred Cellier and B.C. Stephenson. The show was well-attended and raised one hundred guineas for charity.

Sidney worked hard to expand the company for the next ten years, but with his debilitating condition he needed to take a holiday break every few months. He would go with Frances to Torquay, in Devon, where the seaside climate helped him recuperate and where there were various therapeutic facilities available.

In 1933, Sidney became seriously ill from further side effects of the disease, and he died on May 14 aged fifty-three. He had survived over ten years longer than the average prognosis at that time, which was a tribute to the love and care that Frances gave to him over the nineteen years of marriage. Sidney was buried on May 17 in Kettering cemetery.

Frances was devastated, but she was only forty-four years old, and her priority was to keep the company going. As they had no children, the board appointed Frances co-Managing Director with Sidney's brother, Percy to ensure family continuity. It was a smooth transition and the company continued to prosper.

By 1935 Frances was adjusting to her new life as a widow. She enjoyed a comfortable lifestyle, having received a generous inheritance from Sidney. A person that had helped her through her grief was her cousin, Alfred Belch, a Scottish solicitor and shipping consultant, who had travelled widely, and he encouraged her to explore new avenues in her life.

She had always been curious about India from the stories her father and mother had told her as a child. She decided to investigate her family history and on February 28, she sailed to Bombay on RMS *California* to revisit the area where her parents had met and married. India was still under British rule and she was fascinated by the British residents she met living a privileged, opulent lifestyle far away from England in the dying days of the British Raj.

Frances enjoyed another cruise a few years later in April 1938. There had been a resurgence in the popularity of cruising, especially in America. She was recommended by Alfred to try one of the banana boats, RMS *Carare,* run by the Elders and Fyffe line from Avonmouth to Jamaica. The accommodation on board was comfortable, there were only a small number of passengers, and she basked in the warmth, sounds and colour of the West Indies. Two years later the *Carare* was sunk in the Bristol Channel by a German mine.

With the outbreak of World War Two in September 1939, orders flooded in to all the bootmakers in Northamptonshire for the millions of pairs of boots the Army would need for its soldiers, and the company was stretched to full capacity.

In 1949 Frances celebrated her sixtieth birthday and decided she wanted to retire near the sea in Brighton. She sold the Kettering house and bought an elegant, Regency, terraced, three-storey house in Belgrave Place on the seafront in desirable Kemp Town.

Frances also spent more time visiting London, and bought an apartment in a block of large, fashionable flats at 55, Park Lane, not far from where she was married. She took great pleasure in furnishing her new homes, continued her travelling expeditions and participated in fund-raising charity functions, which is where she quite possibly met Lady Weir. She never remarried, and her retirement was comfortable and enjoyable.

On that fateful day on October 22 1958, Frances met Jenny at the airport and they boarded the plane together. They were warmly welcomed by the smiling flight attendant, and ushered to their seats near the front of the plane. It was a happy atmosphere on board, and they were excited about their trip to Capri. There was a well-dressed obviously newly wed couple sitting nearby, totally absorbed in each other's company, already sipping champagne.

At sixty-nine years old Frances was the oldest casualty on board. She was buried with her beloved Sidney in Kettering cemetery.

The Radio Technician and the Teleprinter Operator
COLSTON LUXTON AND ROBERT BRUCE

The Radio Technician
COLSTON GEORGE LUXTON

On October 22 1958 Colston Luxton travelled the twenty miles from his cottage in Bovingdon, Hertfordshire to London Airport to catch flight BE142 to Naples and Malta. It is thought he was travelling on the plane with Robert Bruce, as both men worked for BEA and Robert was travelling to Naples. George had been through many traumas in his forty-three years, and he was looking forward to a relaxing trip.

Colston George Luxton, (always known as George) was born in Bristol on October 1 1915 and was baptised at the parish church of St Werburgh. He came from a well-travelled family.

His grandfather, Charles Veale Luxton was born in 1849 in Cullompton, Devon, thirteen miles north-east of Exeter and was a cooper by trade. The job of barrel making is a skilled and ancient art. Staved vessels held together with metal or wooden hoops were recorded as being used by the Egyptians, and preserved casks dating back to 200BC have been found in Europe. The staves are strips of wood usually heated or steamed to make them pliable and are bent into shape and kept in position by the hoops. All manner of wooden containers were made this way, such as casks, barrels, tubs, churns and hogsheads. Sometime in the 1870s, Charles set out by ship to

Newfoundland to seek new business opportunities.

The island of Newfoundland is not for the faint-hearted. Situated on the easternmost edge of Canada, it has a harsh climate with short, cool summers, a lot of rain, clawing mists and dense fog, and brutally cold winters, where the temperature can drop to minus-30 degrees. It lies in an area where two Atlantic currents meet – the cold, Labrador Current flowing south from the Arctic Ocean and the warm Gulf Stream, which flows northward from the Gulf of Mexico.

The richness of these two currents combined with the underwater plateaus south-east of the island called the Grand Banks make the waters around Newfoundland one of the world's richest fishing grounds. The abundance of Atlantic cod, swordfish and haddock in the nutrient-filled waters attracts seals, dolphins and whales to feed on the huge shoals. The fishing industry generated many support businesses and plenty of work for skilled tradesmen, including coopers, who made the barrels for storing and transporting the salted fish.

In 1824 Newfoundland was officially recognised as a British colony and in 1855 became self-governing. In 1869 it voted against a confederacy with Canada, only becoming a province in 1949. Fishing was a booming industry and there was enormous export demand from Europe. Timber mills sprang up, canning factories were built and railways were constructed in the 1880s, attracting many immigrants, especially from Ireland, which was still recovering from the devastating famine years.

Charles worked in Newfoundland for several years, married a local girl, Matilda, in the 1870s and together they had eight children. George's father, William was born in

Newfoundland in 1881, as was his eldest sister, Sabina. Charles travelled back and forth to England. His daughter, Caroline was born in his home town of Cullompton, and their other five children were born in Bristol.

In 1900, at the age of nineteen, William apparently decided not to continue in his father's footsteps but enlisted as a private in the 6th Battalion of the Dragoon Guards, a cavalry regiment of the British Army. The Boer War had started the previous year and was not going well for the British, who badly under-estimated the effectiveness of the hit-and-run guerrilla tactics of the Boers.

William served in South Africa from October 11 1899 until May 2 1902 and was awarded both the Queen's South Africa Medal and the King's South Africa Medal. We can assume he would have signed up for fifteen years.

After leaving the Army, William became a chauffeur in Bristol. On January 3 1914 he married Gertrude Knott at the Church of the Holy Nativity in Knowle, and on October 1 the following year their son, Colston George was born. In 1938 he and Gertrude were living at 85, Mina Road. William retired on his Army pension as a Chelsea Pensioner and died in 1938 at the age of fifty-seven.

Little else is known of George's early life. He was brought up in Bristol and in 1939 he married twenty-one-year-old Lilian Neal. They lived at 43 Marshfield Road and George worked as a bus conductor.

George was unlucky in love. After only six years of marriage, Lilian died at the young age of twenty-seven early in 1945. They did not have children. A few months later he met Margaret Sweeting and after a whirlwind courtship they married in June 1945 in Weston-Super-Mare. This also ended in tragedy when she died seven years later in Amersham in Buckinghamshire aged thirty-three, again with no children.

By 1952 it is thought that George had joined BEA as a radio technician, and was living near Bovingdon, where BEA had a large maintenance facility at the local RAF airbase. In 1952 he married his third wife, Elizabeth Hopkinson in Hemel Hempstead, but the marriage broke down after a few years and they divorced.

George's fourth and final marriage was in 1957 at the age of forty-two when he married thirty-year-old Doreen Benns. They married in Watford, bought a small cottage in Flaunden Lane in Bovingdon and it seemed that George was at last enjoying a stable and happy period in his life. It was made even better when Doreen confirmed she was expecting twins.

Bovingdon is a quiet village with a history going back eight hundred years. The medieval St Lawrence Church of the early 1200s was entirely rebuilt in 1845. It has the largest open churchyard in Hertfordshire covering over four acres. For centuries this rural village had a population of just a few thousand but this increased in 1942 when the RAF built a large base with a runway 1,634 yards long and two secondary runways. It was first used by RAF Bomber Command and then taken over by the United States Air Force in late 1942 supporting the Eighth Air Force bomber crews.

The base was also used to train American journalists to cover the air war over Europe, including Walter Cronkite and

James Denton Scott, who flew and reported on combat missions. Several film stars were assigned to the base, including Clark Gable, James Stewart and William Holden.

Bovingdon had a large maintenance facility which BEA and BOAC took over after the war. They used it as their worldwide base and supplied the smaller hubs in Europe, North Africa and the Middle East. George was based here, specialising in the maintenance of radio equipment, and would travel to the hubs when required.

In October 1958 he was requested to take some equipment to Tripoli, so he booked flight BE142 to Malta, with a connecting flight to Libya, and this would leave on October 22.

On the afternoon of October 22, Doreen was alone at the cottage in Bovingdon settling down to watch the much-anticipated international football match at Wembley between England and Russia. The stadium was full, with 100,000 fans driving on the English side captained by Billy Wright. Famous names of the day were playing, including Tom Finney, Johnny Haynes and Bobby Charlton, who was now fully fit after the trauma of the Munich air crash.

It was a tense first half, with the Russians failing to get through the excellent England defence, apart from one move ending in a magnificent save by Colin McDonald. In the dying moments of the first half, Finney and Haynes charged down the left wing, and it was Haynes that rocketed the ball into the net, leaving the Russian goalkeeper, Belyayev stranded. The stadium erupted and the whistle was blown for half-time.

Doreen did not see the second half, when England scored another four goals to make it 5–0, with Haynes scoring a hat-trick. As she got up to make a cup of tea, a news flash came up on the screen at Wembley stadium. It said there had been a mid-air collision over Italy involving a BEA Viscount on its way to Naples. With her heart pounding she rang BEA. They confirmed the worst, and that there were no survivors.

George was flown back a week later and was buried at St Lawrence Church. The trauma that Doreen went through resulted in her losing the twins. She never remarried. She lived in Bovingdon for the rest of her life and died in 2018.

The Teleprinter Operator
ROBERT BRUCE

R obert decided to change the date of his flight to Naples to October 22 at the last minute. His friend, Colston Luxton, who also worked for BEA, suggested he fly with him that day as he was also going to Naples, and then on to Malta and Tripoli. Robert was working in the BEA headquarters in Lower Regent Street and had taken digs in Comeragh Road, West Kensington, so it was an easy journey on the BEA bus to London Airport. He was looking forward to spending a few hours with his colleague, and it would be a good start to his holiday in Italy.

Robert Bruce was a proud Scot, born in 1930 in Willowbrae, in south-east Edinburgh. It is a pleasant area about one mile east of Edinburgh Castle, adjacent to Holyrood Park and only a mile from Portobello, a small, seaside town and fashionable bathing resort on the Firth of Forth. Little is known of Robert's early life except that his father was William and his mother, Jessie. They had four daughters, Margaret, Gertie, Martha and Chrissie, before Robert arrived a few years later. He was the baby of the family and was cossetted mercilessly by his elder sisters. Sadly, his father died early in his life.

During Robert's childhood he would no doubt have been spent many adventurous days exploring Holyrood Park, with its 650 acres of hills, crags and earthworks, lochs and basalt cliffs. A notable landmark it the 822-foot-high hill called Arthur's Seat, a basalt lava plug of an extinct volcano that was last active around 335 million years ago. It has many legends attached to it and over the years its mystery has provided a popular setting for authors, including Robert Louis Stevenson and Ian Rankin.

It was a natural magnet for kids and a popular walking spot for the citizens of Edinburgh, with the hills relatively easy to climb and the summit providing excellent panoramic views of the city and beyond. The remains of an Iron Age fort can still be seen on top of Dunsapie crag, and Duddingston Loch, the only natural freshwater loch in the city, was popular for fishing, and became a skating rink when there were colder winters. The park also has a bird sanctuary, established in 1925, covering an area of sixty-four acres and includes the largest heronry in the Lothians.

Holyrood Park experienced the only air-raid on Edinburgh in World War One, when a German Zeppelin drifted across and dropped a few bombs in April 1916.

Robert was nine years old when World War Two started. If he had stood on Arthur's Seat he would have seen the German bombers heading for the factories of Glasgow and fires flickering from the bombed-out docks at Leith. Edinburgh had no significant industry and was of little interest to the Germans.

We can assume that Robert spent his early years at school in the city and as a young teenager became interested in new technology. The next we know of him is when he moved to London and was working as a teleprinter operator in the head office of BEA in Lower Regent Street.

Teleprinters evolved from the telegraphic system that had been patented by Samuel Morse in 1840. The first public demonstration on January 11 1838 was at the Speedwell Ironworks in Morristown, New Jersey, in the United States of America. By 1842, Morse had convinced Congress to give him a grant of 30,000 dollars to construct a thirty-eight-mile telegraph line between Washington and Baltimore, alongside the railroad. By 1850 twelve thousand miles of cable had been laid. Within a few years this revolution in communications had spread to Europe and South America.

Émile Baudot (1845–1903) is credited as being one of the pioneers of digital communication. In 1874 the Frenchman invented a five-unit code sent from a keyboard, less complicated than the Morse system that used sequences of dots and dashes. A receiving teleprinter decoded the incoming message and printed it out onto paper tape. By the early 1900s, the Baudot system was being used extensively throughout Europe and across the globe. In 1924 the International Telegraphic Alphabet No 2 (ITA2) was introduced and became standard for Western Union and across America.

Teleprinter machines in 1930 were large and heavy but very robust and capable of running for a month at a time. They were used during World War Two and some remained in production until 1962. By the 1950s, the telex system had developed into a global teleprinter network and was used for most of the twentieth century, until superseded by the internet. In 1958, Robert would have been using this system at BEA, who had been developing its reservation system. It would be 1965 before early computers would be used.

Robert was popular, good looking and enjoyed his job. It is said he enjoyed regaling the girls with tales of his possible ancestor and namesake, Robert the Bruce (1274–1329), whose statue he would have seen set in the wall of Edinburgh Castle.

Robert, King of Scots fought and beat the 20,000-strong English army led by Edward II at the Battle of Bannockburn on June 24 1314. When he died in 1329, his heart was taken on pilgrimage to Jerusalem in a casket by Scottish knight, Sir James Douglas and after his death, was brought back to Scotland and buried in Melrose Abbey, where it remains to this day. His body was buried in a stone vault beneath the floor of Dunfermline Abbey in a lavish ceremony. The Abbey was sacked in 1560 and left in ruins, but in 1818 workmen rediscovered the vault and Robert the Bruce was reinterred in 1819. It is now a popular pilgrimage for those wanting an independent Scotland.

On October 22 Robert and Colston met at London Airport and they boarded the plane together, looking forward to catching up on the flight to Naples.

Robert could not match the life of his hero Robert the Bruce, but his death was as deeply felt by his family in Edinburgh when they heard the tragic news that day of the loss of flight BE142. His funeral was held two weeks later in Edinburgh.

He was just twenty-eight years old.

COLLEAGUES

The Lawyer and the Accountant
JOHN PRINCE AND REUBEN SILBURN

The Lawyer
JOHN PRINCE

Early on October 22 1958, a taxi picked up John Prince from his comfortable, suburban, detached house in Shire Lane, Chorleywood, Hertfordshire, to take him to London Airport. He arrived slightly before 08.00 to meet up with his colleague from the British Petroleum Company (BP), Reuben Silburn, to take flight BE142 first to Naples, then to Malta. From there they would catch a connecting flight to Tripoli, where they were due to attend an important meeting with the Libyan government to finalise negotiations for oil exploration concessions. It had been sixteen years since John had been to the North African coast, and that was in very different circumstances.

In 1958 John was only thirty-five years old, but he had already experienced an extraordinarily full life. He was born Jack Prince on December 12 1922 in Darwen, Lancashire, a small industrial town with around 35,000 inhabitants, twenty-one miles north-west of Manchester, between Blackburn and Bolton.

For centuries Darwen had been an agricultural market town, but being located on the River Darwen, its location made it ideal for textile manufacture. With the Industrial Revolution and the building of the Leeds and Liverpool canal in 1850, thousands of jobs were created in the new cotton mills across Lancashire. The largest mill in Darwen was India Mill, built by Eccles Shorrock in 1865, with an iconic chimney that still stands proud today. Samuel Crompton, the inventor of the revolutionary spinning mule lived in the town for a few years.

At the turn of the twentieth century several members of the Prince family worked in the mills. Jack's father, John Henry Prince was a labourer in the dye works and his mother, Dora was a supervisor in charge of sixteen looms. It was a hard life, working gruelling twelve hour shifts from six in the morning to six at night in noisy, dirty conditions for low wages.

John and Dora married in 1922 when she was nineteen years old. He was a handsome man, and talented – he could play the piano by ear with no formal training. But John had a drink problem, probably exacerbated by playing the piano in pubs to earn a little extra money, and could be violent. Jack's brother, Owen was born in 1927, but the marriage did not survive. By 1934 John and Dora were divorced and she met George Hollings, who was a successful fish distributor in the area, a kind man and very supportive to her two boys.

Jack attended the local school and was a bright and attentive child, and despite the problems at home, won a scholarship to Darwen Grammar School. He matriculated and left school at fifteen to work as a clerk in the local Town Hall. With his wages he was able to contribute to the household expenses and at the same time, start night classes to continue his education. These studies continued through the first two years of World War Two. He successfully completed his exams and prepared to apply to university to read Law.

Being young and fit, these plans had to be postponed when he was called up to fight for his country, and joined the Royal Navy as an ordinary seaman in the middle of 1941. He was sent to HMS *Raleigh* at Torpoint, on the border of Devon and Cornwall, to undergo basic training. The base had been commissioned in January 1940 and the faculty had a permanently moored training ship, HMS *Brecon* on the adjacent River Tamar. A few months before Jack arrived, on April 28 1941, forty-four sailors and twenty-one Royal Engineers were killed when a German bomb hit the air-raid shelter in which they were taking cover. Early in 1942 Jack completed his training and was posted to an extraordinary ship.

HMS *Tartar* was given the nickname 'Lucky Tartar' due to her numerous miraculous escapes from dangerous situations in World War Two. The ship was a Tribal-class destroyer built by Swan Hunter at Wallsend in 1936, and commissioned in March 1939. She was 115 metres long, weighed 2,600 tons, had a top speed of 36 knots (41mph) and a maximum range of 5,700 nautical miles.

She was armed with four 120mm MkXII guns, a quadruple 40mm anti-aircraft gun, two quadruple 12.7mm MkIII anti-aircraft machine guns, one quadruple 533mm torpedo tube, and a rack for twenty depth charges and two throwers. She had a complement of 190 officers and ratings, but could carry an extra twenty officers and men if she became the flotilla leader, (which she did in 1944).

The purpose of this class of ship was to counter the larger destroyers that had been built in Germany in the 1930s and to support the existing destroyer flotillas. *Tartar* was the only one of four ships of that class to survive the war.

The captain in 1942 was Commander Richard Taylor White, a popular and decorated officer who was later promoted to Captain. Also on board was a young Sub-Lieutenant, Ludovic Kennedy, who went on to become a celebrated TV personality, journalist and author.

He wrote a book of his memoirs of his time in the Navy entitled, *'Sub-Lieutenant, A Personal Record of the War at Sea 1942'.* His first impression of *Tartar* was as follows: *'I saw my ship for the first time alongside an oiler. She was a fine-looking vessel with sloping bow and gracious lines. Her main armament of 4.7inch guns stood out boldly against the evening sky, the white ensign fluttered at her main mast. I thank God I have not been appointed to a drifter or a trawler…Here was a ship built to attack. Here was power and majesty, sleek and sharp lines and wicked-looking guns; bows that could cut through water like scissors through paper; a streamlined bridge from which to command, and to control forty thousand horse.'*

By 1942 *Tarter* had gained a reputation for fortitude in action. In 1940 she had escorted convoys to Norway, and RMS *Queen Elizabeth* on her maiden voyage from Glasgow through the Western Approaches. She had rescued survivors from a stricken Portuguese merchant ship and in March 1941, had participated in *Operation Claymore,* an attack on fish and glycerine factories in the Lofoten Islands in German-occupied Norway. During the process the officers boarded a trawler and found cogs for an Enigma machine, and an important code book, which was sent to Bletchley Park for decoding.

In May 1941, *Tartar* joined the pursuit for the *Bismarck*, the largest battleship in maritime history, and the crew watched in a mixture of elation and horror as it was scuttled after being crippled by torpedoes dropped by aircraft from the carrier HMS *Ark Royal.*

Tartar was part of the escort for Arctic convoy PQ7B in January 1942 from Hvalfjordur, Iceland to Murmansk, the Russian port high above the Arctic Circle, to provide arms and supplies to the people in the major cities of the USSR who were coming under relentless German bombardment. These convoy runs were extremely hazardous. In mid-winter it took a minimum of two weeks to sail to Murmansk and back, often in bitter, gale force winds and howling storms that created enormous thirty-foot waves.

The atrocious freezing weather created large blocks of ice on the ship's decks, which had to be forcibly removed. Jack, as an ordinary seaman, would have been doing many of the hard physical tasks, including clearing the packed ice. The convoys would frequently come under heavy bombardment and machine-gun fire from the air, and deadly torpedo attacks launched from invisible U-boats.

In March 1942 *Tartar* was part of convoy PQ12 from Reykjavik to Murmansk, and on the return leg was deployed on a search for *Bismarck*'s massive sister ship, *Tirpitz*, which was causing havoc with the convoys. (It was eventually sunk by the RAF in November 1944).

Jack wrote a letter to his mother on July 31, reassuring her as always and telling her a little of the adjustment to his new life on board ship, and the novelty of sleeping in a hammock. *'…We have had another busy day. I am doing harder manual work these days than ever before, but I do not mind that. My hands are becoming much harder and there are cuts all over them! But I am not a clerk or a law student now, I am just an ignorant ordinary seaman, and I do not feel very efficient in my present job as I did in the TCO!* (Town Council Office) *However, I am learning all I can as quickly as possible and trying to live up to your expectations…I am enjoying my duties on The Tartar, and like the life afloat generally.'* Within a few days of writing this he would be involved in his first major conflict.

By June 1942 Malta had been under siege for two years. This tiny island in the middle of the Mediterranean was of huge strategic importance to the Allies, indeed Winston Churchill called it *'an unsinkable aircraft carrier.'* By summer, Malta was getting desperately low on essential supplies, especially fuel.

On August 3, *Tartar* was sent to the Mediterranean as support for *Operation Pedestal*. It was a large force of four aircraft carriers and two battleships, escorting a convoy of fourteen merchant ships, which included an American oil tanker, SS *Ohio,* to deliver fuel and vital supplies.

Six days later the convoy sailed through the Strait of Gibraltar and met formidable opposition. The enemy had spotted them, and over the next six days of ferocious battle, they were attacked by 285 German bombers, 304 fighters, three heavy cruisers, twelve destroyers and twenty-one submarines. One aircraft carrier, two light cruisers, one destroyer and nine merchant ships were sunk and over 500 sailors died, but although badly damaged, *Ohio* got through to Malta, and the enemy suffered heavy losses. *Tartar* was attacked by Italian bombers, and submarines which were driven off by depth charges. They tried to tow the damaged destroyer *Foresight* back to Gibraltar but it was attacked by a German submarine, and they had to scuttle the stricken ship with a torpedo that blew away the entire midships section.

Dora received this letter from Jack on *Tartar* dated August 24. '...*I am safe and sound after three weeks full of hectic events, and I am as fit as ever... Since last I wrote the Tartar has been in action and I have had my baptism of fire – and I was well and truly baptized too! But we came out of it OK, and the ship was hardly scratched, no-one being injured. The ship's company were complimented on their conduct during the action; and I understand the gun crews are to be 'highly recommended' for the part they played. I was scared at times I admit, and I can tell you I wished I was near my mother several times when things were hot. Anyhow, everything turned out to be fine, so there is no need to worry, and I am as sound as ever...As I write to you the mess table keeps trying to come up and hit me in the face and it is impossible for me to write very much. But I know you will not mind so long as you know everything is fine at this end...*' On August 15 *Tartar* returned to England for essential repairs.

With only a few weeks for the crew to recover, *Tartar* was sent to Kirkwall in Scotland in early September to escort Arctic convoy PQ18 to Archangel in Russia. There were forty merchant ships with an escort of forty to fifty ships, including an American carrier and two submarines. They had received information from Bletchley Park that the Germans were preparing a large force to intercept them. PQ18 was attacked by twelve U-boat submarines, 120 long-range bombers, and mines, and was the target for the biggest torpedo attack on any convoy. Thirteen ships were lost and over 500 men died, at a cost of forty-four German aircraft and four U-boats.

Tartar switched to convoy QP14 for the home run to Scotland, but the nightmare voyage continued when they ran into a violent storm and several ships ran aground, with the Luftwaffe launching further waves of attacks on them. Kirkwall must have been a very welcome sight as the remains of the convoy reached port on September 26. Dora received this upbeat letter from Jack that same day.

'I am perfectly safe and well Mother dear, and The Tartar has come through unharmed once again. So you can set your mind at rest, and thank God for further guidance and protection during the past weeks… Once out of the harbour we were told that we were again going out in anger to meet the enemy. Then we learnt that we should be away for about the whole of the month, and that was that. You will have heard on the wireless that last Wednesday and Thursday a large convoy had just fought its way through to Russia. That was my first experience of a Russian convoy, and really was worse than our last operation. I am allowed to tell you that we were attacked by U-boats and aircraft. Mostly we were against torpedo-bombers but we also got a foretaste of high-level and low-level bombers. Altogether they gave us a hard time, but we certainly gave them one too. I cannot remember how many I saw shot down because there were too many hitting the drink. The submarines are the greatest cause for nerve strain, because you do not know they are there until they go into action. However that is another hill climbed, and we are becoming efficient hill-climbers by now!'

Few of the young Royal Navy sailors had left the shores of the British Isles before the war, and to suddenly find themselves sailing the high seas above the Arctic Circle was a totally new and exhilarating experience.

In the same letter written on September 26, Jack, still only nineteen years old, recalled his first impressions. '...*Remember the September holidays we spent at Blackpool several years ago? You said Blackpool was too cold in September! In the Arctic at this time of year the sky becomes semi-dark about midnight, and then for 3 hours the Aurora Borealis colours the sky, gleaming as the green sea. It is a lovely sight. At 3 o'clock in the morning it is light once more, so for 21 hours each day it is daytime! It is very cold and I wear more clothes than all of you at home wear – added together! I kept myself warm. However, my feet were the problem. I wished many times that they were size 4s instead of 8½s because the cold seemed to have too big a surface to attack for my liking...By the way there is another Darwener on board her. I have worked and joked with him for three solid months and then a fortnight ago I discovered we were both natives of Darwen. He is called Teddy Bassett and is a Petty Officer, and lives in Old Lane. I will tell you more about him tomorrow.'*

The Arctic convoys continued their perilous voyages right up to the end of the war in 1945, but that was the last one for *Tartar*. Thousands of men and many ships were lost on the seventy-eight convoys, but the moral boost and political support they gave to the USSR was invaluable, and tied up valuable troops and resources of the Axis powers at a critical time of the war.

It was not until 2013 that the valour of those brave men working under immensely difficult circumstances was finally recognised. The Arctic Star was awarded to all those who were on the convoys for any time between 1939 -1945, and could be awarded posthumously.

The crew had little time to recover before setting sail in October 1942 for the Mediterranean to support another major campaign, *Operation Torch*. This was an Allied invasion of the French colonies of North Africa by over 100,000 American and British troops, supported by 350 warships and 500 transport ships. British forces were advancing in Egypt and the Allies planned to carry out a pincer movement to attack Morocco, Algeria and Tunisia simultaneously.

Casablanca was captured after a short siege with only initial resistance. Oran surrendered after bombardment by British battleships. *Tartar* was with the eastern task force at Algiers and met less opposition as the Jewish French Resistance had staged an uprising in the city, and the Allies achieved a surrender in the first day under Commander of the US 7th Army, General George Patton.

Despite this relatively easy victory, over 1,300 Allied troops were killed and 756 wounded, and four destroyers were lost. The French Vichy forces suffered over 1,000 dead and 2,000 wounded, and much of their fleet was destroyed.

As well as a military victory there were significant political consequences. When Hitler heard of the defeat, his trust of the French Vichy evaporated and German troops occupied their area in the south of France. The French navy scuttled their ships before they could be seized, and all the French North African governments switched their allegiance to the Allies.

In the early summer of 1943 Jack was sent to HMS *Aerial* in Warrington on a Radio Mechanics course. Those selected needed to be academically bright but the subjects were not important. They learnt radio theory, and followed up with a three-month radar course.

It was conducted under great secrecy and never mentioned on paper. No books were allowed to be taken out of the camp and the details of the course were strictly confidential. Although basic RADAR, (Radio Detection and Ranging) using the reflection of radio signals to identify metal targets on a screen, had been used by the RAF and by two ships since 1937, Britain was leading the technology by making portable sets more powerful, with greater range and accuracy. The development of radar was considered a vital weapon against Germany by Churchill, and it was imperative to keep ahead of German research. Its effectiveness was a key factor in the Battle of Britain victory in 1940.

Jack never discussed what he did on that course, but did send a letter dated September 5 wishing his mother a happy birthday, confidently continuing, '...*I am getting along steadily with the course, and I am not anticipating any difficulty in passing the exams. In fact I ordered my Anchor yesterday, (the leading Radio Mechanics badge that I shall be wearing at the end of this course)...*'

With the victory in North Africa complete, the Allies could prepare for the invasion of Sicily and mainland Italy, and *Tartar* was in the thick of it. Many months of complex planning went into *Operation Husky*, led by General Dwight D. Eisenhower, who was Supreme Allied Commander coordinating the army movements of five Allied countries.

Husky began on July 9 1943 with naval and air bombardments, followed by two amphibious assaults and a six-week land campaign.

One landing was on the south-eastern side of the island and the other on the central-southern coast. 160,000 troops, 600 tanks and 14,000 vehicles were sent to combat a combined force of 300,000 Italian and German soldiers and personnel. *Tartar* participated in the initial bombardment and on July 11 went to the aid of survivors of the hospital ship, *Talamba,* which had been sunk by German bombers. They rescued 200.

Two days later *Tartar* towed the destroyer *Eskimo* to Malta for repairs, and returned immediately to Sicily to support the amphibious landings. *Operation Husky* was a decisive Allied victory, but over 5,000 soldiers died with 14,000 wounded. 9,000 Axis troops were killed, 50,000 wounded and over 100,000 captured. 50,000 German and Italian troops withdrew to the mainland to regroup and prepare for the inevitable Allied attack.

On September 3, the invasion of mainland Italy commenced. A controversial diversionary attack started in Calabria with *Operation Baytown,* and *Tartar* gave backup naval support to the landing force. The main attack was preparing to land at Salerno, and the German troops, (the Italians had now surrendered) were ready for them, falling back from Calabria and destroying the bridges behind them.

The Salerno invasion, *Operation Avalanche,* started on September 9, the day after Italy had officially surrendered. *Tartar* sailed from Calabria to support the landing and the beachhead was secured despite heavy resistance.

The Allied army pushed on towards Naples, which fell on October 1. By early October the whole of southern Italy was in Allied hands. *Tartar* returned to Devonport for more repairs and another refit, and some much-needed rest for an exhausted crew.

In March 1944 *Tartar* was deployed as leader of the 10th Destroyer Flotilla with Plymouth Command, which protected coastal shipping and Allied convoys through the English Channel, and started minelaying as part of preparations for the Normandy landings.

On D-Day, June 6 1944, *Operation Neptune* was launched with the largest seaborne invasion in history, involving 195,700 naval personnel and 156,000 soldiers who set out to begin the liberation of German-occupied France. *Tartar* led the 10th Flotilla into the Channel to protect the convoys sailing to the Normandy beachheads.

On June 9 she was in action against German warships. Two German destroyers were sunk, but that day *Tartar*'s luck ran out, and she was damaged by return fire. Her galley and bridge were hit and set on fire. Four men were killed and twelve wounded, including the captain, Commander Jones. Her foremast hung forlornly over the side and all the radar and communications equipment was knocked out. Luckily, Jack was not injured, and *Tartar* returned to Devonport to undergo speedy temporary repairs before resuming operations in the English Channel.

She sunk two minesweepers of the 46th German Flotilla on June 7 off the Channel Islands, and on August 6, along with two Canadian destroyers, attacked a convoy off Saint-

Nazaire, and sank two more minesweepers and five other smaller vessels.

By November, Jack's time on *Tartar* was coming to an end. The ship was due to go in for another three-month refit and had been assigned to serve in the Eastern Fleet. In March 1945 *Tartar* sailed to Trincomalee in Ceylon, (now Sri Lanka) and continued east to participate in the Allied landings at Rangoon, Burma (now Myanmar). She finished her distinguished service being present at the signing of the Japanese Instrument of Surrender in Tokyo Bay on September 2 1945.

For two and a half years Jack had served on HMS *Tartar*, seen action in the frozen wastes of the Arctic and at the siege of Malta. He was there at the decisive Allied push into Italy and was an eye-witness to the historic D-Day landings at Normandy. Against all odds he had survived innumerable aerial and U-boat attacks.

For a young Lancashire lad barely out of his teens, it was a truly extraordinary and heroic wartime career on board this remarkable ship. He returned home to Darwen and was given a hero's welcome, with a double-page spread in the local newspaper.

Jack never went to the Far East. He could see the end of the war coming, and requested to stay in Europe. He now looked forward to peace, and to returning to his studies. When Germany surrendered on May 8 1945, Jack applied for early demobilisation, keen to fulfil his ambition to study for a degree in Law at Manchester University.

He was released from the Royal Navy, and much to his

excitement, his application was accepted to begin his studies in September. He spent three years as an undergraduate at Manchester University and in 1948 achieved a First-Class Bachelor of Laws (Hons.) degree, one of only three out of twenty-nine of his year to obtain a first.

Whilst he was at university it is thought he had digs in or near Heaton Moor College, located in a suburb in Stockport, Greater Manchester, where a good friend of the family, Eliot Roberts was headmaster. From there it was an easy journey to visit Dora and George at weekends, who had moved to Blackpool.

Before Jack joined the Navy, he had met an attractive girl called Ellen, who he mentioned several times in his letters to his brother, Owen. He was clearly very fond of her and there is a photograph of the two of them on a beach looking very happy in each other's company taken around 1940. This was an unusual relationship as Ellen was of mixed race and a friendship like theirs would have attracted much disapproval. It speaks volumes for Jack's strength of character that he dismissed the prejudicial attitudes so prevalent in England at that time. Tragically, Ellen became ill with cancer, and died while Jack was still at university.

Jack continued his legal studies and passed his Law Notes examinations, (equivalent to Bar finals) in 1949 and became a member of Gray's Inn. He commenced pupillage that same year at a legal firm with chambers in King Street, Manchester. He encountered the kind of class prejudice shown to those who did not come from the 'right' family or school, but his natural intelligence, diligence at work and ability to get on with people from all walks of life enabled him to rise above it all.

He was a keen tennis player, and joined the North Shore Young Conservatives in Blackpool, carefully observing all the social games going on around him. It is about this time he decided to adopt the name John, from which Jack was derived.

In 1949 John met Joan Baggaley (née Shackleton) at a function at the Blackpool Conservative Club, of which he was Vice-Chairman. Joan was an attractive, twenty-nine-year old widow who had already had her share of sadness, but was bright, outgoing and good company. She had married Geoffrey Baggaley in 1941 and they had a son, David in 1943.

Geoffrey had joined the Royal Artillery and was part of the Allied force that fought in the battle of Anzio. (Coincidently, Nettuno was the German name for the battle of Anzio.) After their success in North Africa, the retaking of Italy was essential for the Allies to control the Mediterranean. *Operation Shingle* was an ill-conceived plan to draw the German forces south, away from Cassino, to enable the Allies to advance and take Rome.

The Anglo-American forces landed at Anzio on January 22 and were pinned down by heavy German fire on the beachhead for four months. The Germans launched a series of counterattacks in an attempt to break the Allied hold, but the stalemate resulted in thousands of lost lives in scenes reminiscent of the ghastly carnage of World War One trench warfare. The Allies finally launched a successful breakout on May 23.

Lance Bombardier Geoffrey Baggaley was one of 7,000 soldiers who lost their lives at Anzio, and died on April 8 aged twenty-five. Joan had only been married three years, the majority of the time separated from her young husband by war.

John and Joan's relationship blossomed during 1950 and on December 27, they were married in Holy Trinity Church, Blackpool. Joan looked radiant wearing an ankle-length dress of crisp taffeta in deep purple, embellished simply with cream lace on the cowl neckline and on the sleeve cuffs. A fine reception followed at The Cliffs Hotel in Blackpool. A surviving photograph shows the Prince and Shackleton families, and a young David Baggaley, smiling and enjoying the happy day.

John, Joan and David moved to a house in Heaton Moor, and in November 1951 they celebrated the birth of their daughter, Lynda. John continued his work as a lawyer in Manchester, dealing with a wide variety of cases, but more in commercial law than criminal. Some of these cases were heard in London and he would travel there by train from Manchester.

On October 8 1952 he was due to travel to London, but a case had overrun and a colleague agreed to go in his place. The train was involved in one of the world's worst ever railway crashes, a three-train collision at Harrow and Wealdstone station in Middlesex. At 08.19, an overnight express train from Perth crashed at high speed into the rear of a local passenger train standing at the platform. The wreckage blocked adjacent lines and within seconds, another express train, travelling north from Euston to Liverpool, ploughed into the wreckage.

The subsequent inquiry found that the driver of the Perth train had passed a caution signal and two danger signals before hitting the local train. Both the driver and fireman were killed and the reason for his catastrophic errors was never known. There were 112 fatalities, including John's colleague, and 340 people injured. John must have thought once again how lucky he had been in his life.

In 1953 John was offered a job with the Anglo-Iranian Oil Company, which was expanding and recruiting legal advisors. He accepted, and after discussion with Joan, they moved into a flat in Pinner, in north-west London.

This was a crucial time in the development of the oil business in the Middle East. In 1901, William Knox D'Arcy, an eccentric entrepreneur, won a concession to carry out exploration drilling in Persia. It was seven years before he struck rich and founded the Anglo-Persian Oil Company. In 1914, with World War One looming, British industry and the government needed oil. Winston Churchill was Lord of the Admiralty and had persuaded the British Navy to switch from coal to oil, and the government became a major stockholder in the company.

With cars being mass-produced in the 1920s, the oil business boomed for the next twenty years. In 1935, the company was renamed the Anglo-Iranian Oil Company, employing 200,000 people, and operated the world's largest refinery in the world at Abadan.

In 1951, the Prime Minister of Iran, Mohammad Mossaddegh, objected to the enormous amount of money leaving Iran and nationalised the company. He expelled the foreign employees and shut off the UK pipeline. The response was a boycott and a CIA-funded coup against Mossaddegh in August 1953, during which a pro-west regime was installed. A European consortium came in to run the oil company, giving it a new name. British Petroleum was born, and John was there at its birth.

The company diversified into new and emerging markets, creating a globally integrated oil company. Worldwide exploration led to the discovery of huge new oilfields, with BP developing its refining and retail operations as well as production. The company expanded at a frantic pace and an enormous amount of legal work was generated to safeguard its interests.

John travelled extensively, negotiating new exploration and production contracts for the company, particularly in the other areas of the Persian Gulf, especially Kuwait and Bahrain. He was also formulating legal agreements to establish sales and marketing companies in Europe.

In 1956 their son, Christopher was born, and the family moved to a comfortable house in Chorleywood, ideal for transport links to the city and London Airport. For the next two years John was frantically busy. Education of their children was a priority and they made sure that Lynda and David benefitted from the best schooling available.

John was considered one of the most talented and popular legal advisors in BP, and his reputation grew. With his excellent brain, and calm, relaxing manner, he was a skilled and brilliant negotiator, and excelled at getting difficult contracts signed. His devoted secretary, Kaye Norman was convinced that although he was only thirty-five years old, he would go all the way to the top of BP. In 1958, as well as his corporate interests, John was also considering entering politics and standing as a Member of Parliament. He wanted to make a difference.

At the airport on October 22 1958, John phoned Kaye to check on some last-minute details for the meeting, and met Reuben Silburn before checking in. They boarded the plane and settled down for the start of the journey to Libya, relieved that it was only half full. As he looked round at the other passengers he would have noticed a few servicemen, including a young sailor in uniform sitting a few seats further back. He must have reflected on his own time in the Navy, and how much his life had changed since he had last been in North Africa sixteen years earlier, when he had been on the deck of the *Tartar*, watching the troops going ashore to retake Algiers.

The desperately sad, and highly emotional funeral was held at Christ Church, Chorleywood, and John was buried at Chorleywood Lawn cemetery. Mourners representing all stages of his life came to pay their respects. Owen and his wife, Dilys, who ran two grocer's shops in Darwen, Dora and George, who still lived in Blackpool, friends from his university days in Manchester, and close colleagues in BP and London.

Joan's grief was overwhelming. She had lost two husbands by the age of thirty-eight, both killed within three miles of each other in Italy. She never recovered from this devastating blow, and tragically, died from cancer in 1969 at the age of forty-nine.

Their three children went on to have successful and fulfilling lives. David also worked for BP and became the Financial Director of a major finance house. Lynda emigrated to Australia and became successful in the media publishing industry in Sydney, and Christopher followed in his father's footsteps to become a barrister in criminal law. In 2006 he was appointed a Circuit Judge and in 2009 made the Resident Judge at Durham Crown Court and the Honorary Judicial Recorder of Durham.

Their success is a fitting tribute to a very special man.

The Accountant
REUBEN SILBURN

Reuben Silburn arrived at the BEA check-in desk at London Airport just before 08.00 on October 22 1958. He had travelled from his house in Banstead in Surrey, only thirteen miles by train to Victoria, and caught the BEA airbus from South Kensington to the airport. Once checked-in he looked around for his colleague, John Prince, and found him seated in the departure lounge checking their schedule for the next few days.

Both men worked for the British Petroleum Company (BP) and were flying to Tripoli to attend an important meeting with the Libyan government to finalise negotiations for oil exploration concessions. Flight BE142 was scheduled to land at Naples at 12.10, refuel and land in Malta at 14.30. From there they would board another plane to take them to Tripoli and arrive sometime in the late afternoon. It was going to be a long day.

Reuben's father, Harry was born in Northampton in 1869 and had followed in his own father's footsteps and was a shoemaker by trade. Northampton was once described as the 'shoemaking capital of the world,' the home of 'fine English shoes,' and the town has a proud heritage going back some 900 years. By 1891 Harry and his parents were earning a living by making and selling boots in Kettering. There he met and married Elizabeth Howell, who came from the nearby village of Harrowden. They moved to Ilkeston, in Derbyshire where their first daughter, Hilda was born in 1894. Their second, Eunice followed in 1899 and six years later, Reuben, named after his grandfather, arrived on March 23 1905.

Ilkeston's growth and prosperity was largely due to mining. There is evidence of iron working and quarrying dating back to Roman times as there were plentiful supplies of coal and iron ore. The Industrial Revolution arrived in the 1780s and by 1850 several blast furnaces were manufacturing pig iron. There were also spa baths in the town but they were forced to close due to the contamination of the mineral waters by the mining activities.

By 1905 there were many steel companies of various sizes, with the Stanton Ironworks, (later Stanton Staveley) being the largest, employing around 7,000 people. Ilkeston also boasts one of the largest street fairs in Europe. It was granted a Charter by Henry III in 1252 and is still held every October.

Shortly after Reuben was born, the family left Ilkeston and moved out to Aberystwyth on the west coast of Wales, and

Harry ran his own boot-making business from the house in Alexandra Road. When Reuben was only thirteen years old, his mother died, possibly of Spanish flu, and it is thought his father remarried.

By 1930 Reuben had moved to the Midlands and was training as an accountant. That year, at the age of twenty-five, he married Gladys Sanders in Birmingham.

The Wall Street Crash in the autumn of 1929 caused a global recession and throughout the 1930s cities reliant on heavy industry were severely affected. The recession hit Britain particularly badly and the output of the industrial cities of the Midlands and northern England fell by a third by 1932, and unemployment in Britain rose to 3.5 million. Finding a job as a young person with little experience was extremely difficult.

However, by 1933 Reuben had completed his Articles and had qualified as a Chartered Accountant. He and Gladys moved to Streatham in south London, which would have been an easy commute for him into the City.

Over the next six years the global economy slowly recovered, but it took another setback in September 1939 when war was declared with Germany.

Reuben and Gladys moved to Sanderstead, in Surrey, once a small, rural village nestling on the eastern edge of the Purley Downs and now part of the greater suburban area of Croydon, popular with professionals commuting into London from the railway station.

The couple spent the war years there, living in a house they called 'Chevithorne'. There is an indication that Reuben was an Army officer, and would probably have been involved in some administration capacity as he was thirty-four years old and too old to be conscripted.

In 1949 they had moved to Stamford Green in Epsom, a busier commuter town, and after a few more years they moved again to nearby Banstead, just one stop up the railway line to Victoria. Their large, detached house in Fir Tree Avenue would be the last they shared together.

Banstead is another small commuter town situated on the North Downs with a population of less than 20,000 people, located five miles west of Croydon and only thirteen miles to central London. It is mainly residential and had expanded rapidly since the 1920s, with a thriving High Street of shops and restaurants, and is dominated by All Saints Church, which dates back a thousand years. The present church was built between 1100 and 1220AD, with the tower added in the thirteenth century containing room for a peal of eight bells.

Extensive improvements were made in the nineteenth century after it had fallen into disrepair, and its interior is noted for the Arts and Craft style, with the west window designed by Dante Gabriel Rossetti and a figure of John the Baptist designed by William Morris. It was a church that Reuben and Gladys would have known well.

In the early 1950s Reuben was working in the City for the Anglo-Iranian Oil Company, which became the British Petroleum Company in 1953. With many new oil fields being discovered in the Middle East, particularly in Kuwait and Bahrain, the company was rapidly expanding. Reuben was now a senior accountant and advising the vibrant young sales teams on the financial implications of the contracts being negotiated. His colleague, John Prince was a talented young lawyer who was heading up negotiations with the Libyan government and earning a reputation for his excellent negotiating skills and getting contracts signed. Together they would have made a formidable team.

On October 22 1958, Reuben and John boarded flight BE142 to Naples and Malta for what they thought was going to be a long and productive business meeting in Tripoli.

Reuben and Gladys had no children. He was flown back from Italy to London and the funeral was held in All Saints Church in Banstead. A number of BP and BEA representatives attended the small, family service. Gladys never remarried and continued living for many years in Banstead, before retiring to a bungalow on the Kent coast in Deal. She died in 1984 and was buried at All Saints Church with Reuben.

SINGLES

The Steelworker
JOHN BOOTH

On October 21 1958 John Booth set off from Leven, in Fife, on the east coast of Scotland, heading for London. It would take him all day. The Forth Road Bridge, that would eventually open in 1964 and link Fife to Edinburgh, had only just commenced construction, so he had to travel nearly sixty miles over the Kincardine Bridge before reaching the noisy, steam-filled Waverley Station. From there it was a long, seven-and-a-half-hour journey down the east coast of England to King's Cross.

The following morning he arose before dawn and made his way to the BEA office in Cromwell Road, South Kensington, and caught the bus to London Airport for his flight at 08.25. He was working for a specialist steel fabricator in Leven, and was travelling to Malta on flight BE142 for discussions on a new project. He had spent many years visiting companies around Britain and abroad, and was looking forward to his trip to this historical, Mediterranean island.

John Charles W. Booth was born in Kimberworth, a small suburb of Rotherham, Yorkshire on September 13 1919. He came from a hard-working Yorkshire family who had all been involved in the heavy industries that had evolved out of the Industrial Revolution since the late 1700s.

His father, Charles Booth was born in 1889 in Greasebrough, another small suburb of Rotherham, as was his grandfather, Edward, born in 1852. Edward had married Clara when he was twenty-six and they had six children, all born in Potter Hill in Greasebrough, Charles being the youngest.

In 1919, Rotherham was a large, coal mining town situated only ten miles from the steel producing city of Sheffield, linked to each other by the River Don. It was recorded as a Saxon market town situated on a Roman road, and in 1066 was taken over by a Norman lord. In 1480 the Archbishop of York (from Rotherham), built Jesus College as a rival to Oxford and Cambridge, the first brick building in Yorkshire. The monks there taught theology, grammar, writing and religious chants, but the college was dissolved in 1547 during the reign of Edward VI. Parts of its ancient walls can still be seen in the town today.

The surrounding area abounded in mineral wealth, especially coal and good quality iron ore, and as a result, the Industrial Revolution came to the town early, from the middle of the eighteenth century. The Walker family built an empire, with their foundries producing some of the early cast iron bridges and high-quality cannons for the Royal Navy, including those for Nelson's great flagship, HMS *Victory*. The River Don was widened, deepened and in some parts straightened to improve navigation for the barges, and linked with the new canal network being built at that time, which included a branch to Greasebrough.

The first railway stations opened in 1838, the same time as new coalfields were being developed, with direct connections to Sheffield, Manchester and the Midlands. It was a prosperous time. In 1854, another famous company, Samuel

Beale and Co. supplied the wrought iron plates for Isambard Kingdom Brunel's famous steamship, the SS *Great Eastern*. Many more factories were built and the industry expanded rapidly. Effingham Brass Works was established in 1874 by G. and W.G. Gummer Ltd, which exported brass products all round the world, including fittings for luxury hotels, hospitals and ships, and it is likely that this is where Edward Booth worked as a warehouseman in the late nineteenth century.

In 1911, Charles, like his brother George, was working as a cabinet maker, and together with his father, who had retired from his job at the brass works, and his mother, they all lived in Greasebrough. At the age of twenty-two, he married local girl Elizabeth Colley, and four years later young John was born.

Triggered by the Wall Street Crash in 1929, the country was plunged into a deep recession in the 1930s and it lasted almost five years. As exports fell, industrial output declined sharply and many men became unemployed. Many families, particularly those in the industrial heartlands of England, lived on the bread line. The Booth family moved to 318 Wortley Road in Kimberworth, just outside Rotherham, and Charles found work as a railway wagon repairer.

John was twenty years old in 1939, and working as an assistant chemist in the coal gas works. At that time nearly all domestic gas was produced from coal. It contained a toxic mixture of gases including hydrogen, carbon monoxide, methane and ethylene and needed close monitoring. Many accidents occurred in the home from explosions and poisoning, until it was superseded by the far safer natural gas from the North Sea in the 1960s, which was a by-product of drilling for oil.

It is not known if John served in the forces in World War Two. He may well have been an essential worker, but we do know that he married twenty-two-year-old Joan Schofield in Rotherham early in 1941. They celebrated the birth of their daughter, Susan in 1944, and three years later their son, Robin.

By 1958 John was working for Henry Balfour & Co. Ltd. in Leven, travelling to and from the family house in Rotherham. He was an experienced steel erection supervisor and would have been involved in the tender submissions and liaisons with clients, as well as supervising the erection of the steel on site. While he was living in Leven he lodged at Alverton, McDonald Street in nearby Methil, a coal port situated on the coast south of the town.

The company was founded by Henry Balfour in 1810, a pioneering engineer when the first iron foundries were being developed in Scotland. They were specialist boilermakers for all the different types of vessels required for the many new businesses that had developed from the coal and gas industries. In 1896 it became a Public Company, with the castings being carried out at their main Durie foundry on the banks of the River Leven.

By the early twentieth century the company had established a reputation as a specialist fabricator for plant and vessels for gas and oil condensers, the manufacturing of chemicals, and a specialist in the production of equipment for the brewing industry.

In 1933 the company went into a joint venture with the American company, Pfaudler to manufacture glass-lined steel vessels used for brewing. This was the link with Malta.

Due to the large garrison of British servicemen stationed in Malta, there had always been a big demand for beer. Until the twentieth century this was imported from England, but in 1928, L. Ferrugia & Sons, otherwise known as Farsons, built their first brewery at Hamrun, just south of Valletta and produced Farsons Pale Ale. Shortly afterwards, the Malta Export Brewery, another local brewer, produced a Münchener lager beer called Cisk. The following year Farsons merged with H. and G. Simonds, a long-established brewer from Reading that had been supplying beer to the island for many years.

Malta came under relentless and sustained assault from the Germans during World War Two and during a bombing blitz in 1942, the brewery suffered extensive damage.

In 1948 Simonds, Farsons and Cisk merged and constructed a new brewery in Mriehel, to the west of Valletta, and Henry Balfour were involved with the steelwork. In the 1950s the company diversified into soft drinks, additional works were required, and the link with Henry Balfour was continued.

When Simonds Farsons Cisk contacted Henry Balfour to discuss the alterations in October 1958, John was asked to lend his expertise at the discussions in Malta.

At that time the Maltese government was also concerned about the ongoing Cold War crisis, and was considering the construction of underground grain silos in Valletta. It could be a busy trip.

On October 22, having been on the move for the best part of twenty-four hours, John boarded flight BE142 and sat back in his seat and relaxed. He was looking forward to the visit. Malta was warm at this time of year, a far cry from the chilly east coast of Scotland, and he might even have time for a little sightseeing, and a pint of Cisk lager sitting at sunset in the Upper Barrakka Gardens overlooking the magnificent Grand Harbour, bustling with British ships.

John never got to enjoy that view over Grand Harbour. His wife Joan was in the family house in Rotherham and was informed of the tragic news by the local police.

At the end of October, John's coffin was flown back to London. He was taken to Rotherham for another sad funeral, attended by Joan, his two children Susan and Robin, family, friends, and representatives from Henry Balfour and BEA.

The Soldier
ROBERT CHALMERS

On October 21 1958, nineteen-year-old Robert Chalmers arrived at Waverley Station, Edinburgh from Perth to catch the connecting train to London. This large, draughty, Victorian station, which had been built in the late 1860s was bustling with travellers coming and going from its twenty-one platforms. The air resounded with a cacophony of noise – the hissing of giant steam engines belching out thick clouds of smoke, the clanking and screeching of giant wheels on iron tracks, the banging of metal carriage doors, and the shouts and whistles of guards hurrying along stragglers. He found a seat and settled in for the seven-and-a-half-hour journey on the rugged east coast line, travelling through Newcastle, York, Peterborough and finally to King's Cross.

He was smartly dressed in Army uniform, carrying out his National Service, and was on his way to London Airport to fly to Malta, looking forward to a few days leave with his family before starting a tour of duty with the Black Watch regiment in Cyprus.

Robert John Chalmers was born in King George V Hospital in Floriana, Malta on February 7 1939, as the storm clouds of war were gathering over Europe. He was the second generation of Chalmers to be born in Malta. His grandfather, John Harcus Chalmers was a talented artist, musician and baker who was born in Stromness, Orkney, Scotland in 1870. It is thought he was on his way to visit his brother in India in around 1907 when he stopped off at Malta for a few days and paid a visit to the famous bakers, confectioners and tea shop in Kingsway, (now Republic Street) in Valletta called *Blackley's*.

The elegant, double-fronted shop had large, panoramic windows displaying freshly-baked bread, tiered wedding cakes and mouth-watering confectionery. Above the shop was an ornate balcony to which was attached a large coat of arms displaying a Royal Warrant, *By Appointment To H.M. The King*. The shop's founder was Frederic Blackley. On Frederic's death his daughter, Laura Emma Blackley took over the business and by 1893 had formed a partnership with Edwin Herbert Morris. She retired to Cornwall a few years later and ceded her share to Edwin.

Whether John Chalmers' visit was opportune or planned we don't know, but shortly afterwards he was offered a partnership in the business by Edwin, which he accepted. While the shop sold bread and confectionery at the front, upstairs the patrons could enjoy afternoon tea in the elegant and relaxing tea room. It entered a very prosperous period.

John's paintings and watercolours of Malta were of an exceptional quality and using all his artistic skills, his cake decorations became legendary. He became a Master Baker and in 1907 the production of bread moved to the Blackley Bakery at Triq id-Duluri, on the corner of Gwardamangia Hill in Pietà, a suburb just outside Valletta.

The bakery boasted the most advanced machinery of its time for bread-making. The icing on John's personal cake was when he fell in love with Edwin's sister, Gertrude, and married her at St Andrew's Scots Church, Valletta in 1908.

They had a son, William Ian Chalmers, (always known as Ian) who was born in Malta in 1911. After primary schooling in Valletta he was sent to Scotland and educated at Strathallan School, Forgandenny, a few miles south of Perth, a boarding school for boys aged nine to eighteen.

Strathallan was founded in 1913 in Bridge of Allan, near Stirling by a young teacher called Harry Riley. Harry was born in Bradford in 1888 and came from a humble background. He began his teaching career in 1908 in Bridge of Allan, but after his school was merged with another he decided, at the age of twenty-five, to open his own school and started with seven boys. Harry's vision was to create a nurturing and caring school, a very different ethos from the strict Victorian institutions prevalent at that time. He had four key aims. The pupils should be known for who they are, and as individuals, education should be enjoyed and not a drudgery. Education should find character, talent and potential hitherto unknown, and hard work was essential if education was to be the improving and transforming force.

The school was a success, and by 1919 had over one hundred pupils. Harry needed bigger premises and taking a gamble, bought the Freeland estate in Forgandenny, and moved the school to its present location a few miles from Perth.

Ian was an intelligent and hard-working pupil and went on to read medicine at Edinburgh University. There he met Margaret Mackenzie who was undertaking nursing training at the Edinburgh Royal Infirmary. Margaret visited Ian in Malta, where he proposed to her and, like his parents, they married at St Andrew's Scots Church, Valletta in 1938. A year later their first son, Robert was born.

The family settled in a house in Molo Pietà, overlooking the Marsamxett Harbour, and in time, Ian took over the running of the bakery business from his father. Within a year Malta was about to go through its toughest test of survival in its long history, and the Chalmers family were in the thick of it.

The archipelago of Malta comprises Malta, the two adjacent islands of Gozo and Comino and eighteen other little islands. They cover a tiny area of 122 square miles, but over the centuries their strategic location in the Mediterranean between Gibraltar and Egypt has attracted many invaders. Countless rulers have come and gone in its long and complicated history. Inhabitants arrived from Sicily around 3,600BC and built large, mysterious megalithic temples, some of which are still standing in remarkable condition. The Phoenicians colonised the island around 800BC, as Malta was in a perfect position for their Mediterranean trading routes. The eyes of Osiris painted onto traditional Maltese fishing boats are their legacy.

The Romans invaded in 218BC and stayed for 700 vibrant and prosperous years leaving behind towns, roads, villas and antiquities. There is a strong belief that in 60AD Saint Peter was shipwrecked on Malta and brought Christianity to the island. The Arabs invaded in 870AD and although they stayed for a relatively short time, left a permanent influence on the Maltese language.

In 1530 the islands were given to the Order of Saint John by the Holy Roman Emperor Charles V. In the Great Siege of 1565 Christianity and Islam found themselves at the centre of an ideological clash when Suleiman the Magnificent, a famous Sultan of the Ottoman Empire, laid siege to the island with 30,000 men. It was successfully repelled in five months but not after many towns were destroyed and half the knights killed in battle. With the Treaty of Paris in 1814 Malta became a British protectorate.

It was made the headquarters of the Mediterranean fleet, and a large military and naval fortress was created. During World War One Malta became known as the *Nurse of the Mediterranean*, due to the large number of wounded soldiers sent from the killing fields of France to be treated in its hospitals.

In 1937 the threat of war was again looming. After a review, the British Navy decided Malta would be too open and difficult to defend, and moved its headquarters to Alexandria, in Egypt. In the event of war, this left 4,000 soldiers, a small variety of armaments, and six obsolete Gloucester Sea Gladiator biplanes, including three nicknamed Faith, Hope and Charity. (Charity was destroyed in the first air raid, leaving behind Faith and Hope for the island.)

There was also the warship HMS *Terror,* an old *Erebus*-class monitor built in 1916 and recently refitted in Singapore, and a few submarines left to defend the important harbour and a population of 250,000 civilians if attacked. They did not have to wait long.

Malta watched nervously when Britain declared war on Germany in September 1939. Italy joined Germany on June 10 1940 and Mussolini declared war on Malta. Over the next two years Malta faced relentless aerial attacks by the Luftwaffe and the Italian Air Force. Italian bombers from Sicily bombarded the airbases at Luqa, Hal Far and Ta'Qali, immediately establishing air superiority. With no RAF airfields operational at the time, (Luqa was still under construction) they faced limited opposition and the attacks were followed up by raids on the cities, aiming to quickly reduce morale in the civilian population. There was little damage to the harbour and most casualties were civilian.

Many of the locals left the harbour area, where the majority of the population lived and stayed temporarily in the rural areas. The British thought that they could defend Malta from Alexandria as there were adequate ships in the region, but this strategy soon proved to be wrong, and further aircraft and munitions were immediately dispatched to Malta.

On June 19 twelve Fairey Swordfish torpedo bombers flew into Hal Far having escaped from southern France after the French capitulation, and this formed the nucleus of a new naval air squadron. Within days they had raided Sicily, sunk an Italian destroyer, damaged a cruiser, and destroyed oil storage tanks.

By August they were reinforced by Hawker Hurricanes, and 261 Squadron was formed by the RAF. Mussolini considered an invasion of Malta, but due to increasing difficulties in the North Africa campaign, a shortage of fuel, (at that time most of the oil came from Romania) and unexpected resistance from the Maltese forces, the plan was shelved.

By January 1941, the Italians had suffered further defeats in North Africa, and Hitler dispatched General Erwin Rommel and the German Africa Corps to begin a counter offensive to drive the British back into Egypt. Most of their supplies came by sea so it was essential for them to neutralise Malta. The Axis powers resolved to bomb or starve Malta into submission by attacking its ports, towns and vital facilities, and to cut off the Allied shipping supplies to the island.

Malta was about to come under siege and become one of the most heavily bombed countries in the war. During the autumn of 1940 there had been a lull in the attacks and many civilians had drifted back to their houses in the cities. They paid a terrible toll.

On January 6 1941 the British launched *Operation Excess*, a series of convoy operations to deliver supplies to North Africa. Amongst the escort was a new aircraft carrier, HMS *Illustrious*, which was targeted by the Axis bombers. The carrier received six direct hits, killing 126 crew members and suffering serious damage. She limped into Grand Harbour still being pursued by bombers and underwent emergency repairs.

For twelve continuous days, as the dock workers toiled day and night to repair her, German Stukas screamed across the skies and dived down to the docks, leading wave after wave of bombers raining bombs on the dockyard and the surrounding civilian areas. Anti-aircraft guns were brought in from other areas of Malta and crews were sent from *Illustrious* to help man them. The scene was apocalyptic. Panicked dock workers ran for cover and the terrified citizens of Valletta huddled in underground shelters.

The Reverend Reginald Nicholls, the Chancellor of St Paul's Anglican Cathedral wrote, *'The noise in our crypt was just terrible. There were about 250 people huddled together, many of them crying, but many were brave. The roar was like the loudest thunder one has ever heard, but absolutely continuous, and it was not possible really to distinguish the guns from the bombs, except when one fell close to us – about seventy yards. That brought down a block of flats and five people were killed. We sat, holding hands and praying aloud.'*

Malta's oldest urban communities, established in the sixteenth century by the Knights of Malta, were reduced to rubble. Hundreds of local volunteers joined military and civil defence personnel to claw through the wreckage in a desperate attempt to find survivors. Twelve people were rescued forty-eight hours after the raid from a cellar at Two Gates Street, Senglea. One of the survivors, Willie Mizzie wrote, *'For two days we were huddled on top of each other in complete darkness and, as time passed, we suffered from suffocation, and water and food shortage. There was no panic; we just stood there exchanging an occasional word unaware that we were buried under forty feet of rubble. When we had almost given up hope, we felt some gravel filtering into the shelter and shortly afterwards we could see a speck of light through the mound of masonry. The hole was enlarged and we were asked if we were all well.'*

The Chalmers' house at 109, Molo Pietà, (now Triq Marina) was further away from the main areas of attack and marginally safer. When the air raid sirens sounded the alarm, Margaret grabbed infant Robert and rushed to the cellar to shelter. *Blackley's* and the Opera House were amongst those hit during the bombing, but luckily their house and the bakery were not damaged.

During that blitz, Margaret was asked to look after another little boy, the same age as Robert, called Anthony Clover, whose grandparents ran a pharmacy, *Collis and Williams* in Strada Reale, (now 300 Republic Street) near to *Blackley's*. It is almost certain his grandparents were part of the group that took refuge in the crypt of St Paul's Cathedral that terrifying night. Anthony remained with the Chalmers until the end of the war. He vividly recalled *'the skies pockmarked by shells exploding in the anti-aircraft box barrages over Marsamxett harbour, the cloying stink and stinging of the eyes caused by the smoke screen canisters along Ix-Xatt and Sa Maison, and the ripping noise of heavy vehicles on the roads...'*

He described Margaret in 1941 as a strong, tall woman. Later that year, amongst all this chaos she gave birth to their first daughter, Anne. By the end of the war Margaret weighed less than six stone, having given up much of her food quota to Robert, Anne and Anthony. Rationing reduced morale on the island, and all males aged 16 to 56 years old were conscripted. At times there was such a shortage of food, the ration fell to a quarter of that available in Britain.

Throughout the early months of 1941 Axis forces continued to batter the island. Much of the heavy equipment was destroyed in the dock, and another 2,000 buildings were destroyed. The airfields were attacked and all the RAF Wellington bombers were blown up, but by April, the Allies began to have more success at sea, attacking Axis convoys. Much-needed supplies arrived from Egypt and forty-eight new Hurricanes flew in from the *Ark Royal.* By May nearly 60,000 people had left the cities.

In June 1941 Germany attacked the Soviet Union and

withdrew some of their forces from Italy to send to the eastern front. This respite gave Malta a little time to recover. A new AOC (Air Officer Commanding) arrived, Air Commodore Hugh Lloyd. He immediately hung up a sign outside his office saying, *'Less depends on the size of the dog in the fight than on the size of the fight in the dog.'*

Airfields were enlarged and more planes arrived. Malta as a transfer base was strengthened to support the troops struggling against Rommel in Egypt. Convoys with 65,000 tonnes of supplies arrived in July, and the number of aircraft increased to 60 bombers and 120 Hurricanes. In the second half of 1941, 60% of Axis shipping due for North Africa was sunk. The response to this came in December, when the Luftwaffe brought Messerschmitts to Sicily, and U-boats were sent from the Atlantic. Malta was about to experience a second wave of intense siege. On New Year's Day 1942, the air raid sirens sounded for the 1,175th raid of the war. In January alone, 263 bombing missions were carried out on the towns, docks, airfields and military installations by the Axis forces.

The Chalmers family continued to live through this ordeal in Molo Pietà, with Ian keeping the bakery going and Margaret keeping the children safe. In April they were incredibly lucky when a bomb hit the house and destroyed their bedroom minutes after Margaret had taken Robert, Anthony and baby Anne to the safety of the shelter in the cellar. They moved out and stayed in Gwardamangia, close to the bakery. During this time Ian successfully proposed to the Governor of Malta that 'Victory Kitchens' be set up and offered his vans to transport food around Valletta during the All Clear siren signal between air raids.

By early May Spitfires were delivered to Malta, crewed by battle-hardened, experienced pilots. Numerical and technical superiority was demonstrated by the RAF in intense air battles in the skies over the island. Although the tide seemed to be turning in the Allies' favour, the situation for the civilians on the island was dire.

All essential commodities such as food and water had virtually run out, the pumps and distribution system were crippled, all livestock had been slaughtered and the lack of leather meant people were forced to use curtains and old tyres to replace clothing and shoe soles. Starvation was real, and poor nutrition and sanitation led to the outbreak of disease.

Convoys in the Mediterranean continued to come under relentless attacks by air and submarines, but in August, nine merchant ships made it through to Malta, including the large oil tanker SS *Ohio*, which had been badly damaged. This delivery was an immense boost to the islanders' morale. Amongst the escorting destroyers was HMS *Tartar*, and on board a young able seaman called John Prince, who was to be a fellow traveller with Robert on flight BE142 in 1958.

The bombing campaign against Axis shipping met with increasing success, starving supplies to Rommel's army in North Africa, especially of oil. When Rommel launched an offensive against the Allies in September, he was forced to retreat through lack of fuel, and the Allies began their successful counterattack at Alamein on October 23. Morocco, Tunisia and Algeria fell swiftly through *Operation Torch*, and the next convoy to reach Malta from Alexandria on November 20 arrived virtually unscathed. The siege was over.

The last air raid over Malta occurred on July 20 1943, the 3,340th alert since June 11 1940.

Malta was the most-bombed country in Europe during the war. Between June 1940 and April 1944, 1,581 civilians died and 3,780 were injured. Over 30,000 buildings were destroyed or badly damaged, including 5,524 private dwellings, 111 churches, 50 hospitals, 36 theatres, the Opera House and many factories, offices, banks and clubs.

On April 15 1942, King George VI awarded the George Cross to the people of Malta in recognition of their heroism and bravery when they were on the brink of starvation after having been bombed for 156 consecutive day and nights. Today, the George Cross is proudly displayed in the National War Museum in Valletta, and the flag includes the cross in the top left corner of the hoist.

With so much of the island destroyed, the years after the war were very difficult, as people struggled to rebuild their shattered lives. John died in 1946, aged seventy-six, and Ian continued to run the bakery business, with Margaret in charge of the shop in Valletta. That year Ian and Margaret also celebrated the birth of their second daughter, Victoria, followed in 1947 by the birth of Roderick.

After early schooling at Chiswick House School in Valletta, Robert followed in his father's footsteps and attended Strathallan School in Scotland. There he thrived. Tall and athletic, he became a noted sportsman, winning school colours for both rugby and athletics.

He completed his education in the summer of 1957 and

volunteered to undertake his National Service with the famous Black Watch (Royal Highland Regiment), whose garrison was based in Perth. He completed his basic training and crowned his success by winning the 100 yards sprint in the Army Athletics Championship.

In October 1958 the Black Watch were posted to Cyprus, where violent terrorist attacks were being carried out by EOKA, an organisation fighting a military campaign for the liberation of Cyprus from British rule. William and Margaret were immensely proud of Robert and suggested he take a few days leave with them in Malta before starting his tour of duty in Cyprus. All the family would be looking forward to seeing him.

Early on October 22, Robert caught the BEA bus from the London terminal to the airport and boarded BE142 just before eight o'clock. He noted a few other young servicemen in uniform amongst the travellers, and a sister from the Queen Alexandra's Royal Naval Nursing Service. Robert was the youngest person on board, just nineteen years old.

Ian and Margaret went to Luqa airport to meet Robert off BEA flight 142 from Naples. It was due to arrive at 14.30 but after two hours of increasing worry, all those in the arrivals lounge waiting for the flight were called into a private room at the airport by Mr T. Pollock, the BEA manager for Malta. The families were informed individually of the terrible news of the fatal collision over Nettuno. A few hours later they heard on the radio that there were no survivors.

The heartbroken parents returned home to Pietà to break the tragic news to Anne and Victoria, (who had just been

239

picked up from school) and young Roderick. Reverend Adam Currie from St Andrew's Scots Church came to the family immediately, and a procession of close friends followed to offer condolences and support.

A few days later another family friend, Henry Griscti, who was on a business trip in Rome went to the morgue and identified Robert before his remains were flown to Malta on the evening of October 28 and transferred to the mortuary at St Luke's Hospital.

Because Robert had died while in military service, the Army offered to organise the funeral. On October 29 the funeral cortège left St Luke's Hospital and wound its way slowly through the lined streets to Ta'Braxia cemetery led by a funeral gun carriage, a white floral cross placed on the coffin and a large wreath sent by BEA hanging forlornly over the gun barrel.

At Ta'Braxia a lone piper led the mourners, playing a traditional Scottish lament, with eight bearers of 37 Anti-Aircraft Regiment carrying the flag-draped coffin between two bowed-headed lines of gunners standing with their arms reversed. The family following the coffin included Dr and Mrs Chalmers, Anne and Roderick.

The Rev. Adam Currie conducted the service at the graveside. As the coffin was slowly lowered into the grave, three volleys were fired, followed by four Royal Malta Artillery trumpeters sounding the Last Post. Masses of flowers, bouquets and wreaths surrounded the grave, including from the first battalion The Black Watch (Royal Highland Regiment), the Malta Garrison, many family friends, and a bouquet from *Blackley's* bakery.

Fig 46. Malta Dry Dock after bombing raid 1942.

Fig 47. John Vella c. 1925.

Fig 48. Garth Marshallsay 1958
"He saw a clear way ahead"

Fig 49. Richard Golden 1958   Fig 50. Grace Cadger 1958

Fig 51. Eveline Yuille and family 1948

Figs 52–54.
Right:
Captain Giovanni Savorelli
Below left:
Pilot Giorgio Giannotti.
Below right:
Pilot Vittorio Carone

Fig 55. Exterior of Viscount 701C *Sir John Franklin* – Duxford

Fig 56. Interior of Viscount 701C *Sir John Franklin* – Duxford

Above: Fig 57. Cockpit of Viscount 701C *Sir John Franklin* – Duxford.

Left: Fig 58. Radio Officer's position on a Viscount 701C

Below: Fig 59. Sir Leopold McClintock 1819–1907.

Fig 60. Premier
Khrushchev State Visit,
London, April 1956

Fig 61. Cyprus peace talks'
delegation, London,
August 1955

Chicks Survived

SURVIVORS of the crash were numbers of baby chicks which were uninjured and rushing about among the litter of suitcases, burst mailbags, piles of letters addressed to Malta, newspapers, air tickets, shoes, babies' toys and a red sash of the kind worn by Bishops.

The chicks had fallen in a container from a height of 23,500 feet, the altitude at which the collision is believed to have occurred.

Figs 62–63. Crash site in Nettuno 1958

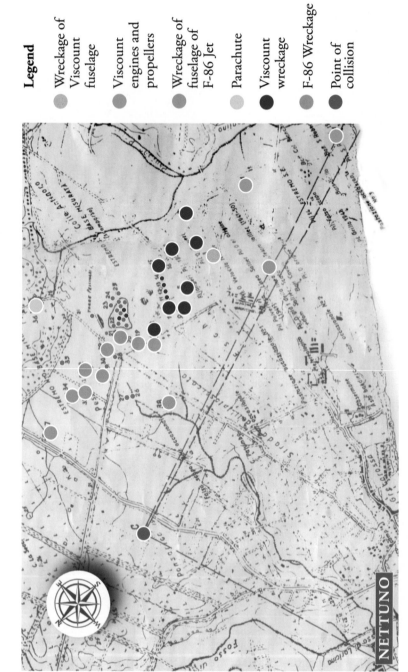

Legend

- ● Wreckage of Viscount fuselage
- ● Viscount engines and propellers
- ● Wreckage of fuselage of F-86 Jet
- ● Parachute
- ● Viscount wreckage
- ● F-86 Wreckage
- ● Point of collision

NETTUNO

Map 3. Location of wreckage of Vickers Viscount 701C and F-86E Sabre jet

Fig 64. 504 US Parachute regiment reserve landing at Nettuno 1944

Fig 65. American military cemetery at Nettuno

Fig 66 and 67. Neptune and the fishing port of Nettuno

Fig 68. Unveiling of the memorial in 2006 by the Bannon family

CAPTAIN / RANK / JESTER   Co-Pilot GEOFFEREY WRIGHT

Radio Officer JAMES BANNON

Flight Attendant ROSEMARY BEVAN
Flight Attendant TERENCE O'GRADY

Mr.W.R.BUCHAN Mrs.W.R.BUCHAN Mr.R.ALLAN Mr.J.C.W.BOOTH Mr.R.BRUCE
Mr.R.A.CHALMERS   Mr.C.D.CUBITT   Mrs.C.D.CUBITT

Mr.A.J.M.DAVIES Mr.B.FOGATY Mr.R.A.GOLDEN
Mrs.J.KAWAJ Mr.G.KIMBLE Mr.L.C.KING

Miss S.MILANI Mrs.M.V.LAROSA
Mr.G.LUXTON Mr.G.MARSHALL SAY
Miss M.L.MATHI SON Mrs.F.MILLER

Mr.J.PRINCE Mr.R.SILBURN
Mr.J.VELLA Miss P.WATSON

ROY J.L.WEIR   Miss E.M.YUILLE

Fig 69. Memorial List

IN MEMORY OF THE PASSENGERS AND CREW OF
BEA VISCOUNT G-ANHC WHO DIED ON WEDNESDAY 22 OCTOBER 1956
AT 11.50 AM FOLLOWING A MID – AIR COLLISION ABOVE THIS SPOT

THESE MOTHERS, FATHERS, SONS, DAUGHTERS, HUSBAND, WIVES
AND LOVED ONES DIED FAR FROM HOME NOT AMONGST STRANGERS,
BUT FRIENDS THEY HAD NEVER YET

RINGRAZIAMO GLI ABITANTI I VIGILI DEL FUOCO I SOLDATI
E I VIGILI URBANI DI NETTUNO CHE HANNO ASSISTITO I MORTI

ERECTED BY THE FAMILY AND RELATIONS OF
JAMES BANNON

CON L'AIUTO DEI NOSTRI AMICI DI NETTUNO
22 OCTOBER 2005

Fig 70. Memorial inscription

Fig 71. Memorial Service at Nettuno in 2008

Fig 72. Memorial Service at Nettuno 2013

Fig 73. Memorial Service at Nettuno 2018

The tragedy had a devastating effect on the family and was made all the worse when Ian died twelve weeks later in January 1959, aged forty-seven. He had been diagnosed with acute leukaemia, but Margaret was convinced he died of a broken heart. A lectern was presented to St Andrew's Scots Church in memory of Robert and has inscribed on the front a small, Black Watch regimental insignia. Above are two stained-glass windows dedicated to his grandparents, John and Gertrude, and close by a communion table dedicated to his father.

Blackley's was sold in the late 1980s but its delicious cakes are still remembered with much affection. It is now a perfumeria but has kept the *Blackley's* sign. The historic bakery fell into disrepair for many years but is now a Grade-2 listed building and is due to be rehabilitated into new offices and apartments.

Both Anne and her sister, Victoria Chalmers followed in their mother's footsteps and took up nursing in Edinburgh and settled there. Roderick became a chartered accountant and moved to Hong Kong with his wife, Mary Rose in 1984, rising to become Chairman of a major multinational company of accountants.

The Hotel Manager
ARNOLD DAVIES

On the morning of October 22 1958, Arnold Davies arrived at London Airport in good spirits. Having lost his mother earlier in the year, it had been a difficult time for him and he was looking forward to spending a few days in Naples for a well-deserved holiday to relax and see the sights. He had travelled up to London by train from his home in Dartington, near Totnes, in Devon, the previous evening. After checking in, he walked through the departure gate to board flight BE142.

Arnold's father, Edmund was born in Ipswich in Suffolk in 1880 and his mother, Harriet came from Frome in Somerset. After leaving home Edmund moved to Kent to work as a bank clerk and on April 29 1911 he married Harriet Marsh at St Barnabas' Church in Bexhill-on-Sea, Sussex. The following year we assume he was transferred to work in Cheltenham, as their first son, Edmund Rupert was born there in 1912, followed by Arnold Joseph on June 28 1914. Little is known of the boys' early lives but it appears they enjoyed a comfortable, middle-class upbringing.

Cheltenham lies on the River Chelt, a small tributary feeding into the mighty River Severn, and had been a sleepy little Gloucestershire village until the discovery of mineral springs in 1732 in a field south of the town, where the Ladies College is now situated. The Pitville Pump Room was built in 1738, followed by assembly rooms and a ballroom, and the town rapidly expanded to cater for the demand for the beneficial waters. Walks, avenues and gardens were created to enhance the restorative experience and the town was given a royal stamp of approval by King George III and his wife Charlotte after a visit there in 1788. A royal crescent was built between 1806 and 1810. With the construction of a racecourse, horse racing became a popular and fashionable pastime and another good income stream for the town. The first railway was opened in 1840, catering for the increasingly large number of tourists and wealthy families who came to retire there.

So many retirees had served in the British colonies that by the end of the century Cheltenham was described as 'the Anglo-Indians' paradise'. Besides the bath houses the town sported a Theatre and Opera House, a municipal art gallery and a free library. However, by the turn of the twentieth century the baths had lost their appeal and the town fell into a steady decline with rising unemployment.

The Cheltenham Festival, a four-day spectacle of world class horse racing held every year in March, began in 1902 and in 1924 huge crowds poured into the town for the first, now legendary, Gold Cup. By 1925 there was little left of the spa business despite the renaming of the railway station from Lansdown to Cheltenham Spa. New light industries sprang up, including pharmaceuticals and foodstuffs and an aircraft components company.

In 1927 the Davies family were living in Pembury House, Cheltenham, a Grade II listed building in fashionable Lansdown Crescent. Edmund was clearly doing well at work as by 1939 he was a bank manager. Arnold had moved to Hampstead by then and was living in digs, working as an apprentice in hotel management. His brother was working as a shipping agent in Birkenhead near Liverpool. It not known where they were during World War Two but both men remained single until 1949, when Edmund married Joan Dixon in Hendon, north London.

Arnold moved to Dartington the same year. His father died in Cheltenham in October 1952, and his mother sold the house and retired to Bath. Arnold lived at Longcause Cross, near to the famous Dartington Hall, and he became treasurer of the Dartington village market, a role that gave him much enjoyment.

Dartington is a small, picturesque village located two miles north-west of Totnes, with a history going back at least 1,000 years. The lands were part of the possessions of the Martin family from the early twelfth century. During the reign of Edward III (1327–1377), ownership of the manor reverted to the Crown, but in 1384 Richard II granted the 1,200-acre estate to his half-brother, John Holand, the 1st Duke of Exeter. He was largely responsible for building the medieval manor house, Dartington Hall, with the Great Hall regarded as being one of the finest buildings of its time in England. After a failed plot to assassinate Richard's successor, Henry IV, the duke was executed in 1400 and his estate again forfeited to the Crown, until the lands and titles were restored to the 2nd Duke of Exeter in 1415, who had distinguished himself in Henry V's service at the Battle of Agincourt.

The estate was owned briefly by two of Henry VIII's wives, Catherine Howard and Catherine Parr until 1559, when the manor became the property of Sir Arthur Champernowne, a vice-admiral under Elizabeth I. The Champernownes were a well-connected, local Devon family and the property remained with them for nearly four hundred years. The agricultural depression in the nineteenth century saw their fortune collapse and in 1925 they sold what remained of their estate.

The Great Hall by this time was in ruins, and much of the estate run down, but it was bought by two wealthy social philanthropists, Leonard and Dorothy Elmhirst, who saw it as a means to foster rural regeneration in an area going through much hardship. They rebuilt the Great Hall, with its massive, seventeen-foot-long fireplace in 1931, and renovated all the courtyard buildings at great expense, using only local materials and timber from the estate. Noted garden designers were brought in to restore and expand the magnificent gardens, clearing the tangled overgrowth and returning them to Grade II status.

A collection of modern buildings were built on the estate in the 1930s designed by the architect William Lescaze (1896–1964). Sixteen charitable programmes were started, including the Schumacher College, an international college for ecological studies. A Home Economics centre focused on modern living, a whole range of classes covered art, pottery and other visual crafts, becoming an exciting and vibrant hub of creative activity, and a wide variety of courses ranging from printmaking to textile design were set up to encourage the study of the arts and ecology.

The first Summer School of Music was established in 1948 and moved to Dartington in 1953. The school gained a reputation for being at the forefront of musical innovation and gave opportunities for young players, conductors and composers to explore their craft.

The international festival attracted many leading musicians and composers of the day to give masterclasses, including the Russian composer and pianist, Igor Stravinsky, who lectured at the school in 1957. It is quite likely that Arnold attended performances there.

In 1967 the Dartington Glass Company was founded and quickly became an instantly recognisable brand, once again generating local jobs in the area and continuing to enhance the pioneering and visionary philosophy of the Elmhirsts.

With so much going on in Dartington, it is hard to imagine that Arnold would not have been involved in the community both socially and professionally. He was a very popular treasurer of the village market. He enjoyed dealing with the smallholders, helping them out with any disputes, problems of transportation, and delivering messages, which he did willingly and with great charm. Under his benign rule the market flourished.

In early 1958 his mother Harriet died in Bath aged seventy-one, and the two sons came into a generous inheritance. Edmund and Joan were living in London and had no children, so the two brothers invested in a large house in Totteridge Lane, Barnet, in north London, which they called Pembury, after their childhood home in Cheltenham. That gave Arnold a reasonable income and allowed him the luxury of a holiday abroad.

On October 22 1958 Arnold decided to travel to Italy to see and absorb the beautiful sights in and around Naples. His hopes and dreams came to a sudden end in the skies above Nettuno on that fateful day.

After the accident, Arnold was flown back to London and his funeral was held at 12.00 on October 31 in St Mary's Church in Dartington. He was forty-four years old. His brother Edmund lost two of his closest family that year. He died twenty years later in 1978.

The Sailor
RICHARD GOLDEN

On Tuesday October 21 1958, Richard Golden boarded his flight at Royal Naval Air Station (RNAS) Lossiemouth, a large, busy Fleet Air Arm base located in Moray in north-east Scotland. He sat down in his seat with a heavy but jubilant heart as he headed for London. It had been a glorious leave in Scotland, finishing on one of the happiest days of his life when his girlfriend, Grace Cadger agreed to marry him. He could still taste their passionate and lingering goodbye kiss at the airport. Grace was the last of the family to see him alive.

Richard Arnold Golden was born in 1932 in the rural hamlet of Dunmoran in the parish of Skreen, in County Sligo, Ireland. His parents, John and Violet Golden were farmers, and brought up their six children, Iris, Arthur, Harold, Vivien, Muriel and Richard in a four-bedroomed, traditional stone farmhouse. It had outstanding views over Sligo Bay of the ancient mountain of Knocknarea to the north-east and the mysterious, legendary Ben Bulben, known as the 'Table Mountain' of County Sligo. In the far distance on a clear day they could see the peaks of the Blue Stack Mountains of Donegal. This is 'Yeats Country', so called after the great Irish poet, W. B. Yeats.

William Butler Yeats's mother, Susan Mary Pollexfen came from a wealthy family who owned a wine, milling and shipping business based in Sligo. Yeats was born in Sandymount, Dublin in 1865 but spent his childhood holidays in Sligo. It was his spiritual home. Its landscape became both literally and symbolically his 'country of the heart', and it influenced his poetry throughout his life.

He was one of the major literary figures of the twentieth century and is the greatest lyric poet that Ireland has produced. Yeats died in Menton in France in 1939, but asked that his body be buried in Sligo, when *'the newspapers have forgotten me.'* Eventually, in 1948 his remains were interred at St Columba's Church, Drumcliffe.

Richard and his siblings had an idyllic childhood on the farm in Dunmoran. The farmhouse was just a short distance from the beach, and they spent endless summer days swimming in the cool, clean water, and exploring the sweeping strand of golden sand that curved round the bay as far as a finger of rock sticking out to sea known locally as 'the local rock'.

At low tide, the exposed rock pools teamed with little fish, crabs and starfish in the crystal water, and were a continuous source of delight to the young and old alike. On the nearby Aughris pier the local fishermen waited patiently to catch the abundant mackerel passing by, watched by inquisitive children eager to learn their techniques. Richard never lost his love for this beautiful spot, or for salmon fishing, and rowing on the inland rivers as they flowed gently towards the sea.

Every morning young Richard walked the narrow, country road from Dunmoran to the little village school in Skreen, which once boasted an ancient abbey, until Viking raiders pillaged and razed it in the ninth century. There is no trace of the abbey left, as the imposing Church of Ireland was built over the remains. This is the church that Richard attended every Sunday.

As a child he may well have played among the ruins of Ardnaglass Castle, originally owned by the powerful O'Dowds family, who were descended from the Kings of Connacht and dominated Mayo and Sligo for centuries. Oliver Cromwell finally defeated them in 1642, following the revolt of Ulster in 1641.

This ancient seaport of Sligo had a population of about 20,000 and although only fifteen miles from Dunmoran, for Richard it was a different world. At sixteen he left school to follow his brother Harold and sister Muriel to the bustling, county town to find work. Harold and Muriel both worked in Henry Lyons & Co. in the town and Richard found a position as an assistant in a draper's shop, W. T. and G. Johnston in O'Connell Street. There he sold cotton, silk, linen and all the accessories to tailors, dressmakers and the general public. It was a modest job but a step onto the first rung of the ladder.

County Sligo has a rich and ancient history. It has one of the largest collections of Neolithic tombs in Ireland dating back to 4000BC, the Carrowmore megaliths just outside Sligo town being the most extensive.

It was known to Phoenician, Greek and Roman traders, and although there are sixth-century references to the Garavogue River that winds through the town to the mouth of Sligo Bay, the town itself is said to have been founded in 1243 by the Norman knight, Maurice Fitzgerald. He built Sligo Castle in 1245 and a Dominican friary, but the

Normans were driven out in 1257 after the battle of Credran Cille. Throughout the medieval period Sligo was almost continuously under native Irish control.

During the Great Famine of 1847 to 1851, over 30,000 people emigrated from the county of Sligo alone, and the decline continued into the middle of the twentieth century. It made a slow recovery after the end of World War Two, but even though many people still travelled to England to find work throughout the 1940s and 50s, Sligo maintained its position as an important harbour and fishing port.

In September 1948, Richard would have seen the boat arriving in Sligo from France carrying Yeats back to his homeland. His coffin was accompanied to St Columba's Church at Drumcliffe by Seán MacBride, the son of Maud Gonne. She was a beautiful, English-born Irish revolutionary, suffragette and actress with whom Yeats was completely infatuated, but who constantly spurned him. He proposed to her four times between 1889 and 1917 and many of his poems are inspired by her. In a last desperate attempt he even half-heartedly proposed to her daughter, with further rejection. Maud was convinced his poetry was the better for it! After a simple service at Drumcliffe, Yeats was buried in the churchyard under the omnipresent gaze of Ben Bulben. In his poem 'Under Ben Bulben' Yeats composed his own epitaph:

Cast a cold eye
On Life, on Death.
Horseman, pass by.

By 1950, Harold had decided to leave Sligo and joined the Royal Navy to see the world. He came back with tantalising stories of what he had seen, and in 1952 persuaded Richard to follow him. Richard enlisted into the Fleet Air Arm in County Derry and was sent to Lossiemouth to train as a radio operator. Harold was based at Portsmouth occasionally, and when he was given leave, Richard would hitch a lift and see his brother for a weekend on the town. It was during one of these visits that Harold ran into a tall, handsome, hell-raising sailor with striking blue eyes who was completing his National Service. His name was Peter O'Toole and when they met up, anything could happen.

Peter Seamus O'Toole had a roller coaster of a life, leaving many stories and much confusion from his colourful time on this earth. His father, Patrick 'Spats' O'Toole was an Irish metal plater and a travelling bookmaker visiting the race courses of Ireland, England and France. As a result there was some confusion as to where his son was actually born. Official records show Peter was born in Leeds in 1932. Others claim Peter's birthplace was Connemara in Country Galway. Either way he was the same age as Richard Golden.

When he was two years old, Peter moved with his mother, Constance and sister, Patricia to Hunslet, south Leeds, where he attended a Catholic school for seven years. He enjoyed asking irreverent questions to the school nuns, much to their consternation. His father often took him out of school to the race courses, where he appeared to gain most of his education.

At the age of fourteen he left school, already getting into scrapes and fights, and was hired as a goffer to journalists on the *Yorkshire Evening Post*. He was interested in amateur dramatics and in 1949 he saw Michael Redgrave on stage as King Lear. Redgrave's performance and powerful command over the audience entranced him, and he dreamed of being on stage himself. This dream was interrupted in 1950 when he was called up for National Service.

The six-foot-two-inch-tall, eighteen-year-old decided he wanted to join the Royal Navy. At the assessment meeting, his fervent imagination went into overdrive. He described in vivid detail to the board that he was the son of a sea captain and came from generations of seafaring men. He claimed the sea was coursing through his blood and he couldn't wait to get on board a ship! The recruitment board was so impressed that he was given a job in the Admiralty, which they soon regretted.

Before long O'Toole was involved in lengthy drinking sessions, brawls and arrests in the various ports to which he was sent. It was during a visit to Portsmouth that Harold and Richard Golden met this wild seaman from Connemara, delighted to meet two Irish boys from the Emerald Isle. Evenings in the pub with O'Toole were legendary, as he entertained everyone with his wild stories and yarns that would invariably disintegrate into brawls.

But within a year O'Toole was gone. His arrests and insubordination were too much for the officers of the Royal Navy and he was discharged for being temperamentally unsuitable for the service. Before he left, an officer enquired what he intended to do. He replied that he wanted to be an actor.

In 1953, after rejection by the Abbey Theatre's drama school in Dublin because he could not speak the native tongue Gaelic, O'Toole joined the Royal Academy of

Dramatic Art (RADA). With contemporaries Alan Bates and Albert Finney, the intake that year was a supremely talented and fiery combination of actors. He graduated from RADA in 1955 and did his apprenticeship at the Bristol Old Vic, where he played over fifty parts. O'Toole appeared in his first film in a minor role playing the bagpipes in the Disney version of *Kidnapped*. In 1960 he was cast to play T. E. Lawrence, (as the third choice) in the epic David Lean film, *Lawrence of Arabia* and shot to international fame.

The film won seven Oscars in 1962 and Peter O'Toole earned his first nomination as Best Actor. He went on to become one of the greatest English-speaking actors of the twentieth century. He died on December 14 2013 aged eighty-one, and requested his ashes go to Connemara, Ireland. By 2020 they had got as far as Dublin. There is a memorial plaque in St Paul's Church in Covent Garden dedicated to him that reads, *'Good night and joy be with you all.'*

When Richard finished his training as a radio operator in Lossiemouth, he returned to Ireland and was stationed at Eglinton base in County Derry. In 1957 he returned for another tour to Lossiemouth, where he met his girlfriend, Grace Cadger, who came from Black Isle near Inverness, and had just qualified as a teacher.

In 1957 the British government began a series of nuclear weapons tests in the South Pacific they called Operation *Grapple*. They were carried out at Malden Island and Christmas Island, (now Kirimati) and Harold was part of an observation team watching the testing of the hydrogen bombs. Nine tests were carried out over 1957/58 culminating in a massive explosion of three megatonnes of TNT. It remains the largest British nuclear weapon ever tested. After major demonstrations, a moratorium on nuclear testing came into effect in October 1958.

Some of the bombs were dropped from a Valiant bomber, exploding in the air and causing a massive fallout of radiation. Many of those observing the tests suffered long-term medical problems as they were inadequately protected. Harold was one of them. Remaining veterans are still fighting for compensation to this day in the highest courts in Britain and Europe.

Richard arrived at London Airport and boarded the Viscount around eight o'clock on October 22. He noticed several other passengers from the military services on board, including a naval nurse in the dark-blue QARNNS uniform. He settled down in his seat still basking in the memories of his last romantic evening with Grace.

Richard's family heard about the terrible accident in Italy later that day listening to the six o'clock news on the radio. They were still not sure if Richard was on board until his uncle and the Garda came to the farmhouse in Dunmoran to confirm the awful news.

This tragedy was especially felt in Sligo as Richard was the fourth victim of a plane crash to come from that town within the last twelve months. Finbar Smyth, manager of the Yeats County Hotel was with Cosmo Meldrum when their Aquila Airways plane crashed in the Solent, off the Isle of Wight on November 15 1957 with a total loss of forty-five lives. Mrs

Irene Brown was in a Vickers Viscount on a Central African Airways flight on August 9 1958, travelling from Wadi Halfa in Sudan to Benghazi, Libya, when it crashed while making its approach to land at Benina airport. Eighteen survived but thirty-six died in the crash.

John and Violet, Richard's parents, never got over their loss. They are buried with Richard and Harold in the Church of Ireland in Skreen, in the glowering shadow of Ben Bulben.

Grace Cadger never married, and kept in touch with the family from that day.

I know that I shall meet my fate
Somewhere among the clouds above;
Those that I fight I do not hate
Those that I guard I do not love;
My country is Kiltartan Cross,
My countrymen Kiltartan's poor,
No likely end could bring them loss
Or leave them happier than before.
Nor law, nor duty bade me fight,
Nor public men, nor cheering crowds,
A lonely impulse of delight
Drove to this tumult in the clouds;
I balanced all, brought all to mind,
The years to come seemed waste of breath,
A waste of breath the years behind
In balance with this life, this death.

'An Irish Airman Foresees His Death'
W. B. Yeats 1919

The Sales Manager
GEORGE KIMBLE

George was given a cheery greeting as he approached the BEA check-in desk at London Airport early on October 22 1958. A popular and well-respected man, he was a senior Sales Manager for BEA and knew many of the staff both in London and abroad from his business trips around Europe. George and his wife, Myrtle lived in a comfortable flat in Tiverton Mansions, Holborn, London WC1. It had been an easy journey for him to the airport that morning, catching the BEA bus link from Cromwell Road in Kensington. He was flying out to Malta as he had organised a small sales conference there for foreign travel agents for BEA.

George Edward Ralph Kimble was born on November 10 1906 in the historic village of Wargrave, a small, riverside village three miles from Henley-on-Thames on the border of Oxfordshire and Berkshire. This ancient village is recorded in the Domesday Book of 1086 as having a population of 250. Wargrave is surrounded by rich, arable farmland, and agriculture has been the main source of employment over the centuries. It was a stop for stagecoaches travelling between Henley and Reading and at one time boasted seven public houses. With the growth of the leisure industry, the marina expanded and chandlery businesses provided services for all types of boats on the river. Wargrave was mentioned in '*Three Men in a Boat*' written by Jerome K. Jerome and like the river, has serenely drifted through its existence largely unaffected by the tribulations of history. This tranquility drew writers and artists to its peaceful surroundings. The village grew steadily during the twentieth century with commuters working in new companies opening west of London towards Reading.

George's parents ran a confectionery shop in the High Street. George had an elder sister, Penelope and another sister, Nora and it is believed the family moved to Littlehampton whilst he was still young. Little is known about his life until 1935 when, at the age of twenty-nine, George married Myrtle Bennett, and for a while they went to live in Hendon, Middlesex.

George had taken an interest in the business of tourism promotion by 1939. We know he had moved to Woolwich in south-east London working as a clerk with the tourism office of Southern Railway (SR), the company formed in 1923 through the amalgamation of several smaller railways, including South Eastern and Chatham Railway (SE&CR) and the London, Brighton and South Coast Railway (LB&SCR).

In the 1930s, the majority of people took their holidays in Britain and a seaside holiday was advertised as healthy and fun. As soon as the first railways were built in the nineteenth century, excursions to the coast quickly became popular with people of all classes eager to get away from the congested and polluted cities. There were four big railway companies, the Great Western (GWR), London, Midland and Scottish (LMSR), London and North Eastern (LNER) and Southern Railway (SR). They vied with each other for business through the advertising medium of posters. The idyllic landscape scenes so liked by the Victorians gave way to pictures of happy, smiling people having fun soaking up the sun in relaxed and inviting surroundings.

The 1930s was a golden age for the British railway poster. Companies employed some of the most talented artists and commercial designers of the age, and copies of their hand-painted posters are highly sought after. The railway companies promoted leisure travel using modernist styles such as Art Deco and Surrealism in bright colours and bold designs.

Probably the most famous holiday advertisement was *'Skegness is so Bracing'* The picture of the red-scarved Jolly Fisherman leaping across the beach was designed by John Hassall and used for decades to encourage people to visit the town. John Barker's poster for Ramsgate depicts elegant, Regency terraces, many serving as boarding houses, the pretty harbour with the lighthouse in the distance, mouth-watering seafood, and the golden beach with the promenade and night-time illuminations in the distance.

Southern Railway promoted popular seaside towns such as Whitstable, Margate, Broadstairs and Folkestone, promising carefree days in the Kent sunshine on pristine, sandy beaches, just an hour or two away on a cheap day return from London. The south-west of England was billed as the more sophisticated Cornish Riviera, the hint of aspirational foreign escapism hiding the time it took to get there.

Up to 1939 railway promotion was highly successful, with trains the main mode of travel, carrying passengers to packed resorts in the summer, and offering enticing weekend breaks.

As soon as the war broke out however, piers were cordoned off, some having entire sections removed, and beaches were mined in anticipation of German invasion in 1940. Blacked-out boarding houses, once hosting carefree holidaymakers now billeted uniformed troops, and picturesque fishing harbours were strung with mines and moored military vessels. Tourism stopped overnight.

At thirty-three, George would have been too old to have been called up during the war, but it is likely that he worked in the stations helping to keep the railways running.

After the war, the Labour government was elected and the railways were nationalised in 1948. George decided on a change, and joined BEA around 1950. By then, demand for flights to Europe was growing fast from both business travellers and holidaymakers, especially to France, Italy and Greece. Malta was also a popular destination, with many servicemen still based there.

BEA had been founded in 1946. By 1950 it had a network of town terminals and sales offices across Britain, and was flying from airports in Liverpool, Manchester, Birmingham, Belfast, Cardiff, Edinburgh and Glasgow. Passengers flew to destinations throughout Europe, and BEA rapidly expanded its routes to North Africa and the Middle East. At the same time, BEA bought shares in many of its European competitors, including Aer Lingus, Alitalia, Gibraltar Airways, Cyprus Airways and thirty-four per cent in Malta Airways.

The booking office in London was at Dorland Hall in Lower Regent Street, and there was a bus link to London Airport running twenty coaches an hour, (replaced by the

West London air terminal in Cromwell Road in October 1957). In 1957 a new mechanical reservation system was introduced called *Flightmaster*, capable of displaying seat availability on 32,000 flights at a time. It was not until 1965 that the first, very basic computer system came into operation. This needed an army of trained clerks to operate it. The drive to promote the company and sell seats was intense, and Sales Managers were set competitive targets.

The rapid expansion, plus the cost of purchasing the new fleet of Viscounts put a lot of pressure on the company finances. In July 1950 BEA earned more than a million pounds in that month alone, but because of its outgoings and overheads was still making a loss. In 1952 it carried more than a million passengers but with its commitment to expansion the losses too increased. It was not until 1955, with the new fleet of Viscounts firmly established, that BEA started to make a profit, and from then on it made steady progress, doubling its passenger numbers in 1956.

In 1958 George would have been based at Dorland Hall, where at that time travel agents had to phone BEA to make every individual booking. By then George had risen through the company to become a senior Sales Manager, in charge of organising events and conferences for the travel agents.

On October 22 George settled into his seat on flight BE142 looking forward to his visit to Malta. While he was there, he could also meet up with his old friend, Mr. T. Pollock, the BEA Manager for Malta and North Africa, someone he had known for twenty-six years.

Later that afternoon at Luqa airport, Mr. T. Pollock had the job that every manager dreaded, to inform the relatives of the passengers who lived in Malta of the tragic news of their loved ones. He broke the awful news to small groups of anxious and tearful colleagues, friends and family of those on board, at the same time knowing that one of his oldest friends had also been on board flight BE142.

George was flown back to London, and was cremated in Southwark, south London. George and Myrtle had no children and Myrtle died in Kensington in 1985.

The Nursing Sister
SHEILA LANE

S heila Lane arrived at the BEA check-in desk at London
Airport on October 22 1958 in plenty of time to catch
flight BE142 to Malta. Punctuality came naturally to her
with her military training. She was smartly dressed in her
dark-blue naval uniform, comprising a jacket with gold-
coloured buttons and a close-fit skirt, a crisp, white shirt and
a dark tie. Her epaulettes showed a crown with an entwined
anchor and a circular red cross below indicating she was in
the Queen Alexandra's Royal Naval Nursing Service
(QARNNS). She had travelled from Sunbury Avenue in Mill
Hill, north-west London, so it had been an easy journey to
the airport. Sheila had made the trip to Malta several times
and was looking forward to getting back to work.

Both Sheila's parents were from London. Her father, Harold
Arthur Lane, (always known as Harry) was born in 1900 and
was a bank manager. Her mother, Janet Hilda Browning was
born in Battersea in 1903, and after they married, they settled
in Hendon, (part of Barnet in north-west London) where
their only child, Sheila Mary was born on June 29 1927.
When war broke out with Germany in 1939, Sheila was
evacuated from London to Penzance in Cornwall to stay with
her grandfather, who was a cleric in the town, where she was
safe from the falling bombs.

In 1946 Sheila returned to London, and at the age of
nineteen went to train as a nurse at the Queen Elizabeth
Hospital for Children in Hackney. Originally the Dispensary

for Women and Children, it was founded by two Quaker sisters, Ellen and Mary Philips in 1867 and renamed the Queen Elizabeth Hospital for Children in 1942.

The east end of London was badly bombed during the war and many houses were damaged or completely destroyed. In the poorer areas of London like Hackney, woeful housing and sanitary conditions combined with the lack of nutritious food led to many health problems for the young children in the area. In 1949, Mary qualified as a children's nurse, and in 1951 passed the exams to become a state registered nurse.

A year later she moved to the internationally renowned St Mary's Hospital in Paddington in the City of Westminster, to gain further experience. This was built in 1845 as a voluntary hospital, giving free medical care to those that could not afford it, and is one of London's earliest teaching hospitals. It gained fame when Alexander Fleming discovered penicillin in his laboratory there in 1928. A wealthy businessman financed a purpose-built private wing in 1937 for celebrities and royalty. Princess Diana gave birth to Princes William and Harry there in 1982 and 1984. After the formation of the NHS in 1948, several local hospitals were affiliated with St Mary's and in the 1950s it became a pioneering hospital for its treatments in reducing the risk of strokes under distinguished consulting surgeon, Felix Eastcoat. It was an exciting place for a young nurse to be in 1952.

In 1954, at the age of twenty-seven, Sheila made the decision to join the forces and enrolled with the Queen Alexandra's Royal Naval Nursing Service (QARNNS). It is not certain the reason why. Maybe she just wanted to see more of the world whilst working, or maybe she was inspired by someone to join. It may have been Dame Doris Beale (1889–1971), who had a similar background to herself.

Doris Beale was born in Forest Hill in London and trained at the London Hospital in Whitechapel in 1912, close to where Sheila had begun her training. She joined the QARNNS in 1917, served in Plymouth, Portsmouth and Gibraltar, and spent two years from 1925 to 1927 at the Royal Naval Hospital (RNH) at Bighi in Malta. In July 1941 she was promoted to Matron-in-Chief of QARNNS, and after her retirement in 1944, continued to work tirelessly, taking trips to the Middle East to see the relief work being carried out by British nurses in 1949, and spending a lot of time with the disabled. She was made a Dame in 1944 and died in 1971.

In 1884 the Naval Nursing Service was introduced to improve the medical care for members of the Royal Navy. It became established as QARNNS in 1910 with Queen Alexandra, the wife of Edward VII, as its President.

Sheila carried out basic military training when she joined, and due to her experience was quickly promoted to Nursing Sister, the equivalent of Lieutenant. She would have first been sent to Royal Navy bases in England for further training, probably Portsmouth or Plymouth, before being posted to RNH Bighi in Malta, following in the footsteps of Dame Doris Beale.

Malta was a busy, bustling island in 1958, and with one of the largest harbours in the world, had been an important base for all the military services, but especially the Royal Navy.

At the outbreak of World War One there were four

hospitals in Malta, at Cottonera, Mtarfa, Forrest and Valletta, with a total of just 268 beds. Four days after the landings at Gallipoli on April 29 1915, 1,000 sick and wounded were sent to Malta. Within a month their number had increased to over 4,000. By the time Gallipoli was evacuated in January 1916, there were 20,000 beds available in Malta, in twenty-eight hospitals and convalescent centres.

The sick and wounded were reaching Malta at the rate of 2,000 a week. They were served by 334 medical officers, 913 nurses and 2,032 staff from across the world. Over 120,000 wounded soldiers of all ranks passed through Malta. For some it was their last resting place. Malta became known as the *Nurse of the Mediterranean*.

Malta was at the heart of the struggle between the Allied and Axis powers for control of the Mediterranean because it was vital for Allied shipping routes and a base for aircraft and submarine operations. From the beginning of World War Two, the German Luftwaffe and the Italian Air Force launched sustained and relentless aerial attacks on the island. Malta came under siege and became the most bombed country in the war. Between June 1940 and April 1944 over 1,500 civilians died, 3,780 were injured and over 30,000 buildings were destroyed, including 50 hospitals.

When Sheila arrived in Malta there was still much evidence of the extensive bomb damage, despite the cleaning up and rebuilding since 1945. Thousands of British servicemen were still based on the island, with many ships using the harbour and dockyard facilities, and the shops, restaurants, and bars were all thriving. However, the decline had started, as the

British government was discussing the withdrawal of troops for an eventual handover to the Maltese authorities, which caused great consternation and resentment. It was the end of the long colonial era, with Malta eventually gaining its independence in 1964.

Sheila was based at RNH Bighi, located in the small town of Kalkara, which proudly overlooks the Grand Harbour to Valletta. It was a 200-bed hospital built in the grounds of an ancient villa, Palazzo Bichi, in 1832, designed in grand Classical style with tall, fluted Doric columns, high floors and large windows. It was further extended in 1901–03 and despite a number of buildings being damaged in the 1942 blitz, it was repaired and operational again after the war, eventually closing down in 1970.

Sheila wore the distinctive QARNNS nursing uniform when working in the hospital. It was a traditional light-blue dress, with a black or red belt buckled round the waist and a white apron, with a watch attached to the breast pocket. The hat was very striking, perched low on the front of the head and expanding like the wings of an exotic bird at the back to keep it secure. In the summer it could be roasting hot, so when off duty, the nurses wore a white, lightweight uniform, with an option of shorts.

On their days off they could walk down the hill from Bighi Hospital to Cospicua and catch the five-minute ferry ride across to Valletta, sitting on the open-top deck taking in the spectacular views on one of the world's best ferry rides. They could walk up to Kingsway, (now called Republic Street), the main thoroughfare to shop, and have a cool drink in Upper Barrakka Gardens overlooking the Grand Harbour, or if the ships were in, watch the antics of the British and American servicemen in Strait Street, (christened The Gut by the Navy), a long, narrow alley full of lively bars and busy restaurants pumping out Elvis Presley's *Jailhouse Rock* or Connie Francis' *Stupid Cupid*, be entertained by the shenanigans of the colourful, local characters selling trinkets on the street corners, and buxom barmaids dreaming of marrying a sailor. They might have a refined tea at *Blackley's* cake shop or alternatively, catch a ferry to the nearby, almost-deserted island of Comino to swim in the pristine, turquoise waters of the Blue Lagoon, explore the secret caves or walk the sculptured cliffs on Gozo, before relaxing in a beachside restaurant eating the catch of the day. It was a good life.

As Sheila boarded flight BE142 to Malta that fateful day, she would have noticed a few other servicemen in uniform from the Army, Navy and Air Force, some looking so young that they must be doing their National Service.

On October 22, Harry and Janet were in Mill Hill when they were told of the catastrophic mid-air crash over Nettuno and the fate of their only child. They would have been given the option for Sheila to be buried in England, or Malta with a military funeral. It is likely that Sheila had made the decision to be buried in Malta, but we will never know.

Sheila's coffin was flown to Malta on the same plane as three other residents, Robert Chalmers, John Vella and Mary La Rosa, arriving at Luqa airport on a BEA Viscount on October 28. She was interred at the Kalkara Naval Cemetery two days later, and the military headstone was engraved with the QARNNS emblem and her name, and the words from the Gospel According to John, *'I am the Resurrection and the Life. He that believeth in me, though he were to die, yet shall he live'*. She was just thirty-one years old.

The Commonwealth War Graves Commission cares for the graves of more than 1,000 British and Commonwealth service personnel in thirteen cemeteries who died during the world wars. The cemetery was begun in 1901 for the burial of Royal Navy personnel who died on Malta. Separate plots were created in the cemetery for officers, Protestants and Roman Catholics. Sheila lies in the Protestant officer's plot.

At St Mary's Church in the little village of Sixpenny Handley are the graves of Harry and Janet Lane, who retired to Dorset in around 1965, but it still leaves the mystery of why Sheila chose to be buried in Malta.

The Maltese Visitor
MARY VASSALLO LA ROSA

Mary arrived early at London Airport on October 22 1958 with her niece, Guilia. She was probably still feeling a bit weak from her recent hospital treatment and was taking everything at an easy pace, ready for her return trip to Malta. Guilia lived in London, so Mary had stayed at her house to recuperate, and they travelled together to the airport. Mary checked in for flight BE142, and sat down with Guilia for one last chat before boarding the plane.

Mary Vassallo La Rosa left us with very few clues to the life she led in Malta. At first we thought that she was a nurse working in England, which would not have been unusual at that time, but hints from newspaper reports showed that she lived in Malta not England. *The Times of Malta* described her as 'returning from a visit to England.'

Mary was born in 1903 in Hamrun, a small town a few miles south of Valletta, with a population of around 10,000 people at that time and expanding. Her family house was situated towards the south end of St Joseph's Road, where an eighteenth-century aqueduct passes by at second floor level, carrying the water from its source in Rabat to Valletta.

Hamrun would not be described as an attractive town. Unlike Valletta or the Three Cities, it has few surviving historical sights and lacks the medieval charm of many other towns on the island. It is dominated by the long, straight St Joseph's Road, lined with a huge variety of shops, bars and other commercial outlets. However, the community has survived many changes and challenges over the centuries and has a unique character of its own, attracting a tough, colourful collection of inhabitants with strong commercial instincts.

When the Knights of St John built a powder magazine there in the seventeenth century, Hamrun became a popular meeting place for Maltese and Sicilian contraband dealers, armed to the teeth and extremely dangerous. There were two main groups, Tas-Sikkina, meaning 'those who carry a knife' and Ta'Werwer, 'those who scare'. It was a popular area for Sicilian immigrants to live in, with generations of men working in the docks as stevedores.

Hamrun boasts several churches. The first Baroque chapel was built in 1736 and unusually, the town has three patron saints, Saint Gaetan, the Immaculate Conception, and Saint Joseph.

In 1883 the Malta Railway Company built an eleven-kilometre-long railway from Valletta, with stations at Floriana, Hamrun, Msida, Birkirkara, Lija, San Antonio, Attard and terminating at Mdina. The name Hamrun was engraved in bold, black letters above the entrance door, and after purchasing a ticket, passengers entered the new platform, which had the luxury of a canopy giving protection from the summer heat and rain. The company lasted only seven years however before being declared insolvent and went out of business in 1890. The government of Malta took over the running of the railway and renovated the line, but competition from the tram and bus services hastened its demise and it closed forever in 1931.

During World War Two, Mary shared the terrifying experience of living through the terrible blitz of 1942 with fellow travellers, John Vella and Robert Chalmers. When the Three Cities – Senglea, Vittoriosa and Cospicua, were badly hit, many families moved away from the harbour towns, and Hamrun, being slightly inland became a popular area for the refugees to stay.

Times were desperate and conditions on the island extremely difficult. With very few supplies getting through to the island, the shops struggled. The cramped rooms above the shops were bursting with families. The brave people of Malta struggled through with little food and water. Fuel was always in short supply and people were forced to improvise clothing and footwear.

In August 1943 the islander's morale was boosted enormously by the arrival of nine merchant ships. The German blockade was broken and another convoy reached Malta in November virtually unscathed. Families could breathe again.

The war left thousands of homes destroyed, but Hamrun was not as badly damaged as other towns around Grand Harbour and businesses were up and running again relatively quickly. A large number of shops sprung up along the length of St Joseph's Road, followed by bars, coffee shops and restaurants serving good, local fare. These shops ignored the popular, commercial brands and specialised in lesser-known but good quality goods, little competition for the trendy, upmarket shops of Valletta, and better value for the locals.

As with other larger towns on Malta, Hamrun has two brass bands from St Gaetan and St Joseph that are an essential part of the noisy, annual festival in August. The bands are decked out in red and blue and the festival atmosphere is a heady cacophony of music, in which the bands compete with each other fiercely. Crowds dance, traditional food and wine is consumed in joyous celebration, and fine beer from the famous local brewery of Simonds Farsons Cisk is drunk in considerable quantities.

Mary never married. She came from a Roman Catholic family, (Malta was over ninety-five per cent Catholic), so it is possible she was the youngest daughter who traditionally looked after the parents in their old age. Many Maltese left the island after the war to find work, and many left Hamrun. In 1931 the population was over 22,000 and this dropped to 16,000 by 1957. We know that Mary's niece, Guilia and her brother, Renato Cerillo, were part of that mass emigration.

Guilia went to London, and Renato gained a degree in Economics and continued with his studies in Canada. He gained his doctorate and went on to teach as a highly respected Professor at Alberta University in Edmonton. They both kept in close touch with the family in Malta and would regularly visit.

On October 22 Guilia gave her aunt a hug at the departure gate, and waved her goodbye as she boarded the plane. Little did she know that she would be returning to Malta for Mary's funeral only seven days later.

Mary's coffin was flown to Malta on the same plane as three other residents, Robert Chalmers, John Vella and Sheila Lane, arriving at Luqa airport on a BEA Viscount on the evening of October 28, and transferred to the mortuary at St Luke's Hospital in Pietà. The following day a solemn Requiem Mass was celebrated at the Santa Maria Addolorata Cemetery chapel in Hamrun, led by Father Agostino Caruana, and Mary was laid to rest.

The Novitiate
GARTH MARSHALLSAY

I t had been a hectic five weeks for Garth, on leave from his
National Service in Malta. He had caught up with friends
and family in Newcastle Upon Tyne and was now on the train
on the way back to London Airport to catch BE142 to Malta.
It was October 21 1958. He looked out of the carriage
window as the train puffed slowly out of Central Station, and
reflected on the momentous decision he had made.

On his way back from Malta, Garth had taken the
opportunity to contact some fellow novitiates in Clare Priory
in Suffolk to meet in Rome and take a tour of the Vatican. He
was amazed when his group was selected for an audience with
Pope Pius XII. It would be an unforgettable and life-changing
experience for him. His Holiness was eighty-two years old
and had been ill for the last few years, suffering from gastritis
and the side effects of cellular rejuvenation injections, but was
determined to keep up his meetings with lay people. That day
in late September would have been one of his last meetings.

Pope Pius XII had been elected on March 2 1939, a few
months before the outbreak of World War Two, and he was
plunged into years of complicated diplomacy and
controversy. Throughout the war he lobbied for peace, helped
with aid to thousands of war refugees, and channelled funds
to America. Many Jewish lives were saved by him and the
Church, but he came in for strong criticism for not wholly
denouncing the genocide of the Jews by the Nazis.

His reticence to speak out was partly due to the fear of the

Nazis taking Vatican City if he did criticise, but also he had no desire to be seen as a martyr. As a result of his silence, he became known as Hitler's Pope, even when Jewish leaders said *'they would never forget what he was doing for our unfortunate brothers and sisters at this most tragic hour.'*

Pope Pius had been through a very turbulent time in history, and was determined to pass on his ideas for a new world to the post-war generation.

Garth's group was ushered into the room, where His Holiness was sitting on a red cushion in a gold-gilded chair, his advisors and doctor nearby. He was looking pale and rather weak, but he welcomed the group, and gave them a short talk covering a wide range of important issues that he wanted them all to contemplate. Garth listened carefully and was mesmorised as he was given a farewell blessing by the Pope.

Three weeks later, on October 9, Pope Pius XII died at Castel Gandolfo. The funeral was spectacular. He was born in Rome in 1876 and spent all his early life in the city. He was a Roman, and the city paid a heartfelt tribute to him as one of their citizens, as well as their Pope. Cardinal Angelo Giuseppe wrote at the time, *'No Roman Emperor had enjoyed such a triumph.'* The new Pontiff, Pope John XXIII, would not be elected until October 28 1958.

Garth Donald Marshallsay was born in Luton, Bedfordshire in April 1938, and had a complicated childhood. His father, Henry (known as Harry) had married his mother, Lily Stone the previous year, but she tragically died when Garth was only three years old.

When World War Two broke out in 1939, his father joined the RAF Police and Garth was looked after by his grandparents, Dr. Sidney Marshallsay and his wife, Rose in Nottingham during the war years. Sidney was a surgeon-dentist and they ran a small family business in the town.

In 1945 Harry was demobbed from the RAF. He remarried, a local girl, Ruth Hatherly on May 18 1945 and they lived in Nottingham. The following year, on April 1 their son, Nigel was born. In 1947 the family moved to Carlisle, where they ran a shop, Struthers Opthalmic Opticians in the Crescent, and Garth attended Grosvenor College School in Carlisle.

It was not a successful marriage. Harry fell in love with another woman, Elsie, and in 1951 Harry and Elsie moved to Newcastle to start a new business, running a public house called *The Brandling Villa* in South Gosforth, which is still thriving today. Thirteen-year-old Garth was sent to the newly-opened Austin Friars School in Carlisle, living with old friends of the family, Mr and Mrs Duncan. His half-brother, Nigel also stayed in Carlisle and attended Grosvenor College School. It was not until March 1956 that Harry finally got a decree absolute and he married Elsie the following month.

It was a disruptive period for both boys, but Garth quickly settled in and enjoyed the solace and stability of Austin Friars School. He was a good pupil.

The school had been opened in 1951 by the friars of the Order of St Augustine, and they were keen to attract new pupils and gave them a warm welcome. Austin Friars offered a boarding education for Catholic boys in Cumbria from the ages of three to eighteen years old, and instilled in them the Augustine doctrine of harmony, of *'being of one mind and one heart, on the way on God.'* There was a strong emphasis on scholarship, theology, science, and the care of those around you. The friars have long since left, but today Austin Friars is a successful independent coeducation day school still educating pupils in accordance with the Augustinian principles of Unity, Truth and Love.

The Augustinian friars are followers of St. Augustine of Hippo, who was born in modern-day Algeria in North Africa in AD354. He was probably a Berber and converted to Christianity in AD386, after leading a normal life of a son from a prosperous family. He had been living with a concubine and was about to get married to another much younger girl in an arranged marriage, but after much thought, decided to become a monk and took a vow of celibacy. He was well-educated, spoke and wrote Latin fluently, and wrote many theological and philosophical works that have influenced scholars and thinkers from all round the world for centuries.

There are two Catholic orders that follow the Rule of St Augustine. The Austin Friars, or Augustinians, are an order founded in 1244 in Tuscany, Italy. They are recognised by the black-belted tunic they adopted in 1256, are based in priories led by a prior, leading a life of prayer and contemplation, but also providing spiritual care for their neighbours.

In Germany the order had established their own printing press by 1479, and the most famous member was Martin Luther, who joined in 1505. Augustinians had started early missionary work in Mexico, throughout South America, and then China, Japan and Africa. During the dissolution of the monasteries in England in the reign of Henry VIII, they were dispersed and nineteen Augustinian houses were dissolved.

It was not until the 1860s that the Augustinians were re-established in England, with the creation of the Augustinian Priory, church and school in Hoxton Square, London in 1864. Today they are well-established in many countries throughout the world.

By the twentieth century the Catholic Church was experiencing a decrease in the number of vocational callings, so Garth's interest in the Augustinians would have been strongly supported by the monks at Austin Friars in Carlisle.

In 1955, at the age of seventeen, Garth had decided he wanted to be a priest. He had discussed this extensively with his teachers at the school, who were very supportive and advised him to go to Clare Priory in Suffolk as a novitiate. He studied there for two years until he was called up for his National Service, which was compulsory for all healthy males between seventeen and twenty-one years old.

National Service had been brought in by the National Service Act 1948, enlisting men to serve in the armed forces for eighteen months. Men were exempt if they worked in any of the three essential services, coal mining, farming and the Merchant Navy. By 1957 National Service was being phased out and the last conscripted serviceman left the armed services in 1963.

Garth enlisted in 1957 and joined the RAF in the Air Traffic Control branch. He carried out his basic training in

England, and was posted to Malta, to the RAF base at Luqa as an assistant air traffic controller.

RAF Luqa was the Mediterranean command headquarters of the RAF during World War Two. During the siege of Malta in 1941 it saw some of the most ferocious air battles of the war. The island and people of Malta were awarded the George Cross by King George VI on April 15 1942 for their heroism during this period.

By 1956, RAF Luqa was being developed as Malta's main civilian airport, but anti-British demonstrations had started on the island calling for strikes and independence. This was the situation when Garth arrived in 1957.

In the 1940s secondary airfields were also built at Ta'Qali, Qrendi and on Malta's second island, Gozo. Garth would have been carrying out his duties around the islands, and watching the rebuilding of the extensive damage inflicted by the relentless German bombardment during the war. He also saw the resulting poverty the war had created.

In his spare time, there was plenty to entertain him. There were pristine beaches, clear blue sea to swim in, family-run restaurants where he could sample the local fare, interesting walks and secret caves to explore. No doubt Garth attended mass in the magnificent St John's Cathedral in Valletta on Sundays.

The Roman Catholic cathedral's austere, fortress-like exterior, designed by Girolamo Cassar and built of Maltese limestone in 1572, is in sharp contrast to the highly ornate interior, decorated mostly by Mattia Preti at the height of the Baroque period (1600–1750). It is considered to be one of the finest examples of high Baroque architecture in Europe.

It was a stunning contrast to what Garth had grown up with in Carlisle, and prepared him for the magnificent opulence of the Vatican.

After his visit to the Vatican in September 1958 and his audience with the Pope, Garth flew to London. First he went back to Carlisle and visited Austin Friars School, where he discussed his future with the friars. He spent some time with Nigel to tell him about his adventures in Malta, and gave him a hand-painted wall tile as a memento. It was not until the last few days of his leave that he went to Newcastle to see Harry, and his stepmother Elsie, that he only distantly knew.

Garth arrived at London Airport in plenty of time on October 22 and boarded the Viscount just after eight o'clock. He was shown to his seat towards the back of the plane by the flight attendant, and noticed several other young servicemen among the passengers, and a sister in the dark-blue uniform of the Queen Alexandra's Royal Naval Nursing Service. He sat back in his seat, looking forward to completing his service in Malta, and starting his new life ahead.

Harry was the first in the family to be informed of the terrible crash in Italy later the same day at his home in Cheltenham Terrace, Heaton, in Newcastle, and that there were no survivors.

Garth's funeral was held in Newcastle, with his grief-stricken family, the friars from his old school, and representatives of BEA attending. As with many other families, twelve-year-old Nigel was not allowed to attend the funeral as he was considered too young. Garth is buried in Long Benton Cemetery in Newcastle, near his father's home. That same year his grandfather, Dr. Sidney Marshallsay also passed away.

A few months later a package arrived at the house for Harry from BEA. It was Garth's Agfa camera that had amazingly survived the crash with minor damage. It was repaired free by Agfa and still works to this day.

Garth had six months left of his National Service and was planning to return to Clare Priory in Suffolk to begin his new life with the Augustinians.

He was twenty years old.

The Boilermaker
JOHN VELLA

On October 22 1958, John Vella arrived early at London Airport to ensure that he caught the 08.25 flight to Malta via Naples. After successful treatment at the Royal Marsden Hospital in Fulham Road, Chelsea, on a cancer in his throat, all he wanted to do was to get back home. The doctors had wanted him to stay in England a little longer to recuperate, but he could not wait to see his family again, so they allowed him to travel with a temporary plastic tube inserted in his trachea. This tiny detail would come to the world's attention by the end of the day.

John was fifty-seven years old. He was born in Cospicua on July 1 1901, one of the Three Cities across the Grand Harbour opposite Valletta, an area popular with families working in the dockyards. His father, Lawrence and mother, Maryanne were also from Cospicua, and he had three older siblings, Joseph, Francis and Concetta. All the men of the family worked in the docks.

Although covering an area of just over a hundred and twenty square miles, Malta's location in the Mediterranean has always been of vital importance. Over the centuries the island had been occupied by countless marauding armies – the Phoenicians, the Romans and the Arabs had all invaded and left their mark. On July 23 1813 Malta became a Crown Colony. The Napoleonic Wars that had begun in 1803 were partially ended by the Treaty of Paris in 1814, and Malta's status as part of the British Empire was confirmed.

The first dry dock in Valletta was opened in 1847 and extended in 1857. The Suez Canal, which connected the Mediterranean to the Red Sea was opened in 1869. It enabled naval ships to pass swiftly from east to west and consequently, Malta became even more of a strategic stronghold.

With the size of ships increasing and the number in the fleet based there, a rapid building programme commenced and a further five dry docks were constructed, along with an assortment of specialised buildings to serve them. Valletta became a mighty military and naval fortress, and the headquarters of the Mediterranean Fleet.

It was a time of prosperity for the island. In February 1883 the Malta railway had opened between Valletta and Mdina, a distance of just eleven kilometres. The journey took around twenty-five minutes and in 1900 an extension was built to the barracks at Mtarfa. As a young boy, John might have seen the little locomotives, built in Leeds, pulling four or five wooden carriages with iron frames on a single one-metre-gauge railway track, slowly winding their way out of Valletta through a tunnel to Hamrun, Fort Salvatore and stopping at eight small stations on the way to Mtarfa. The trains had first and third-class carriages that were lit by candles, until replaced by electric lights in 1900.

In 1905 the first buses were introduced on the island which led to a steady decline in the railway. It eventually closed in 1931.

John was a thirteen-year-old boy and still at school when Archduke Ferdinand of Austria-Hungary was assassinated on June 28 1914. The shocking news caused consternation and concern throughout Europe. The political crisis escalated rapidly and as Malta was the base of the large and powerful British Mediterranean Fleet, the island was immediately affected by the threat of war.

Volunteers were enrolled into the Malta Royal Naval Reserve and for service in the Royal Malta Artillery and the Royal Engineers (Militia). Tempted by the pay, many local men joined the King's Own Malta Regiment of Militia, including 5,600 volunteers in the Maltese Labour Corps to assist the Allies in Gallipoli (1915), Salonika (1917) and Cyprus. Four members of the Vella family, part of the MLC, died in 1918 and are buried in Italy and Greece.

Grand Harbour was closed by a boom defence and put under continuous surveillance. In response to the local resistance, the German navy blocked the approaches to Malta by laying naval mines, which sank numerous ships, including the battleship HMS *Russell* in 1916.

In 1917 twenty aircraft were built by the Seaplane Construction Department. Based at Kalafrana they were used in anti-submarine operations and for the protection of the Allied shipping force. During the war 137,000 wounded were brought to the island's twenty-seven hospitals from the horrific battlefields of France, and Malta became known as *The Nurse of the Mediterranean.*

The war memorial in Floriana commemorated 592 Maltese men who died in the conflict and on it is now inscribed, *'Let me assure you that I am fully conscious of the important and patriotic part that Malta has played during these years of warfare. King George V'*

When the war was over, shortages followed and in 1919 there were riots over the excessive price of bread. This led to greater autonomy for the local population and in 1921 Malta's first parliament was set up.

The dockyards were the powerhouse of Malta's economy and the workforce gained a reputation for militancy in their struggle for fairer wages.

John had started his apprenticeship in the shipyards as a boilermaker, learning the skills required to build, install and maintain the steel containers in all shapes and sizes required in a ship. He learned how to read blueprints, to cut and bend different types of steel, and mastered the skills needed to weld or bolt them together. The work was physically demanding in dirty, noisy and sometimes dangerous conditions, but it was guaranteed and the pay was above average.

John also had a gift for languages. His mother was convinced he could speak seven languages, and he earned a little extra money as an interpreter between the many foreign personnel on the tankers that used the dry dock facilities.

With the recession in the 1930s trade slowed down. The British were slimming the Navy, making business more challenging, but the Vella family struggled through. The situation changed dramatically in 1939 when Britain was forced to declare war on Germany, and Malta was dragged into the conflict when Italy joined Germany on June 10 1940. The people of Malta and especially the dockyard families would now endure three years of hell.

The Axis powers launched bombing raids from Sicily within days of the declaration of war. The airfields at Luqa, Hal Far and Ta'Qali were quickly put out of action and these were followed by attacks on the cities, aimed at demoralising the civilians. There was little damage to the docks, which were protected by anti-aircraft guns, the old warship HMS *Terror* built in 1916 and a few submarines. The RAF rebuilt the airfields, more anti-aircraft guns were brought in to help defend the dockyards and Swordfish bombers carried out retaliatory strikes on enemy bases in Sicily. In 1941 the Germans began a counter offensive against the British in North Africa. For this to succeed it was essential that Malta was neutralised, and an order went out from Nazi headquarters in Berlin to pound it into submission.

It is at this point that the stories of the Vella and Chalmers families intertwined, both families enduring the horrors of the blitz, living just a few miles apart from each other.

On January 10 1941 the aircraft carrier HMS *Illustrious* came under concentrated aerial attack by Axis bombers and was badly damaged. Chased by German Stuka bombers, she made her way towards the dockyard in need of urgent repair. When the stricken carrier limped into Grand Harbour and docked at Palatoria Wharf, the deteriorating weather and the anti-aircraft guns saw off the enemy aircraft, giving the dock workers a window of opportunity to begin the repairs. Hundreds of men huddled at the wharf waiting to board.

The 126 fatalities and scores of injured were taken to the hospitals, and inspection crews went aboard to assess the extensive internal damage, with divers checking the external hull. The carrier's massive metal plates were blackened, twisted and torn with huge gaping holes in the bow and deck. Everywhere there was blood and pieces of human debris. Orders were issued to repair only the worst damage, as the carrier could sail to Alexandria for a substantial refit of its armament. Damaged areas were cut away and temporary patches welded over, requiring all the skills of the engineers, boilermakers, welders, and divers.

They worked in twelve-hour shifts for the next twelve days in cold, atrocious weather while the engines were repaired, the electrics were replaced and vital operating systems checked. As soon as there was the slightest improvement in the weather, they came under further attack from German bombers and fighters, determined the carrier would not sail again. It was one of the rare times the workers welcomed the rain.

On January 19 there were two massive raids involving over eighty enemy aircraft aimed at disabling the carrier. Only one bomb damaged the ship when it landed adjacent to the hull. The explosion threw the ship against the dock wall and she began to list. Some of the bombs weighed 1,000kg, full of high explosives and caused extensive damage to the dockyard. The noise was ear-splitting as earth-shaking explosions sent shards of shattered glass, red-hot metal and lumps of blasted concrete screaming through the air.

We can only imagine how John and his colleagues must have felt amid the apocalyptic chaos, as terrified workers sprinted for shelter when the air raid sirens sounded, clutching their metal helmets and gas masks. One observer noted, *'Forty dockyard workers were huddled in communal prayer in a shelter hewn from rock under heavy bastions, but they could still feel the impact of the bombing. The shelters all had a niche with a holy picture and several candles burning. One man led the invocation and the rest would respond in a nervous chant, invoking images of the earliest Christians who gathered in the catacombs under Rome to pray to avoid persecution from the*

Romans. The whole shelter seemed to be trembling and shuddering as if we were in the middle of a gigantic earthquake... sometimes it felt as if express trains were running at full speed under our feet. Occasionally the sharp blasts of heavy gunfire would penetrate the shelter but were quickly drowned out by the surrounding din.'

By January 23 the mechanics and engineers had successfully done their job and *Illustrious* slipped out of the Grand Harbour at 18.46, escorted by four destroyers, heading for Alexandria. It was a magnificent effort, and Admiral Sir Andrew Cunningham, Commander-In-Chief of the Mediterranean Fleet, gave special praise to Malta's dockyard workers and the anti-aircraft teams for their contribution to the survival of this vital ship.

The Vella family lived in Cospicua, one of Malta's Three Cities, the other two being Senglea and Vittoriosa, which were built and fortified in the sixteenth century and had survived many assaults. Dozens of bombs aimed at *Illustrious* rained down on the little towns destroying hundreds of houses, damaging five hundred and leaving many casualties of all ages crushed under the demolished buildings.

Huge craters were gouged out of the narrow streets, the collapsed buildings were mounds of smouldering rubble and an acrid smell of gas from the burst mains pipes hung in the air. Hundreds of the survivors were homeless and sought shelter with friends and family, walking the streets in shock, clasping pathetic bundles of clothing and anything else they could carry, as volunteers and demolition squads arrived to try to extricate those trapped.

The Vella family were forced to flee, and went to the south of the island to find refuge in Qrendi, where they were given shelter in St Mary's Band Club, close to the centre of the town. They received a warm welcome from the musical family with whom they resided, in which every member played an instrument.

Throughout 1941, as the second wave of the siege intensified, John, his father and two brothers, Joseph and Francis, carried on working at the dockyard. Tragedy struck the family when Joseph was killed in an air raid. By 1942 conditions on the island were grim, with shortages of all essential supplies, including food, clothes and clean water. Poor sanitation led to disease and there was a real threat of starvation.

On April 15 1942, King George VI recognised the valour of the Maltese people in a letter to the Governor. *'To honour the brave people I award the George Cross to the Island Fortress of Malta to bear witness to a heroism and devotion that will long be famous in history.'*

By May the tide had begun to turn in the Allies' favour and in October the first convoys got through. Very slowly conditions on the island improved. On September 2 1945 the war ended and the islanders erupted in celebration. The Band Clubs in Qrendi held an enormous street party in the village square, with much joyous singing and dancing late into the night.

There was peace at last for this shattered island, and the people could start rebuilding their cities and lives.

John was forty-five years old, and his thoughts turned to finding a wife with whom he could start a family and catch up on the life he had lost during the war years. In 1946 he met Theresa Catania, a local tailoress, ten years his junior, and after a whirlwind courtship they married the same year and settled down in Qrendi. In 1947 their first son was born, and they named him Joseph after his late brother.

Tragically, little Joseph died a few days after he was born. The next year their daughter, Mary Anne was born, followed by their second son, Michael, and a third son, Saviour in 1953.

For the next five years John enjoyed the happiest years of his life, relishing the joy of bringing up his children in Qrendi with his close family living nearby. He continued to work in the dockyard, which was rebuilt as a modern, bustling port and provided him with plenty of work.

However, the conditions he had worked in for so many years started to affect his health. Many boilermakers and welders suffered from throat, lung and skin problems after being continually exposed to the fumes and polluted air from working with steel all their lives. Some days John would return from the dock and Theresa would have to pluck out black soot particles from his skin. The problems started as dryness of the throat, with soreness and coughing.

By 1958 his throat had become very painful and after an examination by his doctor he was given some bad news. A throat cancer had developed and an operation to remove it was necessary. He could have the operation in Malta, but he would lose his voice box and the ability to speak. An alternative was to fly to England and have pioneering

291

radiotherapy treatment at the Royal Marsden Hospital, where they could remove the cancer and save his voice.

John immediately opted to go to London. Before he flew, he agreed to have a temporary plastic tube inserted in his throat which would assist his breathing whilst travelling, and with the treatment.

The Royal Marsden Hospital was the first hospital in the world dedicated to the study and treatment of cancer. It was founded as the Free Cancer Hospital in 1851 by surgeon William Marsden (1796–1867). He was born in Sheffield, was apprenticed to a wholesale druggist and left for London in 1816 to become a student of surgery. He qualified and became a Member of the Royal College of Surgeons in 1827. He was a man with a profound social conscience, and after witnessing the difficulties of the poor in obtaining medical treatment, Marsden set up a free hospital for which *poverty and sickness were the only passports.'* He was also greatly influenced by having to watch helplessly as his wife, Elizabeth-Ann died of cancer in 1846. The hospital moved location several times until benefactors dedicated a brand new building in Brompton Road and was granted a Royal Charter in 1910 by King George V.

It was renamed the Royal Marsden Hospital in 1954 in recognition of the vision and commitment of its founder, and it was here that John was admitted early in October 1958.

John responded well to the radiotherapy and wrote to the family saying that he was delighted it had been a success, and felt he had been reborn. The plastic tube was kept in his trachea to help his breathing during the recuperation period.

He had a niece living in England who was married to a

British soldier, and had offered him a place to stay for a few days so she could show him around England. He thanked her but declined the kind invitation as he was missing his family so much. He couldn't wait to get back home.

On October 22, just before eight o'clock John slowly climbed the mobile stairs at the rear of the Viscount to be met by a charming flight attendant. She immediately saw the tube in his throat and paid him special attention. She showed him to his seat, right at the back near her own, where it would be easy for her to keep an eye on him during the flight.

John's wife, Theresa, was waiting at the airport and looking forward to seeing her husband again after his successful operation. After a few very anxious hours she was ushered into the BEA office to be told the terrible news by the manager, Mr. T. Pollock. There were distressing scenes all around the arrivals hall as the horrific news filtered through.

The tragic news of the crash was in the international newspapers that evening, and several reported that one middle-aged man, who was not identified, was found unconscious but miraculously, still alive in the fuselage of the plane after plunging 23,500ft. from the sky. He was reported to have a plastic tube in his neck. This man can only have been John. The tube may somehow have saved him from the effects of the severe decompression that would have occurred at the initial collision. How he survived the impact we will never know. He never regained consciousness and died on the way to the hospital in Nettuno.

John was flown back to Malta from Rome on October 28

with the three other victims from the island, Robert Chalmers, Mary Vassallo La Rosa and Sheila Lane, and they were transferred to the mortuary at St Luke's Hospital in Pietà. The following day John's coffin was placed in a glass hearse drawn by two black horses, and covered with wreaths and bouquets of flowers, including a large wreath from BEA. The desperately sad family cortège wound its way slowly south to Qrendi, entering the village square, where many local friends had gathered to pay their respects with hats removed, heads bowed, many in tears.

It passed St Mary's Band Club flying its flag at half-mast, and paused at the steps of the imposing, Baroque, Parish Church of the Assumption of Mary, consecrated in 1782, where a lone bell tolled slow, melancholy chimes before it continued to the cemetery near the village for the graveside service with the family.

One more day in England and John would have avoided the tragedy of BE142. Another of those on board whose last-minute change to their schedule proved fatal.

The Tea Broker's Daughter
EVELINE YUILLE

Eveline Yuille arrived early at London Airport on Wednesday 22 October 1958 excited at the prospect of her first visit to Italy. It had been a hectic week at the hospital in Worthing and this would be a perfect break for her, to explore and relax on the gorgeous Italian coast of Campania. She checked in at the BEA desk, and made her way to the boarding gate for flight BE142 to Naples. Eveline was only twenty-three years old, but had already experienced many traumas in her short life, and this holiday would be a chance to put all her cares aside and enjoy herself.

Eveline Margaret Yuille was born on December 20 1934 in Eastbourne, Sussex. Her father was George Herbert Yuille, a tea-broker and taster, and her mother was Rosalinda Blow Carrick, whose family ran a successful business in Madras, (now Chennai).

Eveline's grandfather, Herbert Buchanan Yuille came from old, Scottish trading family that specialised in tea. Herbert was born in Edinburgh in 1868, the eighth of ten children. He was educated at St Paul's School but by the early 1880s his family were living in Kensington, London. At the age of seventeen he joined Lloyd, Matheson & Carritt, a tea broking company that flourished after the East India Company lost its monopoly, and one of several that dominated the tea auctions in Calcutta and London.

After six years learning the complex business of the buying and selling of tea, he travelled to India, where it was considered the very best tea in the world was grown, and lived there for the next eleven years. He met Margaret Mabel Sidey and in 1896 they were married at St Paul's Cathedral, Calcutta.

In November that year their first son, Archibald Buchanan was born, and they returned to London in 1902, where he joined George White & Co., an established firm of tea and rubber brokers in Fenchurch Street, established in 1873. Over the next twenty years he rose up through the company to eventually become Director.

The turn of the century was the dawn of a new age – that of the automobile. In 1903 the Ford Motor Company began production of the Model T, and rubber was the commodity that was increasing in demand from this exciting new business.

Rubber originally came from Brazil. It is made from the white sap of the rubber tree called latex and is known to have been used by the Aztecs. By far the largest number of trees were found deep in the Amazon rain forest. When the early European pioneers of the industry arrived in South America during the nineteenth century, the small towns along the River Amazon such as Manaus boomed, and large quantities of rubber were shipped to the factories of Europe. Fortunes were quickly made and the Manaus rubber barons flaunted their wealth, building enormous houses graced with the latest fashion décor from Paris, and ordered the best food and champagne from Europe.

In stark contrast, it was a brutal period for the local people, enslaved on vast plantations and ruthlessly exploited with savage brutality and violence. They were saved unintentionally by an English planter in 1876 called Henry Wickham.

Seeing an opportunity, he collected 70,000 rubber seeds and shipped them back to England. 2,800 of the seeds germinated and were sent to Ceylon (now Sri Lanka), Singapore and Malaya, (now Malaysia). Tea and coffee were the most profitable crops and it was not until 1895 that two coffee planters in Ceylon were persuaded to plant two acres of rubber. After six years it was possible to tap the trees for their sap.

Twelve years later more than 300,000 acres of rubber trees grew in plantations in Ceylon and Malaya. New innovations in production increased efficiency, and output of the highly sought-after crop doubled every two years. Rubber grown in the Far East cost a fraction of that in Brazil, and by 1914 production in South America had dropped 50%.

George White & Co. continued their profitable trade as brokers in tea and quickly moved into the rapidly expanding business of rubber. Herbert was involved from the start. By 1908 he was Chairman of the Rubber Trade Association and became a Director of Eow Seng Rubber Company in Malaya. The same year, his second son, George, Eveline's father, was born in Richmond, London and in 1911 the family moved to a larger house in Northwood, Middlesex.

Archibald had attended Rugby School, and when World War One broke out in July 1914, he was keen to see action. He joined the 8th Battalion East Lancashire Regiment in 1914 and quickly rose to the rank of Captain. Having been wounded in the arm at Contalmaison, near Pozières,

Archibald spent three months in hospital, but by the end of summer he was back in action.

Possibly as a result of the injury to his arm, in the autumn of 1917 Archibald joined the Royal Flying Corps (RFC) and was sent to the Somme in France to join the newly formed 151 Squadron, the first specialist night-fighter unit.

The German Air Service was flying heavy bomber aircraft over both the east and western fronts, the Gotha G.V and the huge Zeppelin-Staaken-R XIV. There was no radar in 1918 and night-flying aids were virtually non-existent. The chance of finding a plane in the dark was remote and even more difficult to shoot down. Archibald shot down two. In July 1918 he damaged a Gotha over Étaples, Belgium and forced it down.

On the night of August 10 1918 he was patrolling the lines on the Somme in a Sopwith Camel, a single-seat biplane fighter aircraft introduced in 1917. He was flying at 8,000ft. near Talmas when he intercepted a Zeppelin-Staaken which had been sent out to attack Doullens. It had a crew of six and was vastly bigger than the Sopwith with more guns, but he decided to attack it nonetheless. The official citation recorded, '...this officer observed an enemy aeroplane in the beams of the searchlight. Three of our Camels were engaging this machine, but not at sufficient range for decisive results. With great gallantry he dived between the nearest Camel and the enemy, thereby exposing himself to the fire of our tracers, and by skilful manoeuvre succeeded in getting under the enemy machine, where he opened fire at twenty-five yards. After three bursts the enemy machine caught fire and crashed. A fine performance deserving the highest praise.'

On April 1 1918 the Royal Air Force was formed by the amalgamation of the RFC and the Royal Naval Air Service. On November 2 1918 Archibald was one of the earliest recipients of the newly created DFC, (Distinguished Flying Cross).

On November 11 1918, peace was declared and Archibald returned to London, settled back into his life as a tea and rubber broker and married Cecilia Frances Silverwood-Cope in 1923. On December 31 1925 the business partnership at George White & Co. between himself and his father Herbert was dissolved and he went on to become an auctioneer of tea.

George was too young to serve in the war, but after he left school he followed in his father and brother's footsteps to join George White & Co. With the increasing demand for tea and a boom in the rubber market in the 1920s, the family prospered and moved to a comfortable house in Queen Anne's Gate in Kensington.

There was a lot for George to learn about tea. It was originally brought to India from China by British colonists, but it was not until the early 1820s that the British East India Company began large scale production in Assam, aiming to break China's monopoly of the market. The high rainfall and acid soils of Darjeeling in the foothills of the Himalayas were the perfect environment for the growing of the tea plant. In 1837 the first tea garden was established at Chabua in Upper Assam, and in 1840 the Assam Tea Company began commercial production in the region. It expanded quickly and after the break-up of the East India Company in 1857, private companies moved in to replace it, and cater for the increasing demand of the British public, helped by the powerful Temperance movement.

The British preferred the robust strength of India teas compared to the subtle China teas and blending different varieties created new tastes. By the end of the nineteenth century, large companies such as Lyons and Liptons dominated the market.

George travelled to India to visit the plantations, talk to the producers and learn the art of tasting.

Tea has four pickings (flushes) a year, the first flush in spring considered the best. The tea taster looks for four key features – appearance, aroma, flavour and the feel in the mouth. Appearance includes the colour, the texture and size of the leaf, and the quality of the tea buds. The clearest spring water has to be used. Hard and boiling water is best for making black tea, and soft and cooler water for green teas. Brew time must be three and a half minutes. The purest white crockery is essential to see the colour and depth. The liquor inspected must be a bright, jewel-like colour, and its appearance shiny and slightly oily. Small fragments of tea are acceptable for clarity. The brew must be held close to the nose and the aroma inhaled. A good slurp is essential, the noisier the better, to take in oxygen, which brings out the flavours. Then you can swallow.

The flavour must hit three marks, the head, which gives the initial impression, the body gives the secondary ring, and the tail reacts to the lingering taste and reveals the complexity of the brew.

Finally, there are the sensations felt after tasting the brew, which indicates the overall strength. Blends continually change and the most experienced tasters take years to master the art.

George travelled to both India and the Far East to practise his specialised skill and on a trip in 1932, he met a vivacious young woman called Rosalinda Blow Carrick, (always known as Linda) through her brother, who was running a successful business in Madras, (now Chennai). She had sailed to Calcutta on the steam ship *Mashobra* on October 31 1931, travelling first class, and stayed with her brother in Calcutta. They were both excellent golfers.

Linda won the Ladies' Championship in Calcutta in 1933 and it is likely that George and Linda met at a golf event. The following year they returned to England and were married in London. Their first daughter, Eveline was born just before Christmas in Eastbourne later that year.

In 1937 their second daughter, Jane was born followed by Sarah Rosalinda, (always known as Sally) in 1938 and the family settled into a house called *Bracondale* in Uckfield, Sussex. Those few years of happiness were soon cut short though as the dark clouds of war gathered once again.

World War Two broke out in Europe on September 1 1939, and when Japan bombed Pearl Harbour and launched simultaneous attacks on Malaya, Singapore and Hong Kong in 1941, it was soon realised that the whole of the Far East and even India was at risk.

The British Army needed soldiers with knowledge and experience of the Far East and although he was thirty-two years old, George was ideal. He signed up with the Bihar Regiment of the Indian Army in 1941 soon after it was raised, and was quickly promoted to Captain.

The Bihar Regiment was an Indian Army infantry regiment that traced its origins back to 1857 when a battalion was raised by the then Governor of Bengal, Lord Clive at Patna. It originally comprised two groups, the North and South Biharis, and also took soldiers from parts of Uttar Pradesh. They were considered fine, brave soldiers and deeply religious, and distinguished themselves in several battles. However, they were offended by the increasingly arrogant and disrespectful attitude of the East India Company, and this led to the Indian Mutiny against the British in 1857. They were brutally put down and disbanded.

It was not until 1941 that the regiment was raised again and recruited into the 19th Hyderabad Regiment. There were two battalions, the first fought in the Burma Campaign against the Japanese and the second was raised in 1942 to fight in Malaya, where they won further honours for gallant action.

It is not known where George was stationed during the war but for a while he would have been based in Calcutta. With his knowledge of Malaya it is likely he was with the second battalion. The Burma campaign ran from December 1941 to September 1945, and was divided into four phases; the first from 1941 to 1942 was the swift and successful invasion of the Japanese from Malaya up to the Indian border, the second was the failed Allied offensives in 1943, the third was the failed Japanese invasion of India after the battles of *Imphal* and *Kohima*, and the fourth was the successful Allied offensive which started in late 1944 and ran through to mid-1945.

After the Americans dropped two nuclear bombs on Hiroshima and Nagasaki on August 6 and 9 1945, the Allies had planned to launch *Operation Zipper* to liberate Malaya and Singapore. 100,000 troops, including the Bihar Regiment were to land at Port Swettenham, (now Port Klang) and Port Dickson on the west Malay coast near to the capital Kuala Lumpur on September 9, but it was forestalled by the Emperor's announcement on August 15 of the surrender of Japan.

The Allies arrived at Penang Island on August 28, which surrendered without resistance. The fleet sailed on to Singapore, arriving on September 4 and the formal surrender was signed at the Singapore City Hall a week later.

In the General Election of July 1945, Winston Churchill, much to his astonishment, was soundly defeated. Clement Attlee led the new Labour government and the rebuilding of the country's economy and bombed-out cities began.

When George returned to England he found a very different country. Everyone was tired of war and looking forward to a better future. As with many servicemen returning from action in the Far East, nobody was interested in their horrific experiences they had seen and endured. He too was no doubt keen to get back to work.

In March 1946, soon after George had returned home to Sussex, Eveline contracted polio while she was at her school in Eastbourne. She was only eleven years old, and naturally he travelled to the school to see her. To his relief he found that her condition was not too serious, and the muscle weakness confined largely to her left hand.

His mother, Margaret had also contracted the disease and was very ill in Crowborough Hospital. He rang his brother Archibald to say he should come to the hospital urgently. That evening he did not feel well himself and decided to postpone travelling to see his mother.

The following day, on March 30, Archibald travelled to Crowborough to see Margaret, but there was no sign of George. He had been admitted to Tonbridge Wells Hospital and his condition had significantly worsened during the day. That night he died. Three days later Margaret died.

It was a terrible blow for the family. It was a devastating trauma for Eveline and her sisters attending the funeral in Crowborough cemetery, having to bury their father, and to have lost their grandmother in the same week.

Linda had three young children to look after, but gradually returned to an active social life, and became a leading light in the Crowborough Golf Club. In 1948 she met Edward Stanton Jerdein, a retired wine and spirit agent who had lost his wife in 1945. He had no children of his own, and he got on well with the three girls. At forty-two, Linda was still a relatively young woman and although Edward was over twenty years older than Linda, she enjoyed his company and the support he gave, and later that year they married.

The girls were all at school and although there is little detail about their lives, they would have enjoyed a stable and comfortable upbringing. Linda continued playing golf to a high standard and in 1949 and 1950 she was crowned Sussex County Ladies' Champion.

Eveline left school in 1952 and maybe because of her own experiences with polio and the national shortage of nursing staff, she decided to become a nurse and trained at Worthing Hospital, not far from the family home at Uckfield.

The National Health Service began on July 5 1948 bringing together doctors, hospital services, pharmacists and community care staff together for the first time. It was a massive challenge and in 1952 it was still being implemented.

A new nursing training syllabus was introduced covering hygiene, nutrition, environmental care and psychological and social care. Further training was given when working on specialist wards. The matron had complete control over the hospital, covering all aspects of patient care, catering, laundry and cleaning. She also controlled the nurses' homes, imposing rules on time-keeping and even what the nurses could wear. They were strict disciplinarians, but very protective of their staff.

It would have been hard training for Eveline as there was a considerable amount of hands-on work to do, such as making the beds, cleaning and emptying bedpans, monitoring their patients' health and even boiling their eggs for breakfast, but it also gave them plenty of time to spend with their patients. The role of a nurse in the 1950s was a very different one compared to that of today, where nurses are highly-qualified graduate technicians monitoring the most advanced equipment and technology, backed up by nursing assistants doing the cleaning, cooking and laundry.

Linda and Edward enjoyed six years of happy marriage, but in 1954 tragedy struck the family again when Linda was diagnosed with leukaemia and died after only a few months at the age of forty-eight. By the age of twenty, Eveline and her two teenage sisters were orphans.

Eveline came from a remarkable and interesting family. They had enjoyed success in the tea industry. Both her father and uncle had distinguished careers in the armed forces. Her early years were dominated by the war, during which she endured long periods of separation from her father. Her mother and two sisters would have gone through years of rationing and the ever-present threat of being hit by a stray bomb. Post-war austerity dominated her teenage years, but she was nurtured and supported by a caring and loving family.

Maybe as a result of all the traumas in her life she found her calling in the nursing service. We know that by 1958 Eveline was working at Worthing Hospital and able to return some of the loving care that she had seen given to her parents.

On October 22, at the age of twenty three, it is quite possible that Eveline was taking her first trip abroad, to experience the vibrancy and culture of Italy, the noise and bustle of Naples and the fascinating ruins of Pompeii, overlooked by a smouldering Mount Vesuvius. There could be an opportunity to take a boat ride across the Bay of Naples to Capri with some of her fellow passengers. Just as she might have been looking forward to having children of her own and enjoying precious time with her sisters, her life was cut short by this tragic event in the skies over Nettuno.

The family had to oversee another heartbreaking funeral at Crowborough cemetery, and see Eveline buried with her father and mother. The grave inscription on the headstone is now fading on the granite, but it reads:

In Precious and Happy Remembrance of George Herbert Yuille
March 30 1946 and of Rosalinda August 11 1954.
Also Eveline Margaret October 22 1958.
To live in the hearts of those we love, is not to die.

4.

AFTERMATH

On October 22 1958 Thomas Watson, the resident engineer for BEA in Italy, decided to go to the coast for the day and take a short break from the bustle of Rome. He caught an early train to Anzio with his wife, Mary, a friend, Jenny Russell visiting from England, and Mr G. Carducci, a colleague from BEA.

At just before midday they took a stroll down to the pier to look at the boats moored in the marina, when suddenly they heard a very loud bang above them. Mary Watson recounted later, *'We were on the pier looking at the boats when we heard an explosion. We looked up and saw a big puff of smoke and silvery pieces floating around the sky. Out of the smoke tumbled a plane, looking like a toy falling slowly to the ground. Nearby some Italian naval men looked up with a pair of binoculars. Then one ran to the nearby fire station and went tearing off in a car. He was closely followed by a fire engine. We did not dream that it was a* (BEA) *Viscount that had crashed until we arrived home and heard a newsflash on the BBC Overseas Service.'*

Many local people witnessed the terrible scene unfolding.

Annibale De Franceschi, a forty-six-year-old farm worker was picking potatoes in a field near to the military base, and heard the explosion.

'I threw myself to the ground, and covered my head with my

hands. I saw two pieces of aeroplane plunging down from the sky. There were a series of heavy thuds, and looking up I saw flames in the gorse several hundred yards away.'

Domenico Cibati was eating lunch of fried fish and pasta in his house when he heard the explosion. *'I heard a noise like a gunshot and ran outside. Part of the wing of the Viscount wing had fallen thirty yards away, and the plane* (fuselage) *was wobbling down from the sky.'*

Mariano De Lucia, a local innkeeper, was standing outside his house with his friend, Dr Mariani Luigi. *'I was standing in the street when suddenly I heard a loud bang and ran for shelter. Very high up I saw two planes had disintegrated. The big one came down in three pieces. The fuselage and wing spiralled down and things seem to be falling out of it all the time.'*

Bellini Luciano, a farmer's son, also heard the explosion and looked up. *'I saw the parachute come down about one kilometre away, and jumped on my motor scooter. I saw the pilot in the tree, in pain and his face was bleeding, and I tried to free him. He told me to be careful as his back and side were injured. An ambulance arrived soon afterwards.'* Captain Savorelli was taken to Nettuno Hospital with a suspected spinal fracture.

The driver of the Commandant of the army base, Amerigo Zaccardi, was standing outside the office when he heard the explosion and he ran over as the fuselage spiralled down ahead of him. *'...At the same time, I also noticed an open parachute, and watched the plane fuselage hit the ground and start to burn. The fire spread to the surrounding moorland.'*

First on the scene of the crash were a group of soldiers who went to the fuselage, lying at an angle in a patch of burning gorse, its starboard engine in flames.

Within minutes the first army fire engines arrived and extinguished the fire with foam and brought out six bodies from the fuselage. Amerigo continued, *'…Once by the fuselage I helped a man who still showed some signs of life. I then drove off in the direction of the parachute.'*

The man who was still alive and unconscious was John Vella from Malta, who had just had cancer treatment in London and a tube was still inserted in his throat, which possibly enabled him to survive the decompression. He died in Nettuno Hospital a few hours later from multiple injuries without regaining consciousness.

An army chaplain walked amongst the wreckage seeking signs of life and gave absolution to the bodies he found.

As they toiled through the wreckage the firemen saw an unbelievable sight. Amongst the twisted metal and scattered luggage and personal effects, dozens of baby chicks were scampering around, scattering in all directions. There had been boxes of day-old chicks in the freight hold and somehow one box had survived the fall. Some chicks fled into the surrounding bush, but the firefighters saved a few lucky ones and laid them in a bed of wadding from a wrecked plane seat.

In the burnt-out cockpit a small, white handkerchief hung limply from one of the controls.

Large numbers of police were drafted in from a nearby police school to assist, and artillerymen from the base cordoned off the area and began the sad task of collecting the bodies. Each location was marked with a red flag and any personal items that could identify the victims were recorded.

Within an hour more fire engines arrived from Rome. The

Town Hall was converted into an emergency centre. Twenty dogs were brought in to find the package that had contained secret equipment for the Royal Navy in Malta which had been in the cockpit with Captain Frank Foster.

They also searched for the diplomatic bag which had contained twenty-thousand pounds in five-pound notes. By the end of the afternoon the package had been found, but the diplomatic bag had split open in the collision and thousands of five-pound notes had fluttered down in the wind, scattering over a wide area. The rain of money falling from the sky caused much local interest, and only sixteen-thousand pounds were ever recovered, despite an intensive search for the rest by the local police.

One by one the ambulances returned to the hospital empty. By late afternoon all the fires had been extinguished, and the remaining bodies recovered. They were put in makeshift coffins and taken by the army in a convoy of lorries to the Town Hall. Many local people lined the route, shocked and bewildered as the sad procession passed slowly along the streets, and bowed solemnly as it passed by.

In its long history this small, medieval town had seen much sadness. Fourteen years earlier, on January 22 1944, a force of 150,000 Allied troops landed on Nettuno and Anzio beaches to start the liberation of mainland Italy. There were over 40,000 casualties on both sides. A large, American cemetery lies just to the north of Nettuno, full of young American soldiers and sailors who had died far from home.

A former schoolroom in the Town Hall was transformed into a temporary chapel. Candles lined either side of the room, and a large, black curtain hung at one end adorned with a sombre crucifix.

The following day, Captain Savorelli was transferred by ambulance to a specialist hospital in Rome. The coffins were transferred to the morgue in Rome by road. Here the bodies were identified, examined and each prepared for their last journey home.

A few relatives and friends started arriving at the morgue to help with the identification process, including those of Desmond and Diana Cubitt, Robert Chalmers, Robert Allan and Mary Mathieson.

There were sixteen crew and passengers whose final destination was to be Malta, but it took some time to identify which passengers were to be buried there. It took nearly a week to confirm those to be sent to Malta. There were four – Robert Chalmers, Sheila Lane, Mary Vassallo La Rosa, and John Vella.

They were flown to Malta on a sister Viscount, RMA *George Vancouver* on the evening of October 28, and even this journey was not without incident. Between Sicily and Malta the plane encountered a violent hailstorm, which was evident from the pitted nose on landing.

The Viscount parked on the floodlit apron outside the air terminal and boxes containing the coffins were unloaded by a heavy-duty fork-lift truck. Relatives and friends stood silently at a distance and watched the unloading, which included large wreaths sent by airline officials and personnel, including that of the Chairman and members of the board of BEA.

The funerals of Robert, John and Mary were carried out the next day, and the interment of Sheila Lane took place on October 30 at Kalkara Naval Cemetery.

5.

THE INQUIRY

When an air accident happens in any part of the world, an inquiry is held to investigate the cause, and it is the responsibility of the country where the accident has occurred to hold the inquiry. Unfortunately, it is a well-practiced procedure. The crash happened at 11.50 GMT and by 19.00 on October 22 1958, the Italian Ministry of Defence had appointed a commission in Rome to start the investigation.

The President of the commission was the Commander-in-Chief of the Air Defence, Domenico Ludovico, and his committee included ten senior experts in different areas of aviation, from aeronautical engineering and construction to flying and air traffic control. They covered both civil and military aircraft. The British Government appointed Mr G. M. Kelly of the Ministry of Transport and Civil Aviation accident branch at Farnborough as its representative on the committee. He flew to Rome that day.

BEA also convened their accident investigation team in London on the afternoon the news came in. The team was led by its Chief Executive, Anthony Millward, with the Chief Accident Investigator, J. W. Gibbs, Director of Flight

Operations, Captain J. W. G. James, and the Chief Pilot, Captain W. Baillie. After Anthony Millward issued a statement to the press expressing his sympathies to the relatives of all those on the plane, the team caught a flight to Rome later that day. The following morning they travelled to Nettuno by train, only an hour from Rome.

At 08.00 on October 23 the commission assembled in Nettuno and formally opened proceedings. It was essential to start interviewing any eyewitnesses within twenty-four hours, in particular the small group of people standing on Anzio pier a few miles to the west, and some Nettuno locals who had seen the explosion. The four Italian jet pilots were key witnesses.

Captain Giovanni Savorelli was too injured to be interviewed and was being transferred to hospital in Rome for further treatment. He was not able to make a statement until March 1959. The three other pilots, Giorgio Giannotti, Siro Sari and Vittorio Carone were available for questioning, but still suffering from shock, and had their statements taken by military personnel at their airbase at Pratica di Mare on the day of the crash.

After an initial briefing the investigation team went to the crash site on the Nettuno army artillery base. It was a scene of devastation. All the fires had been extinguished, but parts were still smouldering, and a pungent, acrid smell hung in the air. The wreckage of the planes and their contents was scattered over a wide area of the artillery range, mostly rough bush and scrubland which, up to that point had been home to the birds and local wildlife.

Two hundred policemen were drafted in from Rome to help the army scour the area covering two square miles. All pieces of wreckage found had to be meticulously recorded with a photograph, and the exact location and condition they were found in.

The remains of the Viscount fuselage looked as though it had been ripped open with a can-opener, with two large, gaping holes peeled back to expose the horror within. Military personnel and police crawled around inside the broken fuselage, brought out the remains of the luggage and personal belongings, and sorted them into piles for collection and identification. Passports, identification cards and small, personal items were kept separately.

The tail section had broken off and was lying at a drunken angle a few hundred yards north, the scarred BEA logo clearly visible and glinting in the autumn sun. Local villagers stood in groups quietly looking on in hypnotised curiosity, awe and sadness. Local journalists were interviewing any witnesses they could find and a camera crew was taking photographs.

One of the Viscount engines, engine three, was still attached to the starboard wing, but the other three could not be found. Divers were summoned in case they had landed in the sea, but within a few days all the engines were located on land. Engine one was found close to the coast. It was soon realised that engine two had been hit by the jet and had disintegrated. Engine four had detached from the wing and was found south of the fuselage.

Three hundred yards east of the fuselage lay the cockpit and the all-important navigation instruments. Strangely, the front nose section of the plane with part of the control panel was intact, but the joy-stick and pilot's seat were missing, leaving a tangle of trailing wires. A small, white handkerchief lay crumpled by the controls.

The state of the separated sections of the plane gave clues as to the exact point of collision, and which direction the planes were heading in at the moment of impact.

The navigational instruments were photographed immediately they were found and showed the direction from the Gyrosyn compass as 123°. This was the direction the Viscount was heading in at the moment of impact, coming from a north-west sector. The Decca system, the radio navigation system used at the time whereby aircraft determined their position from radio signals transmitted from fixed radio beacons, was also recovered. The findings of the detailed examination of these instruments were crucial in the deliberations of the inquiry panel.

The F-86E fighter jet wreckage was found a short distance to the north of the Viscount and was smashed into many fragments. At one end of the crash area, parts of the two planes were still entwined together in their death throes.

The port wing of the F-86E had broken off and was badly damaged, and only a few pieces of wing tank and aileron of the starboard wing had survived intact, indicating it had exploded on impact. The jet engine was wrecked, its parts twisted and broken. The tail unit was badly damaged but the forward intake to the jet engine of the fuselage was intact.

The fighter pilot's seat lay nearby and was examined closely. The ejection cartridge was still intact and unfired, and there were signs of a heavy impact on the underside of the seat. The pilot's straps and the corresponding inertia reel were missing, and only the right part of the safety belt remained. The left part up to the seat attachment was gone.

This was an important find. The press had been reporting that the pilot, Giovanni Savorelli, had ejected before impact and parachuted into the sea. Careful examination of his seat showed that he was still in the plane at impact and had been thrown out attached to his ejector seat. He did not land in the sea. He was recovered from a tree. He remembered nothing of the impact or how the parachute opened. It was a miracle he survived.

The teams worked late into the night on the first day and a vast amount of information was gathered. They started to piece together where, when and how the crash had occurred, but one crucial question remained unanswered – why? It would take days and weeks of detailed forensic examination before the commission could finalise their conclusions.

Anthony Millward met the two teams on site the next day, and late on October 24 he flew back to London. At the airport he made a statement saying, *'We think it most unlikely the Viscount was off course. There was not enough liaison between military and civil* (air traffic) *controls.'* This was picked up by the press around the world and it quickly became an international story.

BEA had a difficult task on their hands trying to reach relatives before the journalists broke the news, and making sure that the newspapers reported the facts correctly. On October 22 late editions contained errors in the number, ages and even the names of the deceased.

BEA tried to withhold the victim's names until the next of kin had been informed, but this proved impossible. Lady Weir's husband, Sir Cecil Weir was en route between Canada and America and could not be contacted. Other relatives were not at home, or did not live at the addresses given, and Leslie King caused complications because he was travelling under his alias, Lee Benson. For a while some of the press reported that thirty-two passengers and crew had died.

The majority of the deceased came from England and Scotland, but there were two from Ireland, one American, two Canadians and three passengers from Malta. BEA sent staff where they could to inform the relatives or relied on the local police to break the terrible news. It was a race against time. Local newspapers rushed to find anyone from their area and fed information to the national papers to make some money from the story. In several cases reporters got to the relatives first, causing unbelievable anguish.

By October 31 the teams at Nettuno had gathered a vast amount of information and the microscopic analysis began. The position of all the major components had been pinpointed, and an accurate calculation made for the exact point where the mid-air collision occurred. Witness statements had been taken and radio recordings between the various traffic controls gathered. The history of each aircraft was minutely examined and the records of each of the main components comprehensively scrutinised.

G-ANHC was a series 701C Viscount and had been built by Vickers at their Hurn factory, near Bournemouth on the south coast in 1954. The engines were Rolls Royce Dart MK 506 and the aeroplane's Certificate of Airworthiness was valid to December 17 1958. The Certificate of Safety had last been issued on October 12 1958 and all had been in order. The Certificate of Airworthiness allowed a maximum weight of 27,216kg. and it was estimated that at the time of the accident the aircraft's weight was approximately 22,800kg.

There was nothing to suspect in the detailed inspections that a mechanical fault caused the collision. In addition, the Viscount had been chosen for several Royal flights and its service history was impeccable.

Information on the F-86E jet aircraft was restricted by the military authorities, but it was a reliable and battle-tested aircraft. It was based at the main air force base in Italy and subject to strict servicing schedules. Although the damage to the aircraft was catastrophic, it could be explained by the force and angle of impact of the collision, and the subsequent explosion.

The thousands of pieces of each aircraft were taken away to a hanger and painstakingly reassembled. There were many gaps remaining where pieces had been completely destroyed, presenting the investigators with an extremely difficult jigsaw puzzle.

After slow and meticulous detective work, the points of collision on each plane were accurately identified, as well as the sequence of destruction, all of which had occurred in less than a second.

The ground-to-air communications transcripts were poured over and showed that the Viscount regularly transmitted the prescribed position reports at the agreed reporting points.

The precise location of the collision was soon established. There was no doubt that the Viscount had made a small deviation from the permitted air corridor, Airway A1, which followed the coast, and had encroached into prohibited military airspace. This was backed up by eyewitnesses who saw the black cloud that followed the explosion over land.

This evidence was supported by the distribution of the wreckage, especially the trajectory of engine 1 and its propeller after they detached at the time of the collision.

The navigational aids were closely scrutinised, both those used by the aircraft and the control centres, but also the direction-finding stations. At that time, many European countries had problems with their civil aircraft having to thread their way through a deadly obstacle course – a number of prohibited flying zones imposed by each other's military services. This was especially problematic over Italy, with the worst congestion in the skies above Rome.

Here the civil corridor, Airway A1 was sixty nautical miles long and just ten nautical miles (eleven miles) wide with a lower limit of 4,000ft. and an upper limit of 23,000ft. It was surrounded by Prohibited Area 15, (the Approach Control Zone of the Pratica di Mare military base) on the south sector, and to the east. Within Area 15 was also Prohibited Area 18, a thirty-mile-long stretch where the Nettuno artillery range was located.

In 1958, the Viscount carried a DECCA navigation system which was a technically reliable system used internationally, (it was used into the 1990s), but at that time there were no stations in Italy using it. The short-range radio navigation system near Rome (Fiumicino) was VOR, (Very High Frequency/ Omni-Directional/ Range), which the Viscount could not receive. The crew therefore used the ADF (Automatic Direction Finding) system, which transmitted signals from radio beacons, in this case from the Ostia and Ponza beacons.

This was an adequate way of determining position but not as accurate. It relied on the experience of the crew to take this into account in their decision making. On the ground the ATC (Air Traffic Control) staff needed to be aware what instrumentation was being used on the planes and its capabilities and limitations. In a nutshell, the Viscount was using one system, Italy was using another and neither could speak to each other.

By March 1959 all the evidence and statements were in and testing completed. The crucial question was, why had G-ANHC made a deviation from Airway A1? There were three hypotheses considered:

The first was a deliberate deviation. This was quickly dismissed as extremely unlikely due to the unquestionable professional reliability, competence and conscientiousness of the captain of the Viscount, Frank Foster. He was one of BEA's most experienced pilots, with 8,314 flying hours behind him, and had flown this route many times.

Although they were running a few minutes late, he simply would not have taken the risk for negligible time savings. He maintained altitude at 23,500ft. at Ostia and had not begun the descent, which was in the original flight plan. This was cleared by Rome ATC, and it would have been a safety decision, keeping G-ANHC well away from the more congested lower levels.

The second hypothesis was that the Viscount had seen the fighter aircraft and had deviated for fear of a collision. This was based on the supposition that the Viscount had seen the fighter ten miles away, and above them, and in the few seconds before the collision was attempting to leave the airway.

This does not stand up to scrutiny because the collision occurred on the nose of the Viscount. From calculations, fifty-five seconds before the collision, the leader of the formation of jets was approximately ten miles from the Viscount and was about to start the final manoeuvre, the *Chandelle*. In reality, neither of the pilots saw each other before the collision.

The third hypothesis was that the Viscount intended to fly along the Ostia-Ponza airway but had gradually and inadvertently drifted east due an error in navigation. There was strong evidence to support this.

On the day of the accident the wind was very irregular in the area. Strong north-easterly winds were blowing over the coast of the Upper Tyrrhenian Sea, but at Rome they were variable and blowing from almost the opposite direction. The conditions the Viscount encountered over Italy were different to the weather report given to the crew on departure.

However, an experienced crew would have made the necessary corrections in accordance with observations of the local conditions. As we know, the Viscount did not carry

VOR equipment, and the radio compass (ADF) was tuned to medium frequency radio beacons which could give less reliable indications of direction. This too could have caused drift over to the eastern edge of the airway.

In the event of these factors being compounded, the three-mile deviation of the Viscount was possible, and made this hypothesis a distinct possibility. Another vital factor in this scenario was that at no time was any warning given by the ATC to the Viscount that it had drifted into Prohibited Area 18.

After lengthy deliberation a vote was cast by the eleven members of the commission on the three hypotheses presented in the inquiry. Four voted for the first, none for the second, and seven for the third.

The translation of the causes of the disaster was as follows:

The disaster was attributed to a fortuitous and fatal conjunction of circumstances, 'An Act of God,' as the 'immediate' cause of the collision occurred without the pilots seeing the aircraft with which their own aircraft was moving into collision. This is certain in the case of the fighter aircraft; it is presumable and probable in the case of the Viscount.

The 'earlier' cause which led to the occurrence of the accident is the deviation from the Airway of the Viscount which found itself in a Prohibited Area reserved for military activity.

The inquiry highlighted the problems and in the final chapter of the report made a series of recommendations. These covered flying over prohibited areas, navigational instrumentation, radar facilities and pilot compliance. No mention was made anywhere in the report of the complete lack of coordination and communication between the military and civil ATC, nor of the structure of the ATC staff in Italy. As the commission was dominated by military personnel, it is understandable.

In the final recommendation it was noted that during the year 1958 alone, Prohibited Area 15 was flown over thirty-six times, including fourteen times after the accident.

The inquiry's recommendations were aimed specifically at Italy, but the report was a wake-up call to all countries and airlines operating in Europe. Ironically, the crash took place during a week when three international and Commonwealth organisations were meeting to discuss air traffic congestion.

On October 21 a division of the International Civil Aviation Organisation (ICAO) concerned with rules of the air met in Montreal for a four-week session. The following day a two-day conference of the Guild of Air Traffic Control officers opened in Southend, and on October 27 the annual meeting of the International Air Transport Association (IATA) met in Delhi.

There was strong criticism of the airways system over Italy, with numerous and consistent complaints having been received from pilots. These included from Italian pilots who had been fighting for years to improve air traffic control in the country. Other European countries also complained of the deadly obstacle course of prohibited zones imposed by each country's military services. Over the next five years major changes were made in the coordination between civil and military Air Traffic Controls, and priority was given to standardise and update instrumentation.

For want of a few seconds, this tragic accident in clear blues skies over Nettuno would never have happened, but the fatal collision was an accident waiting to happen.

6.

CLOSURE

Early one morning in September 2004, Terry Bannon was on his way to work driving slowly down Northumberland Road in Ballsbridge, Dublin, looking for a parking place. After only a few minutes, he found one not too far from his office, and pulled in. On getting out of the car he looked up and saw that he had parked right outside the Italian Embassy.

The anniversary of the air collision over Nettuno that had taken his father, James, was coming up. Terry had been thinking about him that morning, and his disappointment that there had never been a memorial erected to all those on the flight that had died that day. On impulse, he walked into the embassy and asked the receptionist if he could talk to someone about the possibility of erecting one on the crash site in Italy.

He was politely asked to wait, and within a short time he was interviewed by one of the embassy staff. The official listened sympathetically to Terry's story, made some notes, and forwarded the request to the Mayor's office in Nettuno.

A few months later he received a reply from the Mayor, Vittorio Marzoli that he would be happy to meet Terry and discuss what could be done.

In November Terry flew to Rome with his wife, Nuala, with some trepidation that the site of the crash had been developed since 1958. In Rome they caught a train south and were at Nettuno in less than an hour, and found a charming, medieval fishing village overlooking the Mediterranean Sea.

The next day they were greeted warmly by the Mayor and introduced to Massimo De Marco, a member of the local police force who would act as interpreter, and two firefighters, Arnaldo Serra and Aleandro Petriconi who had attended the crash in 1958. They had helped in the removal and laying of the remains in Nettuno town hall, and still had vivid memories of the devastation they encountered.

The Mayor confirmed that the crash site was still part of the army base, and that it would be possible to see the Commandant to confirm if a memorial stone could be erected. A meeting was quickly arranged, and held at the site. Also present at that emotional meeting were the two firefighters, who had not been back to the site since 1958, and were able to pinpoint the exact position of the fuselage and tail. The Commandant immediately approved the spot for the memorial and asked Terry to put forward his idea for a design.

Terry and Nuala returned to Dublin elated, and they decided to enrol for Italian lessons at the Italian Cultural Institute in Dublin. The warmth and cooperation of the Italian authorities they had received was overwhelming and he set to work. By the spring, he was ready to return to Nettuno with a design.

Early in April 2005 Terry returned to Nettuno with his son and presented the design to the Commandant. It was simple and striking, a sculpture based around the upright tail of the

Viscount that had separated from the fuselage. The tail would be carved from one block of stone and sit on a black, limestone base in the oval shape of the unique Viscount window by local sculptor Simone Vellitri. The plot had been confirmed, and the design was sent to the military authorities in Rome for final approval.

After the meeting, Massimo took Terry to a well-known local craftsman to look at the materials available in the area. Stonemasons had worked in this area for thousands of years, drawn to the famous marble quarries around Rome. They chose local granite for the tail. As soon as Rome approved the design, the order for the stone was placed. The base was engraved with the thirty-one names of all those on board, and an epitaph.

On April 29 2006, a large group gathered on the army base at Nettuno and the memorial was unveiled by Terry, his uncle Bill and brother Liam, witnessed by the official Commissario Straordinario, Dr. Maurizio Alicalandro. It was blessed by the local priest and the ceremony was attended by representatives from the military, the Mayor's office, the press and local townspeople, some of whom had witnessed the accident in 1958. Sixteen members of the Bannon family looked on. Many new friends were made that day.

On returning to Ireland, Terry got in touch with the Vickers Viscount Network, who were extremely helpful. Through their website the first contacts were made with families from those on board, including Sally Dowdle, the first relative of a passenger, Brian Fogaty, a young freelance photographer, and Carol Clifford, the daughter of Captain Frank Foster, who lives in South Africa.

In October 2008 everyone gathered to commemorate the 50th anniversary of the accident, and again in 2013. This time Sally was able to attend. Terry and Sally were keen to find other relatives and let them know about the memorial. On returning home they continued the difficult search for more families.

The 60th anniversary commemoration service was held at Nettuno on October 20 2018, with three more representatives of the crew and passengers attending, including myself and my sister, Rosemary. By Terry's side was his now good friend Massimo representing the Mayor's office, and local villagers came with their families to pay their respects.

It was another moving service with more tributes delivered from the newly found families, followed by another long, animated lunch, with personal and fascinating stories exchanged for the first time. Terry and I talked late into the night, and we decided a book had to be written that would tell the story of every person on that flight.

When we returned to England, I began filtering through the information available, and quickly realised the difficult task we had taken on. I started with studying the official inquiry document published in April 1959, which listed all those on board and gave the technical details of the plane and its history. It was the first time I had seen all the names, nationalities, ages and addresses of the victims. It was a strange feeling as the details of people's lives started to emerge from the mists of time after all these years.

More friends were brought in to help with the research, including Jenny Thomas, Sally Dowdle and my cousin,

Russell Kilmister. They navigated through the vast amount of information gleaned on the internet from census returns, the registers of birth, marriages and deaths, family trees, passenger lists, newspaper reports, war service records, history books and archives from companies long since dissolved.

After a year we had found details of every one of the families, but not always finding living contacts. It was especially difficult when there were no descendants to follow up on.

There was also some important technical information about the two planes in the report which needed clarification, and I contacted the Vickers Viscount Network again for further assistance. I had no idea that there are so many dedicated followers of the much-loved Viscount all over the world. These comprised ex-pilots, engineers, maintenance staff, and enthusiasts of the Viscount. Between them they know every detail of the plane, and help to locate, rescue and renovate old Viscounts.

This led me to the Duxford Aviation Society, who had restored a Viscount 701C, the *Sir John Franklin*, registration mark G-ALWF. It was built in 1953, the year before the *Sir Leopold McClintock,* and stood proudly on display in excellent condition at Duxford aerodrome, near Cambridge.

By strange coincidence, both planes were linked to Arctic explorers. In 1857, McClintock led a two-year Arctic expedition in his ship *The Fox* to find Sir John Franklin, who had perished in the ice in 1847 trying to find the elusive North West Passage. His expedition caught the imagination and admiration of the public, and in 1859, he found various artifacts and a document proving Franklin's death in 1847.

On returning to England in 1859 he was knighted and his crew were given a parliamentary reward, as told in the excellent biography *The Arctic Fox* by David Murphy (2004).

I was lucky to have been given a personal tour inside the aircraft, which was a very strange experience and really brought home to me the reality of the crash in 1958. The layout had been amended slightly but the seat layout was the same, as were the famous large, panoramic windows, (which could be used as emergency exits).

I could see the snug area the two pilots squeezed into, the radio officer's section behind them and the seats where the two flight attendants would have been sitting during take-off and landing. The cockpit windows were surprisingly small, limiting the pilots' vision and they certainly would not have been able to see anything above them. There were some original uniforms hanging up in the closet adjacent to the crew area and I began to feel claustrophobic. I was ready to start writing.

As the stories evolved and developed, interesting connections started to emerge, where passengers' lives had unknowingly crossed. One example was during the siege of Malta in 1942 when four of them were within five miles of each other during the blitz, all surviving to meet together on the plane in London sixteen years later. Fate indeed.

An extraordinary range of stories cascaded out from this small number of people, from all walks of life, in different occupations and from places all round the world.

As Malta was the ultimate destination for eleven of the passengers and the crew, the island was present in many of the stories and we realised a trip there was essential. Russell and I paid a visit at the end of the summer in 2020, when there was a window in the pandemic. With the generous help and hospitality of Roderick Chalmers and Michael Vella we visited many places mentioned in the stories, including the docks around the Grand Harbour, *Blackley's* bakery and confectionery shop mentioned in the Chalmers story, and the Three Cities in the Vella and Lane stories. Also, a visit to the recently opened National War Museum gave valuable and dramatic details of life in Malta during World War Two.

The lives, loves, hopes and ambitions of all those on flight BE142 have now been revealed for the first time. With details of their working lives, glimpses into their family histories and with personal recollections from those who loved them, this tribute can now be handed down to new generations.

For the relatives, the chance to share the pain of loss has been truly healing, bringing good out of this tragedy. This was all thanks to one man in Dublin who made it possible by deciding to walk into an embassy and ask a simple question. The memorial in Nettuno has brought thanks and gratitude from their families, bringing life back to those we thought were forgotten. As the memorial inscription says,

These mothers, fathers, sons, daughters and loved ones
Died far from home, not among strangers,
But friends they had never met.

Acknowledgements

First, many thanks to Russell Kilmister, who has been involved with this book from its conception, helped with the research, including the trip to Malta, and once again painstakingly worked as my editor, listened to my stories in various pubs in England and Malta and deflected my assault on the English language.

This book was possible because of Terry Bannon who has worked ceaselessly since 2004 to get a memorial erected, help find the families, contributed to the graphics, and assembled the large number of photographs into an impressive collage for this book. This would not have been possible without the backing of his wife Nuala and the hard work of his family and friends in Ireland.

Many hours of research was undertaken to produce these stories, and my grateful thanks go to Sally Dowdle, Jenny Thomas, Amy Kilmister, Johnathon Smith, Rosemary Jones and Morag Bain in Australia for their invaluable help.

I would also like to thank Brian Burrage at Vickers Viscount Network, Rebecca Ash at the Duxford Aviation Society, Lizzie Pike and Debbie at the National Gliding Association, Glyn Bradley at the Lasham Heritage Centre, staff at the National Archives, Kew, Russell Muscat at Heritage Malta, staff at Malta National Library and the National War Museum in Fort St Elmo, Pat More and Hope Clark at Claridges, London, and HRH Duchess of Cornwall.

Finally, many thanks to my publisher, James Essinger for

his valuable advice and enthusiastic support, and to Rachael and Nat Ravenlock for their excellent work on the typesetting and the cover.

Many families around the world helped furnish details of the stories and I would like to thank all the following families individually.

THE CREW
FRANK FOSTER

With grateful thanks to Carol Clifford, (Frank's daughter) who I was lucky to meet in England when she was visiting from South Africa. Also to Debbie at the National Gliding Association for the use of archive material and contacting retired members, and Glyn Bradney, the secretary of the Heritage Centre at Lasham aerodrome who checked my draft with the archives. He also showed me the actual *Slingsby* prototype that Frank flew in Spain in 1952, exhibited amongst an amazing collection of vintage gliders at Lasham.

GEOFFREY WRIGHT

With grateful thanks to Grahame Wright, (nephew) and his sister, Deborah Siggery for their assistance. Stuart sadly passed away in 2018, but I was very fortunate to speak to Pam before she passed away in 2021.

JIMMY BANNON

With huge thanks to the many members of the Bannon family and friends that have assisted with this story, all coordinated and driven by Terry Bannon, who could not have completed it without the invaluable support of his wife Nuala.

ROSIE BEVAN

With grateful thanks to Veronica Lewis, (sister) who I was lucky enough to meet and had fond memories of Rosie going back to the 1930s, and for the great assistance of Barbara Ogilvy, (Veronica's niece).

TERRY O'GRADY

Many thanks to my sister Rosemary Jones, my cousin Russell Kilmister, and family friend Pauline Potter. Also to Pat and Molly O'Grady for the many stories they told us over the years who I wished I had asked more questions when they were still here.

THE PASSENGERS
EUGENIE KAWAJA/JANE BUCKINGHAM

With grateful thanks to Rebecca Ash, (daughter in England), Yasmin Pereira, (daughter in St Kitts and Nevis), and Lauren Cundari, (cousin in London) for their help in sorting out the fact and fiction of the tragedy of this beautiful, enigmatic woman.

PADDY WATSON

Many thanks to Roger Kinsella, (nephew) who liaised with the family and sent details of Paddy's life, and found a copy of the memorial service at St Bride's Church.

BRIAN FOGATY

With many thanks to Sally Dowdle, (Brian's daughter) for the time she spent with the research, and her patience going through the maze with me. Also for her liaison with her mother, Hazel, and the Fogaty family, and a lucky meeting with Terry O'Neill before he died in 2019. Sally has the cufflinks that her father was wearing on the plane. His camera was never found.

LESLIE KING/ LEE BENSON

Unfortunately we were unable to trace any of the King family, but Lee would have relished that.

CHARLES AND DIANA CUBITT

With grateful thanks to Gerald Cubitt, who I was lucky enough to meet in Suffolk when he was visiting from South Africa. He attended the wedding of Desmond and Diana, and still had copies of newspapers from 1958. Unfortunately, I was unable to make contact with anyone from the Muckerman family.

WILLIAM AND MARGARET BUCHAN

With grateful thanks to John and Anne Achnairn, (niece of Margaret) from the north of Scotland who sent through details of this very interesting and devoted couple.

MARY MATHIESON

With many thanks to Amber and Alex in the St Johns Norway cemetery records office in Toronto, and Victoria Bohm, who is Mary's great-niece living near Toronto, who sent recollections from her mother, Hazel. They still have Mary's bracelet.

Mary's sister-in-law, also called Mary, lived another fifty-eight years and wrote her memoirs in 2014 called *'Stories of my Century'* in which many of the childhood tales are recounted, and recollections of that wonderful visit to Paris. Sadly, she died in 2016 before we could make contact.

ROBERT ALLAN

Unfortunately, we were not able to trace any of the Allan family, but we were lucky enough to find some details from Mary's sister in-law, also called Mary Mathieson, who wrote her memoirs in 2014.

LADY JENNY WEIR

With grateful thanks to Susan Weir, (granddaughter in Australia) who liaised with and sent details from the family of an uplifting story of an amazing life

FRANCES MILLER

With grateful thanks to Babette Stanton, the great-niece of Sidney who liaised with the family and found photographs long forgotten of Frances, another inspiring woman in a heartwarming love story.

COLSTON LUXTON

With thanks to Julie Thumwood, Doreen's niece, who helped us piece together George's complex and tragic life.

ROBERT BRUCE

With grateful thanks to Bruce Tait from Edinburgh, Robert's nephew, the son of Martha, who coordinated with the family to bring together the scattered memories that remain.

JOHN PRINCE

With many thanks to Christopher Prince, (John's son) in Newcastle for his liaison and valuable contributions from the family for a truly remarkable story. They include Lynda Prince, (daughter in Australia), David Baggaley, (stepson), Sue Trude, (niece), and grandchildren Lucy, James and Jon. Also with special thanks to Kaye Norman, (John's secretary in 1958) who sadly passed away in 2020.

REUBEN SILBURN

Unfortunately, we were unable to trace any of the Silburn family except their graves, and BP were unable to help us. Hopefully there are relatives of Eunice or Hilda who may read this.

JOHN BOOTH

We thought we had found the grandchildren of John Booth in Kent, who were intrigued, but unfortunately it was an unrelated branch. Many thanks to Roderick Chalmers, for putting me in contact with retired employees who had been working at the Simonds Farsons Cisk, and remember Henry Balfour working at the brewery.

ROBERT CHALMERS

My cousin Russell and myself were lucky to have an opportunity to visit Malta in a window of the pandemic in 2020, and I am most grateful to Roderick Chalmers, (Robert's brother) for showing us all the areas mentioned in this story, including the location of *Blackley's,* and gathering the information from the family. Also with grateful thanks for contributions by Mary Rose, (sister-in-law), Anne Chalmers, (sister), Victoria Thomas, (sister), and Anthony Clover, (friend).

ARNOLD DAVIES

With grateful thanks to Scott Pettitt in the Devon Heritage Centre, who found the article in the 'News of the Day at Dartington Hall' which gave a tribute to Arnold. Unfortunately, we were unable to track down any of the Davies family.

RICHARD GOLDEN

With grateful thanks to Arthur, (brother), Vivien, (sister), Muriel, (sister), and special thanks to Grace Cadger. Also to Terry Bannon for his coordination with the Golden family in Ireland.

GEORGE KIMBLE

Sadly, we were unable to trace any of George's relatives. The information on Mr. T. Pollock was found in the *Malta Times*.

SHEILA LANE

Unfortunately, we could not track any relatives of Sheila, but we did find her grave at the Royal Navy Capuccini Cemetery, Bighi, in Malta.

MARY VASSALLO LA ROSA

Unfortunately, we were unable to make contact with Mary's family, but when we visited Malta in 2020, we did find the house where she lived in St Joseph's Road, Hamrun, in Malta. We also know that Renato retired to Malta and died in 1991.

GARTH MARSHALLSAY

With grateful thanks to Nigel Marshallsay and his wife Karen for their generous hospitality in Lincoln. Nigel shared his memories of a special brother and found an interesting assortment of photographs of Garth, and the Agfa camera.

JOHN VELLA

With grateful thanks to Michael Vella, (son), Nicolina Vella, (daughter-in-law), Joanne Bonello, (granddaughter) and all the Vella family still living in Qrendi and England, for their hospitality and stories of John when we visited Qrendi during the trip to Malta in 2020. We were able to visit all the places mentioned, including the St Mary's Band Club, which has now moved into a brand new building, and is more popular than ever.

EVELINE YUILLE

With grateful thanks to Sarah Pethybridge, Eveline's niece, who liaised and gathered information from other parts of the family. A detailed and comprehensive family history archive online has also helped us tell this fascinating family story. There we found anecdotes left by Archibald. There are also two small, uplifting postscripts.

In 1970, Archibald's wife died of leukaemia, and three years later he remarried the nurse that bandaged his wounds in the hospital in France in 1916. He died in Chelmsford in

1977, aged eighty. Every year the Sussex County Ladies' Golf Association holds an annual tournament for the *L. Jerdein Memorial* salver in memory of Eveline's mother, Linda.

| FATALITÀ

The details of the cockpit exchanges and the witness statements of the Italian jet pilots are taken from the appendices of the Italian Inquiry document, which I had translated. Many thanks to Dr. Aniello Palma of the University of Kent for helping us with the translation.

| AFTERMATH

The eye-witness statements of the citizens of Nettuno were taken from various Maltese and British newspapers at the time. The Military and Police statements were from the Inquiry document published in April 1959. The details of the funerals in Malta were from the *Times of Malta* dated October 30 1958

| THE INQUIRY

With thanks to the staff at the National Archives at Kew for providing the English translation of the 1959 Italian Inquiry document by the Italian Republic Ministry of Defence sent to the Ministry of Aviation.

CLOSURE

With thanks to Dr David Murphy from the Department of History at Maynooth University, Ireland, for the details of Sir John Franklin and Sir Leopold McClintock from his book of the biography of McClintock called *The Arctic Fox*.

NETTUNO, Italy

In 2018 I was fortunate to meet Massimo De Marco and some of the officials from the Town Hall and the Artillery Army base that have given Terry Bannon so much assistance over the years. They have included the following,

Town Hall Personnel

Mayor Vittorio Marzoli (2005/6), Mayor Alessio Chiavetta (2013) Commissario Straordinario Dr Bruno Strati (2018) Assessore Domenico Cianfriglia

Coordinators and Translators – Massimo De Marco, Simona Andolfi, Ludovica, Domiziana and Simone De Marco

Army Artillery Range

Col. Ing. Antonio Cuozzo (2005/6), Col. Ing. Arturo Salvano (2008), Col. Ing Antonio Affrunti (2013), Col. Ing. Angelo Assorti (2018), Luogotenente Danilo Sollai (2018), Luogotenento Salvatore Megne and his wife Maria Teresa Cristiani

Police Chief

Dr. Giorgio Tomassetti

Clergy

Don Walter Giusti, Don Luca De Donatis, Don Gino Carlino (Military)

Also to the many kind people of Nettuno who have been so supportive over the years, including the staff who run the fine restaurants *Pizzeria Di Peppone* and *Ristoranti Romolo* situated in the village square. Here you can look up to the same clear blue sky where the tragedy happened all those years ago.

Bibliography

| Books referred to in the text

DUXFORD AVIATION SOCIETY, 2017, *The British Airliner Collection*
KENNEDY, L., 1942, *Sub-Lieutenant, A Personal Record of the War at Sea*
MATHIESON, M., 2014, *Stories of My Century*
MORRIN, S., 2007, *The Munich Air Disaster*
MURPHY, D., 2004, *The Arctic Fox*
OWEN, G., 2009, *The Shepperton Story*
ROGERS, A., 2020, *Siege of Malta 1940–42*
STEPHENSON, W., 1976, *A Man Called Intrepid*
WEIR, SIR C., 1953, *Civilian Assignment*
WOODLEY, C., 2001, *The History of British European Airways 1946–1972*

| Newspapers and Magazines referred to in the text

ABERDEEN EVENING EXPRESS, Oct 23 1958
BELFAST TELEGRAPH, Oct 23 1958
BOURNEMOUTH EVENING ECHO, Oct 23 1958
COVENTRY EVENING TELEGRAPH, Oct 23 1958
DAILY EXPRESS, Oct 22 and Oct 23 1958
DAILY MAIL, Oct 23 1958
DAILY SKETCH, Oct 23 1958

DAILY TELEGRAPH, Oct 23 1958
EDINBURGH EVENING NEWS, Oct 23 1958
EVENING STANDARD, Oct 22 1958
FLIGHT GLOBAL MAGAZINE, June 1958
SAILPLANE AND GLIDING MAGAZINE, Oct and
   Nov 1956
SLIGO CHAMPION, Oct 25 1958
SOARING MAGAZINE, Aug 1952
TATLER, Oct 1958
THE TIMES, Oct 23 and 29 1958
TIMES OF MALTA, Oct 23 and 30 1958
WESTERN MAIL, Oct 23 1952

Papers, Articles and Letters in text

BANNON FAMILY, *Letters from Private Collection*
BEVAN FAMILY, *Letters from Private Collection*
CHALMERS FAMILY, *Extracts from Private Collection*
CUBITT FAMILY, *Extracts from Private Collection*
DEVON ARCHIVES, EXETER, DEVON, *Archives of*
   Dartington Hall
FOGATY FAMILY, *Extracts from Private Collection*
FOSTER FAMILY, *Extracts from Private Collection*
GOLDEN FAMILY, *Extracts from Private Collection*
KAWAJA FAMILY. *Extracts from Private Collection*
MALTAGE 30, 2020, *MALTA: War Diary of a George Cross*
MARSHALLSAY FAMILY, *Extracts from Private Collection*
MILLER FAMILY, *Extracts from Family Collection*
NATIONAL ARCHIVES, KEW, LONDON, ITALIAN

REPUBLIC MINISTRY OF DEFENCE, April 1959, *Report of the Inquiry into the accident which occurred over Nettuno on 22 October 1958.*

NATIONAL ARCHIVES, KEW, LONDON, MINISTRY OF TRANSPORT AND CIVIL AVIATION, April 1959, *Civil Aircraft Accident Report of the Inquiry into the Accident over Nettuno on 22 October 1958*

NATIONAL ARCHIVES, KEW, LONDON, MINISTRY OF AVIATION, April 1959, *Background Notes for the Minister of Aviation*

O'GRADY FAMILY, *Letters from Private Collection*

PRINCE FAMILY, *Letters from Private Collection*

TURVEY J. 1945, *Account of the 85th Mountain Regiment Trek over the Mountains to Repina, Italy*

VELLA FAMILY, *Extracts from Private Collection*

WATSON FAMILY, *Extracts from Private Collection*

WEIR FAMILY, *Letters from Private Collection*

WRIGHT FAMILY, *Extracts from Private Collection*

YUILLE FAMILY, *Extracts from Private Collection*

Other references in the text

BICKERSTETH, E.W., 1875 Hymn, *Peace, Perfect Peace*

YEATS, W.B., 1919 Poem, *An Irish Airman Foresees his Death*

YEATS, W.B., 1938 Poem, *Under Ben Bulben*

Index

About the author

The Flight of The Arctic Fox is the third book Rory O'Grady has written since 2010.

The first was written for the consortium that built the award winning Stonecutters Bridge in Hong Kong that he was part of, concluding a successful career in Civil Engineering management working in the UK, Nigeria, Saudi Arabia and Hong Kong.

On returning to the UK from Hong Kong in 2015 he researched and wrote *The Passionate Imperialists*, the biography of Sir Frederick Lugard and his famous wife Dame Flora Shaw, the first female colonial editor of *The Times* to whom he is related by marriage.

Rory retired to Canterbury, Kent, in south-east England and has started research for the next book.

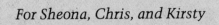

For Sheona, Chris, and Kirsty

ROBERT BURNS

The Kilmarnock Poems

(Poems, Chiefly in the Scottish Dialect, 1786)

Edited, with an introduction and notes, by
DONALD A. LOW
Reader in English Studies, University of Stirling

Dent: London and Melbourne
EVERYMAN'S LIBRARY

© Introduction, notes and editing, J. M. Dent & Sons Ltd, 1985

Phototypeset in 9/12pt Trump Mediaeval by
The Word Factory Ltd., Rossendale, Lancs.
Made and printed in Great Britain by
Richard Clay (The Chaucer Press) plc, Bungay, for
J. M. Dent & Sons Ltd
Aldine House, 33 Welbeck Street, London W1M 8LX
This edition first published in Everyman's Library 1985

British Library Cataloguing in Publication Data
Burns, Robert, *1759–1796*
    The Kilmarnock poems.
    I. Title   II. Low, Donald A.
    821'.6   PR4312.K/

    ISBN 0–460–00343–7
    ISBN 0–460–01343–2

Contents

Preface

What is the unique communicative quality in the genius of Burns which has helped to make his work truly international? The publication at Kilmarnock in 1786 of *Poems, Chiefly in the Scottish Dialect* clearly stands as one of the decisive events in post-mediaeval Scottish literature. Beyond this, though, Burn's poetic fame has gone round the world, so that he is virtually on his own among major poets of the British Isles in being genuinely popular not only throughout Europe and North America, but also in Australasia, in the Soviet Union, and in Japan and the Orient. To date, his poetry has been translated into more than twenty languages.

The present edition of the volume of poems which made Burns famous is true to the original 1786 text, and is the first to be published incorporating both detailed marginal glossing and notes. It seeks to meet an obvious modern need, created by lack of familiarity with eighteenth-century Lowland Scots. My first aim has been to share the pleasure I find in Burns by making it possible for any reader to understand at a glance the literal meaning of the words on the page. (As an alternative or additional resource, the glossary which the poet published with his work in 1786 is reproduced in full in Appendix A.) In my introduction, headnotes to individual poems, and notes, I have tried to provide clear and accurate guidance on some of the many points – biographical, historical, and literary – raised by an endlessly challenging and delightful collection of poems. A Select Bibliography lists further sources of information about Burns and his poetry.

In common with everyone who has worked on Burns during the past seventeen years, I owe a large debt to the editorial labours of the late James Kinsley in *The Poems and Songs of Robert Burns* (3 vols., Oxford, 1968). It is a pleasure for me to acknowledge indebtedness to the scholarship of G. Ross Roy in his revision and expansion of the standard edition of *The Letters of Robert Burns* (2 vols., Oxford, 1985).

The award of sabbatical leave in the spring semester of 1984 has enabled me to complete this edition, work on which has been helped in a variety of ways by the support of the University of Stirling and its Robert Burns Project. My warm thanks for their interest are due to Sir Kenneth Alexander, Principal and Vice-Chancellor of the University; to Mr R. G. Bomont, University Secretary; to Professors T. A. Dunn and A. N. Jeffares of the Department of English Studies; and to our Honorary colleagues, Professor David Daiches and Miss Jean Redpath. The responsibility for errors of fact or interpretation in these pages is of course mine alone.

It was an unforgettable privilege to enjoy the friendship of the late Dr R. S. Gilchrist of Edinburgh, sponsor of the continuing Burns Project at Stirling University. I am only sorry that he did not live to see in its new form a book of poems he loved and wanted to make accessible to all.

Mr W. A. Anderson, Honorary Secretary of the Burns Federation, has very kindly allowed me to make use of a card index to the *Burns Chronicle* (1892 –   ), prepared by his predecessor, the late Mr J. F. T. Thomson; while Mr William Cowan, Honorary Secretary of Irvine Burns Club, has made it easy for me to consult original Burns manuscripts at Irvine used as printer's copy in 1786. For other acts of kindness, I wish to record my gratitude to all those, too numerous to name, who have assisted my research in the British Library, the National Library of Scotland, the Mitchell Library, Glasgow, Stirling University Library (especially Douglas Mack), the Dick Institute, Kilmarnock, and the Burns Cottage Museum, Alloway.

I particularly wish to thank Tina Stewart, of Fortronic Information Systems (Edinburgh), for helping to convert my instinctive enthusiasm for Wang word-processing into practical knowledge; Tony Hewitt and his colleagues in Stirling University's very lively Computer Unit; and – not for the first time – Jocelyn Burton of J. M. Dent, the most helpful and dependable of editors.

No words can adequately sum up what I once again owe in this book to my wife Sheona for her unstinting encouragement, totally positive outlook, and sense of fun. To her, and to Chris and Kirsty, this edition is dedicated.

Chronology

1759   Robert Burns born at Alloway, near Ayr, 25 January.

1766   Burn's father becomes tenant of Mount Oliphant, a farm near Alloway.

1774   Burns writes his first song at harvest-time, to please Nelly Kilpatrick. 'Thus with me began Love and Poesy'.

1777   The family move to Lochlea Farm, by Tarbolton.

1780   Burns is active in founding a Bachelors' Debating Club at Tarbolton.

1784   His father dies at Lochlea. Burns and his brother Gilbert move to Mossgiel Farm, near Mauchline, leased from Gavin Hamilton.

        Reads Fergusson's *Poems*.

1785   Meets Jean Armour, begins to 'puzzle Calvinism with . . . heat and indiscretion', and writes much poetry.

1786   Runs into trouble with Jean Armour's family, vainly tries to forget her in 'all kinds of dissipation and riot', parts from 'Highland Mary', and makes plans to emigrate to Jamaica. *POEMS, CHIEFLY IN THE SCOTTISH DIALECT*, published at Kilmarnock (late July). Burns gives up the idea of emigration, and goes to Edinburgh (November).

1787   First Edinburgh and London editions of *Poems*. Tours the Borders and the Highlands of Scotland, begins to contribute songs to James Johnson's *Scots Musical Museum*, and meets Mrs Agnes McLehose ('Clarinda').

1787–8   Much of this winter spent in Edinburgh.

1788   Burns acknowledges Jean Armour as his wife ('and so farewell Rakery!'), leases the farm of Ellisland, near Dumfries, and is commissioned as an exciseman. From now on, writes more songs than poems.

1789   Begins work in the Excise at a salary of £50 per annum.
Blake, *Songs of Innocence*.

1790   Writes 'Tam o' Shanter'.

1791   Gives up Ellisland in favour of full-time excise work, and
moves to Dumfries. On a visit to Edinburgh, says farewell
to Clarinda.

1792   Burns is asked to contribute songs to George Thomson's *A
Select Collection of Original Scotish Airs* (1793–1818). He
is accused of political disaffection. This charge blows over,
but 'I have set, henceforth, a seal on my lips, as to these
unlucky politics.'

1793   Second Edinburgh edition of *Poems* and first set of
Thomson's *Select Collection* published.

1794   Appointed Acting Supervisor of Excise.
Blake, *Songs of Experience*.

1795   Joins in organizing Dumfries Volunteers. Severely ill with
rheumatic fever.

1796   Burns dies at Dumfries, 21 July.

1798   Wordsworth and Coleridge, *Lyrical Ballads*.

Introduction

When he published *Poems, Chiefly in the Scottish Dialect* at Kilmarnock at the end of July 1786, twenty-seven-year-old Robert Burns believed that he was about to emigrate. Bringing out a book of poems was at once a bid for poetic fame, a poet's farewell to his native Scotland, and an attempt to raise a little cash. Burns's life was in a tangle. There was a spirit of defiance – and more than a hint of desperation – about his frame of mind in the period immediately before and after publication.

Burns's father had died in February 1784, worn out by the struggle to make a living for his family as a tenant farmer in central Ayrshire. Shortly afterwards, Burns and his brother Gilbert took a lease on the farm of Mossgiel, near Mauchline: but poor soil, bad harvests and lack of capital were all against their success. Later, Burns was to comment, 'I entered on this farm with a full resoluton, "Come, go to, I will be wise!" – I read farming books; I calculated crops; I attended markets . . . but the first year from unfortunately buying in bad seed, the second from a lean harvest, we lost half of both our crops; this overset all my wisdom . . .'[1] Then in the spring of 1786 the breaking of his relationship with a local girl made the future seem bleak. Briefly, Burns had wooed and made pregnant Jean Armour, a girl from his own village of Mauchline. The couple wanted to wed, and Burns went so far as to give Jean a document promising marriage (or possibly stating that it had taken place) – which would have been sufficient evidence of their new status in the eyes of the community. But Jean Armour's parents objected to her having anything to do with, let alone marrying, a penniless farmer whose reputation was that of rake and tearaway. The document was destroyed, and Jean was sent away to Paisley and forbidden to have anything more to do with Burns. The episode drove the poet, in his own words, 'into all kinds of dissipation and riot'.

Given this situation of wounded love and pride over Jean Armour, and continuing poverty, it is hardly surprising that Burns should have responded positively – if less than eagerly – to the news that an estate at Port Antonio on Jamaica (owned by a Scotsman from Ayr) was looking for an Assistant Overseer, or Book-keeper. He accepted the suggestion of his friend and landlord, Gavin Hamilton, that the publication of his poems by subscription would help to raise money towards the costs of emigration. In an autobiographical letter to Dr John Moore written in August 1787 Burns explained what his feelings were when he decided on publication:

> Before leaving my native country for ever, I resolved to publish my Poems. – I weighed my productions as impartially as in my power: I thought they had merit; and 'twas a delicious idea that I would be called a clever fellow, even though it should never reach my ears a poor Negro-driver, or perhaps a victim to that inhospitable clime gone to the world of Spirits . . . I was pretty sure my Poems would meet with some applause; but at the worst, the roar of the Atlantic would deafen the voice of Censure, and the novelty of west-Indian scenes make me forget Neglect.[2]

In the event, the extremely favourable reception given to his *Poems* made Burns opt to stay in Scotland. The special pressures of the spring and summer of 1786, which played so large a part in making him take his work to the Kilmarnock printer, gradually receded.

It may be added that Burns had at least toyed with the idea of publication for some time before the Armour crisis decided him on this course. According to his brother Gilbert, he considered publishing his 'Epistle to Davie' immediately after writing it:

> It was, I think, in the summer of 1784 . . . that he repeated to me the principal part of this epistle. I believe the first idea of Robert's becoming an author was started on this occasion. I was much pleased with the epistle and said to him I was of opinion it would bear being printed and that it would be well received by people of taste . . . Robert seemed very well pleased with my

criticism, and we talked of sending it to some magazine;
but as this idea afforded no opportunity of learning how
it would take, the idea was dropped.[3]

The first direct reference by the poet himself to the idea of giving his
poems the permanence of print is in the 'Epistle to James Smith',
written probably in early 1786:

This while my notion's taen a sklent,
To try my fate in guid, black *prent*;
But still the mair I'm that way bent,
    Something cries, 'Hoolie!
.'I red you, honest man, tak tent!
    Ye'll shaw your folly.

Burns's Most Prolific Phase as a Poet

Such was the range and overall excellence of Burns's poetic output
during 1785–6 that it was entirely reasonable that he should think of
publishing his poems. It has been noted that '1785–6 was as much an
annus mirabilis in his career as 1797–8 was in Wordsworth's'.[4]
There were two principal reasons for Burns's surge of creativity at
this time. The first lay in his reading of the brilliantly handled
Scottish poems of Robert Fergusson (1750–74). 'Rhyme,' Burns later
explained, 'except some religious pieces which are in print, I had
given up; but meeting with Fergusson's Scotch Poems, I strung my
wildly-sounding rustic lyre with emulating vigour.'[5] He used an
edition of Fergusson's poems published in 1782; and the evidence of
various references in his writings and also of poems showing the
influence of his 'elder brother in the Muse', points to his having
made this crucial discovery not earlier than 1784.

Essentially, what Fergusson offered him was a challenge.
Fergusson had died tragically young. As Burns saw it, such an example must not be allowed to lapse. Burns was by instinct and by
choice a social poet, quick to catch the rhythms of living speech, and
strongly interested in describing the way of life and the values of
country-dwelling people who shared his background of experience –
an art which he called 'manners-painting'. He found in such poems

as Fergusson's 'Leith Races' and 'The Farmer's Ingle' at once a model and a point of departure, acutely observed socio-descriptive poetry with the potential for being developed further in Burns's hands towards full-blooded satire or explicit celebration.

A second motivating factor was psychological. It seems clear that, following the loss of a strict, respected father, Burns felt a compelling need to come to terms with complex and intense feelings, both of personal liberation, and of remorse at his own sometimes undisciplined conduct. His letters and first Commonplace Book allow us to glimpse a process of adjustment which took place over many months. As a result of this period of inner stock-taking, much of the poetry which Burns wrote during 1785 and 1786 has a new and confident note of authority, that of lived experience. He followed a sure artistic instinct in expressing with extraordinary candour and energy his hard-earned new awareness of his personal and social identity.

Omissions

During his most prolific phase, Burns wrote a number of fine poems which did not find their way into print in 1786. 'Holy Willie's Prayer' is an outstandingly successful verse satire on a named individual, a Mauchline church elder. 'Address to the Unco Guid, or the Rigidly Righteous' and 'The Ordination' are two other examples – the first deftly generalized, the second full of parish particulars – of poems inspired by ecclesiastical attitudes which Burns judged illiberal and worthy of ridicule. Local church affairs offered many subjects for satire; but when it came to selecting poems for publication, he was guided at least to some degree by an instinct for caution. Burns felt that he had gone through trouble enough for his sexual indiscretions, from Kirk Session and James Armour, without risking the loss through legal prosecution of whatever profit his book might bring him. Although in 1787 he was to add to his *Poems* 'Address to the Unco Guid' and 'The Ordination', he did not even then risk publishing 'Holy Willie's Prayer'.

In making his choice for publication, he omitted also all but a handful of the more than thirty songs he had written to pre-existent tunes, including those in a lively low-life cantata, 'Love and Liberty' (often known as 'The Jolly Beggars'). It seems likely that one or two of the songs which eventually found their way into the volume were chosen in some haste – like another category, the epigrams – mainly to increase its length. Excellent individual songs such as, for example, 'Mary Morison', would have added to the appeal of the whole, as 'Corn Rigs' undoubtedly does, but it has to be kept in mind that Burns's aim in 1786 was to provide a volume of *poems*: in that sense, literary convention pointed him in a different direction from his lifelong love of song. As regards 'Love and Liberty', it is of interest that when Burns submitted the manuscript of the cantata to a leading Scottish critic with a view to publishing it in the 1787 edition, the critic in question, Hugh Blair, a Church of Scotland divine, advised against inclusion on the grounds that what the poet had written was 'by much too licentious' to print. Burns then abandoned the idea of bringing before the public this particular work, a masterpiece.

Publication and Reception

In choosing to publish his poems by subscription, Burns followed a common eighteenth-century practice. In this way, an author could take steps in advance to cover himself against loss. John Wilson, printer in Kilmarnock, was the same age as Burns'.[6] He agreed to handle the printing, the responsibility to secure subscribers remaining the poet's own. In mid-April, Burns circulated *Proposals* for publishing by subscription, at three shillings, a stitched octavo volume, *Scotch Poems by Robert Burns*.[7] The *Proposals* – according to which the author had 'not the most distant *mercenary* view in Publishing' – were then vigorously passed about by Burns and by his friends. At this stage, certain individuals were notably successful in helping him. Gavin Hamilton, for instance, obtained the names of forty subscribers, Gilbert Burns seventy, and Robert Aiken, dedicatee of 'The Cotter's Saturday Night', no fewer than a hundred and forty-five names.

Printing of the collection, now entitled *Poems, Chiefly in the Scottish Dialect*, began on about 13 July. Three hundred and fifty people in Ayrshire and neighbouring districts had subscribed in advance for the book when, in an edition of six hundred and twelve copies, it appeared towards the end of the month. Its impact within the region was immediate and dramatic. Burns's first biographer, Robert Heron, describes it in this way:

> Old and young, high and low, grave and gay, learned or ignorant, all were alike delighted, agitated, transported. I was at that time resident in Galloway, contiguous to Ayrshire; and I can well remember, how that even the plough-boys and maid-servants would have gladly bestowed the wages which they earned the most hardly, and which they wanted to purchase the necessary clothing . . . (On a Saturday evening) I opened the volume, by accident, while I was undressing, to go to bed. I closed it not, till a late hour on the rising Sunday morn, after I had read over every syllable it contained.[8]

By 28 August the printer had no more than thirteen copies of the book on his hands, unsold. In the autumn, Burns offered Wilson a second edition. Wilson declined, probably judging that there might be only a limited further sale in the Kilmarnock area. Any disappointment Burns felt at the close of their business relationship did not last long. Wilson and he had served each other well, in professional terms. Burns cleared, by his own statement, twenty pounds from the sale of the Kilmarnock edition.[9] Soon, his thoughts were centred on publishing, without Wilson's help, a new expanded edition of *Poems, Chiefly in the Scottish Dialect*; and this duly appeared in Edinburgh in April 1787. (See Appendix B.)

Comparison with other books printed by Wilson shows that Burns succeeded in eliciting a higher standard of printing lay-out than Wilson's usual. The poet took an active interest throughout: such features as the bold, clear handling of his text, and the consistent use of italics to mark rhetorical emphasis, point to his close involvement. Even more obvious evidence of Burns's determination to reach out to and communicate with his readers is provided by his carefully written Preface, well judged arrangement of the sequence of poems, and helpful Glossary of Lowland Scots. (Burns's Preface and Glossary are reproduced in Appendix A.)

Before long, Burns's work was being enthusiastically spoken of in Edinburgh. A chance incident which helped to make him decide to stay in Scotland took place a few weeks after publication. Dr George Lawrie, minister of Loudoun in Ayrshire, had sent a copy of the *Poems* to Dr Thomas Blacklock, a much respected blind poet from Ayrshire living in the capital. On 4 September, Blacklock wrote in glowing terms about the work:

> There is a pathos and delicacy in his serious poems; a vein of wit and humour in those of a more festive turn, which cannot be too much admired, nor too warmly approved; and I think I shall never open the book without feeling my astonishment renewed and increased . . .

He would see to it that the book reached the hands of Hugh Blair, the critic, and he added,

> It were . . . much to be wished, for the sake of the young man, that a second edition, more numerous than the former, could immediately be printed; as it appears certain that its intrinsic merit, and the exertions of the author's friends, might give it a more universal circulation than any thing of the kind which has been published within my memory.[10]

This letter was sent by Lawrie to Gavin Hamilton, who showed it to Burns. The latter's autobiographical letter to Dr John Moore, written in August 1787, shows with what excitement he reacted to Blacklock's praise:

> I had taken the last farewell of my few friends; my chest was on the road to Greenock; I had composed my last song I should ever measure in Caledonia, 'The gloomy night is gathering fast', when a letter from Dr Blacklock to a friend of mine overthrew all my schemes by rousing my poetic ambition. – The Doctor belonged to a set of Critics for whose applause I had not even dared to hope. – His idea that I would meet with every encouragement

for a second edition fired me so much that away I posted
to Edinburgh without a single acquaintance in town, or a
single letter of introduction in my pocket.[11]

Reviews of the Kilmarnock edition began to appear in October 1786.
In the eyes of James Sibbald's *Edinburgh Magazine*, Burns was 'a
striking example of native genius bursting through the obscurity of
poverty and the obstructions of a laborious life'. In December there
appeared in *The Lounger*, also published in Edinburgh, a long essay
in praise of Burns which was to prove influential far beyond Scotland. Its anonymous author, Henry Mackenzie – whose novel *The
Man of Feeling* Burns prized 'next to the Bible' – described the poet
in a memorable phrase as 'this Heaven-taught ploughman'.[12] The
implication that Burns owed everything to inspiration, and nothing
to familiarity with earlier Scottish and English poetry, was mis-
leading, but in terms of public relations Mackenzie's way of paying
tribute to his achievement proved triumphantly successful.
Edinburgh took up the ploughman poet as if he were her own; and
Burns was well and truly launched on the way to fame. Within a few
months, his poetry was being eagerly read in England by William
Cowper, who wrote to Samuel Rose on 27 August 1787,

> Poor Burns loses much of his deserved praise in this
> country through our ignorance of his language. I despair
> of meeting with any Englishman who will take the pains
> that I have taken to understand him. His candle is bright,
> but shut up in a dark lantern. I lent him to a very
> sensible neighbour of mine; but his uncouth dialect
> spoiled all; and before he had half read him through he
> was quite *ram-feezled* (exhausted).

Then in December 1787, Dorothy Wordsworth wrote to Jane Pollard
that her brother William had recommended the Kilmarnock edition
to her: 'he had read it and admired many of the pieces very much'.

Language and Style

If Cowper had a point in 1787, it is much more urgent two hundred years later that Burns's poems be accompanied by the kind of glossing which is easy to take in at a glance. Hence the translations of Scots words as they occur in this, the first separately published modern edition (as distinct from facsimile) of the Kilmarnock poems to have appeared. Burns himself wrote about wishing to publish his work while ever-changing language and manners allowed his meaning to be understood. Significantly, he included in the 1787 Edinburgh edition of his *Poems* an enlarged Glossary; he knew that even among his fellow-Scots some readers would otherwise be unable to make complete sense of the poems in Lowland Scots. Today, almost all readers, non-Scots and Scots alike, need even quite basic information, so rapid and continuous has been the decline in knowledge of the Lowland Scots tongue.[13]

Burns is at his best as a poet in Scots, simply because it was the language he spoke and heard every day of his life. Originally, Scots and northern English were variant forms of the same language. Never native to the Highlands, where Gaelic was spoken, Scots became firmly established in Lowland Scotland. As used by the poets of the late Middle Ages and early Renaissance, Dunbar, Henryson and Lyndsay, it is a flexible and copious literary language, drawing on a long tradition of spoken language development. The choice, by the Scottish Reformers, of English as the language of religious usage, the Union of the Crowns in 1603, and the Union of Parliaments in 1707, all had the effect of reducing the status of Scots, which in time gradually ceased to be a complete national language. Already by Burns's age – despite a brave attempt at literary revival by Allan Ramsay in the early eighteenth century – the Scots language was appreciably less rich or 'dense' in vocabulary and idiom than it had been in centuries past, and the process had begun of progressive fragmentation into a variety of dialects.

Belonging as he did, however, to an ancient and proud country district, Burns had the advantage of growing up with a relatively strong linguistic inheritance. It probably helped him in his assimilation and discovery over the years of the varied possibilities open to a poet using Scots that while his mother was a native Ayrshire woman, with a stock of songs and proverbial sayings, his father was an incomer from another notably well endowed linguistic area, the north-east of Scotland; and one moreover who insisted that his family acquire skills in the reading and writing of English. As a poet, Burns became confident and fluent in English, although as Scott noted 'he never seems to have been completely at his ease when he had not the power of descending at pleasure into that which was familiar to his ear, and to his habits'. In Scots he is totally at home, enriching the spoken dialect of Ayrshire with a judicious selection of words drawn from other sources, including his reading of Ramsay, Fergusson, and older Scottish poets. He does not need to strain after effect through any parade either of inkhorn terms or of local words, but instead is guided by what is appropriate in specific contexts. The lexical level varies in particular poems according to what Burns wishes to express. One poem which makes exceptionally interesting use of words and phrases he associated specifically with Ayrshire farmers of the older generation is 'The Auld Farmer's New-Year-Morning Salutation to His Auld Mare, Maggie'. 'Halloween' is an unusually and consciously difficult poem, in terms of vocabulary, because the poet has an antiquarian purpose and is deliberately recording as many local superstitions as he can; whereas 'To a Louse' is obviously much closer to the kind of Scots conversational idiom likely to have been understood anywhere in Scotland in 1786.

The poem which opens the collection offers immediate evidence of Burns's assurance and poise in handling language. Like many of his poems – the best-known example of all is 'Tam o' Shanter' – 'The Twa Dogs' is a poem for the speaking voice. Burns derives his mastery of pitch and timing from long practice not only in writing verse, but in listening to his countrymen speak: a finely tuned ear for Lowland Scots in combination with Scottish English enables him to capture the rhythms and idiom of actual spoken usage. Here are the first twelve lines:

'Twas in that place o' Scotland's isle,
That bears the name o' Auld King Coil,
Upon a bonie day in June,
When wearing thro' the afternoon,
Twa Dogs, that were na thrang at hame,
Forgather'd ance upon a time.

The first I'll name, they ca'd him *Caesar*,
Was keepit for his Honor's pleasure;
His hair, his size, his mouth, his lugs,
Shew'd he was nane o' Scotland's dogs,
But whalpit some place far abroad,
Whare sailors gang to fish for Cod.

Interestingly, the only Scots words – as distinct from the Scots forms 'na', 'hame', and 'ance' – which are used in the first verse paragraph are two adjectives, the widely known 'bonie' (lovely, attractive), and 'thrang' (busy, occupied). Yet, such is the significance of a distintive form of pronunciation, allied to the opening reference to Scotland, that the six lines are unmistakably the work of a native Scots poet. ('Auld King Coil', in line 2, is an eighteenth-century Ayrshire insider's way of denoting Kyle, the district where the poet was born.) Burns's exceptionally accurate sense of verbal phrasing is in operation throughout. For example, at the end of the single-sentence paragraph there is a slight quickening and then a slowing up, as casual description ('that were na thrang') is followed by deliberate emphasis ('Forgather'd ance'). It is one of the characteristic signs of the poet's control of his diction that 'ance upon a time' is spoken with a tiny but noticeable stress on 'ance', followed by a pause and then by the throwaway 'upon a time'. Substitute 'once upon a time' and the effect of the last line is lost.

Possibly the best single piece of advice for anyone coming to Scots poetry for the first time is to try reading the words aloud. Burns is writing about 'twa dogs'. The correct way to pronounce the noun is shown by the rhyme with 'lugs' (ears). In the preceding couplet, the rhyme gives another clue to pronunciation – 'pleasure' has a long ee sound. Here the vital information 'they ca'd him Caesar' is presented as it might be in real-life conversation, casually and almost as an afterthought. However, Burns also manages to convey through the matter-of-fact sounding collocation 'they ca'd him Caesar' a very Scottish recognition of the fact that 'Caesar' is no usual name for a dog in this society. There is already a hint, in 'Caesar . . . keepit for his Honor's pleasure', of the reductive power which lies ahead in 'The Twa Dogs'. What a grand name and style of life, the poet implies! He then makes a point of mentioning that Caesar has been 'whalpit' (whelped or born) across the Atlantic, 'Whare sailors gang to fish for Cod' – another deliberate touch of down-to-earth realism, reinforcing the reader's sense of an outlook on life which rejects all mere affectation.

As the poem develops, its language offers many individual clues to what could be called its incremental social meaning, like those mentioned above. Through his sure and varied knowledge of idiom, Burns works cumulatively to build up a strong and entirely distinctive poetic viewpoint on the action, often by creating unexpected groups of words drawn from different speech registers and placed together with ironic effect. It quickly becomes clear that Caesar is wise, friendly, and completely unsnobbish (such are not necessarily the attributes of his owner the laird or landowner). He may have begun life as 'nane o' Scotland's dogs', and now he belongs to a member of the gentry; but for all his exotic and aristocratic background, thanks to his naturally sociable attitude he is thoroughly at home in all the usual meeting-places of men and dogs, 'at kirk or market, mill or smiddie', and at once shows himself ready to spend the afternoon on equal terms with a 'ploughman's collie'. Caesar, in other words, is noble in nature as well as in name, an emperor indeed among dogs through his canine magnanimity. Luath – and Burns's implied readers – listen to what he has to say, therefore, with affection and respect.

The contents of the 1786 volume admirably represent both in scope and in quality the poetry Burns had written by this date. Strongly original satire can be seen at many points: it is to the fore in the genial dialogue between Caesar and Luath, in 'The Holy Fair', a rollicking – and for that very reason, devastating – exposé of hypocrisy in action at a typical Ayrshire convention, and in the disrespectful stance towards inherited religious taboo which Burns adopts in the 'Address to the Deil':

> An' now, auld *Cloots*, I ken ye're thinkan,
> A certain *Bardie's* rantin, drinkin,
> Some luckless hour will send him linkan,
>   To your black pit;
> But faith! he'll turn a corner jinkan,
>   An' cheat you yet.

Burns's 'manner-painting' strain, about which he writes in 'The Vision', is seen in 'The Cotter's Saturday Night', an essentially realistic if also idealized picture of family life among the rural poor (which at once established itself as a popular favourite on publication), and in 'Halloween', where he supplies a detailed narrative account of particular local customs and superstitions. Poems such as 'The Auld Farmer's New-Year-Morning Salutation to His Auld Mare, Maggie' and 'To a Mouse, on Turning Her up in Her Nest, with the Plough', show the generous, swiftly inclusive sympathy of someone who understands that animals deserve to be treated as our fellow-creatures.

Burns found the exercise of writing in verse to a friend congenial therapy. Revealingly, there are no fewer than seven verse-epistles in the Kilmarnock edition. His main literary model in composing these poems for Sillar, Lapraik and others was a celebrated exchange of verse-epistles between two vernacular Scottish poets of his own century, Allan Ramsay, and William Hamilton of Gilbertfield.[14] Just as his predecessors had done, Burns saw the need for those who wanted to write in Scots to encourage each other, as poets, and also as human beings. He developed a very flexible style in his verse epistles, one which allowed for the expression alike of the concerns of friendship, of personal ambition, and of social complaint. His art conceals art, so that the impression created is frequently one of wholly spontaneous, improvised composition:

> Just now I've taen the fit o' rhyme,
> My barmie noddle's working prime,
> My fancy yerket up sublime
>   Wi' hasty summon;
> Hae ye a leisure-moment's time
>   To hear what's comin?

None of Burns's contemporaries could rival such relaxed fluency. Of the major English poets of the next century, only Byron would develop an intimate colloquial style to compare with that of Burns the natural communicator – as exemplified, for instance, in a passage from his first verse-epistle to John Lapraik, in which he dismisses, in characteristic manner, pedantry and the deadweight of learned tradition:

> I am nae *Poet*, in a sense,
> But just a *Rhymer* like by chance,
> An' hae to Learning nae pretence,
>   Yet, what the matter?
> Whene'er my Muse does on me glance,
>   I jingle at her.
>
> Your Critic-folk may cock their nose,
> And say, 'How can you e'er propose,
> You wha ken hardly *verse* frae *prose*,
>   To mak a *sang*?'
> But by your leaves, my learned foes,
>   Ye're maybe wrang.
>
> What's a' your jargon o' your Schools,
> Your Latin names for horns an' stools;
> If honest Nature made you *fools*,
>   What sairs your Grammars?
> Ye'd better taen up *spades* and *shools*,
>   Or *knappin-hammers*.
>
> A set o' dull, conceited Hashes,
> Confuse their brains in *Colledge-classes*!
> They *gang in* Stirks, and *come out* Asses,
>   Plain truth to speak;
> An' syne they think to climb Parnassus
>   By dint o' Greek!
>
> Gie me ae spark o' Nature's fire,
> That's a' the learning I desire;
> Then tho' I drudge thro' dub an' mire
>   At pleugh or cart,
> My Muse, tho' hamely in attire,
>   May touch the heart.

Just as Byron was to attain his full poetic identity only with the discovery of *ottava rima*, so Burns – from early in his career – felt especially at home with the stanza used here, 'Standart Habby'. Earlier Scottish poets had already begun to widen the range of this verse form beyond its original use for comic elegy. Burns carried the process much further, so that it became second nature with him to think of employing 'Standart Habby' in a serious poem like 'The Vision', or in a deftly controlled satire for a particular occasion like 'To a Louse', as well as in verse epistles. 'Poor Mailie's Elegy' shows that he did not lose touch with vernacular literary tradition.

It is easy to underestimate the significance of social as distinct from literary, factors inspiring Burns. With regard to song-writing, there was usually a girl, or a tune, or a joke – quite often a combination of two of these. Immediacy mattered to him. The stimulus came from a wish to please an individual, or rhyme for his own amusement, or match words to a much-loved melody. He wrote a certain number of songs in English – 'From thee, Eliza, I must go' is an example – but his instinctive wish was to use Scots words, or Scotticized English, for Scots tunes; for he had grown up in a living tradition of the playing of Scots melodies and singing of Scots songs. In his first Commonplace Book he comments directly on the suitability of Scots as the language for Scots melodies,

> There is a certain irregularity in the old Scotch Songs, a redundancy of syllables with respect to that exactness of accent & measure that the English Poetry requires, but which glides in, most melodiously with the respective tunes to which they are set. There is a degree of wild irregularity in many of the compositions & Fragments which are daily sung to them by my compeers, the common people – a certain happy arrangement of old Scotch syllables, & yet, very frequently, nothing, not even *like* rhyme, or sameness of jingle at the ends of the lines. – This has made me sometimes imagine that perhaps it might be possible for a Scotch Poet, with a nice, judicious ear, to set compositions to many of our most favourite airs, particularly that class of them mentioned above, independent of rhyme altogether.[15]

When Burns wrote about the songs being sung by the common people daily, he had in mind casual workaday situations, as well as occasions like the 'hearty yokin at sang about' described in his first 'Epistle to Lapraik'. One of the great attractions of song was precisely that he could hum a tune and think of words while out in the fields. Later on, when he was a busy exciseman, hurrying about the countryside on horseback, he would have little time to write long poems – but songs went with him everywhere, because the tunes were in his head. In this way, he was able to fulfil his ambition to bring together the best of Scottish song in *The Scots Musical Museum* (1787–1803).

Whereas in poetry Burns's main debt is to Fergusson, as a songwriter he owes more to the example of Allan Ramsay, who wrote songs himself and edited *The Tea-Table Miscellany*, an influential anthology of Scots songs (1724–1737). However, despite his obligation to a patriotic enthusiast who did much to make vernacular song popular in the drawing-rooms of Edinburgh, Burns at his best differs radically from Ramsay in his approach to the creation of songtexts, being much more vigorous, and less inclined merely to gratify a continuing taste for pastoral prettiness.

One song in the Kilmarnock collection which illustrates Burns's lyrical gift is 'It was upon a Lammas night', set to the traditional Scottish air, 'Corn Rigs'. Here his starting-point is the final song, a mildly amusing pastoral pastiche, in Ramsay's *The Gentle Shepherd* (1725):

> My Patie is a Lover gay,
>   His mind is never muddy;
> His breath is sweeter than new Hay,
>   His Face is fair and ruddy:
> His Shape is handsome, middle Size;
>   He's comely in his Wauking:
> The shining of his Een surprise;
>   'Tis Heaven to hear him tawking.
> Last Night I met him on a Bawk,
>   Where yellow Corn was growing,
> There mony a kindly Word he spake,
>   That set my Heart a glowing.

He kiss'd, and vow'd he wad be mine,
 And loo'd me best of ony,
That gars me like to sing since syne,
 O Corn-riggs are bonny.
Let Lasses of a silly Mind,
 Refuse what maist they're wanting;
Since we for yielding were design'd,
 We chastly should be granting.
Then I'll comply, and marry Pate,
 And syne my Cockernonny,
He's free to touzel air or late,
 Where Corn-riggs are bonny.

Guided by the tune, Burns writes out of his own experience. He turns the situation of Ramsay's song, writes from the male point of view, and conveys an unmistakable sexual swagger. He is a participant rejoicing in conquest, and his song is personal from beginning to end:

It was upon a Lammas night,
 When corn rigs are bonie,
Beneath the moon's unclouded light,
 I held awa to Annie:
The time flew by, wi' tentless head,
 Till 'tween the late and early;
Wi' sma' persuasion she agreed,
 To see me thro' the barley . . .

CHORUS

Corn rigs, an' barley rigs,
 An' corn rigs are bonie:
I'll ne'er forget that happy night,
 Amang the rigs wi' Annie.

Staying close to folk tradition, he has replaced a rather contrived, coy lyric with one which is characteristically jaunty and direct. In this way a fine melody is passed on, and Burns has simplified and deepened the communicative form.

Burns's world-wide popularity owes much to the simplicity of utterance of songs like 'It was upon a Lammas night'. It is sometimes forgotten, however, that his distinctive 'voice', whether in lyric or satire, resulted from commitment to his art, as well as from an immediately attractive personal candour. He is in no sense a provincial simpleton or mere literary curiosity. His is an achieved simplicity: because he had true things to say and wanted to share his ideas, he had worked his way through the traps of poetic artifice which caught so many British poets in his century. Credit for the renewal of energy and simplicity in British poetry in the late eighteenth century tends to be given automatically to Blake, Coleridge and Wordsworth alone, by English and American critics who assume that the use of Scots disqualifies Burns from full consideration. But the dates of original publication speak for themselves. Two hundred years on, the range and quality of Burns's poetic achievement in the 1786 volume seem more impressive than ever.

1. Burns to Dr J. Moore, 2 August 1787, *Letters of Robert Burns*, ed. J. De Lancey Ferguson and G. Ross Roy (1985), I. 143. (Moore, 1729–1802, was a widely travelled Scots doctor and man of letters, with his medical practice in London. His first novel *Zeluco* (1786) had considerable success, and was to provide Byron with hints for the character of Childe Harold. He was father of Sir John Moore, hero of Corunna.)

2. Burns to Moore, *Letters*, op. cit., I. 144–5.

3. *The Works of Robert Burns*, ed. James Currie, 2nd edition (1801), vol. iii, pp. 380–1.

4. John Butt, *The Mid-Eighteenth Century* (*Oxford History of English Literature*, vol. viii, 1979), p. 159.

5. Burns to Moore, *Letters*, op. cit., I. 143.

6. On Wilson, see Frances M. Thomson, 'John Wilson, an Ayrshire printer, publisher and bookseller', *The Bibliotheck*, vol. v (1967–70), pp. 41–61; and Farquhar McKenzie, 'John Wilson, 1759–1821', *Burns Chronicle*, 3rd series, vol. xxii (1973), pp. 1–5.

7. 'April 14th, 1786. / PROPOSALS, / FOR PUBLISHING BY SUBSCRIPTION, / SCOTCH POEMS, / BY ROBERT BURNS. / The Work to be elegantly printed in One Volume, Octavo. Price Stitched *Three Shillings*. As the Author has not the most distant *Mercenary* view in

Publishing, as soon as so many Subscribers appear as will defray the *necessary* Expence, / The Work will be sent to the Press. / Set out the brunt side o' your shin, / For pride in *Poets* is nae sin; / *Glory's* the Prize for which *they* rin, / And *Fame's* their jo; / And wha blaws best the Horn shall win: / And wharefore no? Ramsay.' The only known surviving copy of Burns's *Proposals* is in the Burns Cottage Museum, Alloway.

8. 'A Memoir of the Life of the Late Robert Burns' (1797); D. A. Low, ed., *Robert Burns: The Critical Heritage* (1974), p. 122. On the evidence for and against 31 July as the date of publication, see J. W. Egerer, *A Bibliography of Robert Burns* (1964), p. 4.

9. Burns to Moore, *Letters*, op. cit., I. 145; and cf. letter to Robert Aiken, c. 8 October 1786 (*Letters*, op. cit., I. 57): 'I was with Wilson, my printer, t'other day, and settled all our bygone matters between us. After I paid him all demands, I made him the offer of the second edition, on the hazard of being paid out of *the first and readiest*, which he declines. By his account, the paper of a thousand copies would cost about twenty-seven pounds, and the printing about fifteen or sixteen: he offers to agree to this for the printing, if I will advance for the paper, but this you know is out of my power; so farewell hopes of a second edition till I grow richer! an epocha which, I think, will arrive at the payment of the British national debt.' Wilson's account for printing the Kilmarnock edition is reproduced in J. D. Ross, *The Story of the Kilmarnock Burns* (1933), pp. 59–60.

10. F. B. Snyder, *The Life of Robert Burns* (1932), p. 154.

11. Burns to Moore, *Letters*, op. cit., I. 145.

12. Mackenzie's *Lounger* essay is reprinted, along with the comments of other contemporaries of Burns cited in this paragraph, in D. A. Low, ed., *Robert Burns: The Critical Heritage* (1974).

13. For a detailed account of Burns's handling of Scots, see David Murison's essay 'The Language of Burns' in D. A. Low, ed., *Critical Essays on Robert Burns* (1975), pp. 54–69. Murison notes that 'in his complete works he employs over 2,000 peculiarly Scots words (the average Scots speaker today would have about 500 at the most)' (p. 63).

14. The 'familiar epistles' exchanged by Hamilton and Ramsay are reprinted in the Scottish Text Society edition of *The Works of Allan Ramsay*, vol. i (ed. Burns Martin and John W. Oliver, 1951), pp. 115–37.

15. *Robert Burns's Commonplace Book, 1783–5*, ed. J. C. Ewing and D. Cook (Glasgow, 1938), reprinted with introduction by David Daiches (1965), p. 38.

Select Bibliography

Texts

Poems, Chiefly in the Scottish Dialect (Kilmarnock, 1786). No previous modern edition, but frequently reissued in facsimile. See G. Ross Roy, 'Some notes on the facsimiles of the Kilmarnock Burns', *The Bibliotheck*, vol. iv (1963–6). Recent facsimiles include those by the Scolar Press (Menston, 1971; also prints the poems which Burns added in 1787), and by Famedram (Gartocharn, [1977]).

The Poems and Songs of Robert Burns, ed. James Kinsley, 3 vols. (Oxford, 1968). The standard complete edition of Burns's poetry, chronologically arranged.

The Letters of Robert Burns, ed. J. De Lancey Ferguson and G. Ross Roy, 2 vols. (Oxford, 1985). The standard edition of the poet's correspondence, now completely revised.

Robert Burns's Commonplace Book, 1783–85, ed. J. C. Ewing and D. Cook (Glasgow, 1938); repr., with introduction by D. Daiches (London, 1965). Offers fascinating insights into the making of the poet.

Biography and Criticism

Mary Ellen Brown, *Burns and Tradition* (London, 1984). A study of Burns's relationship to folk tradition, including his role as collector and editor of Scottish song.

Thomas Crawford, *Burns: A Study of the Poems and Songs* (Edinburgh, 1960, repr. 1978). Contains the most detailed critical analysis to date.

Thomas Crawford, *Society and the Lyric. A Study of the Song Culture of Eighteenth-Century Scotland* (Edinburgh, 1979). Shows how Burns's songs were the culmination of a rich song tradition.

David Daiches, *Robert Burns* (1950, rev. 1966, repr. 1981). Lively biographical and critical study.

Catarina Ericson-Roos, *The Songs of Robert Burns: A Study of the Unity of Poetry and Music* (Uppsala, 1977). Valuable for its emphasis on song as an integrated art form.

J. W. Egerer, *A Bibliography of Robert Burns* (Edinburgh, 1964). Aims to list every significant original appearance of poetry or prose to 1802; most 'complete' editions to 1953.

R. D. S. Jack and Andrew Noble (ed.) *The Art of Robert Burns* (London and Totowa, N.J., 1982). A wide-ranging collection of critical essays.

James Kinsley, *Burns and the Peasantry, 1785*, Warton Lecture on English Poetry, British Academy, 1974. Stimulating on Burns as 'social poet'.

Maurice Lindsay, *The Burns Encyclopaedia*, 3rd edition (London, 1980). A useful reference work, by the author of *Robert Burns: The Man, His Work, The Legend* (1954, rev. 1979).

Donald A. Low (ed.), *Robert Burns: The Critical Heritage* (London and Boston, 1974). Includes the first reviews and much early criticism.

Donald A. Low (ed.), *Critical Essays on Robert Burns* (London and Boston, 1974). Considers various aspects of Burns's achievement as poet and song-writer.

David Murison, *The Guid Scots Tongue* (Edinburgh, 1977). A helpful introductory guide to Lowland Scots, by a former editor of *The Scottish National Dictionary*, 10 vols., 1929–76.

Franklyn B. Snyder, *The Life of Robert Burns* (New York, 1932; repr. Hamden, Conn., 1968). Still the most thoroughly documented life of the poet.

John Strawhorn (ed.), *Ayrshire in the Time of Robert Burns* (Ayr, 1959). Valuable sourcebook on Burns's regional background.

Map

Armstrongs' Map of Ayrshire (1775), in six sheets. Facsimile published by Ayrshire Archaeological & Natural History Society.

Cassette

Poems chiefly in the Scottish dialect: a selection from the Kilmarnock Edition read by members of the Irvine Burns Club, Scotsoun (1975) SSC IBC 008.

Note on the Text

The text used throughout as copy for this edition is that published in *Poems, Chiefly In the Scottish Dialect* (1786). While not a facsimile, the Everyman edition seeks to be faithful in its essentials to the original. Burns's carefully revised holograph manuscripts of six poems ('The Twa Dogs', 'Scotch Drink', 'The Author's Earnest Cry and Prayer', 'The Holy Fair', 'Address to the Deil' and 'The Cotter's Saturday Night'), used as printer's copy in 1786 and now in the safe keeping of Irvine Burns Club, have been consulted. Capitals, italics and other features which clearly belong in an integral way to the Kilmarnock edition text have been retained. Single rather than double inverted commas have been used to enclose reported speech and quotations, 'its' and 'it's' have been conventionally differentiated, and minor printing errors have been silently corrected (cf. list by D. McNaught in the *Burns Chronicle*, vol. xix, 1910, pp. 75–6).

Titles of individual poems are given in full in the text. Some have been shortened on the Contents pages, e.g. 'The Twa Dogs' for 'The Twa Dogs, A Tale'. All footnotes in the text are Burns's own as printed in 1786. The letter (B) in the margin of a poem denotes the poet's explanation of the meaning of a Scots word or phrase in his 1786 (or expanded 1787) Glossary.

Appendix C contains a finding-list of poetic manuscripts. Some of the more significant textual changes made by the poet before or after first publication are cited in the notes; but no attempt has been made to duplicate James Kinsley's exhaustive study of early textual variants (1968). It is worth noting that one important group of manuscripts is published in its entirety in *Burns Holograph Manuscripts in the Kilmarnock Monument Museum*, ed. David Sneddon, Kilmarnock, 1889.

Burns's Scots

The marginal glosses which accompany the text of the Scots poems in this edition aim to gloss, on its first occurrence in each poem, every word which is likely to be unfamiliar to the modern reader. To avoid unnecessary repetition, the most common words are given in the list below. Most of the words listed are variant forms of words which are well known in English, but a few Lowland Scots words without equivalent English forms (e.g. 'unco') are included. Burns's own glossary, as printed in 1786, is reproduced in Appendix A, and the poet's use of Lowland Scots is fully discussed in the introduction.

List of Common Words

a' *all*
ae *one*
aff *off*
aft(en) *often*
amaist *almost*
amang *among*
ance *once*
ane *one*
auld *old*
awa *away*
ay(e) *always*
baith *both*
ben *indoors/within*
bluid *blood*
bon(n)ie *attractive*
braw *fine/splendid*
ca' *call/name*
cauld *cold*
countra *country*
fa' *fall*
frae *from*
gae, gaen, gaun *go, gone*
gang *etc go*
gat *got*
gie *etc give*
guid *good*
hae *have*
hame *home*
ither, *other, each other*
ilk(a) *each/every*
ken *know*

lang(er) *long(er)*
mair *more*
maist *most, almost*
maun *must*
meikle/mickle/muckle *much*
monie/mony *many*
na, nae, nane, naething *not, no, none, nothing*
onie/ony *any*
owre *over, too*
sae *so*
sang *song*
sic/sich *such*
sma' *small*
tae *to*
taen *taken*
thegither *together*
tither *the other*
twa *two*
unco *very, odd*
wa' *wall*
wad *would, would have*
wee *small*
weel *well*
wha/whase *who, whose*
whare *where*
why(i)les *now, at times/ sometimes*
yon *that*

POEMS,

CHIEFLY IN THE SCOTTISH DIALECT
(KILMARNOCK, 1786)

THE TWA DOGS, A TALE

'TWAS in that place o' Scotland's isle,
That bears the name o' auld king COIL,
Upon a bonie day in June,
When wearing thro' the afternoon,
Twa Dogs, that were na thrang at hame,   busy
Forgather'd ance upon a time.

 The first I'll name, they ca'd him *Caesar*,
Was keepet for His Honor's pleasure;
His hair, his size, his mouth, his lugs,   ears
Shew'd he was nane o' Scotland's dogs,
But whalpet some place far abroad,   whelped
Where sailors gang to fish for Cod.

 His locked, letter'd, braw brass-collar
Shew'd him the *gentleman* an' *scholar*;
But tho' he was o' high degree,
The fient a pride na pride had he,   not a bit of
But wad hae spent an hour caressan,
Ev'n wi' a Tinkler-gipsey's *messan*:   mongrel
At Kirk or Market, Mill or Smiddie,   church, smithy
Nae tawted *tyke*, tho' e'er sae duddie,   matted cur, ragged
But he wad stan't, as glad to see him,   stood
An' stroan't on stanes an' hillocks wi' him.   watered, stones

 The tither was a *ploughman's collie*,
A rhyming, ranting, raving billie,   merry, fellow
Wha for his friend an' comrade had him,
And in his freaks had *Luath* ca'd him,   odd notions
After some dog in *Highland sang,
Was made lang syne, lord knows how lang.   long ago

10 (line marker)
20 (line marker)

*Cuchullin's dog in Ossian's Fingal.

He was a gash an' faithfu' *tyke*,   wise, dog
30   As ever lap a sheugh or dyke.   leapt, ditch, stone wall
His honest, sonsie, baws'nt face   pleasant, white-striped
Ay gat him friends in ilka place;
His breast was white, his towzie back,   shaggy
Weel clad wi' coat o' glossy black;
His gawsie tail, wi' upward curl,   cheerful
Hung owre his hurdies wi' a swirl.   buttocks

Nae doubt but they were fain o' ither,   fond of
An' unco pack an' thick thegither;   very intimate together
Wi' social nose whyles snuff'd an' snowket;   sniffed, poked about
40   Whyles mice and modewurks they howket;   moles, dug
Whyles scour'd awa in lang excursion,   ranged
An' worry'd ither in diversion;
Till tir'd at last wi' mony a farce,
They set them down upon their arse,
An' there began a lang digression
About the *lords o' the creation*.

CAESAR

I've aften wonder'd, honest *Luath*,
What sort o' life poor dogs like you have;
An' when the *gentry's* life I saw,
50   What way *poor bodies* liv'd ava.   folk, at all

Our *Laird* gets in his racked rents,
His coals, his kane, an' a' his stents: payment in kind, dues
He rises when he likes himsel;
His flunkies answer at the bell;
He ca's his coach; he ca's his horse;
He draws a bonie, silken purse
As lang's my tail, whare thro' the steeks,   stitches
The yellow letter'd *Geordie* keeks.   guinea, peeps

Frae morn to een it's nought but toiling,   evening
60   At baking, roasting, frying, boiling;
An' tho' the gentry first are steghan,   cramming

Yet ev'n the *ha' folk* fill their peghan   servants, stomach
Wi' sauce, ragouts, an' sic like trashtrie,   trash
That's little short o' downright wastrie.   waste/extravagance
Our *Whipper-in*, wee, blastet wonner,   hunt-servant, wonder
Poor worthless elf, it eats a dinner,
Better than ony *Tenant-man*
His Honor has in a' the lan':
An' what poor *Cot-folk* pit their painch in,   cottagers, put, paunch
70   I own it's past my comprehension.

LUATH

     Trowth, Caesar, whyles they're fash't enough;   indeed, troubled
A *Cotter* howkan in a sheugh,
Wi' dirty stanes biggan a dyke,   building
Bairan a quarry, an' sic like,   clearing
Himsel, a wife, he thus sustains,
A smytrie o' wee, duddie weans,   swarm, children
An' nought but his han'-daurk, to keep   labour of his hands
Them right an' tight in thack an' raep.   thatch and rope

     An' when they meet wi' sair disasters,   sore
80   Like loss o' health or want o' masters,
Ye maist wad think, a wee touch langer,
An' they maun starve o' cauld and hunger:
But how it comes, I never kent yet,
They're maistly wonderfu' contented;
An' buirdly chiels, and clever hizzies,   well-built lads, wenches
Are bred in sic a way as this is.

CAESAR

     But then, to see how ye're negleket,
How huff'd, an' cuff'd, an' disrespeket!   scolded
L—d man, our gentry care as little
90   For *delvers*, *ditchers*, an' sic cattle;   beasts
They gang as saucy by poor folk,
As I wad by a stinkan brock.   badger

I've notic'd, on our Laird's *court-day*,   rent-day
An' mony a time my heart's been wae,   sad
Poor *tenant bodies*, scant o' cash,
How they maun thole a *factor's* snash;   endure, insolence
He'll stamp an' threaten, curse an' swear,
He'll *apprehend* them, *poind* their gear;   seize, distrain
While they maun stan', wi' aspect humble,
100   An' hear it a', an' fear an' tremble!

I see how folk live that hae riches;
But surely poor-folk maun be wretches!

LUATH

They're no sae wretched's ane wad think;   as one would
Tho' constantly on poortith's brink,   poverty
They're sae accustom'd wi' the sight,
The view o't gies them little fright.

Then chance and fortune are sae guided,
They're ay in less or mair provided;
And tho' fatigu'd wi' close employment,
110   A blink o' rest's a sweet enjoyment.

The dearest comfort o' their lives,
Their grushie weans an' faithfu' wives;   thriving
The *prattling things* are just their pride,
That sweetens a' their fire side.

An' whyles twalpennie-worth o' *nappy*   twelvepenny, ale
Can mak the bodies unco happy;   folk
They lay aside their private cares,
To mind the Kirk and State affairs;
They'll talk o' *patronage* an' *priests*,
120   Wi' kindling fury i' their breasts,
Or tell what new taxation's comin,
An' ferlie at the folk in LON'ON.   marvel

As bleak-fac'd Hallowmass returns,
They get the jovial, rantan *Kirns*,   harvest-homes
When *rural life*, of ev'ry station,
Unite in common recreation;
Love blinks, Wit slaps, an' social Mirth
Forgets there's *care* upo' the earth.

    That *merry day* the year begins,
130 They bar the door on frosty win's;
The nappy reeks wi' mantling ream,   smokes, foam
An' sheds a heart-inspiring steam;
The luntan pipe, an' sneeshin mill,   smoking, snuff-box
Are handed round wi' right guid will;
The cantie, auld folks, crackan crouse,   lively, talking
          cheerfully
The young anes rantan thro' the house——   romping
My heart has been sae fain to see them,   glad
That I for joy hae barket wi' them.

    Still it's owre true that ye hae said,
140 Sic game is now owre aften play'd;   often
There's monie a creditable *stock*
O' decent, honest, fawsont folk,   respectable
Are riven out baith root an' branch,   torn
Some rascal's pridefu' greed to quench,
Wha thinks to knit himsel the faster
In favor wi' some *gentle Master*,
Wha aiblins thrang a *parliamentin*,   perhaps
For Britain's guid his saul indentin——   soul, pledging

CAESAR

Haith lad ye little ken about it;   'a petty oath' (B)
150 *For Britain's guid*! guid faith! I doubt it.
Say rather, gaun as PREMIERS lead him,   going
An' saying *aye* or *no's* they bid him:
At Operas an' Plays parading,
Mortgaging, gambling, masquerading:

Or maybe, in a frolic daft,
To HAGUE or CALAIS takes a waft,   sea-trip
To make a *tour* an' tak a whirl,   go on the Grand
To learn *bon ton* an' see the worl'.   Tour

    There, at VIENNA or VERSAILLES,
160 He rives his father's auld entails;   splits, estate
Or by MADRID he takes the rout,   succession
To thrum *guittars* an' fecht wi' nowt;   road
Or down *Italian Vista* startles,   fight, cattle
Wh-re-hunting amang groves o' myrtles:
Then bowses drumlie *German-water*,   boozes, cloudy
To mak himsel look fair and fatter,
An' purge the bitter ga's an' cankers,   galls
O' curst *Venetian* b-res an' ch-ncres.   cracks, ulcers

For Britain's guid! for her destruction!
170 Wi' dissipation, feud an' faction!

LUATH
    Hech man! dear sirs! is that the gate,   way
They waste sae mony a braw estate!
Are we sae foughten and harass'd   worn out
For gear to gang that gate at last!   wealth

    O would they stay aback frae courts,
An' please themsels wi' countra sports,
It wad for ev'ry ane be better,
The *Laird*, the *Tenant*, an' the *Cotter*!
For thae frank, rantan, ramblan billies,   these
180 Fient haet o' them's ill hearted fellows;   not one
Except for breakin o' their timmer,   timber
Or speakin lightly o' their *Limmer*,   mistress
Or shootin of a hare or moorcock,
The ne'er-a-bit they're ill to poor folk.   not in the least

But will ye tell me, master *Caesar*,
Sure *great folk's* life's a life o' pleasure?
Nae cauld nor hunger e'er can steer them,   affect
The vera thought o't need na fear them.   frighten

CAESAR
L—d man, were ye but whyles where I am,
190   The *gentles* ye wad neer envy them!   'great folks' (B)

It's true, they need na starve or sweat,
Thro' Winter's cauld, or Summer's heat;
They've nae sair-wark to craze their banes,   hard work, bones
An' fill *auld-age* wi' grips an' granes;   gripes and groans
But *human-bodies* are sic fools,
For a' their colledges an' schools,
That when nae *real* ills perplex them,
They *mak* enow themsels to vex them;   enough
An' ay the less they hae to sturt them,   trouble
200   In like proportion, less will hurt them.

A country fellow at the pleugh,   plough
His *acre's* till'd, he's right eneugh;
A country girl at her wheel,
Her *dizzen's* done, she's unco weel;   dozen cuts of yarn
But Gentlemen, an' Ladies warst,   worst of all
Wi' ev'n down *want o'wark* are curst.   sheer lack of
                                                             work
They loiter, lounging, lank an' lazy;
Tho' deil-haet ails them, yet uneasy;   damn-all
Their days, insipid, dull an' tasteless,
210   Their nights, unquiet, lang an' restless.

An' ev'n their sports, their balls an' races
Their galloping thro' public places,
There's sic parade, sic pomp an' art,
The joy can scarcely reach the heart.

The *Men* cast out in *party-matches*,   fall out, card-contests
Then sowther a' in deep debauches.   patch up
Ae night, they're mad wi' drink an' wh-ring,
Niest day their life is past enduring.   next

    The *Ladies* arm-in-arm in clusters,
220 As great an' gracious a' as sisters;
But hear their *absent thoughts* o' ither,
They're a' run deils an' jads thegither.   all complete hussies
Whyles, owre the wee bit cup an' platie,
They sip the *scandal-potion* pretty;
Or lee-lang nights, wi' crabbet leuks,   live-long, cross looks
Pore owre the devil's *pictur'd beuks*;   playing-cards
Stake on a chance a farmer's stackyard,
An' cheat like ony *unhang'd blackguard*.

    There's some exceptions, man an' woman;
230 But this is Gentry's life in common.

    By this, the sun was out o' sight,
An' darker gloamin brought the night: twilight
The *bum-clock* humm'd wi' lazy drone,   beetle
The kye stood rowtan i' the loan;   cattle, lowing, pasture
When up they gat an' shook their lugs,
Rejoic'd they were na *men* but *dogs*;
And each took off his several way,
Resolv'd to meet some ither day.

SCOTCH DRINK

Gie him strong Drink until he wink,
  That's sinking in despair;
An' liquor guid to fire his bluid,
  That's prest wi' grief an' care:
There let him bowse an' deep carouse,
  Wi' bumpers flowing o'er,
Till he forgets his loves or debts,
  An' minds his griefs no more.

Solomon's Proverbs, xxxi. 6, 7

LET other Poets raise a fracas
'Bout vines, an' wines, an' druken *Bacchus*,   drunken
An' crabbed names an' stories wrack us,   ill-natured
          An' grate our lug,   ear
I sing the juice *Scotch bear* can mak us,   barley
          In glass or jug.

O thou, my MUSE! guid, auld SCOTCH DRINK!
Whether thro' wimplin worms thou jink,   twisting tubes, slip
                                                 fast
Or, richly brown, ream owre the brink,   froth
10   In glorious faem,   foam
Inspire me, till I *lisp* an' *wink*,
          To sing thy name!

Let husky Wheat the haughs adorn,   level land by a river
And Aits set up their awnie horn,   oats, bearded
An' Pease an' Beans, at een or morn,   evening
          Perfume the plain,
Leeze me on thee *John Barleycorn*,   you delight me
          Thou king o' grain!

On thee aft Scotland chows her cood,   chews, cud
20 In souple scones, the wale o' food!   pliable, choice
Or tumbling in the boiling flood
          Wi' kail an' beef;   vegetable broth
But when thou pours thy strong *heart's blood*,
          There thou shines chief.

Food fills the wame, an' keeps us livin;   stomach
Tho' life's a gift no worth receivin,
When heavy-dragg'd wi' pine an' grievin;
      But oil'd by thee,
The wheels o' life gae down-hill, scrievin,   gliding swiftly
30   Wi' rattlin glee.

Thou clears the head o' doited Lear;   stupified learning
Thou chears the heart o' drooping Care;
Thou strings the nerves o' Labor-sair,   -hard
      At's weary toil;
Thou ev'n brightens dark Despair,
      Wi' gloomy smile.

Aft, clad in massy, siller weed,   silver dress
Wi' Gentles thou erects thy head;   'great folks' (B)
Yet humbly kind, in time o' need,
40   The *poor man's* wine;
His wee drap pirratch, or his bread,   drop of, porridge
      Thou kitchens fine.   seasons

Thou art the life o' public haunts;
But thee, what were our fairs and rants?   without, sprees
Ev'n godly meetings o' the saunts,   saints/'the elect'
      By thee inspir'd,
When gaping they besiege the *tents*,   'field pulpit' (B)
      Are doubly fir'd.

That *merry night* we get the corn in,
50 O sweetly, then, thou reams the horn in! horn vessel
Or reekan on a *New-year-mornin*   smoking
      In cog or bicker,   wooden drinking cups
An' just a wee drap *sp'ritual burn* in,   water used in brewing
      An gusty sucker!   tasty sugar

When Vulcan gies his bellys breath,
An' Ploughmen gather wi' their graith,   ploughing gear
O rare! to see thee fizz an' freath   froth
    I' the lugget caup!   wooden dish with handles
Then *Burnewin* comes on like Death   'burn-wind'/blacksmith
60   At ev'ry chap.   stroke

Nae mercy, then, for airn or steel;   iron
The brawnie, banie, ploughman-chiel   bony, -lad
Brings hard owrehip, wi' sturdy wheel,   over the hip
    The strong forehammer,   sledge-hammer
Till block an' studdie ring an' reel   anvil
    Wi' dinsome clamour.   noisy

When skirlin weanies see the light,   yelling infants
Thou maks the gossips clatter bright,   neighbour-women chatter
How fumbling coofs their dearies slight,   clowns
70   Wae worth them for't!   cursed be
While healths gae round to him wha, *tight*,   virile
    Gies famous sport.   gives

When neebors anger at a plea,   neighbours
An' just as wud as wud can be,   angry
How easy can the *barley-brie*   whisky
    Cement the quarrel!
It's aye the cheapest Lawyer's fee
    To taste the barrel.

Alake! that e'er my *Muse* has reason,
80 To wyte her countrymen wi' treason!   blame
But monie daily weet their weason   wet, gullet
    Wi' liquors nice,
An' hardly, in a winter season,
    E'er spier her price.   ask

Wae worth that *Brandy*, burnan trash!
Fell source o' monie a pain an' brash!   severe, illness
Twins monie a poor, doylt, druken hash   deprives, muddled,
     O' half his days;   drunken waster
An' sends, beside, auld *Scotland's* cash
90   To her warst faes.   worst foes

Ye Scots wha wish auld Scotland well,
Ye chief, to you my tale I tell,
Poor, plackless devils like *mysel*,   penniless
     It sets you ill,
Wi' bitter, dearthfu' *wines* to mell,   meddle
     Or foreign gill.   measure

May *Gravels* round his blather wrench,   urinary pains,
An' *Gouts* torment him, inch by inch,   bladder
Wha twists his gruntle wi' a glunch   snout, frown
100   O' sour disdain,
Out owre a glass o' *Whisky-punch*
     Wi' honest men!

O *Whisky*! soul o' plays an' pranks!
Accept a *Bardie's* gratefu' thanks!   poet's
When wanting thee, what tuneless cranks   noises
     Are my poor Verses!
Thou comes—— they rattle i' their ranks
     At ither's arses!

Thee *Ferintosh*! O sadly lost!   a whisky
110 Scotland lament frae coast to coast!
Now colic-grips, an' barkin hoast,   cough
     May kill us a';
For loyal Forbes' *Charter'd boast*
     Is ta'en awa!

Thae curst horse-leeches o' th'Excise,	those
Wha mak the *Whisky stells* their prize!	stills
Haud up thy han' *Diel*! ance, twice, *thrice*!	hold, Devil
There, sieze the blinkers!	spies/cheats
An' bake them up in brunstane pies	brimstone
120   For poor d—n'd *Drinkers*. | |

Fortune, if thou'll but gie me still	give
Hale breeks, a scone, an' *whisky gill*,	intact breeches
An' rowth o' *rhyme* to rave at will,	abundance
Tak a' the rest,	
An' deal't about as thy blind skill	
Directs thee best.	

THE AUTHOR'S EARNEST CRY AND PRAYER, TO THE RIGHT HONORABLE AND HONORABLE, THE SCOTCH REPRESENTATIVES IN THE HOUSE OF COMMONS

Dearest of Distillation! last and best! ——
—— *How art thou lost!* ——

Parody on Milton

YE *Irish lords*, ye *knights* an' *squires*,	
Wha *represent* our *Brughs* an' *Shires*,	burghs
An' dousely manage our affairs	decorously
In *Parliament*,	
To you a simple Bardie's pray'rs	poet's
Are humbly sent.	

Alas! my roupet *Muse* is haerse!	husky, hoarse
Your Honors' hearts wi' grief 'twad pierce,	it would
To see her sittan on her arse	
10 Low i' the dust,	
An' scriechan out prosaic verse,	screeching
An' like to brust!	burst

Tell them wha hae the chief direction,
Scotland an' *me's* in great affliction,
E'er sin' they laid that curst restriction
     On AQUAVITAE;   *water of life/*
                       whisky
An' rouse them up to strong conviction,
     An' move their pity.

Stand forth and tell yon PREMIER YOUTH,
20   The honest, open, naked truth:
Tell him o' mine an' Scotland's drouth,   *thirst*
     His servants humble:
The muckle devil blaw you south,   *great, blow*
     If ye dissemble!

Does ony *great man* glunch an' gloom?   *frown*
Speak out an' never fash your thumb.   *pay heed/bother*
Let *posts* an' *pensions* sink or swoom   *swim*
     Wi' them wha grant them:
If honestly they canna come,
30   Far better want them.

In gath'rin votes you were na slack,
Now stand as tightly by your tack: *leasehold/tenure*
Ne'er claw your lug, an' fidge your back,   *scratch, ear, shrug*
     An' hum an' haw,
But raise your arm, an' tell your crack   *story/scandalous*
     Before them a'.   *tale*

Paint Scotland greetan owre her thrissle;   *weeping, thistle*
Her *mutchkin stowp* as toom's a whissle;   *¼-pint measure,*
                            empty as, whistle
An' d—mn'd Excise-men in a bussle   *commotion*
40   Seizan a *Stell*,   *still*
Triumphant crushan't like a muscle   *crushing it, mussel*
     Or laimpet shell.   *limpet*

Then on the tither hand present her,
A blackguard *Smuggler*, right behint her,
An' cheek-for-chow, a chuffie Vintner,
      Colleaguing join,
Picking her pouch as bare as Winter,
      Of a' kind coin.

Is there, that bears the name o' SCOT,
But feels his heart's bluid rising hot,
To see his poor, auld Mither's *pot*,
      Thus dung in staves,
An' plunder'd o' her hindmost groat,
      By gallows knaves?

Alas! I'm but a nameless wight,
Trode i' the mire out o' sight!
But could I like MONTGOMERIES fight,
      Or gab like BOSWELL,
There's some *sark-necks* I wad *draw* tight,
      An' *tye* some *hose* well.

God bless your Honors, can ye see't,
The kind, auld, cantie Carlin greet,
An' no get warmly to your feet,
      An' gar them hear it,
An' tell them, wi' a patriot-heat,
      Ye winna bear it?

Some o' you nicely ken the laws,
To round the period an' pause,
An' with rhetoric clause on clause
      To mak harangues;
Then echo thro' Saint Stephen's wa's
      Auld Scotland's wrangs.

Margin glosses:

-by-jowl, fat-faced
conspiring

blood

beaten into

fellow

talk eloquently
collars

pleasant old
woman, weep

get them to

will not

wrongs

Dempster, a true-blue Scot I'se warran;   I will warrant

Thee, aith-detesting, chaste *Kilkerran*;   oath-

An' that glib-gabbet Highland Baron,   smooth-tongued

        The Laird o' *Graham*;

And ane, a chap that's d—mn'd auldfarran,   old-fashioned/ 'sagacious'

        Dundas his name.

Erskine, a spunkie norland billie;   spirited northern lad

80 True Campbells, *Frederick* an' *Ilay*;

An' Livistone, the bauld *Sir Willie*;   bold

        An' monie ithers,

Whom auld Demosthenes or Tully   Cicero

        Might own for brithers.   brothers

Arouse my boys! exert your mettle,

To get auld Scotland back her *kettle*!   cauldron

Or faith! I'll wad my new pleugh-pettle,   wager, plough-spade

        Ye'll see't or lang,   before long

She'll teach you, wi' a reekan whittle,   smoking knife

90   Anither sang.

This while she's been in crankous mood,   captious

Her *lost Militia* fir'd her bluid;

(Deil na they never mair do guid,   May they never prosper at all

        Play'd her that pliskie!)   [who], trick

An' now she's like to rin red-wud   run stark mad

        About her *Whisky*.

An' L—d! if ance they pit her till't,   put, to it

Her tartan petticoat she'll kilt,

An' durk an' pistol at her belt,   dirk

100   She'll tak the streets,   take to

An' rin her whittle to the hilt,   run

        I' th' first she meets!

For G—d-sake, Sirs! then speak her fair,
An' straik her cannie wi' the hair,   stroke gently
An' to the *muckle house* repair,   Parliament
     Wi' instant speed,
An' strive, wi' a your Wit an' Lear,   Learning
     To get remead.   redress

Yon ill-tongu'd tinkler, *Charlie Fox,*   that low tinker/rascal
110 May taunt you wi' his jeers an' mocks;
But gie him't het, my hearty cocks!   hot
     E'en cowe the cadie!   trounce, rascal
An' send him to his dicing box,
     An' sportin lady.

Tell yon guid bluid o' auld *Boconnock's,*
I'll be his debt twa mashlum bonnocks,   mixed meal bannocks
An' drink his health in auld *Nanse Tinnock's*
     Nine times a week,
If he some scheme, like tea an' winnocks,   windows
120   Wad kindly seek.

Could he some *commutation* broach,
I'll pledge my aith in guid braid Scotch,   broad Scots
He need na fear their foul reproach
     Nor erudition,
Yon mixtie-maxtie, queer hotch-potch,   confused
     The *Coalition.*

Auld Scotland has a raucle tongue;   rough
She's just a devil wi' a rung;   cudgel
An' if she promise auld or young
130   To tak their part,
Tho' by the neck she should be strung,
     She'll no desert.

*A worthy old Hostess of the Author's in *Mauchline*, where he sometimes studies Politics over a glass of guid, auld *Scotch Drink.*

And now, ye chosen FIVE AND FORTY,
May still your Mither's heart support ye;   mother's
Then, tho' a *Minister* grow dorty,   supercilious
    An' kick your place,
Ye'll snap your fingers, poor an' hearty,
    Before his face.

God bless your Honors, a' your days,
140 Wi' sowps o' kail and brats o' claise,   sups, broth, rags, clothes
In spite o' a' the thievish kaes   jackdaws
    That haunt St *Jamie's*!
Your humble Bardie sings an' prays
    While *Rab* his name is.

POSTSCRIPT

Let half-starv'd slaves in warmer skies,
See future wines, rich-clust'ring, rise;
Their lot auld Scotland ne'er envies,
    But blythe an' frisky,
She eyes her freeborn, martial boys,
150   Tak aff their Whisky.   drink

What tho' their Phoebus kinder warms,
While Fragrance blooms an' Beauty charms!
When wretches range, in famish'd swarms,
    The scented groves,
Or hounded forth, *dishonor* arms
    In hungry droves.

Their *gun's* a burden on their shouther;   shoulder
They downa bide the stink o' *powther*;   cannot endure, powder
Their bauldest thought's a hank'ring swither,   boldest, hesitant uncertainty
160   To stan' or rin,
Till skelp— a shot— they're aff, a' throw'ther,   smack, in confusion
    To save their skin.

But bring a SCOTCHMAN frae his hill,
Clap in his cheek a *Highland gill*,   quarter mutchkin
Say, such is royal GEORGE'S will,

An' there's the foe,
He has nae thought but how to kill
    Twa at a blow.

Nae cauld, faint-hearted doubtings tease him;
170 Death comes, wi' fearless eye he sees him;
Wi' bluidy han' a welcome gies him;
    An' when he fa's,   *falls*
His latest draught o' breathin lea'es him   *leaves*
    In faint huzzas.

Sages their solemn een may steek,   *eyes, shut*
An' raise a philosophic reek,   *smoke*
An' physically causes seek,
    In *clime* an' *season*,
But tell me *Whisky's* name in Greek,
180   I'll tell the reason.

SCOTLAND, my auld, respected Mither!
Tho' whyles ye moistify your leather,   *moisten, throat*
Till whare ye sit, on craps o' heather   *tops*
    Ye tine your dam;   *lose [i.e. pass water]*
FREEDOM and WHISKY gang thegither,
    Tak aff your *dram*!

THE HOLY FAIR

A robe of seeming truth and trust
  Hid crafty observation;
And secret hung, with poison'd crust,
  The dirk of Defamation:
A mask that like the gorget show'd,
  Dye-varying, on the pigeon;
And for a mantle large and broad,
  He wrapt him in Religion.

Hypocrisy A-La-Mode

I

UPON a simmer Sunday morn,	summer
When Nature's face is fair,	
I walked forth to view the corn,	
An' snuff the callor air.	sniff, fresh
The rising sun, owre GALSTON Muirs,	over
Wi' glorious light was glintan;	
The hares were hirplan down the furrs,	moving unevenly forward, furrows
The lav'rocks they were chantan	larks
Fu' sweet that day.	very

II

10 As lightsomely I glowr'd abroad	gazed intently
To see a scene sae gay,	
Three *hizzies*, early at the road,	wenches
Cam skelpan up the way.	hurrying
Twa had manteeles o' dolefu' black,	capes
But ane wi' lyart lining;	grey
The third, that gaed a wee a-back,	a little in the rear
Was in the fashion shining	
Fu' gay that day.	

III

The *twa* appear'd like sisters twin,	
20 In feature, form an' claes;	clothes
Their visage wither'd, lang an' thin,	
An' sour as ony slaes:	sloes

The *third* cam up, hap-step-an' -loup,   hop-step-and-jump
 As light as ony lambie,   little lamb
An' wi' a curchie low did stoop,   curtsy
 As soon as e'er she saw me,
  Fu' kind that day.

IV

Wi' bonnet aff, quoth I, 'Sweet lass,
 I think ye seem to ken me;
30 I'm sure I've seen that bonie face,
 But yet I canna name ye.'
Quo' she, an' laughan as she spak,   said, spoke
 An' taks me by the han's,   hands
'Ye, for my sake, hae gien the feck   have given most
 Of a' the *ten comman's*   commandments
  A screed some day.'   tear/rent

V

'My name is FUN — your cronie dear,
 The nearest friend ye hae;
An' this is SUPERSTITION here,
40 An' that's HYPOCRISY.
I'm gaun to ********* *holy fair*,   [Mauchline]
 To spend an hour in daffin: frolic
Gin ye'll go there, yon runkl'd pair,   if, that wrinkled
 We will get famous laughin
  At them this day.'

VI

Quoth I, 'With a' my heart, I'll do't;
 I'll get my Sunday's sark on,   shirt
An' meet you on the holy spot;
 Faith, we'se hae fine remarkin!'   we'll, entertainment
50 Then I gaed hame at crowdie-time,   breakfast-time
 An' soon I made me ready;
For roads were clad, frae side to side,
 Wi' monie a wearie body,   person
  In droves that day.

VII

Here, farmers gash, in ridin graith,   smart, habit
   Gaed hoddan by their cotters;   jogging, cottagers
There, swankies young, in braw braid-claith,   strapping lads, broadcloth
   Are springan owre the gutters.
The lasses, skelpan barefit, thrang,   hurrying, barefoot, in a crowd
60   In silks an' scarlets glitter;
Wi' *sweet-milk cheese*, in monie a whang,   thick slice
   An' *farls*, bak'd wi' butter,   bits of oaten bannock
      Fu' crump that day.   'hard and brittle' (B)

VIII

When by the *plate* we set our nose,
   Weel heaped up wi' ha'pence,
A greedy glowr *black-bonnet* throws,
   An' we maun draw our tippence.   twopence
Then in we go to see the show,
   On ev'ry side they're gath'ran;
70   Some carryan dails, some chairs an' stools,   deal planks
   An' some are busy bleth'ran   chatting hard
      Right loud that day.

IX

Here stands a shed to fend the showr's,
   An' screen our countra Gentry;
There, *racer Jess*, an' twathree wh—res,   two or three
   Are blinkan at the entry.
Here sits a raw o' tittlan jads,   row, gossiping hussies
   Wi' heaving breasts an' bare neck;
An' there, a batch o' *Wabster lads*,   weaver
80   Blackguarding frae K*******ck   roistering, [Kilmarnock]
      For *fun* this day.

X

Here, some are thinkan on their sins,
   An' some upo' their claes;
Ane curses feet that fyl'd his shins,   fouled
   Anither sighs an' prays:

On this hand sits an *Elect* swatch,   sample
    Wi' screw'd-up, grace-proud faces;   sanctimonious
On that, a set o' chaps, at watch,
    Thrang winkan on the lasses   throng
90   To *chairs* that day.

XI

O happy is that man, an' blest!
    Nae wonder that it pride him!
Whase ain dear lass, that he likes best,   own
    Comes clinkan down beside him!   sitting smartly
Wi' arm repos'd on the *chair-back*,
    He sweetly does compose him;
Which, by degrees, slips round her *neck*
    An's loof upon her *bosom*   palm
         Unkend that day.   unknown

XII

100 Now a' the congregation o'er
    Is silent expectation;
For ****** speels the holy door,   [Moodie] climbs
    Wi' tidings o' s—lv—t—n.
Should *Hornie*, as in ancient days,   Satan
    'Mang sons o' G— present him,
The vera sight o' ******'s face,
    To's ain *het hame* had sent him   hot home [Hell]
         Wi' fright that day.

XIII

Hear how he clears the points o' Faith
110   Wi' rattlin an' thumpin!
Now meekly calm, now wild in wrath,
    He's stampan, an' he's jumpan!
His lengthen'd chin, his turn'd up snout,
    His eldritch squeel an' gestures,   hideous
O how they fire the heart devout,
    Like *cantharidian* plaisters
         On sic a day!

XIV

But hark! the *tent* has chang'd its voice;   'field pulpit' (B)
   There's peace an' rest nae langer;
120 For a' the *real judges* rise,
   They canna sit for anger.
***** opens out his cauld harangues,   [Smith]
   On *practice* and on *morals*;
An' aff the *godly* pour in thrangs,
   To gie the jars an' barrels
      A lift that day.

XV

What signifies his barren shine,
   Of *moral pow'rs* an' *reason*?
His English style, an' gesture fine,
130 Are a' clean out o' season.
Like SOCRATES or ANTONINE,
   Or some auld pagan heathen,
The *moral man* he does define,
   But ne'er a word o' *faith* in
      That's right that day.

XVI

In guid time comes an antidote
   Against sic poosion'd nostrum;   poisoned remedy
For *******, frae the water-fit,   [Peebles], river-mouth
   Ascends the *holy rostrum*:
140 See, up he's got the word o' G—,
   An' meek an' mim has view'd it,   demure
While COMMON-SENSE has taen the road,
   An' aff, an' up the *Cowgate*
      Fast, fast that day.

XVII

Wee ****** niest the Guard relieves,   [Miller], next
   An' Orthodoxy raibles,   gabbles
Tho' in his heart he weel believes,
   An' thinks it auld wives' fables:

But faith! the birkie wants a *Manse*,   fellow
150   So, cannilie he hums them;   dextrously, takes
      Altho' his *carnal* Wit an' Sense   them in
        Like hafflins-wise o'ercomes him   in half measure/
          At times that day.   partly

XVIII

Now, butt an' ben, the Change-house fills,   in outer and inner
    Wi' *yill-caup* Commentators: room, tavern
Here's crying out for bakes an' gills,   ale-cup
    An' there the pint-stowp clatters;   biscuits, drams
While thick an' thrang, an' loud an' lang,   -measure
    Wi' *Logic*, an' wi' *Scripture*,   closely engaged
160 They raise a din, that, in the end,   together
      Is like to breed a rupture
        O' wrath that day.

XIX

Leeze me on Drink! it gies us mair   I'm all for
    Than either School or Colledge:
It kindles Wit, it waukens Lear,   wakens Learning
    It pangs us fou o' Knowledge.   stuffs, full
Be't *whisky-gill* or *penny-wheep*,   small beer
    Or ony stronger potion,
It never fails, on drinkin deep,
170   To kittle up our *notion*,   rouse, fancy
      By night or day.

XX

The lads an' lasses, blythely bent
    To mind baith *saul* an' *body*,   soul
Sit round the table, weel content,
    An' steer about the *toddy*.   whisky, hot water
On this ane's dress, an' that ane's leuk,   and sugar
    They're makin observations;   expression
While some are cozie i' the neuk,
    An' forming *assignations*   corner
180   To meet some day.

XXI

But now the L—'s ain trumpet touts,   blasts
   Till a' the hills are rairan,   roaring
An' echoes back return the shouts;
   Black ****** is na spairan: [Russel], sparing
His piercin words, like Highlan swords,
   Divide the joints an' marrow;
His talk o' H—ll, whare devils dwell,
   Our vera *'Sauls does harrow'
      Wi' fright that day!

XXII

190 A vast, unbottom'd, boundless *Pit*,
   Fill'd fou o' *lowan brunstane*,   blazing brimstone
Whase raging flame, an' scorching heat,
   Wad melt the hardest whun-stane!   whinstone
The *half asleep* start up wi' fear,
   An' think they hear it roaran,
When presently it does appear,
   'Twas but some neebor *snoran*   neighbour snoring
      Asleep that day.

XXIII

'Twad be owre lang a tale to tell,
200   How monie stories past,
An' how they crouded to the yill,   crowded, ale
   When they were a' dismist:
How drink gaed round, in cogs an' caups, dishes, bowls
   Amang the furms an' benches;   forms
An' *cheese* an' *bread*, frae women's laps,
   Was dealt about in lunches,
      An' dawds that day.   hunks

*Shakespeare's Hamlet

XXIV

In comes a gawsie, gash *Guidwife*,   jovial, neat matron
  An' sits down by the fire,
210 Syne draws her *kebbuk* an' her knife;   then, cheese
  The lasses they are shyer.
The auld *Guidmen*, about the *grace*,   husbands
  Frae side to side they bother,
Till some ane by his bonnet lays,
  An' gies them't, like a *tether*,   rope
    Fu' lang that day.   very

XXV

Waesucks! for him that gets nae lass,   alas
  Or lasses that hae naething!
Sma' need has he to say a grace,
220 Or melvie his braw claithing!   'soil with meal' (B), clothing
O *Wives* be mindfu', ance yoursel,
  How bonie lads ye wanted,
An' dinna, for a *kebbuck-heel*,   do not, heel of cheese
  Let lasses be affronted
    On sic a day!

XXVI

Now *Clinkumbell*, wi' rattlan tow,   bellringer, rope
  Begins to jow an' croon;   toll and sound
Some swagger hame, the best they dow,   are able
  Some wait the afternoon.
230 At slaps the billies halt a blink,   gaps in dyke, fellows
  Till lasses strip their shoon: shoes
Wi' *faith* an' *hope*, an' *love* an' *drink*,
  They're a' in famous tune
    For crack that day.   chat

XXVII

How monie hearts this day converts,
  O' sinners and o' Lasses!
Their hearts o' stane, gin night are gane,   stone, by nightfall, gone
  As saft as ony flesh is.   soft

There's some are fou o' *love divine*;
240   There's some are fou o' *brandy*;
An' monie jobs that day begin,   intrigues
    May end in *Houghmagandie*   fornication
        Some ither day.

ADDRESS TO THE DEIL

O Prince , O chief of many throned pow'rs,
That led th'embattl'd Seraphim to war —

                Milton

O THOU, whatever title suit thee!
Auld Hornie, Satan, Nick, or Clootie,   Cloven-hoof
Wha in yon cavern grim an' sootie,
    Clos'd under hatches,
Spairges about the brunstane cootie,   bespatters,
                      brimstone tub
    To scaud poor wretches!   scald

Hear me, *auld Hangie*, for a wee,   Hangman
An' let poor, *damned bodies* bee;
I'm sure sma' pleasure it can gie,
10   Ev'n to a *deil*,   devil
To skelp an' scaud poor dogs like me,   smack
    An' hear us squeel!

Great is thy pow'r, an' great thy fame;
Far kend an' noted is thy name;
An' tho' yon *lowan heugh's* thy hame,   blazing pit
    Thou travels far;
An' faith! thou's neither lag nor lame,   backward
    Nor blate nor scaur.   bashful, afraid

Whyles, ranging like a roaran lion,
20 For prey, a' holes an' corners tryin;
Whyles, on the strong-wing'd Tempest flyin,
          Tirlan the *kirks*;   uncovering,
                                                 churches
Whyles, in the human bosom pryin,
          Unseen thou lurks.

I've heard my rev'rend *Graunie* say,   grandmother
In lanely glens ye like to stray;   lonely
Or where auld, ruin'd castles, gray,
          Nod to the moon,
Ye fright the nightly wand'rer's way,
30   Wi' eldritch croon.   unearthly moan

When twilight did my *Graunie* summon,
To say her pray'rs, douse, honest woman!   sober
Aft 'yont the dyke she's heard you bumman,   behind, wall,
                                               humming
          Wi' eerie drone;
Or, rustling, thro' the boortries coman,   elder trees
          Wi' heavy groan.

Ae dreary, windy, winter night,
The stars shot down wi' sklentan light,   slanting
Wi' you, *mysel*, I gat a fright,
40   Ayont the lough;   beyond, loch
Ye, like a *rash-buss*, stood in sight,   clump of rushes
          Wi' waving sugh.   sound of wind

The cudgel in my neive did shake,   fist
Each bristl'd hair stood like a stake,
When wi' an eldritch, stoor *quaick, quaick*, harsh
          Amang the springs,
Awa ye squatter'd like a *drake*,   'flutter in water' (B)
          On whistling wings.

Let *Warlocks* grim, an' wither'd *Hags*,
50 Tell how wi' you on ragweed nags,   ragwort
They skim the muirs an' dizzy crags,   moors

Wi' wicked speed;
And in kirk-yards renew their leagues,
    Owre howcket dead.   *exhumed*

Thence, countra wives, wi' toil an' pain,
May plunge an' plunge the *kirn* in vain;   *churn*
For Oh! the yellow treasure's taen
    By witching skill;
An' dawtet, twal-pint *Hawkie's* gane   *spoiled, twelve-,*
60   As yell's the Bill.   *cow / milkless as, bull*

Thence, mystic knots mak great abuse,
On *Young-Guidmen*, fond, keen an' croose;   *-husbands,*
When the best *wark-lume* i' the house,   *confident / work-loom*
    By cantraip wit,   *magic*
Is instant made no worth a louse,
    Just at the bit.   *critical moment*

When thowes dissolve the snawy hoord,   *thaws, snowy drift*
An' float the jinglan icy boord,   *(on), cracking,*
Then, *Water-kelpies* haunt the foord,   *surface / waterhorse*
70   By your direction,   *demons, ford*
An' nighted Trav'llers are allur'd
    To their destruction.

An' aft your moss-traversing *Spunkies*   *wills o' the wisp*
Decoy the wight that late an' drunk is:
The bleezan, curst, mischievous monkies   *blazing*
    Delude his eyes,
Till in some miry slough he sunk is,
    Ne'er mair to rise.

When MASONS' mystic *word* an' *grip*,
80 In storms an' tempests raise you up,
Some cock or cat, your rage maun stop,
    Or, strange to tell!
The *youngest Brother* ye wad whip
    Aff straught to *H—ll*.   *straight*

Lang syne in EDEN's bonie yard,   long ago, garden
When youthfu' lovers first were pair'd,
An' all the Soul of Love they shar'd,
   The raptur'd hour,
Sweet on the fragrant, flow'ry swaird, sward
90   In shady bow'r.

Then you, ye auld, snick-drawing dog! latch-
Ye cam to Paradise incog,   unknown
An' play'd on man a cursed brogue, trick
   (Black be your fa'!)
An' gied the infant warld a shog, world, shock
   'Maist ruin'd a'.

D'ye mind that day, when in a bizz, remember, stir
Wi' reeket duds, an' reestet gizz, smoky clothes, 'cured' wig
Ye did present your smoutie phiz, ugly face
100   'Mang better folk,
An' sklented on the *man of Uzz*, directed aslant
   Your spitefu' joke?

An how ye gat him i' your thrall,
An' brak him out o' house an' hal',
While scabs an' botches did him gall, 'angry tumours' (B)
   Wi' bitter claw,   scratching
An' lows'd his ill-tongu'd, wicked *Scawl* loosed, abusive woman
   Was warst ava?   worst of all

But a' your doings to rehearse,
110 Your wily snares an' fechtin fierce, fighting
Sin' that day *MICHAEL did you pierce,
   Down to this time,
Wad ding a' *Lallan* tongue, or *Erse*, weary, Lowland, Gaelic
   In Prose or Rhyme.

*Vide Milton, Book 6th

An' now, auld *Cloots*, I ken ye're thinkan,
A certain *Bardie's* rantin, drinkin,   poet
Some luckless hour will send him linkan,   going briskly
        To your black pit;
But faith! he'll turn a corner jinkan,   side-stepping
120   An' cheat you yet.

But fare-you-weel, auld *Nickie-ben*!
O wad ye tak a thought an' men'!   and mend
Ye aiblins might – I dinna ken –   perhaps
        Still hae a *stake* –   chance
I'm wae to think upo' yon den,   unhappy
        Ev'n for your sake!

The Death and Dying Words of
POOR MAILIE,
The Author's Only Pet Yowe,
An Unco Mournfu' Tale

As MAILIE, an' her lambs thegither,
Was ae day nibbling on the tether,
Upon her cloot she coost a hitch,   hoof, cast
An' owre she warsl'd in the ditch: struggled
There, groaning, dying, she did ly,
When *Hughoc he cam doytan by.   blundering

    Wi' glowrin een, an' lifted han's,   eyes, hands
Poor *Hughoc* like a statue stan's;
He saw her days were near hand ended,   almost
10   But, waes my heart! he could na mend it!   woe is
He gaped wide, but naething spak,   spoke
At length poor *Mailie* silence brak.   broke

*A neibor herd-callan.

'O thou, whase lamentable face
Appears to mourn my woefu' case!
My *dying words* attentive hear,
An' bear them to my *Master* dear.

'Tell him, if e'er again he keep
As muckle gear as buy a *sheep*,   money
O, bid him never tye them mair,
20   Wi' wicked strings o' hemp or hair!
But ca them out to park or hill,
An' let them wander at their will:
So, may his flock increase an' grow
To *scores* o' lambs, an' *packs* of woo'!   wool

'Tell him, he was a Master kin',   kindly
An' ay was guid to me an' mine;
An' now my *dying* charge I gie him,
My helpless *lambs*, I trust them wi' him.

'O, bid him save their harmless lives,
30   Frae dogs an' tods, an' butchers' knives!   foxes
But gie them guid *cow-milk* their fill,
Till they be fit to fend themsel;
An' tent them duely, e'en an' morn,   tend
Wi' taets o' *hay* an' ripps o' *corn*.   tufts, handfuls

'An' may they never learn the gaets,   ways
Of ither vile, wanrestfu' *Pets*!   restless
To slink thro' slaps, an' reave an' steal,   gaps, plunder
At stacks o' pease, or stocks o' kail.   green kale
So may they, like their great *forbears*,
40   For monie a year come thro' the sheers:
So *wives* will gie them bits o' bread,
An' *bairns* greet for them when they're dead.   weep

'My poor *toop-lamb*, my son an' heir,   ram-
O, bid him breed him up wi' care!
An' if he live to be a beast,
To pit some havins in his breast!   put, sense

An' warn him ay at riding time,
To stay content wi' *yowes* at hame;
An' no to rin an' wear his cloots,   run, hooves
50 Like ither menseless, graceless brutes.   ill-bred, senseless

   'An' niest my *yowie*, silly thing,   next, young ewe
Gude keep thee frae a *tether string*!
O, may thou ne'er forgather up,
Wi' onie blastet, moorlan *toop*;   accursed, ram
But ay keep mind to moop an' mell,   nibble, mix
Wi' sheep o' credit like thysel!

   'And now, *my bairns*, wi' my last breath,
I lea'e my blessin wi' you baith:
An' when ye think upo' your Mither,   mother
60 Mind to be kind to ane anither.   remember

   'Now, honest Hughoc, dinna fail,   don't
To tell my Master a' my tale;
An' bid him burn this cursed *tether*,
An' for thy pains thou'se get my blather.'   you will, bladder

   This said, poor *Mailie* turn'd her head,
An' clos'd her een amang the dead!

POOR MAILIE'S ELEGY

LAMENT in rhyme, lament in prose,
Wi' saut tears trickling down your nose;   salt
Our *Bardie's* fate is at a close,   poet's
        Past a' remead!   cure
The last, sad cape-stane of his woes;   coping-stone
        Poor Mailie's dead!

It's no the loss o' warl's gear,   worldly property
That could sae bitter draw the tear,
Or make our *Bardie*, dowie, wear   sad
10   The mourning weed:
He's lost a friend and neebor dear,   neighbour
          In *Mailie* dead.

Thro' a' the town she trotted by him;   village/farm
A lang half-mile she could descry him;
Wi' kindly bleat, when she did spy him,
          She ran wi' speed:
A friend mair faithfu' ne'er came nigh him,
          Than *Mailie* dead.

I wat she was a *sheep* o' sense,   know
20   An' could behave hersel wi' mense: discretion
I'll say't, she never brak a fence,   broke
          Thro' thievish greed.
Our *Bardie*, lanely, keeps the spence,   lonely, inner room
          Sin' *Mailie's* dead.

Or, if he wanders up the howe,   valley
Her living image in *her yowe*,   ewe
Comes bleating till him, owre the knowe,   to
          For bits o' bread;
An' down the briny pearls rowe   roll
30   For *Mailie* dead.

She was nae get o' moorlan tips,   offspring, tups
Wi' tauted ket, an' hairy hips;   matted fleece
For her forbears were brought in ships,
          Frae 'yont the TWEED: beyond
A bonier *fleesh* ne'er cross'd the clips   fleece, shears
          Than *Mailie's* dead.

Wae worth that man wha first did shape,   woe to
That vile, wanchancie thing – *a raep*!   unlucky, rope
It maks guid fellows girn an' gape,   'twist the features
                                                in rage' (B)

40   Wi' chokin dread;
    An' *Robins's* bonnet wave wi' crape
         For *Mailie* dead.

    O, a' ye *Bards* on bonie DOON!
    An' wha on AIRE your chanters tune!
    Come, join the melancholious croon   moan
         O' *Robin*'s reed!
    His heart will never get aboon!   above
         His *Mailie's* dead!

TO J. S****

Friendship, mysterious cement of the soul!
Sweet'ner of Life, and solder of Society!
I owe thee much——

                         Blair

    DEAR S****, the sleest, pawkie thief,   cleverest, humorous
    That e'er attempted stealth or rief,   plunder
    Ye surely hae some warlock-breef   charm/wizard-spell
         Owre human hearts;
    For ne'er a bosom yet was prief   proof
         Against your arts.

    For me, I swear by sun an' moon,
    And ev'ry star that blinks aboon,   above
    Ye've cost me twenty pair o' shoon   shoes
10   Just gaun to see you;
    And ev'ry ither pair that's done,
         Mair taen I'm wi' you.

    That auld, capricious carlin, *Nature*,   old woman
    To mak amends for scrimpet stature,   stunted
    She's turn'd you off, a human-creature

On her *first* plan,
And in her freaks, on ev'ry feature,
She's wrote, *the Man*.

Just now I've taen the fit o' rhyme,
20 My barmie noddle's working prime,   *yeasty brain*
  My fancy yerket up sublime   *stirred*
    Wi' hasty summon:
Hae ye a leisure-moment's time
    To hear what's coming?

Some rhyme a neebor's name to lash;   *neighbour*
Some rhyme, (vain thought!) for needfu' cash;
Some rhyme to court the countra clash,   *invite, talk*
    An' raise a din;
For me, an *aim* I never fash;   *bother about*
30   I rhyme for *fun*.

The star that rules my luckless lot,
Has fated me the russet coat,   *poor man's rural wear*
An' damn'd my fortune to the groat;   *small coin*
    But, in requit,   *by way of compensation*
Has blest me with a *random-shot*
    O' countra wit.

This while my notion's taen a sklent,   *slant/turn*
To try my fate in guid, black *prent*;   *print*
But still the mair I'm that way bent,
40   Something cries, 'hoolie!   *'take leisure, stop!' (B)*
I red you, honest man, tak tent!   *advise, take care*
    Ye'll shaw your folly.   *show*

'There's ither Poets, much your betters,
Far seen in *Greek*, deep men o' *letters*,   *well-versed*
Hae thought they had ensur'd their debtors,   *insured as*
    A' future ages;
Now moths deform in shapeless tatters,
    Their unknown pages.'

Then farewell hopes of Laurel-boughs,
50   To garland my poetic brows!
Henceforth, I'll rove where busy ploughs
      Are whistling thrang,   *busily*
An' teach the lanely heights an' howes   *lonely, hollows*
      My rustic sang.

I'll wander on with tentless heed,   *careless*
How never-halting moments speed,
Till fate shall snap the brittle thread;
      Then, all unknown,
I'll lay me with th'*inglorious dead*,
60   Forgot and gone!

But why, o' Death, begin a tale?
Just now we're living sound an' hale;
Then top and maintop croud the sail,   *crowd*
      Heave *Care* o'er-side!
And large, before Enjoyment's gale,
      Let's tak the tide.

This life, sae far's I understand,   *so far as*
Is a' enchanted fairy-land,
Where Pleasure is the Magic-wand,
70   That, wielded right,
Maks Hours like Minutes, hand in hand,
      Dance by fu' light.   *full*

The *magic-wand* then let us wield;
For, ance that five an' forty's speel'd,   *climbed*
See, crazy, weary, joyless Eild,   *Old Age*
      Wi' wrinkl'd face,
Comes hostan, hirplan owre the field,   *coughing, limping*
      Wi' creeping pace.

When ance *life's day* draws near the gloamin,   *twilight*
80   Then fareweel vacant, careless roamin;
An' fareweel chearfu' tankards foamin,

An' social noise;
An' fareweel dear, deluding woman,
      The joy of joys!

O *Life*! how pleasant in thy morning,
Young Fancy's rays the hills adorning!
Cold-pausing Caution's lesson scorning,
      We frisk away,
Like school-boys, at th'expected warning,
90   To joy and play.

We wander there, we wander here,
We eye the *rose* upon the brier,
Unmindful that the *thorn* is near,
      Among the leaves;
And tho' the puny wound appear,
      Short while it grieves.

Some, lucky, find a flow'ry spot,
For which they never toil'd nor swat;   sweated
They drink the *sweet* and eat the *fat*,
100   But care or pain;   without
And haply, eye the barren hut,
      With high disdain.

With steady aim, Some Fortune chase;
Keen hope does ev'ry sinew brace;
Thro' fair, thro' foul, they urge the race,
      And seize the prey:
Then canie, in some cozie place,   cautious,
      They close the *day*.   comfortable

And others, like your humble servan',
110 *Poor wights*! nae rules nor roads observin;   fellows
To right or left, eternal swervin,
      They zig-zag on;
Till curst with Age, obscure an' starvin,
      They aften groan.

Alas! what bitter toil an' straining —
But truce with peevish, poor complaining!
Is Fortune's fickle *Luna* waning?   Moon
    E'en let her gang!
Beneath what light she has remaining,
120   Let's sing our Sang.

My pen I here fling to the door,
And kneel, 'Ye *Pow'rs*', and warm implore,
'Tho' I should wander *Terra* o'er,   Earth
    In all her climes,
Grant me but this, I ask no more,
    Ay rowth o' rhymes.   plenty

'Gie dreeping roasts to *countra Lairds*,   dripping
Till icicles hing frae their beards;   hang
Gie fine braw claes to fine *Life-guards*,   clothes
130   And *Maids of Honor*;
And yill an' whisky gie to *Cairds*,   ale, tinkers
    Until they sconner.   feel disgust

'A *Title*, DEMPSTER merits it;
A *Garter* gie to WILLIE PIT;
Gie Wealth to some be-ledger'd Cit,   townsman
    In cent per cent;
But give me real, sterling Wit,
    And I'm content.

'While ye are pleas'd to keep me hale,   healthy
140 I'll sit down o'er my scanty meal,
Be't *water-brose*, or *muslin-kail*,   -porridge, meatless
    Wi' chearfu' face,   broth
As lang's the Muses dinna fail
    To say the grace.'

An anxious e'e I never throws   eye
Behint my lug, or by my nose;   ear
I jouk beneath Misfortune's blows   dodge

        As weel's I may,
Sworn foe to *sorrow*, *care*, and *prose*,
150   I rhyme away.

O ye, douse folk, that live by rule,   sedate
Grave, tideless-blooded, calm and cool,
Compar'd wi' you – O fool! fool! fool!
       How much unlike!
Your hearts are just a standing pool,
        Your lives, a dyke!   stone wall

Nae hare-brain'd, sentimental traces,
In your unletter'd, nameless faces!
In *arioso* trills and graces
160   Ye never stray,
But *gravissimo*, solemn basses
       Ye hum away.

Ye are sae *grave*, nae doubt ye're *wise*;
Nae ferly tho' ye do despise   wonder
The hairum-scairum, ram-stam boys,   wild, reckless
       The rambling squad:
I see ye upward cast your eyes –
      – Ye ken the road –

Whilst I – but I shall haud me there –   hold
170 Wi' you I'll scarce gang *ony where* –
Then *Jamie*, I shall say nae mair,
       But quat my sang,   end
Content *with* YOU to mak a *pair*,
       Whare'er I gang.

A DREAM

Thoughts, words and deeds, the Statute blames with reason;
But surely Dreams *were ne'er indicted Treason.*

On Reading, in the Public Papers, the Laureate's Ode, with the other
Parade of June 4th, 1786, the Author was no sooner dropt asleep, than
he imagined himself transported to the Birthday Levee; and, in his
dreaming Fancy, made the following Address.

I

GUID-MORNIN to your MAJESTY!
   May heaven augment your blisses,
On ev'ry new *Birth-day* ye see,
   A humble Bardie wishes!   poet
My Bardship here, at your Levee,
   On sic a day as this is,
Is sure an uncouth sight to see,
   Amang thae Birth-day dresses   those
      Sae fine this day.

II

10 I see ye're complimented thrang,   busily
   By many a *lord* an' *lady*;
'God save the King' 's a cuckoo sang
   That's unco easy said ay:
The *Poets* too, a venal gang,
   Wi' rhymes weel-turn'd an' ready,
Wad gar you trow ye ne'er do wrang,   make, believe,
   But ay unerring steady,   wrong
      On sic a day.

III

For me! before a Monarch's face,
20   Ev'n *there* I winna flatter;   will not
For neither Pension, Post, nor Place,
   Am I your humble debtor:

So, nae reflection on YOUR GRACE,
　　Your Kingship to bespatter;
There's monie *waur* been o' the Race,　　　worse
　　And aiblins *ane* been better　　　perhaps one
　　　　　Than You this day.　　　[Charles Stewart]

IV

'Tis very true, my sovereign King,
　　My skill may weel be doubted;
30　But *Facts* are cheels that winna ding,　　fellows, will not be
　　An' downa be disputed:　　　shifted
Your *royal nest*, beneath *Your* wing,　　cannot
　　Is e'en right reft an' clouted,　　　torn, patched
And now the third part o' the string,
　　An' less, will gang about it
　　　　　Than did ae day.

V

Far be't frae me that I aspire
　　To blame your Legislation,
Or say, ye wisdom want, or fire,
40　　To rule this mighty nation;
But faith! I muckle doubt, my SIRE,
　　Ye've trusted 'Ministration,
To chaps, wha, in a *barn* or *byre*,　　cow-shed
　　Wad better fill'd their station
　　　　　Than *courts* yon day.

VI

And now Ye've gien auld *Britain* peace,
　　Her broken shins to plaister;　　plaster
Your sair taxation does her fleece,
　　Till she has scarce a tester:　　sixpence
50　For me, thank God, my life's a *lease*,
　　Nae *bargain* wearing faster,
Or faith! I fear, that, wi' the geese,
　　I shortly boost to pasture　　must
　　　　　I' the craft some day.　　croft

VII

I'm no mistrusting *Willie Pit*,
   When taxes he enlarges,
(An' *Will's* a true guid fallow's get   fellow's son
   A Name not Envy spairges)   bespatters
That he intends to pay your *debt*,
60   An' lessen a' your *charges*;
But, G—d-sake! let nae *saving-fit*
   Abridge your bonie *Barges*
      An' *Boats* this day.

VIII

Adieu, my LIEGE! may Freedom geck   exult
   Beneath your high protection;
An' may Ye rax Corruption's neck,   wring
   And gie her for dissection!
But since I'm here, I'll no neglect,
   In loyal, true affection,
70 To pay your QUEEN, with due respect,
   My fealty an' subjection
      This great Birth-day.

IX

Hail, *Majesty most Excellent*!
   While Nobles strive to please Ye,
Will Ye accept a Compliment,
   A simple Bardie gies Ye?
Thae bonie Bairntime, Heav'n has lent,   offspring
   Still higher may they heeze Ye   lift
In bliss, till Fate some day is sent,
80   For ever to release Ye
      Frae Care that day.

X

For you, young Potentate o' W—,   [Wales]
   I tell your *Highness* fairly,
Down Pleasure's stream, wi' swelling sails,
   I'm tauld ye're driving rarely;   told

But some day ye may gnaw your nails,
    An' curse your folly sairly,   *sorely*
That e'er ye brak Diana's *pales*,   *broke*
    Or rattl'd dice wi' *Charlie*
90   By night or day.

XI

Yet aft a ragged *Cowte's* been known,   *colt*
    To mak a noble *Aiver*;   *'old horse'* (B)
So, ye may dousely fill a Throne,   *decorously*
    For a' their clish-ma-claver: *gossip*
There, Him at *Agincourt* wha shone,
    Few better were or braver;
And yet, wi' funny, queer *Sir *John*,
    He was an unco shaver   *joker*
        For monie a day.

XII

100 For you, right rev'rend O——,   [Osnaburg]
    Nane sets the *lawn-sleeve* sweeter,   *becomes*
Altho' a ribban at your lug   *ear*
    Wad been a dress compleater:
As ye disown yon paughty dog,   *insolent*
    That *bears* the Keys of Peter,
Then swith! an' get a *wife* to hug,   *quickly*
    Or trouth! ye'll stain the *Mitre*
        Some luckless day.

XIII

Young, royal TARRY-BREEKS, I learn,   *'tar-trousers'*
110   Ye've lately come athwart her;
A glorious †*Galley*, stem and stern,
    Weel rigg'd for *Venus barter*;
But first hang out that she'll discern
    Your *hymeneal Charter*,

---

*Sir John Falstaff, Vide Shakespeare.

†Alluding to the Newspaper account of a certain royal Sailor's Amour.

Then heave aboard your *grapple airn*,   grappling-iron
   An', large upon her *quarter*,   quarter-deck
      Come full that day.

XIV

Ye lastly, bonie blossoms a',
   Ye *royal Lasses* dainty,
120 Heav'n mak you guid as weel as braw,
   An' gie you *lads* a plenty:
But sneer na *British-boys* awa;
   For King's are unco scant ay,
An' German-Gentles are but *sma'*,   -'great folks' (B)
   They're better just than *want ay*   none
      On onie day.

XV

God bless you a'! consider now,
   Ye're unco muckle dautet;   spoiled
But ere the *course* o' life be through,
130   It may be bitter sautet: salted
An' I hae seen their *coggie* fou,   dish, full
   That yet hae tarrow't at it,   who, 'murmured' (B)
But or the *day* was done, I trow,   before
   The laggen they hae clautet   bottom of dish, scraped
      Fu' clean that day.   very

THE VISION

DUAN FIRST*

THE sun had clos'd the *winter-day*,
The Curlers quat their roaring play,   *left*
And hunger'd Maukin taen her way   *the hare*
      To kail-yards green,   *kitchen-gardens*
While faithless snaws ilk step betray   *snows*
      Whare she has been.

The Thresher's weary *flingin-tree*,   *flail*
The lee-lang day had tir'd me;   *all day through*
And when the Day had clos'd his e'e,   *eye*
10   Far i' the West,
Ben i' the *Spence*, right pensivelie,   *'into the parlour' (B)*
      I gaed to rest.

There, lanely, by the ingle-cheek,   *lonely*
I sat and ey'd the spewing reek,   *smoke*
That fill'd, wi' hoast-provoking smeek,   *cough-, smoke*
      The auld, clay biggin;   *building*
And heard the restless rattons squeak   *rats*
      About the riggin.   *roof*

All in this mottie, misty clime,   *dusty*
20 I backward mus'd on wasted time,
How I had spent my *youthfu' prime*,
      An' done nae-thing,
But stringing blethers up in rhyme   *nonsense/idle talk*
      For fools to sing.

Had I to guid advice but harket,   *listened*
I might, by this, hae led a market,   *by now*
Or strutted in a Bank and clarket   *written up*

*Duan, a term of Ossian's for the different divisions of a digressive Poem. See his Cath-Loda, vol. 2 of McPherson's Translation.

My *Cash-Account*;
While here, half-mad, half-fed, half-sarket,   half-clothed
30   Is a' th' amount.   ('-shirted')

I started, mutt'ring blockhead! coof!   fool!
And heav'd on high my wauket loof;   calloused palm
To swear by a' yon starry roof,
          Or some rash aith,   oath
That I, henceforth, would be *rhyme-proof*
          Till my last breath —

When click! the *string* the *snick* did draw;   latch
And jee! the door gaed to the wa';   with a swing
And by my ingle-lowe I saw,   firelight
40   Now bleezan bright,   blazing
A tight, outlandish *Hizzie*, braw,   shapely, wench
          Come full in sight.

Ye need na doubt, I held my whisht;   kept silent
The infant aith, half-form'd, was crusht;
I glowr'd as eerie's I'd been dusht,   'pushed by a ram'
          In some wild glen;   (B)
When sweet, like *modest Worth*, she blusht,
          And stepped ben.   within

Green, slender, leaf-clad *Holly-boughs*
50 Were twisted, gracefu', round her brows,
I took her for some SCOTTISH MUSE,
          By that same token;
And come to stop those reckless vows,
          Would soon been broken.

A 'hare-brain'd, sentimental trace'
Was strongly marked in her face;
A wildly-witty, rustic grace
          Shone full upon her;
Her *eye*, ev'n turn'd on empty space,
60   Beam'd keen with *Honor*.

Down flow'd her robe, a *tartan* sheen,
Till half a leg was scrimply seen;   barely
And such a *leg*! my BESS, I ween,
      Could only peer it;   equal
Sae straught, sae taper, tight and clean,   straight, shapely
      Nane else came near it.

Her *Mantle* large, of greenish hue,
My gazing wonder chiefly drew;
Deep *lights* and *shades*, bold-mingling, threw
70   A lustre grand;
And seem'd, to my astonish'd view,
      A *well-known* Land.

Here, rivers in the sea were lost;
There, mountains to the skies were tost:
Here, tumbling billows mark'd the coast,
      With surging foam;
There, distant shone, *Art's* lofty boast,
      The lordly dome.

Here, DOON pour'd down his far-fetch'd floods;
80 There, well-fed IRWINE stately thuds:
Auld, hermit AIRE staw thro' his woods,   crept
      On to the shore;
And many a lesser torrent scuds,
      With seeming roar.

Low, in a sandy valley spread,
An ancient BOROUGH rear'd her head;
Still, as in *Scottish Story* read,
      She boasts a *Race*,
To ev'ry nobler virtue bred,
90   And polish'd grace.

DUAN SECOND

With musing-deep, astonish'd stare,
I view'd the heavenly-seeming *Fair*;
A whisp'ring *throb* did witness bear
     Of kindred sweet,
When with an elder Sister's air
     She did me greet.

'All hail! *my own* inspired Bard!
In me thy native Muse regard!
Nor longer mourn thy fate is hard,
     Thus poorly low!
I come to give thee such *reward*,
     As *we* bestow.

'Know, the great *Genius* of this Land,
Has many a light, aerial band,
Who, all beneath his high command,
     Harmoniously,
As *Arts* or *Arms* they understand,
     Their labors ply.

'They SCOTIA'S Race among them share;
Some fire the *Sodger* on to dare;   soldier
Some rouse the *Patriot* up to bare
     Corruption's heart:
Some teach the *Bard*, a darling care,
     The tuneful Art.

''Mong swelling floods of reeking gore,
They ardent, kindling spirits pour;
Or, mid the venal Senate's roar,
     They, sightless, stand,
To mend the honest *Patriot-lore*,
     And grace the hand.

100

110

120

'Hence, FULLARTON, the brave and young;
Hence, DEMPSTER'S truth-prevailing tongue;
Hence, sweet harmonious BEATTIE sung
   His "Minstrel lays";
Or tore, with noble ardour stung,
   The *Sceptic's* bays.

'To lower Orders are assign'd,
The humbler ranks of Human-kind,
The rustic Bard, the lab'ring Hind,
130   The Artisan;
All chuse, as, various they're inclin'd,
   The various man.

'When yellow waves the heavy grain,
The threat'ning *Storm*, some, strongly, rein;
Some teach to meliorate the plain,
   With *tillage-skill*;
And some instruct the Shepherd-train,
   Blythe o'er the hill.

'Some hint the Lover's harmless wile;
140 Some grace the Maiden's artless smile;
Some soothe the Lab'rer's weary toil,
   For humble gains,
And make his *cottage-scenes* beguile
   His cares and pains.

'Some, bounded to a district-space,
Explore at large Man's *infant race*,
To mark the embryotic trace,
   Of *rustic Bard*;
And careful note each op'ning grace,
150   A guide and guard.

'*Of these am I* – COILA my name;
And this district as mine I claim,
Where once the *Campbells*, chiefs of fame,

Held ruling pow'r:
I mark'd thy embryo-tuneful flame,
        Thy natal hour.

'With future hope, I oft would gaze,
Fond, on thy little, early ways,
Thy rudely-caroll'd, chiming phrase,
160   In uncouth rhymes,
Fir'd at the simple, artless lays
        Of other times.

'I saw thee seek the sounding shore,
Delighted with the dashing roar;
Or when the *North* his fleecy store
        Drove thro' the sky,
I saw grim Nature's visage hoar,
        Struck thy young eye.

'Or when the deep-green-mantl'd Earth,
170 Warm-cherish'd ev'ry floweret's birth,
And joy and music pouring forth,
        In ev'ry grove,
I saw thee eye the gen'ral mirth
        With boundless love.

'When ripen'd fields, and azure skies,
Call'd forth the *Reaper's* rustling noise,
I saw thee leave their ev'ning joys,
        And lonely stalk,
To vent thy bosom's swelling rise,
180   In pensive walk.

'When *youthful Love*, warm-blushing, strong,
Keen-shivering shot thy nerves along,
Those accents, grateful to thy tongue,
        Th'adored *Name*,
I taught thee how to pour in song,
        To soothe thy flame.

'I saw thy pulse's maddening play,
Wild-send thee Pleasure's devious way,
Misled by Fancy's *meteor-ray*,
  By Passion driven;
But yet the *light* that led astray,
  Was *light* from Heaven.

'I taught thy manners-painting strains,
The *loves*, the *ways* of simple swains,
Till now, o'er all my wide domains,
  Thy fame extends;
And some, the pride of *Coila's* plains,
  Become thy friends.

'Thou canst not learn, nor I can show,
To paint with *Thomson's* landscape-glow;
Or wake the bosom-melting throe,
  With *Shenstone's* art;
Or pour, with *Gray*, the moving flow,
  Warm on the heart.

'Yet all beneath th'unrivall'd Rose,
The lowly Daisy sweetly blows;
Tho' large the forest's Monarch throws
  His army shade,
Yet green the juicy Hawthorn grows,
  Adown the glade.

'Then never murmur nor repine;
Strive in thy *humble sphere* to shine;
And trust me, not *Potosi's mine*,
  Nor *King's regard*,
Can give a bliss o'ermatching thine,
  A *rustic Bard*.

'To give my counsels all in one,
Thy *tuneful flame* still careful fan;
Preserve *the dignity of Man*,

220   With Soul erect;
       And trust, the UNIVERSAL PLAN
              Will all protect.

       '*And wear thou this*' – She solemn said,
       And bound the *Holly* round my head:
       The polish'd leaves, and berries red,
              Did rustling play;
       And, like a passing thought, she fled,
              In light away.

THE following POEM will, by many
Readers, be well enough understood; but, for
the sake of those who are unacquainted with
the manners and traditions of the country
where the scene is cast, Notes are added, to
give some account of the principal Charms
and Spells of that Night, so big with
Prophecy to the Peasantry in the West of
Scotland. The passion of prying into Futurity
makes a striking part of the history of
Human-nature, in its rude state, in all ages
and nations; and it may be some
entertainment to a philosophic mind, if any
such should honor the Author with a
perusal, to see the remains of it, among the
more unenlightened in our own.

HALLOWEEN*

Yes! let the Rich deride, the Proud disdain,
The simple pleasures of the lowly train;
To me more dear, congenial to my heart,
One native charm, than all the gloss of art.

Goldsmith

I

UPON that *night*, when Fairies light
    On *Cassilis Downans*† dance,
Or owre the lays, in splendid blaze,   leas
    On sprightly coursers prance;
Or for *Colean*, the rout is taen,

---

* Is thought to be a night when Witches, Devils, and other mischief-making beings, are all abroad on their baneful, midnight errands: particularly, those aerial people, the Fairies, are said, on that night, to hold a grand Anniversary.

† Certain little, romantic, rocky, green hills in the neighbourhood of the ancient seat of the Earls of Cassilis.

Beneath the moon's pale beams;
There, up the *Cove*,* to stray an' rove,
   Amang the rocks an' streams
      To sport that night.

II

10 Amang the bonie, winding banks,
   Where *Doon* rins, wimplin, clear,   runs, winding
Where BRUCE† ance rul'd the martial ranks,
   An' shook his *Carrick* spear,
Some merry, friendly, countra folks,
   Together did convene,
To *burn* their nits, an' *pou* their stocks,   nuts, pull
   An' haud their *Halloween*   hold/keep
      Fu' blythe that night.   very

III

   The lasses feat, an' cleanly neat,   spruce
20   Mair braw than when they're fine;   in their finery
Their faces blythe, fu' sweetly kythe,   show
   Hearts leal, an' warm, an' kin':   loyal, kindly
The lads sae trig, wi' wooer-babs,   trim, love-knots
   Weel knotted on their garten,   garters
Some unco blate, an' some wi' gabs,   shy, chatter
   Gar lasses hearts gang startin   make
      Whyles fast at night.

* A noted cavern near Colean-house, called the Cove of Colean; which, as well as Cassilis Downans, is famed, in country story, for being a favourite haunt of Fairies.

† The famous family of that name, the ancestors of ROBERT the great Deliverer of his country, were Earls of Carrick.

IV

Then, first an' foremost, thro' the kail,   greens
　　Their *stocks** maun a' be sought ance;
30 They steek their een, an' grape an' wale,   shut, eyes, grope, choose
　　For muckle anes, an' straught anes.   big, straight
Poor hav'rel *Will* fell aff the drift,   foolish, lost the way
　　An' wander'd thro' the *Bow-kail*,   cabbage
An' pow't, for want o' better shift,   pulled, choice
　　A *runt* was like a sow-tail   cabbage stalk [which]
　　　　Sae bow't that night.   bent

V

Then, straught or crooked, yird or nane,   earth
　　They roar an' cry a' throw'ther;   in confusion
The vera *wee-things*, toddlan, rin,
40 　　Wi' stocks out owre their shouther: shoulder
An' gif the *custock's* sweet or sour,   if, pith
　　Wi' joctelegs they taste them;   pocket-knives
Syne coziely, aboon the door,   then snugly, above
　　Wi' cannie care, they've plac'd them   knowing
　　　　To lye that night.

* The first ceremony of Halloween, is pulling each a *Stock*, or plant of kail. They must go out, hand in hand, with eyes shut, and pull the first they meet with: its being big or little, straight or crooked, is prophetic of the size and shape of the grand object of all their Spells – the husband or wife. If any *yird*, or earth, stick to the root, that is *tocher*, or fortune; and the taste of the *custoc*, that is, the heart of the stem, is indicative of the natural temper and disposition. Lastly, the stems, or to give them their ordinary appellation, the *runts*, are placed somewhere above the head of the door; and the christian names of the people whom chance brings into the house, are, according to the priority of placing the *runts*, the names in question.

VI

The lasses staw frae 'mang them a',   stole
   To pou their *stalks o' corn;**
But *Rab* slips out, an' jinks about,   dodges
   Behint the muckle thorn:
50 He grippet *Nelly* hard an' fast;
   Loud skirl'd a' the lasses;   screamed
But her *tap-pickle* maist was lost,   top-most grain
   When kiutlan in the *Fause-house*†   cuddling
      Wi' him that night.

VII

The auld Guidwife's weel-hoordet *nits*‡   mistress, hoarded
   Are round an' round divided,
An' monie lads an' lasses fates
   Are there that night decided:
Some kindle, couthie, side by side   sociably
60   An' *burn* thegither trimly;
Some start awa, wi' saucy pride,
   An' jump out owre the chimlie   fire-place
      Fu' high that night.

VIII

Jean slips in twa, wi' tentie e'e;   watchful, eye
   Wha 'twas, she wadna tell;
But this is *Jock*, an' this is *me*,
   She says in to hersel: whispers

---

* They go to the barn-yard, and pull each, at three several times, a stalk of Oats. If the third stalk wants the *top-pickle*, that is, the grain at the top of the stalk, the party in question will want the Maidenhead.

† When the corn is in a doubtful state, by being too green, or wet, the Stack-builder, by means of old timber, &c. makes a large apartment in his stack, with an opening in the side which is fairest exposed to the wind: this he calls a *Fause-house*.

‡ Burning the nuts is a favourite charm. They name the lad and lass to each particular nut, as they lay them in the fire; and according as they burn quietly together, or start from beside one another, the course and issue of the Courtship will be.

He bleez'd owre her, an' she owre him,   blazed
  As they wad never mair part,
70 Till fuff! he started up the lum,   chimney
  An' *Jean* had e'en a sair heart   sore
    To see't that night.

IX

Poor Willie, wi' his *bow-kail runt*,   cabbage
  Was *brunt* wi' primsie *Mallie*;   burnt, prim
An' *Mary*, nae doubt, took the drunt,   huff
  To be compar'd to *Willie*:
Mall's nit lap out, wi' pridefu' fling,   leapt
  An' her ain fit, it brunt it;   own foot
While *Willie* lap, an' swoor by *jing*,   leapt, swore
80   'Twas just the way he wanted
    To be that night.

X

Nell had the *Fause-house* in her min',
  She pits hersel an' *Rob* in;   puts
In loving bleeze they sweetly join,
  Till white in ase they're sobbin: ashes
Nell's heart was dancin at the view;
  She whisper'd *Rob* to leuk for't: look
Rob, stownlins, prie'd her bonie mou,   by stealth, kissed, mouth
  Fu' cozie in the neuk for't,   corner
90   Unseen that night.

XI

But *Merran* sat behint their backs,
  Her thoughts on *Andrew Bell*;
She lea'es them gashan at their cracks,   leaves, gossiping, talk
  An' slips out by hersel:

She thro' the yard the nearest taks,
　　An' for the *kiln* she goes then,
An' darklins grapet for the *bauks*,   in the dark, groped, beams
　　And in the *blue-clue** throws then,
　　　　Right fear't that night.   thoroughly afraid

XII

100 An' ay she *win't*, an' ay she swat,   wound, sweated
　　I wat she made nae jaukin;   know, trifling
Till something *held* within the *pat*,   pot
　　Guid L—d! but she was quaukin!   quaking
But whether 'twas the *Deil* himsel,   Devil
　　Or whether 'twas a *bauk-en'*,   beam-end
Or whether it was *Andrew Bell*,
　　She did na wait on talkin
　　　　To spier that night.   ask

XIII

Wee *Jenny* to her Graunie says,
110 　'Will ye go wi' me Graunie?
I'll *eat the apple*† at the *glass*,
　　I gat frae uncle Johnie:'
She fuff't her pipe wi' sic a lunt,   puffed, smoke
　　In wrath she was sae vap'rin,   vapouring
She notic't na, an aizle brunt   red ember, burned
　　Her braw, new, worset apron   worsted
　　　　Out thro' that night.

* Whoever would, with success, try this spell, must strictly observe these directions. Steal out, all alone, to the *kiln*, and, darkling, throw into the *pot*, a clew of blue yarn: wind it in a new clew off the old one; and towards the latter end, something will hold the thread: demand, *wha hauds?* i.e. who holds? and answer will be returned from the kiln-pot, by naming the christian and sirname of your future Spouse.

† Take a candle, and go, alone, to a looking glass: eat an apple before it, and some traditions say you should comb your hair all the time: the face of your conjugal companion, *to be*, will be seen in the glass, as if peeping over your shoulder.

XIV

'Ye little Skelpie-limmer's-face!   naughty hussy's
    I daur you try sic sportin,   dare
120 As seek the *foul Thief* onie place,
    For him to spae your fortune: tell
Nae doubt but ye may get a *sight*!
    Great cause ye hae to fear it;
For monie a ane has gotten a fright,
    An liv'd an' di'd deleeret,   delirious
        On sic a night.

XV

'Ae Hairst afore the *Sherra-moor*,   harvest, Sheriffmuir
    I mind't as weel's yestreen,   remember, last night
I was a gilpey then, I'm sure,   girl
130   I was na past fyfteen:
The Simmer had been cauld an' wat,   wet
    An' *Stuff* was unco green;   grain
An' ay a rantan *Kirn* we gat,   rollicking harvest-home
    An' just on *Halloween*
        It fell that night.

XVI

'Our *Stibble-rig* was *Rab M'Graen*,   chief harvester
    A clever, sturdy fellow;
His Sin gat *Eppie Sim* wi' wean,   child
    That liv'd in Achmacalla:
140 He gat *hemp-seed*,* I mind it weel,
    An' he made unco light o't;
But monie a day was *by himsel*,   beside himself

---

* Steal out, unperceived, and sow a handful of hemp seed; harrowing it with
any thing you can conveniently draw after you. Repeat, now and then,
'Hemp seed I saw thee, Hemp seed I saw thee; and him (or her) that is to be
my true-love, come after me and pou thee.' Look over your left shoulder,
and you will see the appearance of the person invoked, in the attitude of
pulling hemp. Some traditions say, 'come after me and shaw thee,' that is,
show thyself; in which case it simply appears. Others omit the harrowing,
and say, 'come after me and harrow thee.'

He was sae sairly frighted   sorely
    That vera night.'

XVII

Then up gat fechtan *Jamie Fleck*,   fighting
    An' he swoor by his conscience,
That he could *saw hemp-seed* a peck;   sow
    For it was a' but nonsense:
The auld guidman raught down the pock,   master, reached,
                                              bag
150   An' out a handfu' gied him;
Syne bad him slip frae 'mang the folk,   then
    Sometime when nae ane see'd him,
        An' try't that night.

XVIII

He marches thro' amang the stacks,
    Tho' he was something sturtan;   afraid
The *graip* he for a *harrow* taks,   dung-fork
    An' haurls at his curpan: drags, rump
And ev'ry now an' then, he says,
    'Hemp-seed I saw thee,   sow
160 An' her that is to be my lass,
    Come after me an' draw thee
        As fast this night.'

XIX

He whistl'd up *lord Lenox' march*,
    To keep his courage cheary;
Altho' his hair began to arch,
    He was sae fley'd an' eerie: badly scared
Till presently he hears a squeak,
    An' then a grane an' gruntle;   groan, grunt
He by his showther gae a keek,   shoulder, look
170   An' tumbl'd wi' a wintle   roll
        Out owre that night.

XX

He roar'd a horrid murder-shout,
  In dreadfu' desperation!
An' young an' auld come rinnan out,
  An' hear the sad narration:
He swoor 'twas hilchan *Jean M'Craw*,   limping
  Or crouchie *Merran Humphie*,   hump-backed
                                         Marion
Till stop! she trotted thro' them a';
  An' what was it but *Grumphie*   the pig
180   Asteer that night?   astir

XXI

Meg fain wad to the *Barn* gaen,   have gone
  To *winn three wechts o' naething*;*   winnow, sievefuls
But for to meet the Deil her lane,   all by herself
  She pat but little faith in: put
She gies the Herd a pickle nits,   shepherd, few
  An' twa red cheeket apples,
To watch, while for the *Barn* she sets,
  In hopes to see *Tam Kipples*
         That vera night.

XXII

190 She turns the key, wi' cannie thraw,   cautious twist
  An' owre the threshold ventures;
But first on *Sawnie* gies a ca',   Sandy
  Syne bauldly in she enters: boldly
A *ratton* rattl'd up the wa',   rat
  An' she cry'd, L—d preserve her!

---

* This charm must likewise be performed, unperceived and alone. You go to
the *barn*, and open both doors; taking them off the hinges, if possible; for
there is danger, that the Being, about to appear, may shut the doors, and do
you some mischief. Then take that instrument used in winnowing the
corn, which, in our country-dialect, we call a *wecht*; and go thro' all the
attitudes of letting down corn against the wind. Repeat it three times; and
the third time, an apparition will pass thro' the barn, in at the windy door,
and out at the other, having both the figure in question, and the appearance
or retinue, marking the employment or station in life.

An' ran thro' midden-hole an' a',   gutter at foot of a
   An' pray'd wi' zeal and fervour,   dunghill
     Fu' fast that night.

XXIII

They hoy't out Will, wi' sair advice;   urged
200   They hecht him some fine braw ane;   promised
It chanc'd the *Stack* he *faddom't thrice*,*
   Was timmer-propt for thrawin: timber-propped
                against bending
He taks a swirlie, auld *moss-oak*,   gnarled
   For some black, grousome *Carlin*;   old woman
An' loot a winze, an' drew a stroke,   let out an oath
   Till skin in blypes cam haurlin   shreds, peeling
     Aff's nieves that night.   fists

XXIV

A wanton widow *Leezie* was,
   As cantie as a kittlen;   lively, kitten
210 But Och! that night, among the shaws,   woods
   She gat a fearfu' settlin!
She thro' the whins, an' by the cairn,   gorse
   An' owre the hill gaed scrievin,   careering
Whare *three Lairds' lan's* met at a burn,†   lands
   To dip her *left sark-sleeve* in,   shirt-
     Was bent that night.

XXV

Whyles owre a linn the burnie plays,   waterfall, little
   As thro' the glen it wimpl't;   stream
Whyles round a rocky scar it strays;

---

* Take an opportunity of going, unnoticed, to a *Bear-stack*, and fathom it three times round. The last fathom of the last time, you will catch in your arms, the appearance of your future conjugal yoke-fellow.

† You go out, one or more, for this is a social spell, to a south-running spring or rivulet, where 'three Lairds' lands meet,' and dip your left shirt-sleeve. Go to bed in sight of a fire, and hang your wet sleeve before it to dry. Ly awake; and sometime near midnight, an apparition, having the exact figure of the grand object in question, will come and turn the sleeve, as if to dry the other side of it.

220	Whyles in a wiel it dimpl't;	eddy
	Whyles glitter'd to the nightly rays,	
	Wi' bickerin, dancin dazzle;	rushing
	Whyles cooket underneath the braes,	hid, hillsides
	Below the spreading hazle	
	Unseen that night.	

XXVI

	Amang the brachens, on the brae,	coarse ferns
	Between her an' the moon,	
	The Deil, or else an outler Quey,	young cow in the open
	Gat up an' gae a croon:	
230	Poor *Leezie's* heart maist lap the hool	leapt out of skin
	Near lav'rock-height she jumpet,	lark-height
	But mist a fit, an' in the *pool*,	foot
	Out owre the lugs she plumpet,	ears
	Wi' a plunge that night.	

XXVII

	In order, on the clean hearth-stane,	
	The *Luggies** three are ranged;	wooden dishes
	And ev'ry time great care is taen,	
	To see them duly changed:	
	Auld, uncle *John*, wha *wedlock's joys*,	
240	Sin' *Mar's-year* did desire,	1715 (Mar's Rising)
	Because he gat the toom dish thrice,	empty
	He heav'd them on the fire,	
	In wrath that night.	

* Take three dishes; put clean water in one, foul water in another, and leave the third empty: blindfold a person, and lead him to the hearth where the dishes are ranged; he (or she) dips the left hand: if by chance in the clean water, the future husband or wife will come to the bar of Matrimony, a Maid; if in the foul, a widow; if in the empty dish, it foretells, with equal certainty, no marriage at all. It is repeated three times; and every time the arrangement of the dishes is altered.

XXVIII

Wi' merry sangs, an' friendly cracks,
    I wat they did na weary;   *am sure*
And unco tales, an' funnie jokes,
    Their sports were cheap an' cheary:
Till *butter'd So'ns,** wi' fragrant lunt,   *porridge, steam*
    Set a' their gabs a steerin;   *tongues, wagging*
250 Syne, wi' a social glass o' strunt,   *liquor*
    They parted aff careerin
        Fu' blythe that night.

THE AULD FARMER'S NEW-YEAR-MORNING SALUTATION TO HIS AULD MARE, MAGGIE, ON GIVING HER THE ACCUSTOMED RIPP OF CORN TO HANSEL IN THE NEW-YEAR

A *Guid New-year* I wish you Maggie!
Hae, there's a ripp to thy auld baggie: *fist of unthreshed corn, belly*
Tho' thou's howe-backet, now, an' knaggie,   *'sunk in the back' (B), bony*
    I've seen the day,
Thou could hae gaen like ony staggie   *colt*
        Out owre the lay.   *outfield*

Tho' now thou's dowie, stiff an' crazy,   *sickly, infirm*
An' thy auld hide as white's a daisie,
I've seen thee dappl't, sleek an' glaizie,   *glittering smooth like glass*
10   A bonie gray:
He should been tight that daur't to *raize* thee,   *capable, dared, provoke*
        Ance in a day.

---

* Sowens, with butter instead of milk to them, is always the *Halloween Supper*.

Thou ance was i' the foremost rank,
A *filly* buirdly, steeve an' swank,   stately, strong, agile
An' set weel down a shapely shank,
     As e'er tread yird;   earth
An' could hae flown out owre a stank,   pool of standing water
     Like onie bird.

     It's now some nine-an'-twenty year,
20   Sin' thou was my *Guidfather's Meere*;   father-in-law's mare
He gied me thee, o' tocher clear,   dowry
     An' fifty mark;
Tho' it was sma', 'twas *weel-won* gear,   property
     An' thou was stark.   strong

When first I gaed to woo my *Jenny*,
Ye then was trottan wi' your Minnie: mother
Tho' ye was trickie, slee an' funnie,   clever
     Ye ne'er was donsie;   ill-tempered
But hamely, tawie, quiet an' cannie,   'that handles quietly' (B)
30   An' unco sonsie.   tractable

That *day*, ye pranc'd wi' muckle pride,
When ye bure hame my bonie *Bride*:   bore
An' sweet an' gracefu' she did ride
     Wi' maiden air!
KYLE-STEWART I could bragged wide,   have challenged
     For sic a *pair*.

Tho' now ye dow but hoyte and hoble,   can only move clumsily
An' wintle like a saumont-coble,   roll, salmon-boat
That day, ye was a jinker noble,   high-spirited beast
40   For heels an' win'!   wind
An' ran them till they a' did wauble   wobble
     Far, far behin'!

When thou an' I were young an' skiegh,   mettlesome
An' *Stable-meals* at Fairs were driegh,   dreary

How thou wad prance, an' snore, an' sciegh, *snort, neigh*
  An' tak the road!
Towns-bodies ran, an' stood abiegh, *town folk, at a shy distance*
  An' ca't thee mad.

When thou was corn't, an' I was mellow, *fed with corn*
50 We took the road ay like a Swallow:
 At *Brooses* thou had ne'er a fellow, *wedding-races*
  For pith an' speed; *energy*
But ev'ry tail thou pay't them hollow, *beat*
  Whare'er thou gaed.

The sma', droot-rumpl't, hunter cattle, *with drooping haunches, beasts*
Might aiblins waur't thee for a brattle; *perhaps, beat, short race*
But *sax Scotch mile*, thou try't their mettle, *six*
  An' gart them whaizle: *made, wheeze*
Nae whip nor spur, but just a wattle *stick*
60   O' saugh or hazle. *willow*

Thou was a noble *Fittie-lan'*, *rear left plough horse*
As e'er in tug or tow was drawn! *leather or rope*
Aft thee an' I, in aught hours gaun, *eight*
  On guid March-weather,
Hae turn'd *sax rood* beside our han', *by ourselves*
  For days thegither.

Thou never braing't, an' fetch't, an' flisket, *drew unsteadily, gasped, fretted*
But thy *auld tail* thou wad hae whisket,
An' spread abreed thy weel-fill'd *brisket*, *abroad, breast*
70   Wi' pith an pow'r,
Till sprittie knowes wad rair't an' risket *rushy, hillocks, roared, torn underfoot*
  An' slypet owre. *fallen*

When frosts lay lang, an' snaws were deep, *snows*
An' threaten'd *labor* back to keep,
I gied thy *cog* a wee-bit heap *dish*

Aboon the timmer;   above, wooden edge
I ken'd my *Maggie* wad na sleep
    For that, or Simmer.   without, before
                                          summer

In *cart* or *car* thou never reestet;   stood restive
80 The steyest brae thou wad hae fac't it;   stiffest hill
Thou never lap, an' sten't, an' breastet, leapt, reared, pulled
                                          forward
    Then stood to blaw;   blow
But just thy step a wee thing hastet,
    Thou snoov't awa.   went steadily on

My Pleugh is now thy *bairn-time* a';   plough-team, brood
Four gallant brutes, as e'er did draw;
Forby sax mae, I've sell't awa,   beside six more,
                                          sold
    That thou hast nurst:
They drew me thretteen pund an' twa,   thirteen
90   The vera warst.   worst

Monie a sair daurk we twa hae wrought,   hard day's labour
An' wi' the weary warl' fought!   world
An' monie an' *anxious day*, I thought
    We wad be beat!
Yet here to *crazy Age* we're brought,   infirm
    Wi' something yet.

An' think na, my auld, trusty *Servan'*,
That now perhaps thou's less deservin,
An' thy *auld days* may end in starvin', old age
100   For my last fow,   firlot
A heapet *Stimpart*, I'll reserve ane   measure of
                                          grain/quarter peck
    Laid by for you.

We've worn to crazy years thegither;   lived
We'll toyte about wi' ane anither;   totter/walk like old
                                          age
Wi' tentie care I'll flit thy tether,   watchful, change
    To some hain'd rig,   reserved field
Whare ye may nobly rax your leather,   stretch, skin
    Wi' sma' fatigue.

THE COTTER'S SATURDAY NIGHT
INSCRIBED TO R. A****, Esq

Let not Ambition mock their useful toil,
  Their homely joys, and destiny obscure;
Nor Grandeur hear, with a disdainful smile,
  The short and simple annals of the Poor.

                              Gray

I

MY lov'd, my honor'd, much respected friend,
  No mercenary Bard his homage pays;
With honest pride, I scorn each selfish end,
  My dearest meed, a friend's esteem and praise: reward
To you I sing, in simple Scottish lays,
  The *lowly train* in life's sequester'd scene;
The native feelings strong, the guileless ways,
  What A**** in a *Cottage* would have been;
Ah! tho' his worth unknown, far happier there
    I ween!   believe

II

10 November chill blaws loud wi' angry sugh;   blows, rushing sound
  The short'ning winter-day is near a close;
The miry beasts retreating frae the pleugh;   plough
  The black'ning trains o' craws to their repose: crows
The toil-worn COTTER frae his labor goes,   farm tenant/ cottager
  This night his weekly moil is at an end,   drudgery
Collects his *spades*, his *mattocks* and his *hoes*,
  Hoping the *morn* in ease and rest to spend,
And weary, o'er the moor, his course does
    homeward bend.

III

At length his lonely *Cot* appears in view,   cottage
20 Beneath the shelter of an aged tree;
The expectant *wee-things*, toddlan, stacher   stagger
    through

To meet their *Dad*, wi' flichterin noise   fluttering
   and glee.
His wee-bit ingle, blinkan bonilie,   little bit of fire
   His clean hearth-stane, his thrifty *Wifie's*   stone
   smile,
The *lisping infant*, prattling on his knee,
   Does a' his weary *kiaugh* and care beguile,   'carking anxiety' (B)
And makes him quite forget his labor and his toil.

IV

Belyve, the *elder bairns* come drapping in,   soon, dropping
   At *Service* out, amang the Farmers roun';
30 Some ca' the pleugh, some herd, some tentie rin   drive, careful, run
   A cannie errand to a neebor town: quiet, neighbouring
Their eldest hope, their *Jenny*, woman-grown,
   In youthfu' bloom, Love sparkling in her e'e,   eye
Comes hame, perhaps, to shew a braw new gown,   good-looking
   Or deposite her sair-won penny-fee,   hard-won
To help her *Parents* dear, if they in hardship be.

V

With joy unfeign'd, *brothers* and *sisters* meet,
   And each for other's weelfare kindly spiers: asks
The social hours, swift-wing'd, unnotic'd fleet;
40 Each tells the uncos that he sees or hears.   news/uncommon things
The Parents partial eye their hopeful years;
   Anticipation forward points the view;
The *Mother*, wi' her needle and her sheers,
   Gars auld claes look amaist as weel's the new;   makes, clothes
The *Father* mixes a' wi' admonition due.

VI

Their Master's and their Mistress's command,
   The *youngkers* a' are warned to obey;
And mind their labors wi' an eydent hand,   diligent
   And ne'er, tho' out of sight, to jauk or play: 'dally, trifle' (B)
50 'And O! be sure to fear the LORD alway!

And mind your *duty*, duly, morn and night!
Lest in temptation's path ye gang astray,
  Implore his *counsel* and assisting *might*:
They never sought in vain that sought the
    LORD aright.'

VII

But hark! a rap comes gently to the door;
  Jenny, wha kens the meaning o' the same,
Tells how a neebor lad came o'er the moor,
  To do some errands, and convoy her hame.   escort
The wily Mother sees the *conscious flame*
60   Sparkle in *Jenny's* e'e, and flush her cheek,
With heart-struck, anxious care enquires his
      name,
    While *Jenny* hafflins is afraid to speak;   half
Weel-pleas'd the Mother hears, it's nae wild,
    worthless *Rake*.

VIII

With kindly welcome, *Jenny* brings him ben;
  A *strappan youth*; he takes the Mother's eye;
Blythe *Jenny* sees the *visit's* no ill taen;
  The Father cracks of horses, pleughs and kye.   talks, cattle
The *Youngster's* artless heart o'erflows wi' joy,
  But blate and laithfu', scarce can weel behave;   shy, bashful
70 The Mother, wi' a woman's wiles, can spy
    What makes the *youth* sae bashfu' and sae grave;
Weel-pleas'd to think her *bairn's* respected like
      the lave.   rest

IX

O happy love! where love like this is found!
  O heart-felt raptures! bliss beyond compare!
I've paced much this weary, *mortal round*,
  And sage EXPERIENCE bids me this declare –
'If Heaven a draught of heavenly pleasure spare,
  One *cordial* in this melancholy *Vale*,

'Tis when a youthful, loving, *modest* Pair,
80   In other's arms, breathe out the tender tale,
Beneath the milk-white thorn that scents the
    ev'ning gale.'

X

Is there, in human form, that bears a heart--
    A Wretch! a Villain! lost to love and truth!
That can, with studied, sly, ensnaring art,
    Betray sweet Jenny's unsuspecting youth?
Curse on his perjur'd arts! dissembling smooth!
    Are *Honor, Virtue, Conscience*, all exil'd?
Is there no Pity, no relenting Ruth,
    Points to the Parents fondling o'er their Child?
90   Then paints the *ruin'd Maid*, and *their*
    distraction wild!

XI

But now the Supper crown their simple board,
    The healsome *Porritch*, chief of SCOTIA'S food: wholesome, porridge
The soupe their *only Hawkie* does afford,   drink, cow
    That 'yont the hallan snugly chows her cood: beyond, partition, chews, cud
The *Dame* brings forth, in complimental mood,
    To grace the lad, her weel-hain'd kebbuck, fell,   -kept, cheese, pungent
And aft he's prest, and aft he ca's it guid;
    The frugal *Wifie*, garrulous, will tell,
How 'twas a towmond auld, sin' Lint was i'   twelvemonth, flax, flower
    the bell.

XII

100   The chearfu' Supper done, wi' serious face,
    They, round the ingle, form a circle wide;
The Sire turns o'er, with patriarchal grace,
    The big *ha'-Bible*, ance his *Father's* pride: hall-
His bonnet rev'rently is laid aside,
    His *lyart haffets* wearing thin and bare;   grey, temples
Those strains that once did sweet in ZION
    glide,

He wales a portion with judicious care;   chooses
'*And let us worship GOD!*' he says with
        solemn air.

XIII

They chant their artless notes in simple guise;
110   They tune their *hearts*, by far the noblest aim:
Perhaps *Dundee's* wild warbling measures rise,
        Or plaintive *Martyrs*, worthy of the name;
Or noble *Elgin* beets the heaven-ward flame,   'adds fuel to' (B)
        The sweetest far of SCOTIA'S holy lays:
Compar'd with these, *Italian trills* are tame;
        The tickl'd ears no heart-felt raptures raise;
Nae unison hae they, with our CREATOR'S
        praise.

XIV

The priest-like Father reads the sacred page,
        How *Abram* was the Friend of GOD on high;
120   Or, *Moses* bade eternal warfare wage,
        With *Amalek's* ungracious progeny;
Or how the *royal Bard* did groaning lye,
        Beneath the stroke of Heaven's avenging ire;
Or *Job's* pathetic plaint, and wailing cry;
        Or rapt *Isaiah's* wild, seraphic fire;
Or other *Holy Seers* that tune the *sacred lyre*.

XV

Perhaps the *Christian Volume* is the theme,
        How *guiltless blood* for *guilty man* was shed;
How HE, who bore in heaven the second name,
130   Had not on Earth whereon to lay His head:
How His first *followers* and *servants* sped;
        The *Precepts sage* they wrote to many a land:
How *he*, who lone in *Patmos* banished,
        Saw in the sun a mighty angel stand;
And heard great *Bab'lon's* doom pronounc'd
        by Heaven's command.

XVI

Then kneeling down to HEAVEN'S ETERNAL KING,
   The *Saint*, the *Father*, and the *Husband* prays:
Hope 'springs exulting on triumphant wing,'*
   That *thus* they all shall meet in future days:
140 There, ever bask in *uncreated rays*,
   No more to sigh, or shed the bitter tear,
Together hymning their CREATOR'S praise,
   In *such society*, yet still more dear;
While circling Time moves round in an eternal
     sphere.

XVII

Compar'd with *this*, how poor Religion's pride,
   In all the pomp of *method*, and of *art*,
When men display to congregations wide,
   Devotion's ev'ry grace, except the *heart*!
The POWER, incens'd, the Pageant will desert,
150 The pompous strain, the sacerdotal stole;
But haply, in some *Cottage* far apart,
   May hear, well pleas'd, the language
     of the *Soul*;
And in His *Book of Life* the Inmates poor enroll.

XVIII

Then homeward all take off their sev'ral way;
   The youngling *Cottagers* retire to rest:
The Parent-pair their *secret homage* pay,
   And proffer up to Heaven the warm request,
That HE who stills the *raven's* clam'rous nest,
   And decks the *lily* fair in flow'ry pride,
160 Would, in the way *His Wisdom* sees the best,
   For *them* and for their *little ones* provide;
But chiefly, in their hearts with *Grace divine*
     preside.

* Pope's Windsor Forest.

XIX

From scenes like these, old SCOTIA'S grandeur
    springs,
    That makes her lov'd at home, rever'd abroad:
Princes and lords are but the breath of kings,
    'An honest man's the noblest work of GOD:'
And *certes*, in fair Virtue's heavenly road,
    The *Cottage* leaves the *Palace* far behind:
What is a lordling's pomp? a cumbrous load,
170   Disguising oft the *wretch* of human kind,
Studied in arts of Hell, in wickedness refin'd!

XX

O SCOTIA! my dear, my native soil!
    For whom my warmest wish to heaven is sent!
Long may thy hardy sons of *rustic toil*,
    Be blest with health, and peace, and sweet
        content!
And O may Heaven their simple lives prevent
    From *Luxury's* contagion, weak and vile!
Then howe'er *crowns* and *coronets* be rent,
    A *virtuous Populace* may rise the while,
180 And stand a wall of fire around their
        much-lov'd ISLE.

XXI

O THOU! who pour'd the *patriotic tide*,
    That stream'd thro' great, unhappy
        WALLACE' heart;
Who dar'd to, nobly, stem tyrannic pride,
    Or *nobly die*, the second glorious part:
(The Patriot's GOD, peculiarly thou art,
    His *friend, inspirer, guardian* and *reward*!)
O never, never SCOTIA'S realm desert,
    But still the *Patriot*, and the *Patriot-Bard*,
In bright succession raise, her *Ornament*
        and *Guard*!

TO A MOUSE,
On turning her up in her Nest,
with the Plough, November, 1785

WEE, sleeket, cowran, tim'rous *beastie*,   sleek, fearful, little creature
   O, what a panic's in thy breastie!   little breast
Thou need na start awa sae hasty,
       Wi' bickering brattle!   sound of scamper
I wad be laith to rin an' chase thee,   loath, run
       Wi' murd'ring *pattle*!   plough-staff

I'm truly sorry Man's dominion
Has broken Nature's social union,
An' justifies that ill opinion,
10   Which makes thee startle,
At me, thy poor, earth-born companion,
       An' *fellow-mortal*!

I doubt na, whyles, but thou may *thieve*;
What then? poor beastie, thou maun live!
A *daimen-icker* in a *thrave*   occasional ear, 24 sheaves
       'S a sma' request:
I'll get a blessin wi' the lave,   what's left/the rest
       An' never miss't!

Thy wee-bit *housie*, too, in ruin!
20 Its silly wa's the win's are strewin!   frail, winds
An' naething, now, to big a new ane,   build
       O' foggage green!   rank grass
An' bleak *December's winds* ensuin,
       Baith snell an' keen!   bitter

Thou saw the fields laid bare an' wast,   waste
An' weary *Winter* comin fast,
An' cozie here, beneath the blast,
       Thou thought to dwell,
Till crash! the cruel *coulter* past   iron cutter of plough
30   Out thro' thy cell.

That wee-bit heap o' leaves an' stibble,   stubble
Has cost thee monie a weary nibble!
Now thou's turn'd out, for a' thy trouble,
      But house or hald,   without refuge
To thole the Winter's *sleety dribble*,   endure
      An' *cranreuch* cauld!   hoar-frost

But Mousie, thou art no thy-lane,   not alone
In proving *foresight* may be vain:
The best laid schemes o' *Mice* an' *Men*,
      Gang aft agley,   awry
An' lea'e us nought but grief an' pain,
      For promis'd joy!

Still, thou art blest, compar'd wi' *me*!
The *present* only toucheth thee:
But Och! I *backward* cast my e'e,   eye
      On prospects drear!
An' *forward*, tho' I canna *see*,
      I *guess* an' *fear*!

EPISTLE TO DAVIE,
A BROTHER POET

January ——

I

WHILE winds frae off BEN-LOMOND blaw,   blow
And bar the doors wi' driving snaw,   snow
   And hing us owre the ingle,   make us hang, fireside
I set me down, to pass the time,
And spin a verse or twa o' rhyme,
   In hamely, *westlin* jingle.   westland
While frosty winds blaw in the drift,   fallen snow
   Ben to the chimla lug,   in, chimney corner
I grudge a wee the *Great-folk's* gift,
   That live sae bien and snug: comfortable

I tent less, and want less   heed
    Their roomy fire-side;
But hanker, and canker,   become peevish
    To see their cursed pride.

II

It's hardly in a body's pow'r,   person's
To keep, at times, frae being sour,
    To see how things are shar'd;
How *best o' chiels* are whyles in want,   fellows
While *Coofs* on countless thousands rant,   fools, roister
20   And ken na how to wair't: spend
But DAVIE lad, ne'er fash your head,   trouble
    Tho' we hae little gear,   money
We're fit to win our daily bread,
    As lang's we're hale and fier: healthy, sound
     'Mair spier na, nor fear na,'*   ask
      Auld age ne'er mind a feg;   fig
     The last o't, the warst o't,   worst
      Is only but to beg.

III

To lye in kilns and barns at e'en,
30 When banes are craz'd, and bluid is thin,   bones
    Is, doubtless, great distress!
Yet then *content* could make us blest;
Ev'n then, sometimes we'd snatch a taste
    Of truest happiness.
The honest heart that's free frae a'
    Intended fraud or guile,
However Fortune kick the ba',   ball
    Has ay some cause to smile: always
     And mind still, you'll find still,   remember
40   A comfort this nae sma';
     Nae mair then, we'll care then,
      Nae *farther* we can fa'.

* Ramsay.

IV

What tho', like Commoners of air,
We wander out, we know not where,
    But either house or hal'?   *without, refuge*
Yet *Nature's* charms, the hills and woods,
The sweeping vales, and foaming floods,
    Are free alike to all.
In days when Daisies deck the ground,
50   And Blackbirds whistle clear,
With honest joy, our hearts will bound,
    To see the *coming* year:
      On braes when we please then,   *hill-sides*
        We'll sit and *sowth* a tune;   'try over with a low whistle' (B)
      Syne *rhyme* till't, we'll time till't   *then, to it*
        And sing't when we hae done.

V

It's no in titles nor in rank;
It's no in wealth like *Lon'on Bank*,
    To purchase peace and rest;
60 It's no in makin muckle, *mair*:
It's no in books; it's no in Lear,   *learning*
    To make us truly blest:
If Happiness hae not her seat
    And center in the breast,
We may be *wise*, or *rich*, or *great*,
    But never can be *blest*:
      Nae treasures, nor pleasures
        Could make us happy lang;   *for long*
      The *heart* ay's the part ay,
70   That makes us right or wrang.   *wrong*

VI

Think ye, that sic as *you* and *I*,
Wha drudge and drive thro' wet and dry,
    Wi' never-ceasing toil;
Think ye, are we less blest than they,
Wha scarcely tent us in their way,

As hardly worth their while?
Alas! how aft, in haughty mood,
　GOD'S creatures they oppress!
Or else, neglecting a' that's guid,
80　　They riot in excess!
　　　Baith careless, and fearless,
　　　　Of either Heaven or Hell;
　　　Esteeming, and deeming,
　　　　It a' an idle tale!

VII

Then let us chearfu' acquiesce;
Nor make our scanty Pleasures less,
　By pining at our state:
And, ev'n should Misfortunes come,
I, here whae sit, hae met wi' some,
90　　An's thankfu' for them yet.   and am
They gie the wit of *Age* to *Youth*;
　They let us ken oursel;
They make us see the naked truth,
　The *real* guid and ill.
　　Tho' losses, and crosses,
　　　Be lessons right severe,
　　There's *wit* there, ye'll get there,
　　　Ye'll find nae other where.

VIII

But tent me, DAVIE, *Ace o' Hearts*!
100　(To say aught less wad wrang the *cartes*,   cards
　And flatt'ry I detest)
This life has joys for you and I;
And joys that riches ne'er could buy;
　And joys the very best.
There's a' the *Pleasures o' the Heart*,
　The *Lover* and the *Frien'*;
Ye hae your MEG, your dearest part,
　And I my darling JEAN!

It warms me, it charms me,
110   To mention but her *name*:
    It heats me, it beets me,   kindles
          And sets me a' on flame!

IX

O, all ye *Pow'rs* who rule above!
O THOU, whose very self art *love*!
    THOU know'st my words sincere!
The *life blood* streaming thro' my heart,
Or my more dear *Immortal part*,
    Is not more fondly dear!
When heart-corroding care and grief
120   Deprive my soul of rest,
Her dear idea brings relief,
    And solace to my breast.
          Thou BEING, Allseeing,
               O hear my fervent pray'r!
          Still take her, and make her,
               THY most peculiar care!

X

All hail! ye tender feelings dear!
The smile of love, the friendly tear,
    The sympathetic glow!
130 Long since, this world's thorny ways
Had number'd out my weary days,
    Had it not been for you!
Fate still has blest me with a friend,
    In ev'ry care and ill;
And oft a more *endearing* band,
    A *tye* more tender still.
          It lightens, it brightens,
               The tenebrific scene,   dark, gloomy
          To meet with, and greet with,
140   My DAVIE or my JEAN!

XI

O, how that *name* inspires my style!
The words come skelpan, rank and file,   spanking
  Amaist before I ken!
The ready measure rins as fine,   runs
As *Phoebus* and the famous *Nine*   as if
  Were glowran owre my pen.   gazing
My spavet *Pegasus* will limp,   spavined/halting
  Till ance he's fairly het;   hot
And then he'll hilch, and stilt, and jimp,   hobble, limp, jump
150 And rin an unco fit: uncommon pace
    But least then, the beast then,   lest
      Should rue this hasty ride,
    I'll light now, and dight now,   wipe
      His sweaty, wizen'd hide.

THE LAMENT

Occasioned by the Unfortunate Issue of
A FRIEND'S AMOUR

Alas! how oft does goodness wound itself!
And sweet Affection *prove the spring of Woe!*

             Home

I

O Thou pale Orb, that silent shines,
  While care-untroubled mortals sleep!
Thou seest a *wretch*, who inly pines,
  And wanders here to wail and weep!
With Woe I nightly vigils keep,
  Beneath thy wan, unwarming beam;
And mourn, in lamentation deep,
  How *life* and *love* are all a dream!

II

I joyless view thy rays adorn,
    The faintly-marked, distant hill:
I joyless view thy trembling horn,
    Reflected in the gurgling rill.
My fondly-fluttering heart, be still!
    Thou busy pow'r, Remembrance, cease!
Ah! must the agonizing thrill,
    For ever bar returning Peace!

III

No idly-feign'd, poetic pains,
    My sad, lovelorn lamentings claim:
No shepherd's pipe – Arcadian strains;
    No fabled tortures, quaint and tame.
The *plighted faith*; the *mutual flame*;
    The *oft-attested Powers above*;
The promis'd Father's tender name;
    These were the pledges of my love!

IV

Encircled in her clasping arms,
    How have the raptur'd moments flown!
How have I wish'd for Fortune's charms,
    For her dear sake, and her's alone!
And, must I think it! is she gone,
    My secret-heart's exulting boast?
And does she heedless hear my groan?
    And is she ever, ever lost?

V

Oh! can she bear so base a heart,
    So lost to Honor, lost to Truth,
As from the *fondest lover* part,
    The *plighted husband* of her youth?
Alas! Life's path may be unsmooth!
    Her way may lie thro' rough distress!
Then, who her pangs and pains will soothe,
    Her sorrows share and make them less?

VI

Ye winged Hours that o'er us past,
  Enraptur'd more, the more enjoy'd,
Your dear remembrance in my breast,
  My fondly-treasur'd thoughts employ'd.
That breast, how dreary now, and void,
  For her too scanty once of room!
Ev'n ev'ry *ray* of *Hope* destroy'd,
  And not a *Wish* to gild the gloom!

VII

The morn that warns th'approaching day,
50 Awakes me up to toil and woe:
I see the hours, in long array,
  That I must suffer, lingering, slow.
Full many a pang, and many a throe,
  Keen Recollection's direful train,
Must wring my soul, ere Phoebus, low,
  Shall kiss the distant, western main.

VIII

And when my nightly couch I try,
  Sore-harass'd out, with care and grief,
My toil-beat nerves, and tear-worn eye,
60 Keep watchings with the nightly thief:
Or if I slumber, Fancy, chief,
  Reigns, haggard-wild, in sore afright:
Ev'n day, all-bitter, brings relief,
  From such a horror-breathing night.

IX

O! thou bright Queen, who, o'er th'expanse,
  Now highest reign'st, with boundless sway!
Oft has thy silent-marking glance
  Observ'd us, fondly-wand'ring, stray!
The time, unheeded, sped away,
70 While Love's *luxurious pulse* beat high,
Beneath thy silver-gleaming ray,
  To mark the mutual-kindling eye.

X

Oh! scenes in strong remembrance set!
   Scenes, never, never to return!
Scenes, if in stupor I forget,
   Again I feel, again I burn!
From ev'ry joy and pleasure torn,
   Life's weary vale I'll wander thro';
And hopeless, comfortless, I'll mourn
80   *A faithless woman's broken vow.*

DESPONDENCY,
AN ODE

I

OPPRESS'D with grief, oppress'd with care,
A burden more than I can bear,
   I set me down and sigh:
O Life! Thou art a galling load,
Along a rough, a weary road,
   To wretches such as I!
Dim-backward as I cast my view,
   What sick'ning Scenes appear!
What Sorrows *yet* may pierce me thro',
10   Too justly I may fear!
     Still caring, despairing,
       Must be my bitter doom;
     My woes here, shall close ne'er,
       But with the *closing tomb!*

II

Happy! ye sons of Busy-life,
Who, equal to the bustling strife,
   No other view regard!
Ev'n when the wished *end's* deny'd,
Yet while the busy *means* are ply'd,
20   They bring their own reward:
Whilst I, a hope-abandon'd wight,

Unfitted with an *aim*,
Meet ev'ry sad-returning night,
  And joyless morn the same.
    You, bustling and justling,
      Forget each grief and pain;
    I, listless, yet restless,
      Find ev'ry prospect vain.

III

How blest the Solitary's lot,
Who, all-forgetting, all-forgot,
  Within his humble cell,
The cavern wild with tangling roots,
Sits o'er his newly-gather'd fruits,
  Beside his crystal well!
Or haply, to his ev'ning thought,
  By unfrequented stream,
The *ways of men* are distant brought,
  A faint-collected dream:
    While praising, and raising
      His thoughts to Heaven on high,
    As wand'ring, meand'ring,
      He views the solemn sky.

IV

Than I, no *lonely Hermit* plac'd
Where never human footstep trac'd,
  Less fit to play the part,
The *lucky moment* to improve,
And *just* to stop, and *just* to move,
  With *self-respecting* art:
But ah! those pleasures, Loves and Joys,
  Which I too keenly taste,
The *Solitary* can despise,
  Can want, and yet be blest!
    He needs not, he heeds not,
      Or human love or hate;
    Whilst I here, must cry here,
      At perfidy ingrate!

V

V

Oh, enviable, early days,
When dancing thoughtless Pleasure's maze,
  To Care, to Guilt unknown!
60 How ill exchang'd for riper times,
To feel the follies, or the crimes,
  Of others, or my own!
Ye tiny elves that guiltless sport,
  Like linnets in the bush,
Ye little know the ills ye court,
  When Manhood is your wish!
    The losses, the crosses,
      That *active man* engage;
    The fears all, the tears all,
70   Of dim declining *Age!*

MAN WAS MADE TO MOURN,
A DIRGE

I

WHEN chill November's surly blast
  Made fields and forests bare,
One ev'ning, as I wand'red forth,
  Along the banks of AIRE,
I spy'd a man, whose aged step
  Seem'd weary, worn with care;
His face was furrow'd o'er with years,
  And hoary was his hair.

II

Young stranger, whither wand'rest thou?
10   Began the rev'rend Sage;
Does thirst of wealth thy step constrain,
  Or youthful Pleasure's rage?

Or haply, prest with cares and woes,
    Too soon thou hast began,
To wander forth, with me, to mourn
    The miseries of Man.

III

The Sun that overhangs yon moors,
    Out-spreading far and wide,
Where hundreds labour to support
20   A haughty lordling's pride;
I've seen yon weary winter-sun
    Twice forty times return;
And ev'ry time has added proofs,
    That Man was made to mourn.

IV

O Man! while in thy early years,
    How prodigal of time!
Misspending all thy precious hours,
    Thy glorious, youthful prime!
Alternate Follies take the sway;
30   Licentious Passions burn;
Which tenfold force gives Nature's law,
    That Man was made to mourn.

V

Look not alone on youthful Prime,
    Or Manhood's active might;
Man then is useful to his kind,
    Supported is his right:
But see him on the edge of life,
    With Cares and Sorrows worn,
Then Age and Want, Oh! ill-match'd pair!
40   Show Man was made to mourn.

VI

A few seem favourites of Fate,
In Pleasure's lap carest;
Yet, think not all the Rich and Great,
Are likewise truly blest.
But Oh! what crouds in ev'ry land,
All wretched and forlorn,
Thro' weary life this lesson learn,
That Man was made to mourn!

VII

Many and sharp the num'rous Ills
50   Inwoven with our frame!
More pointed still we make ourselves,
Regret, Remorse and Shame!
And Man, whose heav'n-erected face,
The smiles of love adorn,
Man's inhumanity to Man
Makes countless thousands mourn!

VIII

See, yonder poor, o'erlabour'd wight,
So abject, mean and vile,
Who begs a brother of the earth
60   To give him leave to toil;
And see his lordly *fellow-worm*,
The poor petition spurn,
Unmindful, tho' a weeping wife,
And helpless offspring mourn.

IX

If I'm design'd yon lordling's slave,
By Nature's law design'd,
Why was an independent wish
E'er planted in my mind?
If not, why am I subject to
70   His cruelty, or scorn?
Or why has Man the will and pow'r
To make his fellow mourn?

X

Yet, let not this too much, my Son,
  Disturb thy youthful breast:
This partial view of human-kind
  Is surely not the *last*!
The poor, oppressed, honest man
  Had never, sure, been born,
Had there not been some recompence
  To comfort those that mourn!

80

XI

O Death! the poor man's dearest friend,
  The kindest and the best!
Welcome the hour, my aged limbs
  Are laid with thee at rest!
The Great, the Wealthy fear thy blow,
  From pomp and pleasure torn;
But Oh! a blest relief for those
  That weary-laden mourn!

WINTER,
A DIRGE

I

THE Wintry West extends his blast,
  And hail and rain does blaw;   blow
Or, the stormy North sends driving forth,
  The blinding sleet and snaw: snow
While, tumbling brown, the Burn comes down,
  And roars frae bank to brae;   hillside
And bird and beast, in covert, rest,
  And pass the heartless day.

II

'The sweeping blast, the sky o'ercast,'*
10   The joyless *winter-day,*
Let others fear, to me more dear,
     Than all the pride of May:
The Tempest's howl, it *soothes* my soul,
     My *griefs* it seems to join;
The leafless trees my fancy please,
     Their *fate* resembles mine!

III

Thou POW'R SUPREME, whose mighty Scheme,
     These *woes* of mine fulfil;
Here, firm, I rest, they *must* be best,
20   Because they are *Thy* Will!
Then all I want (Oh, do thou grant
     This one request of mine!)
Since to *enjoy* Thou dost deny,
     Assist me to *resign!*

A PRAYER,
IN THE PROSPECT OF DEATH

I

O THOU unknown, Almighty Cause
     Of all my hope and fear!
In whose dread Presence, ere an hour,
     Perhaps I must appear!

II

If I have wander'd in those paths
     Of life I ought to shun;
As *Something,* loudly, in my breast,
     Remonstrates I have done;

* Dr. Young

III

Thou know'st that Thou hast formed me,
10   With Passions wild and strong;
And list'ning to their witching voice
        Has often led me wrong.

IV

Where human *weakness* has come short,
        Or *frailty* stept aside,
Do Thou, ALL-GOOD, for such Thou art,
        In shades of darkness hide.

V

Where with *intention* I have err'd,
        No other plea I have,
But, *Thou art good;* and Goodness still
20   Delighteth to forgive.

TO A MOUNTAIN-DAISY,

On turning one down, with the Plough,
in April —— 1786

WEE, modest, crimson-tipped flow'r,
Thou's met me in an evil hour;
For I maun crush amang the stoure   dust
        Thy slender stem:
To spare thee now is past my pow'r,
        Thou bonie gem.

Alas! it's no thy neebor sweet,   neighbour
The bonie *Lark*, companion meet!
Bending thee 'mang the dewy weet!   wet
10   Wi's spreckl'd breast,
When upward-springing, blythe, to greet
        The purpling East.

Cauld blew the bitter-biting *North*
Upon thy early, humble birth;
Yet chearfully thou glinted forth
    Amid the storm,
Scarce rear'd above the *Parent-earth*
    Thy tender form.

The flaunting *flow'rs* our Gardens yield,
High-shelt'ring woods and wa's maun shield,
But thou, beneath the random bield   shelter
    O' clod or stane,   stone
Adorns the histie *stibble-field*,   bare, stubble-
    Unseen, alane.   alone

There, in thy scanty mantle clad,
Thy snawie bosom sun-ward spread,   snowy
Thou lifts thy unassuming head
    In humble guise;
But now the *share* uptears thy bed,   ploughshare
    And low thou lies!

Such is the fate of artless Maid,
Sweet *flow'ret* of the rural shade!
By Love's simplicity betray'd,
    And guileless trust,
Till she, like thee, all soil'd, is laid
    Low i' the dust.

Such is the fate of simple Bard,
On Life's rough ocean luckless starr'd!
Unskilful he to note the card
    Of *prudent Lore*,
Till billows rage, and gales blow hard,
    And whelm him o'er!

Such fate to *suffering worth* is giv'n,
Who long with wants and woes has striv'n,
By human pride or cunning driv'n

To Mis'ry's brink,
Till wrench'd of ev'ry stay but HEAV'N,
He, ruin'd, sink!

Ev'n thou who mourn'st the *Daisy's* fate,
50   *That fate is thine* – no distant date;
Stern Ruin's *plough-share* drives, elate,
    Full on thy bloom,
Till crush'd beneath the *furrow's* weight,
    Shall be thy doom!

TO RUIN

I

ALL hail! inexorable lord!
At whose destruction-breathing word,
  The mightiest empires fall!
Thy cruel, woe-delighted train,
The ministers of Grief and Pain,
  A sullen welcome, all!
With stern-resolv'd, despairing eye,
  I see each aimed dart;
For one has cut my *dearest tye*,
10   And quivers in my heart.
    Then low'ring, and pouring,
      The *Storm* no more I dread;
    Tho' thick'ning, and black'ning,
      Round my devoted head.

II

And thou grim Pow'r, by Life abhorr'd,
While Life a *pleasure* can afford,
  Oh! hear a wretch's pray'r!
No more I shrink appall'd, afraid;
I court, I beg thy friendly aid,
20   To close this scene of care!

When shall my soul, in silent peace,
  Resign Life's *joyless* day?
My weary heart its throbbings cease,
  Cold-mould'ring in the clay?
    No fear more, no tear more,
        To stain my lifeless face,
    Enclasped, and grasped,
        Within thy cold embrace!

EPISTLE
TO A YOUNG FRIEND

May —— 1786

I

I Lang hae thought, my youthfu' friend,
  A Something to have sent you,
Tho' it should serve nae other end
  Than just a kind memento;
But how the subject theme may gang,
  Let time and chance determine;
Perhaps it may turn out a Sang;
  Perhaps, turn out a Sermon.

II

Ye'll try the world soon my lad,
10   And ANDREW dear believe me,
Ye'll find mankind an unco squad,
  And muckle they may grieve ye:
For care and trouble set your thought,
  Ev'n when your end's attained;
And a' your views may come to nought,
  Where ev'ry nerve is strained.

III

I'll no say, men are villains a';
    The real, harden'd wicked,
Whae hae nae check but *human law*,
20   Are to a few restricked:
But Och, mankind are unco weak,
    An' little to be trusted;
If *Self* the wavering balance shake,
    It's rarely right adjusted!

IV

Yet they wha fa' in Fortune's strife,
    Their fate we should na censure,
For still th'*important end* of life,
    They equally may answer:
A man may hae an *honest heart*,
30   Tho' Poortith hourly stare him;   poverty
A man may tak a neebor's part,   neighbour's
    Yet hae nae *cash* to spare him.

V

Ay free, aff han', your story tell,   offhand
    When wi' a bosom crony;
But still keep something to yoursel
    Ye scarcely tell to ony.
Conceal yoursel as weel's ye can
    Frae critical dissection;
But keek thro' ev'ry other man,   look/pry
40   Wi' sharpen'd, sly inspection.

VI

The *sacred lowe* o' weel plac'd love,   flame
    Luxuriantly indulge it;
But never tempt th'*illicit rove*,   attempt
    Tho' naething should divulge it:
I waive the quantum o' the sin;   amount
    The hazard of concealing;
But Och! it hardens *a' within*,
    And petrifies the feeling!

VII

To catch Dame Fortune's golden smile,
    Assiduous wait upon her;
50 And gather gear by ev'ry wile,   money/property
    That's justify'd by Honor:
Not for to *hide* it in a *hedge*,
    Nor for a *train-attendant*;
But for the glorious priviledge
    Of being *independant*.

VIII

The fear o' Hell's a hangman's whip,
    To haud the wretch in order;   hold
But where ye feel your *Honor* grip,
60   Let that ay be your border:
Its slightest touches, instant pause –
    Debar a' side-pretences;
And resolutely keep its laws,
    Uncaring consequences.

IX

The great CREATOR to revere,
    Must sure become the *Creature*;
But still the preaching cant forbear,
    And ev'n the rigid feature:
Yet ne'er with Wits prophane to range,
70   Be complaisance extended;
An *atheist-laugh's* a poor exchange
    For *Deity offended*!

X

When ranting round in Pleasure's ring,   frolicking
    Religion may be blinded;
Or if she gie a *random-fling*,
    It may be little minded;
But when on Life we're tempest-driven,
    A Conscience but a canker –
A correspondence fix'd wi' Heav'n,
80   Is sure a noble *anchor*!

XI

Adieu, dear, amiable Youth!
   Your *heart* can ne'er be wanting!
May Prudence, Fortitude and Truth
   Erect your brow undaunting!
In *ploughman phrase* 'GOD send you speed,'
   Still daily to grow wiser;
And may ye better reck the *rede*,   heed the advice
   Than ever did th' *Adviser*!

ON A SCOTCH BARD
GONE TO THE WEST INDIES

A' ye wha live by sowps o' drink,   mouthfuls
A' ye wha live by crambo-clink,   rhyme
A' ye wha live and never think,
      Come, mourn wi' me!
Our *billie's* gien us a' a jink,   comrade, slip
      An' owre the Sea.

Lament him a' ye rantan core,   merry company
Wha dearly like a random-splore;   frolic
Nae mair he'll join the *merry roar*,
10   In social key;
For now he's taen anither shore,
      An' owre the Sea!

The bonie lasses weel may wiss him,   wish
And in their dear *petitions* place him:
The widows, wives, an' a' may bless him,
      Wi' tearfu' e'e;   eye
For weel I wat they'll sairly miss him   know
      That's owre the Sea!

O Fortune, they hae room to grumble!
20 Hadst thou taen aff some drowsy bummle,   bungler
Wha can do nought but fyke an' fumble,   fuss
    'Twad been nae plea;
But he was gleg as onie wumble,   nimble, gimlet
    That's owre the Sea!

Auld, cantie KYLE may weepers wear,   cheerful
An' stain them wi' the saut, saut tear: salt
'Twill mak her poor, auld heart, I fear,
    In flinders flee: fragments
He was her *Laureat* monie a year,
30   That's owre the Sea!

He saw Misfortune's cauld *Nor-west*
Lang-mustering up a bitter blast;
A Jillet brak his heart at last,   jilt
    Ill may she be!
So, took a birth afore the mast,   berth
    An' owre the Sea.

To tremble under Fortune's cummock;   cudgel
On scarce a bellyfu' o' *drummock*,   meal and water
Wi' his proud, independant stomach,
40   Could ill agree;
So, row't his hurdies in a *hammock*,   rolled, buttocks
    An' owre the Sea.

He ne'er was gien to great misguidin,
Yet coin his pouches wad na bide in;   pockets
Wi' him it ne'er was *under hidin*;
    He dealt it free:
The *Muse* was a' that he took pride in,
    That's owre the Sea.

Jamaica bodies, use him weel,
50 An' hap him in a cozie biel: wrap, shelter
Ye'll find him ay a dainty chiel,   pleasant fellow

An' fou o' glee: full
He wad na wrang'd the vera *Diel*,   wronged, very,
      That's owre the Sea.   Devil

Fareweel, my *rhyme-composing billie*!   fellow
Your native soil was right ill-willie;   unkind
But may ye flourish like a lily,
      Now bonilie!
I'll toast you in my hindmost *gillie*,   last gill
60   Tho' owre the Sea!

A DEDICATION
TO G**** H******* Esq;

EXPECT na, Sir, in this narration,
A fleechan, fleth'ran *Dedication*,   flattering,
To roose you up, an' ca' you guid,   wheedling
An' sprung o' great an' noble bluid;   praise
Because ye're sirnam'd like *His Grace*,
Perhaps related to the race:
Then when I'm tir'd – and sae are *ye*,
Wi' monie a fulsome, sinfu' lie,
Set up a face, how I stop short,
10   For fear your modesty be hurt.

   This may do – maun do, Sir, wi' them wha
Maun please the Great-folk for a wamefou;   bellyful
For me! sae laigh I need na bow,   low
For, LORD be thanket, *I can plough*;
And when I downa yoke a naig,   cannot, small horse
Then, LORD be thanket, *I can beg*;
Sae I shall say, an' that's nae flatt'rin,
It's just *sic Poet* an' *sic Patron*.

The Poet, some guid Angel help him,
20 Or else, I fear, some *ill ane* skelp him!   slap
    He may do weel for a' he's done yet,
    But only – he's no just begun yet.

    The Patron, (Sir, ye maun forgie me,   forgive
    I winna lie, come what will o' me)   will not
    On ev'ry hand it will allow'd be,
    He's just – nae better than he should be.

    I readily and freely grant,
    He downa see a poor man want;
    What's no his ain, he winna tak it;   own
30 What ance he says, he winna break it;
    Ought he can lend he'll no refus't,   anything
    Till aft his guidness is abus'd;
    And rascals whyles that do him wrang,   wrong
    Ev'n *that*, he does na mind it lang: remember
    As Master, Landlord, Husband, Father,
    He does na fail his part in either.

    But then, nae thanks to him for a' that;
    Nae *godly symptom* ye can ca' that;
    It's naething but a milder feature,
40 Of our poor, sinfu', corrupt Nature:
    Ye'll get the best o' moral works,
    'Mang black *Gentoos*, and Pagan *Turks*,
    Or Hunters wild on *Ponotaxi*,
    Wha never heard of Orth-d-xy.
    That he's the poor man's friend in need,
    The GENTLEMAN in word and deed,
    It's no through terror of D-mn-t-n;
    It's just a carnal inclination,
    And Och! that's nae r-g-n-r-t-n!

50 Morality, thou deadly bane,
    Thy tens o' thousands thou hast slain!
    Vain is his hope, whase stay an' trust is,
    In *moral* Mercy, Truth and Justice!

No – stretch a point to catch a plack;   farthing
Abuse a Brother to his back;
Steal thro' the *winnock* frae a wh-re,   window
But point the Rake that taks the *door*;
Be to the Poor like onie whunstane,   whinstone
And haud their noses to the grunstane;   hold, grindstone
60   Ply ev'ry art o' *legal* thieving;
No matter – stick to *sound believing*.

Learn three-mile pray'rs, an' half-mile graces,
Wi' weel spread looves, an' lang, wry faces;   palms
Grunt up a solemn, lengthen'd groan,
And damn a' Parties but your own;
I'll warrant then, ye're nae Deceiver,
A steady, sturdy, staunch *Believer*.

O ye wha leave the springs o' C-lv-n,
For *gumlie dubs* of your ain delvin!   muddy puddles, digging
70   Ye sons of Heresy and Error,
Ye'll *some day* squeel in quaking terror!
When Vengeance draws the sword in wrath,
And in the fire throws the *sheath*;
When Ruin, with his sweeping *besom*,
Just frets till Heav'n commission gies him;
While o'er the *Harp* pale Misery moans,
And strikes the ever-deep'ning tones,
Still louder shrieks, and heavier groans!   }

Your pardon, Sir, for this digression,
80   I maist forgat my *Dedication*;
But when Divinity comes cross me,
My readers then are sure to lose me.

So Sir, you see 'twas nae daft vapour,   whimsy
But I maturely thought it proper,
When a' my works I did review,
To *dedicate* them, Sir, to YOU:
Because (ye need na tak it ill)
I thought them something like *yoursel*.

Then patronize them wi' your favor,
90   And your Petitioner shall ever –
I had amaist said, *ever pray*,
But that's a word I need na say:
For prayin I hae little skill o't;
I'm baith dead-sweer, an' wretched ill o't;   very reluctant, poor at it
But I'se repeat each poor man's *pray'r*,   I'll
That kens or hears about you, Sir –
'May ne'er Misfortune's gowling bark,   yelling
Howl thro' the dwelling o' the CLERK!
May ne'er his gen'rous, honest heart,
100   For that same gen'rous spirit smart!
May K******'s far-honor'd name   [Kennedy's]
Lang beet his hymeneal flame,   feed
Till H*******'s, at least a diz'n,   [Hamilton's] dozen
Are frae their nuptial labors risen:
Five bonie Lasses round their table,
And sev'n braw fellows, stout an' able,
To serve their King an' Country weel,
By word, or pen, or pointed steel!
May Health and Peace, with mutual rays,
110   Shine on the ev'ning o' his days;
Till his wee, curlie *John's* ier-oe,   }   great-grandchild
When ebbing life nae mair shall flow,   }
The last, sad, mournful rites bestow!' }

I will not wind a lang conclusion,
With complimentary effusion:
But whilst your wishes and endeavours,
Are blest with Fortune's smiles and favours,
I am, Dear Sir, with zeal most fervent,
Your much indebted, humble servant.

120   But if, which Pow'rs above prevent,
That iron-hearted Carl, *Want*,   fellow
Attended, in his grim advances,
By *sad mistakes*, and *black mischances*,

While hopes, and joys, and pleasures fly him,
Make you as poor a dog as I am,
Your *humble servant* then no more;
For who would humbly serve the Poor?
But by a poor man's hopes in Heav'n!
While recollection's pow'r is giv'n,
130   If, in the vale of humble life,
The victim sad of Fortune's strife,
I, through the tender-gushing tear,
Should recognise my *Master dear*,
If friendless, low, we meet together,
Then, Sir, your hand – my FRIEND and BROTHER.

TO A LOUSE,

On Seeing one on a Lady's Bonnet at Church

HA! whare ye gaun, ye crowlan ferlie!   crawling wonder
Your impudence protects you sairly: indeed
I canna say but ye strunt rarely,   strut
     Owre *gawze* and *lace*;
Tho' faith, I fear ye dine but sparely,
     On sic a place.

Ye ugly, creepan, blastet wonner,   wonder
Detested, shunn'd, by saunt an' sinner,   saint
How daur ye set your fit upon her,   dare, foot
10   Sae fine a *Lady*!
Gae somewhere else and seek your dinner,
     On some poor body.

Swith, in some beggar's haffet squattle;   off!, temple, squat
There ye may creep, and sprawl, and sprattle,   scramble
Wi' ither kindred, jumping cattle,   beasts
     In shoals and nations;   families, tribes
Whare *horn* nor *bane* ne'er daur unsettle,   horn, bone
     Your thick plantations.

Now haud you there, ye're out of sight,   keep
20 Below the fatt'rels, snug and tight,   falderals
Na faith ye yet! ye'll no be right,
      Till ye've got on it,
The vera tapmost, towrin height   very topmost
      O' *Miss's bonnet.*

My sooth! right bauld ye set your nose out,   bold
As plump an' gray as onie grozet: gooseberry
O for some rank, mercurial rozet,   resin
      Or fell, red smeddum,   deadly, powder
I'd gie you sic a hearty dose o't,
30   Wad dress your droddum!   thrash, backside

I wad na been surpriz'd to spy
You on an auld wife's *flainen toy*;   flannel cap
Or aiblins some bit duddie boy,   perhaps, small ragged
      On's *wylecoat*;   flannel vest
But Miss's fine *Lunardi*, fye!   balloon bonnet
      How daur ye do't?

O *Jenny* dinna toss your head,   do not
An' set your beauties a' abroad!   abroad
Ye little ken what cursed speed
40   The blastie's makin!   ill-disposed creature
Thae *winks* and *finger-ends*, I dread,   those
      Are notice takin!

O wad some Pow'r the giftie gie us   little gift
To see oursels as others see us!
It wad frae monie a blunder free us
      An' foolish notion:
What airs in dress an' gait wad lea'e us
      And ev'n Devotion!

EPISTLE TO J. L*****K,
AN OLD SCOTCH BARD

April 1st, 1785

WHILE briers an' woodbines budding green,
An' Paitricks scraichan loud at e'en, — partridges, screaming, evening
And morning Poossie whiddan seen, — hare, scudding
    Inspire my Muse,
This freedom, in an *unknown* frien',
    I pray excuse.

On Fasteneen we had a rockin, — Shrove Tuesday, spinning party
To ca' the crack and weave our stockin; — have a chat
And there was muckle fun and jokin,
10   Ye need na doubt;
At length we had a hearty yokin, — set-to
    At *sang about*. — singing in turn

There was ae *sang*, amang the rest,
Aboon them a' it pleas'd me best, — above
That some kind husband had addrest,
    To some sweet wife:
It thirl'd the heart-strings thro' the breast, — thrilled
    A' to the life.

I've scarce heard ought describ'd sae weel,
20 What gen'rous, manly bosoms feel;
Thought I, 'Can this be *Pope*, or *Steele*,
    Or *Beattie's* wark;' — work
They told me 'twas an odd kind chiel — told, fellow
    About *Muirkirk*.

It pat me fidgean-fain to hear't, — put, tingling with pleasure
An' sae about him there I spier't; — asked
Then a' that kent him round declar'd,
    He had *ingine*, — wit
That nane excell'd it, few cam near't,
30   It was sae fine.

That set him to a pint of ale,
An' either douse or merry tale,   *sober*
Or rhymes an' sangs he'd made himsel,
   Or witty catches,
'Tween Inverness and Teviotdale,
   He had few matches.

Then up I gat, an swoor an aith,   *swore, oath*
Tho' I should pawn my pleugh an' graith, *plough, harness*
Or die a cadger pownie's death,   *hawker pony's*
40   At some dyke-back,   *behind a wall*
A *pint* an' *gill* I'd gie them *baith*,
   To hear your crack.   *talk*

But first an' foremost, I should tell,
Amaist as soon as I could spell,
I to the *crambo-jingle* fell,   *rhyming*
   Tho' rude an' rough,
Yet crooning to a body's sel,   *humming, to oneself*
   Does weel eneugh.   *enough*

I am nae *Poet*, in a sense,
50 But just a *Rhymer* like by chance,
An' hae to Learning nae pretence,
   Yet, what the matter?
Whene'er my Muse does on me glance,
   I jingle at her.

Your Critic-folk may cock their nose,
And say, 'How can you e'er propose,
You wha ken hardly *verse* frae *prose*,
   To mak a *sang*?'
But by your leaves, my learned foes,
60   Ye're maybe wrang.   *wrong*

What's a' your jargon o' your Schools,
Your Latin names for horns an' stools;
If honest Nature made you *fools*,

What sairs your Grammars?   *serves*
Ye'd better taen up *spades* and *shools*,   *shovels*
     Or *knappin-hammers*.   *stone-breaking*

A set o' dull, conceited Hashes,   *dunderheads*
Confuse their brains in *Colledge-classes*!
They *gang in* Stirks, and *come out* Asses,   *steers/young bullocks*
70   Plain truth to speak;
An' syne they think to climb Parnassus   *then*
     By dint o' Greek!

Gie me ae spark o' Nature's fire,
That's a' the learning I desire;
Then tho' I drudge thro' dub an' mire   *puddle*
     At pleugh or cart,
My Muse, tho' hamely in attire,
     May touch the heart.

O for a spunk o' ALLAN'S glee,   *spark*
80 Or FERGUSON'S, the bauld an' slee,   *bold, clever*
Or bright L*****K'S, my friend to be,
     If I can hit it!
That would be *lear* eneugh for me,   *learning*
     If I could get it.

Now, Sir, if ye hae friends enow,   *enough*
Tho' *real friends* I b'lieve are few,
Yet, if your catalogue be fow,   *full*
     I'se no insist;   *I'll*
But gif ye want ae friend that's true,   *if*
90   I'm on your list.

I winna blaw about *mysel*,   *will not brag*
As ill I like my fauts to tell;   *faults*
But friends an' folk that wish me well,
     They sometimes roose me;   *praise*
Tho' I maun own, as monie still,
     As far abuse me.

There's ae *wee faut* they whiles lay to me,
I like the lasses – Gude forgie me!   God forgive
For monie a Plack they wheedle frae me,   coin
100   At dance or fair:
Maybe some *ither thing* they gie me
   They weel can spare.

But MAUCHLINE Race or MAUCHLINE Fair,
I should be proud to meet you there;
We'se gie ae night's discharge to *care*,   we'll
   If we forgather,
An' hae a swap o' *rhymin-ware*,
   Wi' ane anither.

The *four-gill chap*, we'se gar him clatter, cup, we'll make
110 An' kirs'n him wi' reekin water;   christen, steaming
Syne we'll sit down an' tak our whitter, draught
   To chear our heart;
An' faith, we'se be *acquainted* better
   Before we part.

Awa ye selfish, warly race,   worldly
Wha think that havins, sense an' grace, manners
Ev'n love an' friendship should give place
   To *catch-the-plack*!   coining money
I dinna like to see your face,   do not
120   Nor hear your crack.

But ye whom social pleasure charms,
Whose hearts the *tide of kindness* warms,
Who hold your *being* on the terms,
   'Each aids the others,'
Come to my bowl, come to my arms,
   My friends, my brothers!

But to conclude my lang epistle,
As my auld pen's worn to the grissle;
Twa lines frae you wad gar me fissle, make, tingle
130   Who am, most fervent,
While I can either sing, or whissle,
   Your friend and servant.

TO THE SAME

April 21st, 1785

WHILE new-ca'd kye rowte at the stake,   *newly calved cattle, low*
An' pownies reek in pleugh or braik,   *ponies, smoke, plough, harrow*
This hour on e'enin's edge I take,   *evening's*
    To own I'm debtor,
To honest-hearted, auld L*****k,
      For his kind *letter*.

Forjesket sair, with weary legs,   *sorely 'jaded with fatigue' (B)*
Rattlin the corn out-owre the rigs,   *ridges*
Or dealing thro' amang the naigs   *distributing, nags*
10   Their ten-hours bite,
My awkwart Muse sair pleads and begs,
      I would na write.

The tapetless, ramfeezl'd hizzie,   *heedless, exhausted hussy*
She's saft at best an' something lazy,   *silly*
Quo' she, 'Ye ken we've been sae busy
      This month an' mair,
That trouth, my head is grown right dizzie,
      An' something sair.'

Her dowf excuses pat me mad;   *weak, put*
20 'Conscience,' says I, 'ye thowless jad!   *spiritless wench*
I'll write, an' that a hearty blaud,   *screed*
      This vera night;   *very*
So dinna ye affront your trade,   *do not*
      But rhyme it right.

'Shall bauld L*****K, the *king o' hearts*,   *bold*
Tho' mankind were a *pack o' cartes*,
Roose you sae weel for your deserts,   *praise*
      In terms sae friendly,
Yet ye'll neglect to shaw your parts   *show*
30   An' thank him kindly?'

Sae I gat paper in a blink,   twinkling
An' down gaed *stumpie* in the ink: worn quill pen
Quoth I, 'Before I sleep a wink,
    I vow I'll close it;
An' if ye winna mak it clink,   will not, rhyme
    By Jove I'll prose it!'

Sae I've begun to scrawl, but whether
In rhyme, or prose, or baith thegither,
Or some hotch-potch that's rightly neither,
40   Let time mak proof;
But I shall scribble down some blether   nonsense
    Just clean aff-loof.   'unpremeditated' (B)

My worthy friend, ne'er grudge an' carp,
Tho' Fortune use you hard an' sharp;
Come, kittle up your *moorlan harp*   tickle
    Wi' gleesome touch!
Ne'er mind how Fortune *waft* an' *warp*;   weave
    She's but a b-tch.

She's gien me monie a jirt an' fleg,   jerk, scare
50   Sin I could striddle owre a rig;   since, straddle
But by the L—d, tho' I should beg
    Wi' lyart pow,   grey head
I'll laugh, an' sing, an' shake my leg,   dance
    As lang's I dow!   can

Now comes the *sax an' twentieth* simmer,   six, summer
I've seen the bud upo' the timmer,   wood
Still persecuted by the limmer   jade
    Frae year to year;
But yet, despite the kittle kimmer,   fickle woman
60   *I, Rob, am here.*

Do ye envy the *city-gent*,
Behint a kist to lie an' sklent,   counter, squint greedily
Or purse-proud, big wi' cent per cent,

An' muckle wame,   big belly
In some bit *Brugh* to represent   small burgh
     A *Baillie's* name?   magistrate's

Or is't the paughty, feudal *Thane*,   haughty
Wi' ruffl'd sark an' glancin cane,   shirt
Wha thinks himsel nae *sheep-shank bane*,   sheep-leg bone
70   But lordly stalks,
While caps an' bonnets aff are taen,
     As by he walks?

'O Thou wha gies us each guid gift!
Gie me o' *wit* an' *sense* a lift,   load
Then turn me, if *Thou* please, *adrift*,
     Thro' Scotland wide;
Wi' *cits* nor *lairds* I wadna shift,   townsmen, change places
     In a' their pride!'

Were this the *charter* of our state,
80 'On pain o' *hell* be rich an' great,'
Damnation then would be our fate,
     Beyond remead;   remedy
But, thanks to *Heav'n*, that's no the gate   way
     We learn our *creed*.

For thus the royal *Mandate* ran,
When first the human race began,
'The social, friendly, honest man,
     Whate'er he be,
Tis *he* fulfils *great Nature's plan*,
90   And none but *he*.'

O *Mandate*, glorious and divine!
The followers o' the ragged Nine,
Poor, thoughtless devils! yet may shine
     In glorious light,
While sordid sons o' Mammon's line
     Are dark as night!

Tho' here they scrape, an' squeeze, an' growl,
Their worthless nievefu' of a *soul*,   fistful
May in some *future carcase* howl,
100   The forest's fright;
Or in some day-detesting *owl*
       May shun the light.

Then may L*****K and B**** arise,
To reach their native, kindred skies,
And *sing* their pleasures, hopes an' joys,
       In some mild sphere,
Still closer knit in friendship's ties
       Each passing year!

TO W. S*****N, OCHILTREE

May —— 1785

I Gat your letter, winsome Willie;
Wi' gratefu' heart I thank you brawlie;   heartily
Tho' I maun say't, I wad be silly,
       An' unco vain,
Should I believe, my coaxin billie,   fellow
       Your flatterin strain.

But I'se believe ye kindly meant it,   I'll
I sud be laith to think ye hinted   should, loath
Ironic satire, sidelins sklented,   sideways directed
10   On my poor Musie;   little Muse
Tho' in sic phraisin terms ye've penn'd it,   extravagant
       I scarce excuse ye.

My senses wad be in a creel,   whirl
Should I but dare a *hope* to speel,   climb
Wi' *Allan*, or wi' *Gilbertfield*,
       The braes o' fame;   slopes
Or *Ferguson*, the writer-chiel,   lawyer-chap
       A deathless name.

(O *Ferguson*! thy glorious *parts*,
20   Ill-suited *law's* dry, musty arts!
My curse upon your whunstane hearts,   whinstone
       Ye Enbrugh Gentry!   Edinburgh
The tythe o' what ye waste at *cartes*   tenth
       Wad stow'd his pantry!)   stored

Yet when a tale comes i' my head,
Or lasses gie my heart a screed,   rent
As whiles they're like to be my dead,   death
       (O sad disease!)
I kittle up my *rustic reed*;   tickle/rouse
30   It gies me ease.

Auld COILA, now, may fidge fu' fain,   tingle with delight
She's gotten *Bardies* o' her ain,   own
Chiels wha their chanters winna hain,   fellows, will not spare
       But tune their lays,
Till echoes a' resound again
       Her weel-sung praise.

Nae *Poet* thought her worth his while,
To set her name in measur'd style;
She lay like some unkend-of isle
40   Beside *New Holland*,   Australia
Or whare wild-meeting oceans *boil*
       Besouth *Magellan*.   south of

Ramsay an' famous *Ferguson*
Gied *Forth* an' *Tay* a lift aboon;   up
Yarrow an' *Tweed*, to monie a tune,
       Owre Scotland rings,
While *Irwin*, *Lugar*, *Aire* an' *Doon*,
       Naebody sings.

Th' *Ilissus*, *Tiber*, *Thames* an' *Seine*,
50   Glide sweet in monie a tunefu' line;
But *Willie* set your fit to mine,   foot

An' cock your crest,   hold up
We'll gar our streams an' burnies shine   make, streamlets
     Up wi' the best.

We'll sing auld COILA'S plains an' fells,
Her moors red-brown wi' heather bells,
Her banks an' braes, her dens an' dells,   hillsides
          Where glorious WALLACE
Aft bure the gree, as story tells,   bore off the prize
60   Frae Suthron billies.   Englishmen

At WALLACE' name, what Scottish blood,
But boils up in a spring-tide flood!
Oft have our fearless fathers strode
          By WALLACE' side,
Still pressing onward, red-wat-shod,   shod with wet
          Or glorious dy'd!   blood

O sweet are COILA'S haughs an' woods,   hollows
When lintwhites chant amang the buds,   linnets
And jinkin hares, in amorous whids,   sporting, gambols
70   Their loves enjoy,
While thro' the braes the cushat croods   wood-pigeon, coos
          With wailfu' cry!

Ev'n winter bleak has charms to me,
When winds rave thro' the naked tree;
Or frosts on hills of *Ochiltree*
          Are hoary gray;
Or blinding drifts wild-furious flee,
          Dark'ning the day!

O NATURE! a' thy shews an' forms
80 To feeling, pensive hearts hae charms!
Whether the Summer kindly warms,
          Wi' life an' light;
Or Winter howls, in gusty storms,
          The lang, dark night!

The *Muse*, nae *Poet* ever fand her,   found
Till by himsel he learn'd to wander,
Adown some trottin burn's meander,
    An' no think lang;
O sweet, to stray an' pensive ponder
90   A heart-felt sang!

The warly race may drudge an' drive,   worldly
Hog-shouther, jundie, stretch an' strive,   push, use elbows
Let me fair NATURE'S face descrive,   describe
    And I, wi' pleasure,
Shall let the busy, grumbling hive
    Bum owre their treasure.   boast

Fareweel, 'my rhyme-composing' brither!   brother
We've been owre lang unkenn'd to ither:
Now let us lay our heads thegither,
100   In love fraternal:
May *Envy* wallop in a tether,   be hanged, noose
    Black fiend, infernal!

While Highlandmen hate tolls an' taxes;
While moorlan herds like guid, fat braxies;   dead sheep
While Terra firma, on her axis,
    Diurnal turns;
Count on a friend, in faith an' practice,
    In ROBERT BURNS.

POSTSCRIPT

My memory's no worth a preen;   pin
110   I had amaist forgotten clean,
Ye bad me write you what they mean
    By this *new-light*,*
'Bout which our *herds* sae aft hae been   shepherds
    Maist like to fight.

* A cant-term for those religious opinions, which Dr Taylor of Norwich has defended so strenuously.

In days when mankind were but callans,   striplings
At *Grammar*, *Logic*, an' sic talents,
They took nae pains their speech to balance,
   Or rules to gie,
But spak their thoughts in plain, braid lallans, vernacular Lowland
                  Scots
120   Like you or me.

In thae auld times, they thought the *Moon*, those
Just like a sark, or pair o' shoon,   shirt, shoes
Woor by degrees, till her last roon   wore out, round
   Gaed past their viewin,
An' shortly after she was done
   They gat a new ane.

This past for certain, undisputed;
It ne'er cam i' their heads to doubt it,
Till chiels gat up an' wad confute it,   fellows
130   An' ca'd it wrang;   wrong
An' muckle din there was about it,
   Baith loud an' lang.

Some *herds*, weel learn'd upo' the beuk, book
Wad threap auld folk the thing misteuk; insist, mistook
For 'twas the *auld moon* turn'd a newk corner
   An' out o' sight,
An' backlins-comin, to the leuk,   backwards–, look
   She grew mair bright.

This was deny'd, it was affirm'd;
140 The *herds* an' *hissels* were alarm'd; flocks
The rev'rend gray-beards rav'd an' storm'd,
   That beardless laddies   boys
Should think they better were inform'd,
   Than their auld daddies.

Frae less to mair it gaed to sticks;
Frae words an' aiths to clours an' nicks; oaths, bumps
An' monie a fallow gat his licks,   punishment

Wi' hearty crunt;	blow
An' some, to learn them for their tricks,	teach
150 Were hang'd an' brunt.	burned

This game was play'd in monie lands,
An' *auld-light* caddies bure sic hands,   rascals, bore
That faith, the *youngsters* took the sands   fled
    Wi' nimble shanks,
Till *Lairds* forbad, by strict commands,
    Sic bluidy pranks.

But *new-light herds* gat sic a cowe,   trouncing
Folk thought them ruin'd stick-an-stowe,   utterly
Till now amaist on ev'ry *knowe*   hillock
160   Ye'll find ane plac'd;
An' some, their *New-light* fair avow,
    Just quite barefac'd.

Nae doubt the *auld-light flocks* are bleatan;
Their zealous *herds* are vex'd an' sweatan;
Mysel, I've ev'n seen them greetan   weeping
    Wi' girnan spite,   complaining
To hear the *Moon* sae sadly lie'd on
    By word an' write.

But shortly they will cowe the louns!   scare, rogues
170 Some *auld-light herds* in neebor towns   neighbouring
Are mind't, in things they ca' *balloons*,
    To tak a flight,
An' stay ae month amang the *Moons*
    An' see them right.

Guid observation they will gie them;
An' when the *auld Moon's* gaun to le'ae them,   leave
The hindmost *shaird*, they'll fetch it wi' them, shard
    Just i' their pouch,   pocket
An' when the *new-light* billies see them,
180   I think they'll crouch!

Sae, ye observe that a' this clatter
Is naething but a 'moonshine matter;'
But tho' dull *prose-folk* latin splatter
    In logic tulzie,   squabble
I hope we, *Bardies*, ken some better
    Than mind sic brulzie.   brawl.

EPISTLE TO J. R******,

ENCLOSING SOME POEMS

O Rough, rude, ready-witted R******,
The wale o' cocks for fun an' drinkin!   choice
There's monie godly folks are thinkin,
    Your *dreams** an' tricks
Will send you, Korah-like, a sinkin,
    Straught to auld Nick's.   straight, Hell

Ye hae sae monie cracks an' cants,   songs, merry tales
And in your wicked, druken rants,   drunken, merry-making
Ye mak a devil o' the *Saunts*,   'Saints'/Elect
10   An' fill them fou;   make, drunk
And then their failings, flaws an' wants,
    Are a' seen thro'.

Hypocrisy, in mercy spare it!
That *holy robe*, O dinna tear it!   do not
Spare't for their sakes wha aften wear it,
    The lads in *black*;
But your curst wit, when it comes near it,
    Rives't aff their back.   tears

Think, wicked Sinner, wha ye're skaithing: hurting
20 It's just the *Blue-gown* badge an' claithing, clothing
O' Saunts; tak that, ye lea'e them naething, leave

---

* A certain humorous *dream* of his was then making a noise in the world.

> To ken them by,
Frae ony unregenerate Heathen,
> Like you or I.

I've sent you here, some rhymin ware,
A' that I bargain'd for, an' mair;
Sae when ye hae an hour to spare,
> I will expect,
Yon *Sang** ye'll sen't, wi' cannie care,   send it, discreet
30   And no neglect.

Tho' faith, sma' heart hae I to sing!
My Muse dow scarcely spread her wing: dares
I've play'd mysel a bonie *spring*,   tune
> An' *danc'd* my fill!
I'd better gaen an' sair't the king,   served
> At Bunker's hill.

'Twas ae night lately, in my fun,
I gaed a rovin wi' the gun,
An' brought a *Paitrick* to the *grun'*,   partridge, ground
40   A bonie *hen*,
And, as the twilight was begun,
> Thought nane wad ken.

The poor, wee thing was *little hurt*;
I *straiket* it a wee for sport,   stroked a little
Ne'er thinkan they wad fash me for't;   trouble
> But, Deil-ma-care!   Devil-me-care
Somebody tells the *Poacher-Court*,   Kirk Session
> The hale affair.   whole

Some auld, us'd hands had taen a note,   experienced
50 That *sic a hen* had got a *shot*;   such and such
I was suspected for the plot;
> I scorn'd to lie;

---

* A *Song* he had promised the Author.

So gat the whissle o' my groat,   lost my money
      An' pay't the *fee*.

But by my *gun*, o' guns the wale,   pick
An' by my *pouther* an' my *hail*,   powder, shot
An' by my *hen*, an' by her *tail*,
      I vow an' swear!
The *Game* shall Pay, owre moor an' *dail*,   dale
60   For this, niest year.   next

As soon's the *clockin-time* is by,   hatching, over
An' the *wee powts* begun to cry,   chicks
L—d, I'se hae sportin by an' by,   I'll have
      For my *gowd guinea*;   gold
Tho' I should herd the *buckskin* kye   American cattle
      For't, in Virginia!

Trowth, they had muckle for to blame!
'Twas neither broken wing nor limb,
But twa-three *draps* about the *wame*   drops, womb
70   Scarce thro' the *feathers*;
An' baith a *yellow George* to claim,   guinea
      An' *thole* their *blethers*!   endure, nonsense

It pits me ay as mad's a hare;   puts
So I can rhyme nor write nae mair;
But *pennyworths* again is fair,
      When time's expedient:
Meanwhile I am, respected Sir,
      Your most obedient.

SONG

Tune, Corn rigs are bonie

I

IT was upon a Lammas night,
  When corn rigs are bonie,   ridges
Beneath the moon's unclouded light,
  I held awa to Annie: took my way
The time flew by, wi' tentless head,   careless
  Till 'tween the late and early;
Wi' sma' persuasion she agreed,
  To see me thro' the barley.

II

The sky was blue, the wind was still,
10 The moon was shining clearly;
I set her down, wi' right good will,
  Amang the rigs o' barley:
I ken't her heart was a' my ain;   own
  I lov'd her most sincerely;
I kiss'd her owre and owre again,
  Amang the rigs o' barley.

III

I lock'd her in my fond embrace;
  Her heart was beating rarely:
My blessings on that happy place,
20 Amang the rigs o' barley!
But by the moon and stars so bright,
  That shone that night so clearly!
She ay shall bless that happy night,
  Amang the rigs o' barley.

IV

I hae been blythe wi' Comrades dear;
  I hae been merry drinking;
I hae been joyfu' gath'rin gear;   money/property
  I hae been happy thinking;

But a' the pleasures e'er I saw,
30 Tho' three times doubl'd fairly,
That happy night was worth them a',
 Amang the rigs o' barley.

CHORUS

Corn rigs, an' barley rigs,
 An' corn rigs are bonie:
I'll ne'er forget that happy night,
 Amang the rigs wi' Annie.

SONG,

COMPOSED IN AUGUST

Tune, I had a horse, I had nae mair

I

NOW westlin winds, and slaught'ring guns westerly
 Bring Autumn's pleasant weather;
And the moorcock springs, on whirring wings,
 Amang the blooming heather:
Now waving grain, wide o'er the plain,
 Delights the weary Farmer;
And the moon shines bright, when I rove at night,
 To muse upon my Charmer.

II

The Partridge loves the fruitful fells;
10 The Plover loves the mountains;
The Woodcock haunts the lonely dells;
 The soaring Hern the fountains:
Thro' lofty groves, the Cushat roves, wood-pigeon
 The path of man to shun it;
The hazel bush o'erhangs the Thrush,
 The spreading thorn the Linnet.

III

Thus ev'ry kind their pleasure find,
   The savage and the tender;
Some social join, and leagues combine;
20   Some solitary wander:
Avaunt, away! the cruel sway,
   Tyrannic man's dominion;
The Sportsman's joy, the murd'ring cry,
   The flutt'ring, gory pinion!

IV

But PEGGY dear, the ev'ning's clear,
   Thick flies the skimming Swallow;
The sky is blue, the fields in view,
   All fading-green and yellow:
Come let us stray our gladsome way,
30   And view the charms of Nature;
The rustling corn, the fruited thorn,
   And ev'ry happy creature.

V

We'll gently walk, and sweetly talk,
   Till the silent moon shine clearly;
I'll grasp thy waist, and fondly prest,
   Swear how I love thee dearly:
Not vernal show'rs to budding flow'rs,
   Not Autumn to the Farmer,
So dear can be, as thou to me,
40   My fair, my lovely Charmer!

SONG
Tune, Gilderoy

I
FROM thee, ELIZA, I must go,
    And from my native shore:
The cruel fates between us throw
    A boundless ocean's roar;
But boundless oceans, roaring wide,
    Between my Love and me,
They never, never can divide
    My heart and soul from thee.

II
Farewell, farewell, ELIZA dear,
10   The maid that I adore!
A boding voice is in mine ear,
    We part to meet no more!
But the latest throb that leaves my heart,
    While Death stands victor by,
That throb, ELIZA, is thy part,
    And thine that latest sigh!

THE FAREWELL
To the Brethren of St. James's Lodge, Tarbolton
Tune, Goodnight and joy be wi' you a'

I
ADIEU! a heart-warm, fond adieu!
    Dear brothers of the *mystic tye*!
Ye favored, *enlighten'd* Few,
    Companions of my social joy!

Tho' I to foreign lands must hie,
    Pursuing Fortune's slidd'ry ba',   slippery ball
With melting heart, and brimful eye,
    I'll mind you still, tho' far awa.   remember

II

Oft have I met your social Band,
10   And spent the chearful, festive night;
Oft, honor'd with supreme command,
    Presided o'er the *Sons of light*:
And by that *Hieroglyphic* bright,
    Which none but *Craftsmen* ever saw!
Strong Mem'ry on my heart shall write
    Those happy scenes when far awa!

III

May Freedom, Harmony and Love
    Unite you in the *grand Design*,
Beneath th' Omniscient Eye above,
20   The glorious ARCHITECT Divine!
That you may keep th' *unerring line*,
    Still rising by the *plummet's law*,
Till *Order* bright, completely shine,
    Shall be my Pray'r when far awa.

IV

And YOU, farewell! whose merits claim,
    Justly that *highest badge* to wear!
Heav'n bless your honor'd, noble Name,
    To MASONRY and SCOTIA dear!
A last request, permit me here,
30   When yearly ye assemble a',
One *round*, I ask it with a *tear*,
    To him, *the Bard, that's far awa*.

EPITAPH ON A HENPECKED COUNTRY SQUIRE

As father Adam first was fool'd,
   A case that's still too common,
Here lyes a man a woman rul'd,
   The devil rul'd the woman.

EPIGRAM ON SAID OCCASION

O Death, hadst thou but spar'd his life,
   Whom we, this day, lament!
We freely wad exchang'd the *wife*,
   An' a' been weel content.

Ev'n as he is, cauld in his graff,   grave
   The *swap* we yet will do't;
Tak thou the Carline's carcase aff,   old woman's
   Thou'se get the *saul o' boot*.   thou'll

ANOTHER

One Queen Artemisa, as old stories tell,
When depriv'd of her husband she loved so well,
In respect for the love and affection he'd show'd her,
She reduc'd him to dust, and she drank up the Powder.

But Queen N**********, of a diff'rent complexion,   [Netherplace]
When call'd on to order the fun'ral direction,
Would have *eat* her dead lord, on a slender pretence,
Not to show her respect, but – *to save the expence*.

EPITAPHS

ON A CELEBRATED RULING ELDER

Here Sowter **** in Death does sleep;	[Hood]
To H—ll, if he's gane thither,	
Satan, gie him thy gear to keep,	money
He'll haud it weel thegither.	hold

ON A NOISY POLEMIC

Below thir stanes lie Jamie's banes;	these stones, bones
O Death, it's my opinion,	
Thou ne'er took such a bleth'ran b—tch,	talkative
Into thy dark dominion!	

ON WEE JOHNIE

Hic jacet wee *Johnie*

Whoe'er thou art, O reader, know,	
That Death has murder'd Johnie;	
An' here his *body* lies fu' low——	very
For *saul* he ne'er had ony.	soul

FOR THE AUTHOR'S FATHER

O ye whose cheek the tear of pity stains,
  Draw near with pious rev'rence and attend!
Here lie the loving Husband's dear remains,
  The tender Father, and the gen'rous Friend.

The pitying Heart that felt for human Woe;
  The dauntless heart that fear'd no human Pride;
The Friend of Man, to vice alone a foe;
  'For ev'n his failings lean'd to Virtue's side.*'

---

* Goldsmith

For R. A. Esq;

Know thou, O stranger to the fame
Of this much lov'd, much honor'd name!
(For none that knew him need be told)
A warmer heart Death ne'er made cold.

For G. H. Esq;

The poor man weeps – here G——N sleeps,   [Gavin]
   Whom canting wretches blam'd:
But with *such as he*, where'er he be,
   May I be *sav'd* or *d——'d*!

A BARD'S EPITAPH

IS there a whim-inspir'd fool,
Owre fast for thought, owre hot for rule,   too
Owre blate to seek, owre proud to snool,   diffident, submit tamely
    Let him draw near;
And o'er this grassy heap sing dool,   lament
      And drap a tear.   drop

Is there a Bard of rustic song,
Who, noteless, steals the crouds among,
That weekly this area throng,   churchyard
10   O, pass not by!
But with a frater-feeling strong,   brother-
      Here, heave a sigh.

Is there a man whose judgment clear,
Can others teach the course to steer,
Yet runs, himself, life's mad career,
    Wild as the wave,
Here pause – and thro' the starting tear,
      Survey this grave.

The poor Inhabitant below
20 Was quick to learn and wise to know,
And keenly felt the friendly glow,
And *softer flame*;
But thoughtless follies laid him low,
And stain'd his name!

Reader attend – whether thy soul
Soars fancy's flights beyond the pole,
Or darkling grubs this earthly hole,
In low pursuit,
Know, prudent, cautious, *self-controul*
30 Is Wisdom's root.

Notes

The Twa Dogs (p. 1). Drafted probably by November 1785, completed by mid-February 1786 (Burns to John Richmond, 17 February 1786; Richmond, 1765–1846, was one of Burns's intimates from the Mauchline period, a lawyer's clerk first in Gavin Hamilton's office there and later in Edinburgh). Burns's brother Gilbert explained that the poet's dog Luath, a great favourite, had been 'killed by the wanton cruelty of some person' the night before their father died (13 February 1784). 'Robert said to me, that he should like to confer such immortality as he could bestow upon his old friend *Luath*, and that he had a great mind to introduce something into the book under the title of *Stanzas to the Memory of a quadruped Friend*; but this plan was given up for the tale as it now stands. Caesar was merely the creature of the poet's imagination.'

Burns knew Fergusson's satirical dialogue poem 'Mutual Complaint of Plainstanes and Causey [pavement and street] in their Mother-tongue' (1773), written, like this poem, in octosyllabic couplets. With the example of Fergusson's deftly rendered colloquial Scots speech in mind, he has created a highly original form of social satire, using canine 'characters' to express pointed criticism. Fergusson has no such animal creations as Burns: indeed, only the Fables of the 15th-century poet Robert Henryson offer anything in Lowland Scots comparable to the astonishingly authentic blend of animal and human characteristics found in Caesar and Luath.

Part of the secret of Burns's success lies in the strategic skill with which he shows Caesar, the rich man's Newfoundland, kept as a pet, to be no stand-offish snob with his nose in the air, but on the contrary a willing companion for the 'gash an' faithfu' *tyke*' Luath, ready to share with him dogs' interests – and to talk – on equal terms. Not only is Caesar's freedom from class pretension in itself a means of commenting on the pettiness of human divisions. His genial outlook wins the goodwill of the reader: he is no biased observer of the life of the gentry, but instead a reliable witness, who can be trusted completely. His revelations carry weight therefore, and when he offers his summing-up, the tone of fair and deliberate judgment damns the life-style of the well-to-do much more effectively than a less carefully dramatized argument could possibly do:

There's some exceptions, man an' woman;
But this is Gentry's life in common.

2. COIL: Kyle, Burns's native, middle district of Ayrshire (cf. 'The Vision'). 'King Kyle' was the land within this district between the Ayr and the Doon.

11. some place far abroad: Newfoundland. 'A large breed of dog, noted for its sagacity, good temper, strength . . .' (*OED*), introduced to Britain in the 18th century.

27. in *Highland Sang*: 'Cuchullin's dog in Ossian's Fingal' (footnote by Burns). Controversy had raged for twenty years over James Macpherson's claim that *Fingal* (1762) was a translation of 'an ancient Epic'. Dr Johnson agreed with David Hume's comment that 'he would not believe the authenticity of *Fingal*, though fifty barearsed highlanders should swear it'.

51. racked rents: Rents in Ayrshire rose sharply in the agrarian revolution, some landlords exploiting the situation very unfairly.

65. Our *Whipper-in*: Hugh Andrew, who served Hugh Montgomerie of Coilsfield, Tarbolton.

96. a *factor*'s snash: 'My father's generous Master died [Provost Fergusson, in 1769]; the farm [Mount Oliphant] proved a ruinous bargain; and, to clench the curse, we fell into the hands of a Factor who sat for the picture I have drawn of one in my Tale of two dogs . . . my indignation yet boils at the recollection of the scoundrel tyrant's insolent, threatening epistles' (Burns to Dr John Moore, 2 August 1787, *Letters* I. 136–7).

119. *patronage* an' *priests*: The Patronage Act of 1712 had reasserted the rights of lay patrons (usually local landowners) to appoint ministers to parishes of the Church of Scotland; but many people fiercely resisted this, believing that the right should lie instead with congregations. Another point of contention concerned the theological outlook of ministers, who were sometimes categorized – according to their beliefs – as 'Auld Licht' (strictly orthodox) or 'New Licht' (liberal).

181. breakin o' their timmer: The common people living on the land were often bitterly opposed to the large-scale tree planting which went on in the second half of the 18th century under the influence of 'improving' lairds. Saplings and young trees planted in country estates were sometimes destroyed under cover of darkness.

Scotch Drink (p. 9). Written between November 1785 and mid-February 1786 (letter to John Richmond, 17 February 1786). On 20 March 1786 Burns wrote to his friend Robert Muir, wine-merchant in Kilmarnock: 'I here inclose my SCOTCH DRINK, and "may the — follow with a blessing for your edification". – I hope, sometime before we have the Gowk [cuckoo], to have the pleasure of seeing you, at Kilm^k; when I intend we shall have a gill between us, in a Mutchkin-stoup; which will be a great comfort and consolation . . .', (*Letters* I. 29). Fergusson's poem 'Caller Water' is Burns's precedent for using the 6–line 'Standart Habby' stanza (see p.34) in a poem celebrating the rejection of wine for another kind of drink. Compare with the opening of 'Scotch Drink', 'Caller Water', ll. 19–24:

> The fuddlin' Bardies now–a–days
> Rin *maukin*–mad in Bacchus' praise,
> And limp and stoiter thro' their lays
>> *Anacreontic*,
> While each his sea of wine displays
>> As big's the Pontic.

17. *John Barleycorn*: The grain from which malt liquor is made.
28. oil'd by thee: cf. Ramsay, 'Epistle to Robert Yarde', lls. 105–8:
    > A cheerfu' Bottle sooths the Mind,
    > Gars Carles grow canty, free and kind;
    > Defeats our Care, and hales our Strife,
    > And brawly oyls the Wheels of Life.
41. pirratch: This form has manuscript authority, though Burns changed it to the more usual *parritch* in his 1787 edition.
70. Wae worth . . . Gies famous sport.: Toned down in 1787 to:
    > Wae worth the name!
    > Nae Howdie [midwife] gets a social night,
    >> Or plack [coin] frae them.
84. spier her price . . . *Brandy*, burnan trash!: In Fergusson's 'A Drink Eclogue', ll. 63–4, whisky says to brandy:
    > For now our Gentles gabbs are grown sae nice,
    > At thee they toot, an' never speer my price.
109. Thee, *Ferintosh*! O sadly lost!: Whisky distilled at Ferintosh on the Cromarty Firth had been exempt from duty since 1695 in reparation for damage (caused in 1689 by the Jacobites) to the estates of Forbes of Culloden, who owned the distillery. In 1785 the exemption was withdrawn. Although more than £20,000 was paid in compensation, the price of whisky rose. Burns's poem reflects the continuing keen interest in the subject in Scotland from the consumer's viewpoint.
115. curst horse–leeches o' th'Excise: Ironical, considering that Burns was later to accept employment himself as an exciseman.

The Author's Earnest Cry and Prayer (p. 13). A note in the 1787 edition indicates the occasion for this poem, 'before the Act anent the Scotch Distilleries, of session 1786; for which Scotland and the Author return their most grateful thanks'. Burns's plea to the Scottish MPs at Westminster was thus highly topical. Feelings had been running high in Scotland since the passing of the Wash Act in 1784, which it was alleged discriminated against Scottish distillers ('that curst restriction', l.15). There were many illicit stills in Scotland at this period, and excisemen who made a practice of seizing stills were very unpopular (cf. 'Scotch Drink', l.115). The legislation of 1786 taxed distillers on the capacity of their stills, and regulated whisky sales between Scotland and England.

Title: cf. 2 *Chronicles* 6:19: '. . . hearken unto the cry and the prayer which thy servant prayeth before thee'.

Epigraph: Burns parodies *Paradise Lost*, ix, 896, 900:

> O fairest of creation! last and best . . .
> How art thou lost . . .

1. YE *Irish lords*: Certain Irish lords had Scottish seats in Parliament, while the eldest sons of Scottish peers were ineligible.

15. that curst restriction: The Wash Act of 1784 had reduced the profits of Scottish distillers.

19. yon PREMIER YOUTH: William Pitt the Younger (b. 1759), prime minister since 1784.

39. d—mn'd Excise-men: Excisemen were engaged in the mid-1780s in a campaign against illicit whisky stills. In view of Burns's later career in the Excise, his comments on excisemen in this poem are charged with unconscious irony.

57. like MONTGOMERIES fight: The Earls of Eglinton. Over the centuries many members of this Ayrshire family had borne arms with distinction. After a long military career, Archibald, the eleventh Earl (1726–96), was appointed governor of Edinburgh Castle in 1782.

58. gab like BOSWEll: James Boswell (1740–95), advocate, biographer of Samuel Johnson, and Laird of Auchinleck in Ayrshire; at this time active in Ayrshire politics. In 1788 Burns sought an introduction, explaining to Bruce Campbell (a mutual acquaintance), 'as I had the honor of drawing my first breath almost in the same Parish with Mr Boswell, my Pride plumes itself on the connection' (letter of 13 November 1788). Boswell endorsed his letter, 'Mr Robert Burns the Poet expressing very high sentiments of me', but he did not invite Burns to meet him.

71. Saint Stephen's wa's: St Stephen's chapel in the palace of Westminster, the House of Commons.

73. *Dempster*: 'Honest George' Dempster (1732–1818), Whig MP for Forfar Burghs, and a noted agricultural improver.

74. *Kilkerran*: Sir Adam Fergusson of Kilkerran, third baronet (1733–1814), MP for Ayrshire 1774–84 and 1790–96; described as 'aith–detesting' perhaps because of his reported way of rebuking his children with the words, 'Dinna think that because I'm no swearin I'm no angry.'

76. *Graham*: James Graham (1755–1836), later third Duke of Montrose. One of Pitt's ministers in 1783, he eventually became Lord Justice-General. Noted for his 'ready elocution'.

78. *Dundas*: Henry Dundas (1742–1811), at this time MP for Midlothian and Treasurer of the Navy under Pitt; a man of exceptional political influence, especially in Scotland.

79. *Erskine*: Thomas Erskine (1750–1823), son of the tenth Earl of Erskine, MP for Portsmouth, 1783, and subsequently Lord Chancellor; 'an honourable politician, an enthusiast for liberty' (*DNB*).

80. Campbels, *Frederic an' Ilay*: Lord Frederick Campbell (1736–1816), third son of the fourth Duke of Argyll, and at this time an MP for Argyll; and Sir Ilay Campbell (1734–1823), member for the Glasgow burghs from 1784, and Lord Advocate.

81. Livistone: Sir William Cuninghame of Milncraig, Ayrshire, and Livingston in Linlithgow; MP for Linlithgow 1774–90.

92. *lost Militia*: In 1782 a militia bill for Scotland, which would have allowed for enlistment from the militia into the army, was opposed by the Scottish representatives at Westminster.

109. *Charlie Fox*: Charles James Fox (1749–1806), Whig leader and gifted rival of Pitt; a notorious gambler and womanizer.

115. *Boconnock's*: The prime minister was a grandson of Robert Pitt of Boconnoc in Cornwall.

119. tea an' winnocks: In an effort to curb smuggling, Pitt's Commutation Act of 1784 slashed the import duty on tea, making up for the loss of revenue by a tax on windows in houses.

126. The *Coalition*: The Fox-North administration of 1783.

133. FIVE AND FORTY: The Scottish representatives in the Commons.

142. St *Jamie's*: Westminster.

176. raise a philosophic reek: Many 18th-century writers argued that climate affected character. Burns may have been familiar with Montesquieu's view, as quoted by Henry Mackenzie in the *Mirror* (27 March 1779), 'difference of climate is the chief, or the only cause of the difference of national characters'.

183–6. Till . . . *dram*!: Burns amended the ending in a holograph note in a copy of his 1793 edition, now in the Huntington Library, to read:

> Till when ye speak, ye aiblins blether;
>   Yet deil-mak-matter!
> FREEDOM and WHISKY gang thegither,
>   Tak aff your whitter.

The Holy Fair (p. 20). 'Composed in 1785' (note by Burns on the Kilmarnock MS), probably after the Mauchline annual Communion, held on the second Sunday in August. Mauchline had only 400 communicant church members, but it is known that in 1786 no fewer than 1,400 received the sacrament, and there is no reason to think such a number was unusual. A Holy Fair went on for several days before reaching its climax in the Communion service; people came from far and wide to hear the 'preachings'. Hence the pretext for communal involvement on the scale and of the boisterous sort described by Burns. In real life, as in Burns's poem, noisy rival factions supported 'Auld Licht' (evangelical) and 'New Licht' (moderate) preachers; hard drinking went on in Nanse Tinnock's tavern next to the churchyard; and many country-dwellers got into the habit of treating the series of religious meetings as a prelude to letting their hair down.

Burns's first aim is to amuse by creating a lively and convivial scene. His companion Fun, however, directs laughter specifically at Superstitition and Hypocrisy (stanzas 3 to 5). 'The Holy Fair' quickly becomes a social satire which turns on a series of contrasts between lofty pretensions and lowly performance, between loudly professed religious motives and actual human inclinations – which prove too strong to resist – to booze, quarrel, and fornicate.

Behind the poem lies a long tradition of Scottish vernacular verse, from the mediaeval 'brawl' poems 'Chrystis Kirk of the Grene' and 'Peblis to the Play' to Robert Fergusson's 'Leith Races' and 'Hallow-Fair'. Burns borrows his metrical form from Fergusson, and broadly keeps to the traditional combination of playful irony and vigorous social description. Certain details point to his also having read *A Letter from a Blacksmith to the Ministers and Elders of the Church of Scotland* (1759). However, 'The Holy Fair' displays a highly original thematic unity. Burns gives depth and meaning to the vividly rendered particulars which belong to his satirical celebration. His early 19th-century biographer J. G. Lockhart noted accurately that, with the publication of this poem, 'national manners were once more in the hands of a national poet'.

Title: 'Holy Fair is a common phrase in the West of Scotland for a sacramental occasion' (Burns, in his 1787 edition).

Epigraph: From a satire by Tom Brown directed against Jeremy Collier, *The Stage Beaux toss'd in a Blanket; or, Hypocrisie Alamode* (1704).

5. GALSTON: A village a few miles north of Mossgiel.

37. My name is FUN: cf. Fergusson's account in 'Leith Races' of his meeting with Mirth, a 'laughing lass', whom he takes as his companion for the day (*Poems*, STS,ii,160–1).

41–5. to ********* *holy fair*: cf. 'Leith Races', ll. 37–45:

> A bargain be't, and, by my feggs,
> > Gif ye will be my mate,
> Wi' you I'll screw the cheery pegs,
> > Ye shanna find me blate;
> We'll reel an' ramble thro' the sands,
> > And jeer wi' a' we meet . . .

cf. also Burns's 'Epistle to J. L*****k', ll. 103–6.

61. *sweet-milk cheese*: A special treat. 'The milk, the cheese, the butter were reserved by the thrifty housewife from the family with jealous care, that they might be converted into cash' (John Mitchell, DD, *Memories of Ayrshire about 1780*, ed. W. K. Dickson, Scottish History Society, Miscellany, vi, 1939, p. 272).

66. *black-bonnet*: The officiating elder wore a black cap of traditional design.

75. *racer Jess*: Janet Gibson, the half-witted daughter of 'Poosie Nansie' (Agnes Gibson), who kept a disreputable tavern in the Cowgate, Mauchline. Jess ran errands for her mother.

86. an *Elect* swatch: Amended in 1787 to 'a Chosen swatch'.

91. O happy is that man, an' blest!: Burns here quotes line 1 of verse 2 from the Scottish Metrical version of Psalm 146, which may be being sung even as the scene he describes is enacted.

102. ****** speels the holy door: Identified as 'Sawnie' in two manuscripts. Alexander Moodie (1728–99), minister of Riccarton from 1762, said once to have preached to his congregation on John 8:44, 'Ye are of your father the devil, and the lusts of your father ye will do.'

103. tidings o' s-lv-t-n: Changed in 1787 to 'tidings o' d-mn-t-n' after Dr Hugh Blair, minister of the High Kirk in Edinburgh and Professor of Rhetoric in Edinburgh University, had objected that the original 'gives just offence. The Author may easily contrive some other Rhyme in place of the word Salv—n.'

104. *Hornie*, as in ancient days: cf. Job 1:6, 'Now there was a day when the sons of God came to present themselves before the Lord, and Satan came also among them.'

116. cantharidian plaisters: Plasters of cantharides (Spanish fly), an aphrodisiac.

122. ***** opens out his cauld harangues: MS 'Geordie begins his . . .' George Smith (d. 1823), a 'New Licht' moderate, minister of Galston.

The preaching of such ministers was dismissed by the 'Auld Licht' evangelicals as insipid, mere morals without faith. Here, Smith's sermon sends off the godly in search of drink.

132. ANTONINE: Roman emperor and reformer.

138. *******, frae the water-fit: MS 'Willy'. Rev. William Peebles (1753–1826), of Newton-upon-Ayr, clerk of the Ayr Presbytery. Burns describes him in 'The Holy Tulzie' as 'shaul' (shallow). Peebles never forgave Burns, and in 1811 published verses scorning 'Burnomania', the rise of the Burns cult.

143. COMMON-SENSE: Traditionally identified as the poet's friend Dr John Mackenzie of Mauchline.

145. Wee ****** niest: MS 'M—R'. Alexander Miller, 'the assistant minister at St Michael's' (Burns, in a copy of the Kilmarnock edition); from 1788 minister of Kilmaurs, where his presentation by the Earl of Eglinton led to violent opposition from the congregation. Miller was short and very stout.

184. Black ******: John Russel (c.1740–1817), previously schoolmaster at Cromarty, ordained as minister at Kilmarnock in 1774; notorious for his severity of temper and doctrine.

188. 'Sauls does harrow': *Hamlet* I, v, 15ff., 'I could a Tale unfold . . . harrow up thy soul.'

226. *Clinkumbell*: The town-crier, bellman.

237. hearts o' stane: Burns plays boldly on Ezekiel 36:26: 'A new heart also will I give you, and a new spirit will I put within you: and I will take away the stony heart out of your flesh, and I will give you an heart of flesh.'

231. lasses strip their shoon . . . : Burns's way of ending 'The Holy Fair' shows that he has borrowed hints from Ramsay's addition to 'Chrystis Kirk of the Grene' (Ramsay, *Works*, STS, i, 73):

> And unko Wark that fell at E'en,
> > Whan Lasses were haff winkin,
> They lost their Feet and baith their Een,
> > And Maidenheads gae'd linkin
> > Aff a' that Day.

Address to the Deil (p. 28). Written in the winter of 1785–6: Burns refers to it as completed in his letter to Richmond of 17 February 1786. While he has no exact model for a comic invocation of this degree of boldness, vernacular Scots tradition is rich in reductive humour concerning the supernatural – born in part out of fear. This humour is made the basis of his art in 'Address to the Deil'. Burns clearly enjoys taking a radically different attitude to his subject from Milton in *Paradise Lost*. The poem begins as an exercise in the medieval craft of 'flyting' or scolding in verse; but as it develops, it anticipates 'Halloween' and 'Tam o' Shanter' as an ironic portrayal of still powerful, though waning, popular beliefs. Burns calls the Devil by a series of familiar, disrespectful nicknames (Hornie, Nick, Clootie, Hangie), bringing him down to his own level and robbing him of dignity. He then goes on to enumerate traditional beliefs concerning the actions of the Devil and of his agents on earth, warlocks and witches, before gently dismissing Satan as an enemy whose measure he has taken.

The poem was more sexually explicit in manuscript, and also more personal, than appears from the printed version. Lines 61–6 originally contained a bawdy joke about a bridegroom interrupted in his love-making by evil spells:

> Thence, knots are coosten, spells contriv'd,
> An' the brisk bridegroom, newly wived
> Just at the kittle point arriv'd,
> > Fond, keen, an' croose,
> Is by some spitefu' jad depriv'd
> > O's warklum's use.

When Burns was revising his *Poems* for the 1787 Edinburgh edition, the critic Hugh Blair suggested that the (toned down) stanza printed in 1786 'had better be left out, as indecent': Burns did not act on this advice. A different motive had in 1786 led the poet to replace manuscript ll. 89–90 containing a direct tribute to Jean Armour:

> Langsyne, in Eden's happy scene,
> When strappin Edie's days were green,
> An' Eve was like my bonie Jean,
> > My dearest part,
> A dancin, sweet, young, handsome quean
> > Wi' guileless heart.

This change seems to have been made shortly before publication – by the summer of 1786 Burns was estranged from Jean. With regard to the stanza immediately following, there was certainly no love lost between Burns and Jean's father; and Burns may also have thought of 'Daddie' Auld, a minister friendly to the Armours, in the role of killjoy 'snick-drawing dog' driving Jean and himself out of Paradise.

Epigraph: *Paradise Lost*, i, 128–9. cf. letter to William Nicol of 18 June 1787, 'I have bought a pocket Milton, which I carry perpetually about with me, in order to study the sentiments – the dauntless magnanimity; the intrepid unyielding independance; the desperate daring, and noble defiance of hardship, in that great Personage, Satan.' (*Letters* I. 123).

1. O Thou: An echo of Pope's way of addressing Swift in *The Dunciad*, i, 19–20:

> O Thou! whatever title please thine ear,
> Dean, Drapier, Bickerstaff, or Gulliver!

2. Auld Hornie: Traditional Scottish nickname for the horned Devil. 'Nick' may be a form of Nicholas (reason obscure), while 'Clootie' means 'cloven-hoofed'.

19. roaring lion: 1 Peter 5:8, 'your adversary the devil, as a roaring lion, walketh about, seeking whom he may devour'.

21. strong-wing'd Tempest: Tradition had it that the Devil raised strong winds.

35. boortries: Elder trees were supposed to give protection against witchcraft.

45. stoor: 'sounding hollow, strong, and hoarse' (B).

50. ragweed: Witches were said to ride on many kinds of steed – animals, enchanted humans, ragwort, ash branches, or straws.

61. mystic knots: Knots devised in malice by witches.

63. *wark-lume*: According to a 17th-century tract, *Satan's Invisible World Discovered*, witches sometimes meddled with the weaver's craft. Burns uses the word with a sexual meaning.

69. *Water-kelpies*: Water-demons in the shape of horses, bent on drowning travellers (traditional in the Scottish Highlands). Burns wrote to Cunningham on 10 September 1792 of 'a Kelpie, haunting the ford, or ferry, in the starless night, mixing thy laughing yell with the howling of the storm' (*Letters* II. 145).

73. *Spunkies*: 'As for Willy and the Wisp, he is a fiery devil, and leads people off their road in order to drown them, for he sparks sometimes at our feet, and then turns before us with his candle, as if he were twa or three miles before us, many a good boat has Spunkie drown'd' (Dougal Graham, *History of Buckhaven in Fifeshire*, 1806).

79. When MASONS' mystic *word* an' *grip*: Burns refers to the Masonic password and handshake as having force to stir up the Devil in a storm; then by contrast to the tradition that a cock, cat, or other unchristened creature was needed in order to appease the Devil. A joke at the expense of Masons, including the poet himself.

85. Lang syne in EDEN'S bonie yard: cf. Fergusson, 'Caller Water', ll. 1-2 (*Poems*, STS, ii, 106):

> When father Adie first pat spade in
> The bonny yeard of antient Eden.

By July 1786 Burns was estranged from Jean Armour, and this stanza replaces one in the Kilmarnock MS (see introductory note, above).

91. snick-drawing: 'An *auld sneck-drawer*, one who, from long experience, has acquired a great degree of facility in accomplishing any artful purpose' (*Jamieson's Scots Dictionary*).

107. lows'd his ill-tongu'd, wicked *Scawl*: cf. Job 2: 8–10, 'Thou speakest as one of the foolish women speaketh.'

111. MICHAEL: cf. *Paradise Lost*, vi, 320, 'then Satan first knew pain . . .'

123–4. Ye aiblins might . . . hae a *stake*: cf. Sterne, *Tristram Shandy*, III, xi: 'I declare, quoth my uncle Toby, my heart would not let me curse the devil himself . . . But he is cursed and damned already, to all eternity, replied Dr Slop. I am sorry for it, quoth my uncle Toby.'

The Death and Dying Words of Poor Mailie (p. 32). Burns's first sustained poem in Scots, included in his First Commonplace Book in an entry dated June 1785, but written considerably earlier. According to his brother Gilbert, he had 'partly by way of frolic, bought a ewe and two lambs from a neighbour, and she was tethered in a field adjoining the house at Lochlea. He and I were going out with our teams, and our two younger brothers to drive for us, at mid-day, when Hugh Wilson, a curious-looking, awkward boy, clad in plaiding, came to us with much anxiety in his face, with the information that the ewe had entangled herself in the tether, and was lying in the ditch. Robert was much tickled with Huoc's appearance and postures on the occasion. Poor Mailie was set to rights, and when we returned from the plough in the evening he repeated to me her *Death and Dying Words* pretty much in the way they now stand.'

Poor Mailie's Elegy (p. 34). Written to accompany *The Death and Dying Words of Poor Mailie*, but possibly not until Burns had decided to publish his poems. Here he follows a very distinctive tradition of comic elegy in Scots, making use of the 6-line stanza employed by Robert Sempill of Beltrees in *The Life and Death of Habbie Simpson* in the late 17th century, and more recently by William Hamilton of Gilbertfield in his *Last Words of Bonny Heck, a Famous Greyhound*. Allan Ramsay, who named the verse form 'Standart Habby' after the first example above, had used it for familiar epistles, as well as for elegy. Fergusson continued this tradition; and Burns in turn widened the range of the stanza still further, handling it so often and with such success that it came to be known after his death as 'the Burns stanza'. See, for example, 'To J.S****' and 'The Vision'.

To J. S**** (p. 36). The first of seven verse-epistles included in *Poems, Chiefly in the Scottish Dialect*. Written when Burns had already decided to publish his poems, in the winter of 1785–6 . . .

> This while my notion's taen a sklent,
> To try my fate in guid, black *prent*. (ll. 37–8)

James Smith, six years younger than Burns, was the son of a merchant in Mauchline, and at this time was himself a draper there. Along with John Richmond and the poet, he was one of the self-styled 'Court of Equity', a 'ramstam' (l. 165) bachelor trio who met in the Whitefoord Arms Inn in Mauchline. Burns celebrated their rakish activities in a riotous mock-trial poem, 'The Court of Equity', which was not published in his lifetime. Smith proved a staunch friend to Burns during his troubles with Jean Armour's family. He worked for a time as a calico-printer in Linlithgow, subsequently emigrating to Jamaica, where he died young.

The poem follows the pattern established in Scots verse-epistles by Ramsay and Fergusson. Beginning with greetings and compliments to Smith, Burns moves on to discuss questions of mutual interest, before returning to a brief final salutation. A particularly lively passage explains Burns's reasons for rhyming (ll. 19-30). His colloquial Scots modulates into lightly accented English in the reflective central part of the poem (ll. 55–120); then he slips back into the vernacular.

14. scrimpet stature: This stanza, with its jest about Smith's diminutive stature, was a late addition to the poem in manuscript.

25. Some rhyme . . . : This much-quoted stanza replaced an earlier manuscript version:

> Some rhyme because they like to clash,
> An' gie a neebor's name a lash;
> An' some (vain thought) for needfu' cash;
> An' some for fame;
> For me, I string my dogg'rel trash
> For fun at hame.

133. DEMPSTER: George Dempster (1732–1818), Whig MP and agricultural improver. cf. 'The Author's Earnest Cry and Prayer', above, l. 73n.

A Dream (p. 42). The poet laureate, Thomas Warton, published a laudatory Pindaric Ode to mark the birthday of King George III on 4 June 1786. This incident must have provoked Burns to write almost at once his very different poem, 'A Dream', because his book was in print by the end of July. 'A Dream' was therefore in its content and allusions the most topical and up-to-date of all the poems included in the Kilmarnock volume. The convention Burns adopts, of free speech within an imagined dream framework, is a common one in satirical journalism of the Georgian period.

Burns's friend Mrs Dunlop advised him to omit 'A Dream' from the second edition of his *Poems*: 'numbers at London are learning Scots to read your book, but they don't like your Address to the King, and say it will hurt the sale of the rest' (letter of 26 February 1787, *Correspondence of Robert Burns and Mrs Dunlop*; ed. William Wallace (1898). pp. 11, 13). Burns rejected her suggestion, replying, 'You are right in your guesses that I am not very amenable to counsel . . . I set as little by kings, lords, clergy, critics, &c. as all these respectable Gentry do by my Bardship' (30 April 1787, *Letters* I. 108).

26. *ane* been better: Burns was a 'sentimental Jacobite', and believed that his father's family had been removed from their land in northeast Scotland because of their loyalty to the Jacobite Earl Marischal.

36. then did ae day: i.e. before the loss of the American colonies.

61. let nae *saving–fit*: A recent proposal had been made to cut down the size of the Navy.

67. gie her for dissection!: Surgeons were allowed, for dissection, the bodies of executed criminals.

79. to release Ye: Burns alludes glancingly to the fact that the Queen had already mothered a large family.

81. young Potentate o' W——: George, Prince of Wales (1762–1830), the future George IV, already a byword for extravagant living, matronly mistresses, and a love of gambling.

88. Diana's *pales*: The boundaries of Diana, goddess of the moon and of the hunt. cf. Shakespeare, *1 Henry IV*, I,ii,25.

89. *Charlie*: Charles James Fox, out-of-office Whig leader and gambling companion of the Prince of Wales.

100. right reverend O—— : Frederick, Duke of York (1763–1827), who while still an infant had been made Bishop of Osnaburg in Westphalia by George III. (Appointed Commander-in-Chief of the British Army in 1798, the Duke had to resign in 1809 as a result of scandal.)

109. royal TARRY–BREEKS: Prince William (1765–1837), later Duke of Clarence and King William IV. His name had recently been linked with that of Sarah Martin, daughter of the Commissioner of Portsmouth Dockyard.

118. Ye . . . bonie blossoms a': The daughters of the royal family were Charlotte (b.1766), Augusta (b.1768), Elizabeth (b.1770), Mary (b.1776), Sophia (b.1777), and Amelia (b.1783).

The Vision (p. 47). Probably written no earlier than August 1785, when Burns noted in his Commonplace Book his disappointment that, despite the varied natural beauty and historic achievements of Ayrshire, 'we have never had one Scotch Poet of any eminence'; then outlined his poetic ambition to 'make the fertile banks of Irvine, the romantic woodlands & sequestered scenes on Aire, and the heathy, mountainous source, & winding sweep of Doon emulate Tay, Forth, Ettrick, Tweed &c.', adding 'no young Poet, nor young Soldier's heart ever beat more fondly for fame than mine'. Burns celebrates different aspects of regional life with enthusiasm in 'The Vision', defining the modest but vital part which he himself is called on to play as 'rustic bard'. Coila watches benevolently over Kyle, Burns's native district of Ayrshire, as one of a force of tutelary spirits, rather as Ariel and other spirits protect humans in *The Rape of the Lock*. After the vernacular Scots opening, Coila speaks dignified English, the language of instruction in Burns's Scotland. Burns arranges the poem, as a note explains, in two 'duans' or sections, on the digressive model of James Macpherson. He owes a general debt in this poem – as does Wordsworth in *The Prelude* – to James Beattie's blank-verse poem 'The Minstrel' (1771–4), which describes how the process of growing up in a country environment inspires the thoughts and feelings of a young poet. The stanza form is 'Standart Habby'.

Additional stanzas existed in manuscript, and the poem was expanded in 1787.

2. their roaring play: Curling, an energetic game played on ice, is sometimes referred to as 'the roaring game'.

3. hunger'd Maukin: cf. Thomson, 'Winter', ll.257–62:

> The hare,
> Though timorous of heart . . .
> . . . the garden seeks,
> Urged on by fearless want.

55. 'hare-brain'd, sentimental trace': Burns quotes from own verse epistle 'To J. S****', l.157.

63. Bess: Elizabeth Paton, servant at Lochlea, bore Burns a child in May 1785, on whose behalf he made a settlement in 1786. Burns was estranged from Jean Armour when the Kilmarnock *Poems* appeared. In later editions he substituted 'Jean' for 'Bess'.

79–82. Doone . . . Irwine . . . Air: Rivers of Ayrshire.

86. An ancient BOROUGH: Ayr.

121. FULLARTON: William Fullarton (1754–1808), of Dundonald, had a varied career as politician, diplomat, and soldier in India before becoming one of the leading agricultural improvers in Ayrshire.

122. DEMPSTER: 'Honest George' Dempster (1732–1818), MP and agricultural improver.
123. BEATTIE: Dr James Beattie (1735–1803), Professor of Moral Philosophy in Aberdeen, author of an *Essay on the Nature and Immutability of Truth* criticizing Hume's scepticism, and poet of *The Minstrel: or, The Progress of Genius* (1771–4).
151. COILA my name: From Kyle, Burns's own district of Ayrshire, between Carrick to the south and Cunningham to the north.
153. once the *Campbells*: Burns's farm Mossgiel, leased from Gavin Hamilton, was part of the Loudoun estate, above the river Irvine to the east of Kilmarnock. The Earls of Loudoun were Campbells, and the Campbell connection went back to the 14th century.
199ff. Thou canst not learn . . .: Burns wrote to Dr John Moore in January 1787: 'my first ambition was, and still my strongest wish is, to please my Compeers, the rustic Inmates of the Hamlet, while ever-changing language and manners will allow me to be relished and understood . . . in a language where Pope and Churchill have raised the laugh, and Shenstone and Gray drawn the tear; where Thomson and Beattie have painted the landskip, and Littleton and Collins described the heart; I am not vain enough to hope for distinguished Poetic fame' (*Letters* I. 88).
213. *Potosi's mine*: silver, gold, and copper mines in Bolivia.

Halloween (p. 55). Probably written in the autumn of 1785: Burns revised and expanded before publication his accompanying footnote commentary on the Halloween rituals he describes in the poem. This is arguably the most thoroughgoing example of 'manners-painting' in the Kilmarnock edition. From start to finish, in both poem and notes, Burns presents a record of social customs in his part of Ayrshire, and explains the various traditions described with the zeal of a folklorist and antiquary. He writes, in part at least, specifically to interest outsiders in a world which he had known as an observer–participant.

It seems likely that he includes in this poem Ayrshire lore from his mother's family. 'Wee Jenny', mentioned in stanza 13, has been identified as his cousin Jenny Broun; likewise, the old woman who recalls 'as weel's yestreen' (l.128) a harvest-home which took place before 1715, may be modelled on a member of the extended family. It is also tempting to assume that the setting of the poem at Cassilis Downans (l.2), and mention of a place 'where three Lairds' lan's meet at a burn' (l.214) (as they did on the boundary of Mount Oliphant) specifically point to places remembered from Burns's boyhood. 'Halloween', however, is a composite picture. All that can safely be said is that personal memories played some part in the making of a poem which is designed to be an authentic and also humorous guide to Ayrshire Halloween traditions.

Epigraph: Goldsmith, *The Deserted Village*, ll. 251–4.

1. that *night*: Halloween, which marks the beginning of the winter half of the year, derives from the great winter feast of the pagan Celts, immediately followed since the 9th century by the Christian festival of All Saints. According to traditional belief in Scotland, spirits are abroad on the night before 1 November, and humans are then able, through use of the proper ritual customs, to ask what the future holds, especially with regard to marriage. The 'mischief night' element symbolizes the activities of the spirits.

5. *Colean*: Culzean Castle, Kirkoswald.

14. *Carrick*: The southern district of Ayrshire.

55. Guidwife's weel-hoordet *nits*: cf. John Mayne's poem, 'Halloween', published in Ruddiman's *Weekly Magazine*, November 1780:

> Plac'd at their head the gudewife sits,
> And deals round apples, pears, and nits . . .

96. for the *kiln*: Where a fire was lit to dry grain, especialy oats. Different types of corn-kiln are described by A. Fenton, in *Scottish Country Life* (1976), pp. 94–6. A common superstition was that there dwelt within the walled kiln, beneath the cross-beams, a 'kiln-carle', hostile when provoked. 'To wind the *blue clue* in the *killpot* on halloween, was a serious matter before Burns made the world laugh at it' (MacTaggart, *Gallovidian Encyclopaedia*, 1824, p.138).

109. Wee *Jenny*: Traditionally identified as Burns's cousin Jenny Broun (b. 1765). Burns may have stayed with the family at Kirkoswald in 1775.

118. Skelpie-limmer's-face: 'a technical term in female scolding' (B.). cf. the gudame's outlook in Fergusson's 'The Farmer's Ingle', l. 60ff.

127. The *Sherra-moor*: Battle of Sheriffmuir (1715), fought between the Earl of Mar's Jacobité troops and pro-Hanoverian forces under the Duke of Argyll.

133. a rantan *Kirn*: A time of celebration on farms. cf. 'The Twa Dogs', l.124.

139. Achmacalla: Probably a name invented for the rhyme.

156. *graip*: An iron-pronged dung-fork.

163. lord Lennox' march: Possibly 'Port Lennox', a march, included in Daniel Dow's *A Collection of Ancient Scots Music* (c.1783) and in

James Bowie's *A Collection of Strathspey Reels and Country Dances* (*c*.1789). Information kindly supplied by Peter Cooke, School of Scottish Studies, Edinburgh. Dr Cooke suggests that Burns may be 'having a little joke about antiquarians', since Dow's book was a specialized collection, primarily of historical interest.

201. he *faddom't thrice*: 'This incantation was performed by measuring or fathoming with the arms round a stack of oats or barley three times, against the sun' (W. Gregor, 1881).

214. *three Lairds' lan's met at a burn*: At Riddicks Moss Burn, the lands of Mount Oliphant, Rozelle and Pleasantfield met.

240. *Mar's-year*: The Earl of Mar led a Jacobite Rising in 1715.

248. *butter'd So'ns*: Sowens is a kind of porridge made by boiling water in which seeds of oats have been steeped for several days.

The Auld Farmer's New-Year-Morning Salutation to His Auld Mare, Maggie (p. 66).

In the Kilmarnock MS, this poem follows *Address to the Deil*, which is mentioned in a letter of 17 February 1786; the likeliest date of composition, therefore, is early 1786. Burns glosses *The Auld Farmer's Salutation* with particular care in the Kilmarnock edition, noting the precise meaning of words as used by farmers in Ayrshire. His aim in the poem, written in the 'Standart Habby' stanza, is to convey the nature of the long and close relationship between farmer and favourite mare. He does this with realism, humour and tenderness. Avoiding excessive sentimentality, he suggests that they have grown old together naturally and with grace. The poem is addressed to Maggie throughout, but – with characteristic country humour – there is a hint that the farmer has affectionately identified together in his mind since his wedding-day (l. 32) Maggie the wedding-gift with his bride Jenny. Jenny has no doubt had to work just as hard as the loyal mare which once belonged to her father.

Title: A 'hansel' is a gift to mark a new beginning or special occasion, particularly a New Year gift.

21. o' tocher clear: Clear of, i.e. quite apart from, dowry.

35. KYLE-STEWART: the northern part of Kyle, Burns's district of Ayrshire, between the rivers Ayr and Irvine.

37. hoyte: 'the motion between a trot and gallop' (B).

51. *Brooses*: races at country-weddings, between the bridegroom's home and the bride's home or church.

57. *Scotch mile*: longer than the standard English mile by some 200 metres.

61. *Fittie-lan'*: The 'fit-o'-land' or left horse of the back pair in the plough team of four, which trod unploughed land while its partner walked in the furrow.

71. Till sprittie knowes . . . : Until rushy hillocks would have roared and torn away easily. An example of apt rural Scots which may have given difficulty even in 1786.

79. *car*: A kind of 'sledge', without wheels, made of two long birch or hazel branches, with wicker cross-pieces. The front ends were tied as shafts to the horse's collar while the rear ends were on the ground.

100. fow: A firlot, equivalent to almost one bushel of wheat or two bushels of barley and oats. Also used in the sense of a 'mow', that which has been forked.

106. To some hain'd rig . . . : The last three lines replace the MS reading:
> An' clap thy back,
> An' mind the days we've haen the gither,
> An' ca' the crack.

The Cotter's Saturday Night (p. 70). Written in the winter of 1785–6 – the setting is November (l. 10) – and mentioned by Burns as complete in his letter to Richmond of 17 February 1786. The father of the household in the poem is modelled at least in part on Burns's own father, William Burnes, who had died in 1784, worn out by toil on poor land. His piety and concern for his children's education led him to compile *A Manual of Religious Belief in a Dialogue between Father and Son*. Burns's brother Gilbert, who shared the same upbringing as the poet, comments on the central action in the poem, 'Robert had frequently remarked to me that he thought that there was something peculiarly venerable in the phrase, "Let us worship God", used by a decent sober head of a family introducing family worship (l. 108). To this sentiment . . . the world is indebted for *The Cotter's Saturday Night*.'

Burns had a model for a naturalistic word-picture of a domestic farm scene in Fergusson's 'The Farmer's Ingle', written like his own poem in Spenserian stanzas. In a number of ways, however, 'The Cotter's Saturday Night' differs sharply from Fergusson's poem. Whereas 'The Farmer's Ingle' is wholly in Lowland Scots, Burns combines the vernacular with extended passages in English. This is because he is concerned to show the nature of the religious outlook and moral values of those he describes, while Fergusson's aim is genre description *per se*. The accepted language for religious and moral reflection in poetry in 18th-century Lowland Scotland was not Scots but English, which had been used in Bible and worship since the time of the Scottish Reformation. Again in contrast to Fergusson, who does not identify any love-interest among the members of his farming family, Burns with the story of Jenny and her wooer introduces a narrative episode centring on romantic love. This helps to broaden his poem's appeal. He has been heavily criticized by a number of 20th-century critics for the rather strained note he strikes in stanza 10 ('Is there, in human-form, that bears a heart – . . .'). But the communicative power of the whole poem is not in doubt. In its ambitious scope and tonal range 'The Cotter's Saturday Night' goes beyond Fergusson's reach in 'The Farmer's Ingle'.

Dedication: R. A****: Robert Aiken (1739–1807), solicitor and surveyor of taxes in Ayr, eldest son of an Ayr shipbuilder, and grandson of James Dalrymple, sheriff-clerk of Ayrshire. He met Burns *c.* 1783, and became a trusted friend and enthusiastic admirer of Burns's poems. He was a talented public speaker and reader of poetry; Burns commented that 'he read me into fame'. Aiken collected the names of 145 subscribers for the Kilmarnock edition.

10. November chill: Burns owes something to the opening of Fergusson's poem 'The Farmer's Ingle':

> Whan gloming grey out o'er the welkin keeks,
> Whan *Batie* ca's his owsen to the byre,
> Whan *Thrasher John*, sair dung, his barn-door steeks,
> And lusty lasses at the dighting tire . . .

but he also has in mind Gray's *Elegy*, ll. 2–3:

> The lowing herd wind slowly o'er the lea,
> The ploughman homeward plods his weary way.

13. black'ning trains: Thomson describes 'a blackening train of clamorous rooks' in 'Winter', ll. 140–1.

21ff. The expectant *wee-things*: Burns's original Scots rendering of a domestic scene which recurs in 18th-century poetry, with its ultimate source in Virgil's *Georgics*, Book II. cf. Gray's 'Elegy', ll. 21–4.

22. flichterin: Glossed by Burns in 1787 as 'to flutter as young nestlings when their dam approaches'.

23. His wee-bit ingle: cf. Ramsay, *The Gentle Shepherd*, I, ii, 179–80:

> In Winter, when he toils thro' Wind and Rain,
> A bleezing Ingle, and a clean Hearth-stane.

26. *kiaugh* and care: Revised in 1793 to 'carking cares', possibly because 'kiaugh' seemed obscure.

48. wi' an eydent hand: cf. 'The Farmer's Ingle', l. 29, 'to labouring lend an eidant hand'.

50. 'fear the LORD alway!': Burns recalls such texts as Psalm 34:9.

73. O happy love!: Burns writes in his first Commonplace Book, April 1783: 'If anything on earth deserves the name of rapture or transport it is the feelings of green eighteen in the company of the mistress of his heart when she repays him with an equal return of affection.'

82ff. Is there, in human form . . . : A modern critic has described this
stanza as 'one of the most nauseating ever published by a reputable
poet' (T. Crawford, *Burns: A Study of the Poems and Songs*, 1960,
p. 179); but the poet's moral reflections held strong appeal for his
contemporaries. James Kinsley accurately comments that the passage is 'an eighteenth-century set piece' (*The Poems and Songs of
Robert Burns*, Oxford, 1968, p. 1115).

93.   *Hawkie*: Cow with the white face, pet name.

96.   weel-hain'd kebbuck: 'If cheese was to be kept for some time . . . all
the whey had to be squeezed out, and pressing was a necessity . . .
Ayrshire or Dunlop cheese became the country's national cheese.'
(A. Fenton, *Scottish Country Life*, 1976, pp. 152, 154.)

111–14. *Dundee . . . Martyrs . . . Elgin*: Old psalm tunes, the first two being
included in the Twelve 'Common Tunes' in the Scottish psalter of
1615, and 'Elgin' in the Scottish Psalter of 1625.

115.   *Italian trills* are tame: Burns agrees with Fergusson ('Elegy on the
Death of Scots Music', ll. 49–54) in deploring the fashionable prefer-
ence for elaborate Italian musical performance over native Scottish
'simplicity'. cf. also William Hamilton of Bangour, who describes in
Ode IV (*Poems on Several Occasions*, 1760) how cottagers

> Had, at the sober-tasted meal,
> Repeated oft, the grateful tale;
> Had hymn'd, in native language free,
> The song of thanks to heaven and thee;
> A music that the great ne'er hear,
> Yet sweeter to th'internal ear,
> Than any soft seducing note
> E'er thrill'd from Farinelli's throat.

117.   Nae unison hae they: The Scottish tradition in psalmody was for
everyone to keep the same pitch and sing together, in unison.

119.   How *Abram*: cf. Genesis 12:1–2.

120–1. *Moses . . . Amalek*: cf. Exodus 17:9, 16.

122.   the *royal Bard* did groaning lye: cf. Samuel 12:10–11, and Psalm 6.

130.   Had not . . . whereon to lay His head: cf. Matthew 8:20, Luke 9:58.

131–2. How . . . to many a land: Burns recalls Acts and the New
Testament epistles.

133.   *he*, who lone in *Patmos*: cf. Revelation 1:8, 19:17.

135.   *Bab'lon's* doom: cf. Revelation 18:10.

138.   springs exulting: *Windsor Forest*, ll. 111–12.

141.   No more . . . the bitter tear: cf. Isaiah 25:8; Revelation 7:17.

142.   hymning their CREATOR'S praise: cf. *Paradise Lost*, vii, 258–9:
'. . . hymning prais'd God and his Works, Creatour him they sung.'

153. *Book of Life*: cf. Revelation 3:5, 13:8.

158. HE who stills the *raven's* clam'rous nest: cf. Job 38:41, 'Who pro-
videth for the raven his food? when his young ones cry unto God . . .'

159. And decks the *lily* fair: cf. Matthew 6:28, 'Consider the lilies of the
field . . .'

163. From scenes like these: Burns echoes Thomson, 'Summer', ll.
423–4:

> A simple scene! yet hence Britannia sees
> Her solid grandeur rise.

165. Princes and lords: cf. Goldsmith, *The Deserted Village*, ll. 53–5:

> Princes and lords may flourish, or may fade;
> A breath can make them, as a breath has made:
> But a bold peasantry . . .

166. An honest man . . . : An echo of Pope, *Essay on Man*, iv, 248.

168. The *Cottage* leaves the *Palace*: Perhaps suggested by Fergusson's
'Retirement', ll. 45–8:

> In yonder lowly cot delight to dwell,
> And leave the statesman for the labouring hind,
> The regal palace for the lowly cell.

172. O SCOTIA!: Fergusson had written in 'The Farmer's Ingle', ll.
113–17:

> May SCOTIA'S simmers ay look gay and green,
>   Her yellow har'sts frae scowry blasts decreed;
> May a' her tenants sit fu' snug and bien,
>   Frae the hard grip of ails and poortith freed,
>   And a lang lasting train o' peaceful hours succeed.

181. the *patriotic tide*: William Wallace, victor of Stirling Bridge, was
executed by Edward I of England in 1305. 'The story of Wallace
poured a Scottish prejudice in my veins which will boil along there
till the flood-gates of life shut in eternal rest' (*Letters* I. 136).

188. the *Patriot*, and the *Patriot-Bard*: cf. Coila's speech to the poet in
'The Vision', l. 109ff.

To a Mouse (p. 77). Dated by the poet November 1785. Burns's brother
Gilbert stated that the 'verses to the *Mouse* and *Mountain-daisy*' were
composed . . . 'while the author was holding the plough'. John Blane, who
worked with Burns as gaudsman (driving the horses in front of the plough),
commented many years after the event that he, being only a lad, had actually
started to run after the mouse with the intention of killing it, when he was
checked by Burns; the latter then became 'thoughtful and abstracted'. Whatever the degree of accuracy of Blane's recollection, *To a Mouse* conveys very

directly Burns's tender concern for a defenceless creature. Drawing aptly and unobtrusively on the Bible, and also on the poet's reading of Johnson's *Rasselas*, it wryly underlines two ideas – the unity of creation, and the vulnerability of human beings as well as of small animals.

6. pattle: A small long-handled spade carried on a plough to clear it of mud, a plough-staff.

7–8. Man's dominion . . . Nature's social union: The idea of man as tyrant over the rest of creation is common in 18th-century poetry. cf. Pope, *Essay on Man*, iii, 147–64, and Thomson's *Seasons, passim*, e.g. 'Spring', ll. 702–5.

15. *daimen-icker*: Ayrshire Scots, denoting an occasional ear of corn. thrave: two stooks of corn, or 24 sheaves, a measure of straw or fodder.

17. I'll get a blessin wi' the lave: cf. 'When thou cuttest down thine harvest in thy field, and hast forgot a sheaf in the field, thou shalt not go again to fetch it: it shall be for the stranger, for the fatherless, and for the widow: that the Lord thy God may bless thee in all the work of thine hands' (Deuteronomy 24:19).

22. foggage: 'rank grass which has not been eaten in summer, or which grows among grain, and is fed on by horses and cattle after the crop is removed' (*Jamieson's Scots Dictionary*).

43–8. Still, thou art blest, compar'd wi' me!: cf. Johnson, *Rasselas*, chapter 2, 'As he passed through the fields, and saw the animals around him, "Ye," said he, "are happy, and need not envy me that walk thus among you, burdened with myself; nor do I, ye gentle beings, envy your felicity, for it is not the felicity of man. I have many distresses from which ye are free; I fear pain when I do not feel it; I sometimes shrink at evils recollected, and sometimes start at evils anticipated: surely the equity of Providence has balanced peculiar sufferings with peculiar enjoyments.'

Epistle to Davie (p. 78). Burns dates the finished poem January 1785, but part of it was drafted the previous year, probably before the idea of its inclusion in a verse epistle had occurred to him. His brother Gilbert commented, 'It was, I think, in the summer of 1784, when in the intervals of harder labour Robert and I were weeding in the garden, that he repeated to me the principal part of the *Epistle*.' By 'the principal part', Gilbert seems to have had in mind 'the poet pointing out the consolations that were in store for him when he should go a-begging', i.e. stanzas 2 to 7 or a sequence within them. The introductory and concluding stanzas, including the tribute to Jean Armour (l. 108ff.), were written later.

A tenant farmer's son, like Burns, David Sillar (1760–1830) was at this time a grocer in Irvine. He was a keen fiddler, as well as a poet; a manuscript of this poem is entitled 'An Epistle to Davy, a brother Poet, Lover, Ploughman and Fiddler'. A point of particular interest in the poem is that ll. 53–4,

> We'll sit and *sowth* a tune;
> Syne *rhyme* till't . . .

were to be fulfilled when Sillar's original tune 'A Rosebud' was used by Burns for his song 'A Rosebud by My Early Walk', first published in volume ii of *The Scots Musical Museum* (1788). Burns wrote a second Epistle to Davie before the Kilmarnock *Poems* were published. Sillar's own *Poems* appeared at Kilmarnock in 1789.

The 14-line stanza Burns uses here had been employed, as he himself noted, in Alexander Montgomerie's poem 'The Cherrie and the Slae', which he knew from Ramsay's anthology, *The Ever Green*. Ramsay himself had handled this complicated verse form in such poems as 'The Poet's Wish: An Ode', and Burns builds on Ramsay's example, seeking to link in fluent unity sestet, quatrain, and 'wheel' (with its demanding internal rhymes in ll. 11 and 13). It is arguable that the form does not allow him to achieve a conversational tone to the same degree as 'Standart Habby'; but any slight air of strain is limited to the 'wheel' at the end of certain stanzas.

1. frae off BEN-LOMOND: The winds blow from the north. Ben Lomond is in the Trossachs, to the north-east of Loch Lomond. It can be seen on the horizon from various points in Ayrshire.

7. blaw in the drift: The sense is that snow is driven by the wind right into the fireside.

25. 'Mair spier na, nor fear na,': From Ramsay's 'The Poet's Wish', ll. 53–6:

> Mair speer na, and fear na,
> But set thy mind to rest,
> Aspire ay still high'r ay,
> And always hope the best.

29. kilns: cf. 'Halloween', l. 96 and note.

54. *sowth* a tune: cf. an entry in the poet's First Commonplace Book: '. . . these old Scottish airs are so nobly sentimental that when one would compose to them; to south the tune, as our Scotch phrase is, over and over, is the readiest way to catch the inspiration'.

56ff. It's no in titles . . . : cf. Fergusson, 'Against Repining at Fortune', l. 41ff:

> 'Tis not in richest mines of Indian gold,
> That man this jewel happiness can find,
> If his unfeeling breast, to *virtue* cold,
> Denies her entrance to his ruthless mind.

> Wealth, pomp and honor are but gaudy toys;
> Alas! how poor the pleasures they impart!
> *Virtue's* the sacred source of all the joys
> That claim a lasting mansion in the heart.

77–80. Alas! how aft . . . : 'Moral indignation has caused Burns to slip unconsciously into the intonation of the Scottish Metrical Psalms' (T. Crawford, *Burns: A Study of the Poems and Songs*, 1960, p. 88).

91, 97. wit: Here 'knowledge, insight, understanding'.

107. MEG: Margaret Orr, a servant at Stair House. According to local tradition, Burns helped to bring the couple together.

108. my darling JEAN: Jean Armour, Burns's future wife.

130–2. Long since . . . for you: cf. Sterne, *A Sentimental Journey:* '. . . illusions, which cheat expectation and sorrow of their weary moments! – long – long since had ye number'd out my days, had I not trod so great a part of them upon this enchanted ground'.

The Lament (p. 83). Written in the spring or summer of 1786 out of Burns's distress over the attitude shown to him by Jean Armour and her parents: the 'friend' of the title is a fiction. The first of a group of poems in the collection all of which reflect in varying degrees either Burns's low spirits specifically at this time ('The Lament', 'Despondency, an Ode', 'To a Mountain-Daisy'), or more generally the melancholy side of his nature expressed for other reasons ('Man Was Made to Mourn', 'Winter, A Dirge', 'A Prayer in the Prospect of Death', 'To Ruin'). Burns chooses English in these poems as the accepted language in which to express moral sentiment. Interestingly, A. L. Taylor has argued that the arrangement of poems in the Kilmarnock edition 'reveals Burns as a creative editor, using his poems to hint at a story as if they were a sequence of sonnets' (*Burns Chronicle*, 3rd series, vol. xii, 1963.) Whatever importance should be attached to alleged cryptic autobiography in the edition as a whole, there can be no doubt that 'The Lament' is a cry from the heart. Burns commented in 1787 in a letter to Dr John Moore: ''Twas a shocking affair, which I cannot yet bear to recollect; and had very nearly given [me] one or two of the principal qualifications for a place among those who have lost the chart and mistake the reckoning of Rationality' (*Letters*, I. 144). What took place was this. Jean Armour's pregnancy became known to her parents in March, causing her father to faint from shock. In April he persuaded the Ayr lawyer Robert Aiken to cut out the names of the couple from a document which Burns had given to Jean promising marriage or stating that it had taken place. The Armours had hopes that a suitor in Paisley more acceptable to themselves than Burns might still marry Jean, despite her pregnancy, and sent her to relatives in that town: this plan came to nothing. Burns meanwhile ran into 'all kinds of dissipation and riot, Mason-meetings, drinking matches, and other mischief, to drive her out of my head, but all in vain'. James Armour applied for a warrant against Burns, and when his *Poems* came out, the poet was virtually in hiding. He escaped any action at law, but, like Jean, was summoned before the Kirk Session, guardians of sexual *mores*. (Twins were born to Jean on 3 September. The next summer she was pregnant by Burns again, and in the spring of 1788 became Mrs Burns.) Burns retained 'The Lament' in unchanged form in later editions of his *Poems*. The metre of this poem is 'ballat royal', rhyming *ababbcbc*, a favourite with medieval Scots poets and with King James VI, who wrote, 'For any heich and grave suiectis . . . use this kynde of verse, callit Ballit Royal.' Burns had come across examples of the form in Ramsay's *Ever Green*.

Epigraph: From John Home, *Douglas: A Tragedy*, 1757 (Home's *Works*, ed. Mackenzie, 1822, i, 307).

  54. Recollection's direful train: cf. Goldsmith, *The Deserted Village*, l. 81, 'Remembrance wakes with all her busy train'.

Despondency (p. 86). Probably written like the preceding poem primarily to express Burns's hurt feelings over the Armour affair (see especially stanza 4). The stanza is that of Alexander Montgomerie's poem 'The Cherrie and the Slae', a combination of sestet, quatrain, and 'wheel'. cf. 'Epistle to Davie', where it is used for a quite different poetic purpose.

  7–10. Dim-backward . . . fear: Burns possibly has in mind *Rasselas*, chapter 2. cf. note on 'To a Mouse', ll. 39–40.

  22. Unfitted with an *aim*: cf. Burns to Moore, 'The great misfortune of my life was, never to have AN AIM' (letter of August 1787).

  31ff. Within his humble cell . . . : 18th-century literature contains many passages praising a retired country life. cf. here Parnell, 'The Hermit', ll. 3–4:

> The moss his bed, the cave his humble cell,
> His food the fruits, his drink the crystal well.

cf. also Fielding, *Tom Jones*, Book viii, chapter 15, 'a curious Discourse between Mr Jones and the Man of the Hill'.

Man Was Made to Mourn (p. 88). Copied into the poet's first Commonplace Book in August 1785. There Burns names as the tune for his 'song' the Irish air 'Peggy Bawn'. A letter to Mrs Dunlop of 16 August 1788 shows how strongly Burns felt on this subject: 'Man is by no means a happy creature. – I do not speak of the Selected Few, favored by partial Heaven . . . I speak of the neglected Many, whose nerves, whose sinews, whose days, whose thoughts . . . are sacrificed and sold to these few bloated Minions of Heaven! – if I thought you had never seen it, I would transcribe you a stanza of an old Scots Ballad called "The life and ages of Man" . . . I had an old Grand uncle, with whom my Mother lived a while in her girlish years . . . long blind ere he died . . . his most voluptuous enjoyment was to sit down and cry, while my Mother would sing the simple old song.' The poet's brother Gilbert comments that, 'Burns could not well conceive a more mortifying picture of human life, than a man seeking work. In casting about in his mind how this sentiment might be brought forward, the elegy *Man was made to Mourn*, was composed.'

Tune, 'Peggy Bawn':

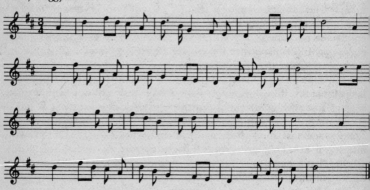

5. I spy'd a man, whose aged step: Like the 'hermit' mentioned in the previous poem, the elderly sage who meets and gives advice to a younger man is a common figure in 18th-century poetry. cf. Coleridge's ancient mariner, and Wordsworth's leech-gatherer.

17. yon moors: The manuscript reading 'Carrick Moors' shows that Burns originally had in mind the estate of the Earl of Cassillis.

34. Manhood's active might: Burns borrows this phrase from Shenstone, *Elegies*, xi, stanza 12.

55. Man's inhumanity to Man: cf. Edward Young, *Night Thoughts*, viii, 104–5, 'Man's . . . endless inhumanities on Man'.

60. To give him leave to toil: De Quincey refers to 'those groans which ascended to heaven from [Burns's] over-burthened heart – those harrowing words, "*To give him leave to toil*", which record almost a reproach to the ordinances of God' (*Collected Writings of Thomas De Quincey*, ed. Masson, Edinburgh, 1899, ii, p. 137).

Winter (p. 91). 'The eldest of my printed pieces' (Burns to Dr Moore, August 1787). In his first Commonplace Book, the title is 'Song – (Tune McPherson's Farewell)', and the entry is dated April 1784. There Burns comments, 'As I am, what the men of the world, if they knew of such a man would call a whimsical Mortal; I have various sources of pleasure & enjoyment which are, in a manner, peculiar to myself; or some here & there such other out-of-the-way person. – Such is the peculiar pleasure I take in the season of Winter, more than the rest of the year – This, I believe, may be partly owing to my misfortunes giving my mind a melancholy cast; but there is something even in the –

> "–Mighty tempest & the hoary waste
>   Abrupt & deep stretch'd o'er the buried earth–"

which raises the mind to a serious sublimity, favorable to every thing great & noble. – There is scarcely any earthly object gives me more – I don't know if I should call it pleasure, but something which exalts me, something which enraptures me – than to walk in the sheltered side of a wood or high plantation, in a cloudy, winter day, and hear a stormy wind howling among the trees & raving o'er the plain. – It is my best season for devotion; – my mind is rapt up in a kind of enthusiasm to Him who, in the pompous language of Scripture, "walks on the winds of the wind". – In one of these seasons, just after a tract of misfortunes, I composed the following SONG – (Tune McPherson's Farewel).' 'Winter' may have been written in 1781–2.

In responding positively to the severe beauty of winter (cf. 'In . . . the hoary majesty of WINTER, the poet feels a charm unknown to the rest of his species', letter to Margaret Kennedy, autumn 1785), Burns is at one with earlier Scottish poets, including James Thomson, whose poem *The Seasons* he knew and admired.

Tune, 'McPherson's Farewell':

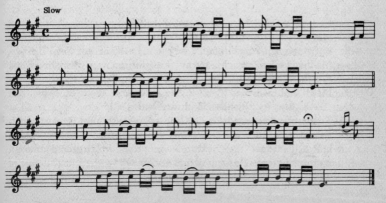

A Prayer, in the Prospect of Death (p. 92). An entry in the first Commonplace Book, dated August 1784, describes this as 'A prayer, when fainting fits, & other alarming symptoms of a Pleurisy or some other dangerous disorder, which indeed still threaten me, first put Nature on the alarm'. The poem may have been written much earlier than August 1784. Burns wrote to his father from Irvine on 27 December 1781, 'The weakness of my nerves has so debilitated my mind that I dare not, either review past events, or look forward into futurity . . . I am quite transported at the thought that ere long, perhaps very soon, I shall bid an eternal adiew to all the pains, & uneasiness & disquietudes of this weary life.' While the poet has in mind Pope's *Universal Prayer*, which is more than once echoed in his poem, his metre is that of the Scottish metrical psalms.

To a Mountain-Daisy (p. 93). Written in April 1786, during Burns's trouble with Jean Armour's family. He wrote to John Kennedy from Mossgiel on 20 April, '. . . I have here, likewise, inclosed a small piece, the very latest of my productions. I am a good deal pleas'd with some sentiments myself, as they are just the native querulous feelings of a heart, which, as the elegantly melting Gray says, "Melancholy has marked for her own".' (Kennedy, 1757–1812, was factor to the Earl of Dumfries, and later to the Earl of Breadalbane; he received copies of several of Burns's poems in manuscript and was active in securing subscriptions for the Kilmarnock edition.) *To a Mountain-Daisy* won the praise of early reviewers, Henry Mackenzie drawing attention to it as an example of 'the tender and the moral'. Recent critics, however, have tended to prefer *To a Mouse* – on which, to some degree, the later poem is modelled – as being stronger in diction and less strained in sentiment than *To a Mountain-Daisy*.

To Ruin (p. 95). Undated, but probably belonging to Burns's unhappy period learning flax-dressing in Irvine in 1781–2. 'My Partner was a scoundrel of the first water who made money by the mystery of thieving . . . I was obliged to give up business; the clouds of misfortune were gathering thick round my father's head, the darkest of which was, he was visibly far gone in a consumption; and to crown all, a belle–fille whom I adored and who had pledged her soul to me in the field of matrimony, jilted me with peculiar circumstances of mortification [cf. ll.9–10]. – The finishing evil that brought up the rear of this infernal file was my hypochondriac complaint being irritated to such a degree, that for three months I was in [a] diseased state of body and mind' (letter to Dr John Moore, August 1787). The stanza is that of 'Epistle to Davie' and of 'Despondency, an Ode'.

Epistle to a Young Friend (p. 96). Dated in the MS at Kilmarnock 15 May 1786. The 'young friend' of the title was Ayr lawyer Robert Aiken's son Andrew, subsequently a merchant in Liverpool and British consul in Riga. (After Burns's death, William Niven of Kirkoswald claimed that the poem was originally addressed to him. He had, however, kept no copy to make good his case.)

The double stanza, with feminine rhyme, was familiar to Burns from the example of Ramsay.

In preparing the poem for publication, Burns reversed the order of stanzas 3 and 4, and omitted a MS stanza after 6:

> If ye hae made a step aside,
> > Some hap-mistake, o'ertaen you;
> Yet, still keep up a decent pride,
> > An' ne'er owre far demean you.
> Time comes wi' kind, oblivious shade,
> > An' daily darker sets it;
> An', if nae mae mistakes are made,
> > The world soon forgets it.

15. views: Plans, purposes.

87–8. may ye better reck the *rede*: cf. *Hamlet*, I, iii,47–51:

> Doe not as some ungracious Pastors doe,
> Shew me the steepe and thorny way to Heaven;
> Whilst like a puft and recklesse Libertine
> Himselfe, the Primrose path of dalliance treads,
> And reaks not his own reade.

On a Scotch Bard Gone to the West Indies (p. 99). Written when Burns had decided to emigrate. His earliest reference to the idea is in a letter of c. 20 April 1786 to John Arnot: 'Already the holy beagles, the houghmagandie pack [fornication pack, i.e. the kirk session], begin to snuff the scent, & I expect every moment to see them cast off, & hear them after me in full cry [because of Jean Armour's pregnancy]: but as I am an old fox, I shall give them dodging and doubling for it; &, by & bye, I intend to earth among the mountains of Jamaica' (*Letters* I. 37). The position Burns had in view was that of book-keeper on a plantation at Port Antonio. By the time of publication of his *Poems*, he had 'orders within three weeks at farthest to repair aboard the Nancy, Captn Smith, from Clyde, to Jamaica, and to call at Antigua' (to John Richmond, 30 July 1786). The date of sailing was put off from week to week, however, and by early October 'the feelings of a father' prevented Burns from emigrating (letter to Robert Aiken, c. 8 October). He did not entirely give up the idea even then, writing to James Smith as late as June 1787 'if I do not fix, I will go for Jamaica'.

Turning on a theme which to most people would not immediately suggest humour, 'On a Scotch Bard Gone to the West Indies' is nevertheless a defiantly playful poem, a fluent and full-blooded exercise in Scots comic elegy. On the stanza, see introductory note on 'Poor Mailie's Elegy', p. 143.

20ff. Hadst thou taen aff some drowsy bummle: Burns boasts about his own sexual prowess ('gleg as onie wumble'), contrasted with 'some drowsy' bungler.

25. KYLE may weepers wear: Burns's native district of Ayrshire. 'Weepers' were thin stripes of linen worn on the cuffs to denote mourning.

33. A Jillet: Jean Armour.

56. Your native soil was right ill-willie: Burns has in mind his own Ayrshire parish, and long experience of uneconomic farms.

A Dedication To G**** H******* Esq (p. 101). In a verse epistle to Hamilton dated 3 May 1786, Burns writes

> The PRAY'R still, you share still,
> Of grateful MINSTREL BURNS.

This reference to what appears here between ll. 90 and 112 of the 'Dedication' shows that at least one part of it, if not the entire poem, was drafted before 3 May. One argument in favour of such a date for the whole poem is that Burns's *Proposals* for publishing his work were in print by 15 April; it is known that Gavin Hamilton was active in distributing copies. It is possible, however, that the 'Dedication' as a whole belongs to May or even June – Burns may have worked his 'prayer' for Hamilton and his family into a new poetic context for the occasion. The poems went to the printer in mid-June. Hans Hecht was probably right to argue that Burns's original intention was to end the Kilmarnock collection with the 'Dedication'; he added a further group of poems on finding that he had not enough copy to make up the book to the length envisaged (Hecht, *Robert Burns*, 1936, p.95).

Gavin Hamilton (1751–1805), who sublet Mossgiel to Burns and his brother Gilbert in 1784, was a 'writer' (solicitor), living in Beechgrove, the so-called 'Castle of Mauchline', next to the village churchyard. He came of an Episcopalian family, and he himself sympathized with the Moderate rather than with the 'Auld Licht', tightly orthodox, wing of the Church of Scotland. These were two of the factors behind a long and bitter wrangle between Mauchline Kirk Session and Hamilton, which resulted in Hamilton's appealing over the heads of the Session to the Presbytery of Ayr and thus being granted by the Session in July 1785 a certificate that he was 'free from public scandal or ground of Church censure' known to them. Burns, who rejoiced in Hamilton's refusal to yield during this affair, wrote one of his most biting satires, 'Holy Willie's Prayer', to mark the discomfiture of Willie Fisher, an elder who had been particularly hostile to Hamilton. (The Session did not give up easily, prosecuting Hamilton for causing his servants to dig new potatoes in his garden on the 'last Lord's day' of July 1787.)

As in 'The Twa Dogs', Burns uses the octosyllabic couplet. His original plan may have been to open and close the collection with poems using this metre.

5. sirnam'd like *His Grace*: When questioned by the Duke of Hamilton about their relationship, Gavin Hamilton's father John is said to have replied that 'it would be needless to seek the root among the branches'.

28. He downa see a poor man want: Burns is at pains to make clear that Hamilton is generous to those in need because Mauchline Kirk Session had accused Hamilton of fraudulently retaining money collected for the parish poor.

42. *Gentoos*: Pagan Hindus, in contrast to Moslems (from Portuguese *gentio*, 'gentile').

43. *Ponotaxi*: Probably Cotopaxi, a volcano in the Andes.

48. This line was dropped from subsequent editions.

67–77. O ye wha leave the springs o' C-lv-n: Hugh Blair advised Burns to omit this paragraph from his 1787 Edinburgh *Poems*: 'The Poem will be much better without it, and it will give offence by the ludicrous views of the punishments of Hell.' Burns did not act on his advice.

77–80. digression . . . Divinity: See introductory note.

97. the CLERK: Hamilton was clerk of local courts.

100. K******'s: Hamilton's wife was Helen Kennedy of Daljarrock.

102. at least a diz'n: Hamilton had in fact two daughters, and two sons.

To a Louse (p. 105). Probably written in late 1785. That year saw several balloon flights over Scotland by the Italian Vincenzo Lunardi, who gave his name to a balloon-shaped bonnet (l. 35): the gently satirical poem is up-to-date in its reference to fashion. In 18th-century Scotland the louse was a common sight. Burns enjoys the idea that this particular louse evidently does not know its place; it is no respecter of Jenny's airs and graces. The success of the poem comes from Burns's mastery of the 'Standart Habby' verse form. He creates, and manages to sustain, a familiar conversational tone, almost a church whisper, by turns 'shocked' and amused, to match the cheeky movement of the louse on the unsuspecting girl's showy bonnet; and incidentally comments on the congregation's response to Jenny:

> Thae *winks* and *finger-ends*, I dread,
>   Are notice takin!

Burns's intimate way of speaking to the louse, as to a naughty child, is reminiscent of the technique used in 'Address to the Deil'.

Epistle to J. L***k** (p. 107). John Lapraik (1727–1807) was a tenant-farmer who had fallen on hard times: in 1785 he was imprisoned for debt in Ayr. While in prison, he wrote poetry for diversion. Following Burns's example, he published *Poems on Several Occasions* at Kilmarnock in 1788. His last years were spent as postmaster and innkeeper in Muirkirk.

Burns's first epistle to Lapraik shows him taking the initiative in contacting a stranger, a fellow-poet of the district, and defining his own characteristic priorities as a writer. The opening describes a 'rocking', a particular kind of social evening when songs and stories were to the fore. Burns responds to the personal (husband to wife) motif in the song by Lapraik which he hears sung. (Years later, he was to send a version of Lapraik's song to James Johnson for inclusion in *The Scots Musical Museum*.) He then goes on to project an image of himself as a spontaneous and instinctive 'rhymer', with no need for academic or critical pretensions ('Gie me ae spark o' Nature's fire . . .', ll. 73–8). His hope is to catch a spark of the inspiration which burns in Allan Ramsay and Fergusson. Reaffirming his wish to meet Lapraik as a friend and 'hae a swap o' *rhyming-ware*', he strongly rejects by contrast the values of people whose efforts are directed towards money-making.

7. a rockin: The Rev. John Sheppard of Muirkirk described a rocking as taking place 'when neighbours visit one another in pairs, or three or more in company, during the moonlight of winter or spring . . . The custom seems to have arisen when spinning on the *rock* or *distaff* was in use, which therefore was carried along with the visitant to a neighbour's house, [and] still prevails, though the *rock* is laid aside' (*Memories of Ayrshire about 1780*, ed. W. Kirk Dickson, Scottish History Society, Miscellany vi, 1939, p. 288).

13. ae *sang*: 'When I upon thy bosom lean', said to have been written when Lapraik's wife had been fretting over their misfortunes. Lapraik included the song in his *Poems on Several Occasions* (Kilmarnock, 1788), and Burns supplied an improved version in Scots for *The Scots Musical Museum* (no. 205, 1780).

21–2. *Pope . . . Steele . . . Beattie*: Here as examples of writers skilled in expressing moral sentiments. Burns was familiar with the poetry of Pope, and with Steele's periodical essays. James Beattie (1735–1803), professor of moral philosophy at Aberdeen, was best known for his blank verse poem, *The Minstrel*, although he also wrote Scots verse.

24. About *Muirkirk*: Lapraik lived at Dalfram, on Ayr Water, about nine miles from Mauchline, and near the village of Muirkirk.

28–30. The version of these lines in the first Commonplace Book reads:
> He was a devil
> But had a frank & friendly heart
> Discreet & civil.

45. *crambo-jingle*: cf. Hamilton of Gilbertfield, Epistle 1 to Allan Ramsay, ll. 49–50:
> At Crambo then we'll rack our Brain,
> Drown ilk dull Care and aiking Pain.

61f. What's a your jargon: cf. Pomfret, *Reason* (1700), ll. 57–8:
> What's all the noisy jargon of the schools
> But idle nonsense of laborious fools . . .

73. Gie me ae Spark: cf. Sterne, *Tristram Shandy*, III, xii, 'Great Apollo! if thou art in a giving humour – give me – I ask no more, but one stroke of native humour, with a single spark of thy own fire along with it.'

79. ALLAN: Allan Ramsay.

80. FERGUSSON: Robert Fergusson. 'Rhyme, except some religious pieces, which are in print, I had given up; but meeting with Fergusson's Scotch Poems, I strung anew my wildly-sounding, rustic lyre with emulating vigour' (letter to John Moore, August 1787).

103. MAUCHLINE Race or MAUCHLINE Fair: In suggesting a convivial meeting between poets, Burns follows the example of Hamilton of Gilbertfield in his first Epistle to Ramsay. Hamilton writes, 'At Edinburgh we'll hae a Bottle of reaming claret' (l.45).

To the Same (p. 111). Burns follows up in his second epistle to Lapraik by condemning mere materialistic or snobbish values and once again asserting the strong claims of poetry and human fellowship:
> The social, friendly, honest man . . .
> 'Tis *he* fulfils *great Nature's plan*,
> And none but *he*.

Two points of particular interest in this poem are the admission – in April 1785, when he was particularly prolific – that his Muse had recently been very busy (ll. 15–16), and the emphasis on writing as a form of improvisation:
> Sae I've begun to scrawl, but whether
> In rhyme, or prose, or baith thegither . . .
> Let time mak proof.

1. new-ca'd kye: Burns is probably recalling a line of Ramsay's, 'And late calf'd Cows stand lowing near their Home' (*Works*, STS, i, 111).
6. kind *letter*: Lapraik's reply, now lost, was in prose, not verse.
8. Rattlin the corn: Burns describes spring sowing.
19. Her dowf excuses pat me mad: c.f. the teasing relationship between poet and Muse in Ramsay's 'Answer II' to Hamilton of Gilbertfield, l. 25ff.
49. She's gien me monie a jirt an' fleg: The image comes from ploughing, as Burns recalls jolting moments in his life, when he has met hidden 'stones'.
69. nae *sheep-shank bane:* The sense is 'no small beer'.
87. The social . . . man: cf. Pope, *Essay on Man*, iv, 341–60:

> God will favour and approve the man
> Who most observes and best pursues his plan:
> His plan, that ev'ry creature, ev'ry soul,
> Should spread the good which he designs the whole;
> To this, that action, passion, reason tend;
> VIRTUE the means, and HAPPINESS the end.

To W. S***** (p.114). William Simson (1758–1815), the son of a farmer at Ochiltree, five miles south of Burns's home at Mossgiel, studied at Glasgow University with a view to entering the ministry, but instead became schoolmaster at Ochiltree. According to tradition, he wrote to Burns to praise 'The Holy Tulzie', a hard-hitting church satire (not included in the Kilmarnock edition). Someone with his knowledge of the Church of Scotland was clearly in a good position to appreciate the postscript to this epistle, with its satire on the current ecclesiastical division between 'Auld Lichts' and 'New Lichts' as 'moonshine matter' (l. 182). Whether or not the postscript was added as an afterthought, Burns follows a sound instinct in keeping it separate from the main part of the poem, in which he expresses friendship and his delight in poetry and in nature, themes belonging to the main tradition of the verse epistle in 18th-century Scotland.

13. in a creel: Confused, in a whirl, lit. in a basket (full of stones). A 'creeling' took place on the second day after a wedding, as a means of showing whether the marriage had been consummated. A basket of stones being placed on the bridegroom's back, 'if he has acted a manly Part, his young Wife with all imaginable Speed cuts the Cords, and relieves him from the Burthen' (Ramsay, *Works*, STS, i, 78).
15. *Allan . . . Gilbertfield*: The Scottish poets Allan Ramsay and William Hamilton of Gilbertfield.
17. the writer-chiel: Robert Fergusson had worked as a copyist in the

Commissary Office in Edinburgh, for which he was paid a penny a page.

31. COILA: The Muse of Kyle, Burns's district of Ayrshire. cf. 'The Vision'.

40. *New Holland*: Australia. The Dutch had discovered the western coasts of the southern continent on their voyages round the Cape of Good Hope to the East Indies.

42. *Magellan*: In 1520 Ferdinand Magellan discovered the strait between South America and Tierra del Fuego.

44f. *Forth an' Tay*: cf. a passage in Burns's First Commonplace Book: 'we have never had one Scotch Poet of any eminence, to make the fertile banks of Irvine, the romantic woodlands & sequestered scenes on Aire, and the heathy, mountainous source, & winding sweep of Doon emulate Tay, Forth, Ettrick, Tweed &c this is a complaint I would gladly remedy'. In his poem 'Hame Content', ll. 75–82, Fergusson asks if the Arno and

> Tiber are 'mair sweet and gay
> Than Fortha's haughs or banks o' Tay'.

61. At WALLACE' name: William Wallace, Scottish patriot, executed by Edward I of England in 1305. Burns wrote to Moore, 'The two first books I ever read in private, and which gave me more pleasure than any two books I ever read again, were the life of Hannibal and the history of Sir William Wallace ... The story of Wallace poured a Scotish prejudice in my veins which will boil along there till the flood-gates of life shut in eternal rest' (August 1787, *Letters* I. 136).

73f. Ev'n winter bleak has charms ... cf. 'Winter, A Dirge' and introductory note; and Thomson, 'Autumn', ll. 1302–30:

> To Nature's voice attends from month to month,
> And day to day, through the revolving year –
> Admiring, sees her in her every shape; ...
> Even Winter wild to him is full of bliss.

88. An' no think lang: cf. Alexander Ross, 'The Fortunate Shepherd', ll. 731–2:

> While Henny's ay the burthen o' his sang,
> And ever keeps his mind frae thinking lang.

92. Hog-shouther: 'a kind of horse play by justling with the shoulder; to justle' (B).

103. While Highlandmen hate tolls an' taxes: One legacy of Culloden was that Hanoverian rule was resented. Despite problems of communication, Highlanders preferred the old drove roads of Scotland to expensive turnpike trusts.

104. braxies: Sheep that have died of 'the braxy', an internal infection.

Burns refers to a common belief among shepherds that eating braxy was not a health risk.

112. this *new-light*: William Taylor of Norwich argued in *The Scripture Doctrine of Original Sin proposed to free and candid Examination* (1740) that in interpreting scripture 'we ought not to admit anything contradictory to the common sense and understanding of mankind'. His book was widely accepted as summing up the 'New Light Rationalism'.

119. in plain, braid lallans: Burns's contemporary Henry Mackenzie noted that 'though our books be written in *English*, our conversation is in *Scotch* . . . we have a suit for holidays and another for working-days' (*The Mirror*, no. 83, 22 February 1780).

152. bure sic hands: Fought with such vigour.

170. things they ca' *balloons*: Balloon flights were making news in 1785. cf. 'To a Louse', introductory note.

Epistle to J. R****** (p. 120). Written probably late in 1784. The poem was occasioned by the pregnancy of Burns's serving-girl at Lochlea, Elizabeth Paton, who bore him a daughter on 22 May 1785. Burns recounts the episode in sporting metaphors, from love-making to the predictable reaction of the parish elders to an unmarried girl's pregnancy. This masculine humour no doubt appealed strongly to John Rankine (d.1810), a tenant farmer in Adamhill, Tarbolton, one of Burns's 'ramstam' cronies of the Lochlea years. Hugh Blair, Edinburgh professor and critic, was shocked by the poem, however. He advised against keeping it in the 1787 edition in these terms: 'The description of shooting the hen is understood, I find, to convey an indecent meaning, tho' in reading the poem . . . I took it literally, and the indecency did not strike me. But . . . the whole poem ought undoubtedly to be left out of the new edition.' Burns did not act on his advice, and the epistle remained in all editions of his poems published in his lifetime.

4. *dreams*: Burns's early 19th-century editor Allan Cunningham supplies details: 'Lord K— [who] was in the practice of calling all his familiar acquaintances . . . "damned brutes" was rebuked by Rankine, who said, 'I dreamed I was dead, and that for keeping other than good company on earth I was damned. When I knocked at hell-door . . . quoth Satan, "ye canna be here; ye're ane of Lord K—'s damned brutes – hell's fou o' them already!"'

5. Korah-like, a sinkin: Korah and his people did not 'die the common death of all men'. 'The earth opened her mouth, and swallowed them up, and their houses, and . . . all their goods' (Numbers 16:29–33).

20. *Blue-gown* badge: Like the badge and clothing of the King's bedesmen, licensed beggars in Scotland since the Middle Ages.
36. *Bunker's hill:* Sir William Howe gained a British victory at Bunker Hill in the American War of Independence.
47. *Poacher-Court:* The Kirk Session had power to require sexual transgressors to pay fines and to sit on the 'stool of repentance' before the congregation.
65. *buckskin* kye: American plantation slaves. 'Buckskin' was a nickname applied to American troops during the War of Independence. cf. Burns to Dr Moore, letter of August 1787, 'I resolved to publish my Poems . . . 'twas a delicious idea that I should be called a clever fellow, even tho' it should never reach my ears a poor Negrodriver.' (*Letters* I. 144).
75. *pennyworths* again is fair: Value for money.

Song, It was upon a Lammas night (p. 123). Burns stated that this song was written before his twenty-third year: the actual time of composition is unrecorded. He was to note many years after 1786, 'All the old words that ever I could meet to this [air] were the following, which seem to have been an old chorus:-

> O corn rigs and rye rigs,
>   O corn rigs are bonie,
> And when'er you meet a bonnie lass,
>   Preen up her cockernony.

He also knew Ramsay's song 'My Patie Is a Lover Gay' from *The Gentle Shepherd*, which ends

> Then I'll comply and marry Pate,
>   And syne my cockernony
> He's free to touzle air and late
>   Where corn rigs are bony.

In performance, this is one of Burns's most successful love-songs, proving that he was able even at this early date to match his words to the spirit of a traditional tune. In comparison with Ramsay's song, 'It was upon a Lammas night' is thoroughly personal. Whereas Ramsay offers a conventional example of pastoral verse love-description, tinged with genteel eroticism, Burns writes in the first person and achieves a note of delight in remembered passion. The identity of Annie is not known, although the youngest daughter of John Rankine (see previous poem and introductory note) later claimed the honour. The tune probably originated in Scotland, although its 17th-century printings are English.

Tune, 'Corn rigs are bonie':

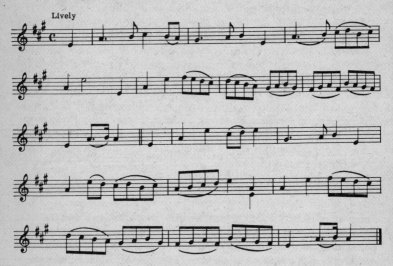

1. Lammas: 1 August, harvest festival when new bread was consecrated. Here the sense is 'late summer', or more specifically 'harvest night in August'.
2. rigs: Broad arable ridges which sloped towards ditches.
5. head: Burns changed this word to 'heed' in the 1793 edition. The phrase 'tentless heed' occurs in 'To J. S****', l. 55.

Song, 'Now westlin winds' (p. 124). Written in 1775 at the time of Burns's infatuation with Peggy Thomson of Kirkoswald. 'I spent my seventeenth summer,' he wrote in his autobiographical letter to Dr Moore in August 1787, 'on a smuggling [coast] a good distance from home at a noted school, to learn Mensuration, Surveying, Dialling, &c . . . I went on with a high hand in my Geometry; till the sun entered Virgo, a month which is always a carnival in my bosom, a charming Fillette who lived next door to the school overset my Trigonomertry, and set me off in a tangent from the sphere of my studies.' Later, he tried out a modification of this early song in honour of Jean Armour; no known copy survives. Going back to the same song, Burns then sent a version which has a number of Scots words in place of the original English diction to be printed in *The Scots Musical Museum* (vol. iv, 1792, no. 351). Unusually for a love-song, 'Now westlin winds' includes four lines of protest against the 'slaught'ring guns' of sportsmen (ll. 21–4).

Tune, 'I had a horse, I had nae mair':

Very slow

Song, 'From thee, Eliza' (p. 126). The first stanza suggests a date of composition shortly before the Kilmarnock *Poems* were published, and the position of the song in the collection immediately before 'The Farewell' also seems to point to the summer of 1786. If so, possibly 'Eliza' is Elizabeth Miller of Mauchline: in a letter to Smith dated 11 June 1787, Burns refers to 'my quondam Eliza'. However, any such identification is speculative, and it must be remembered that elsewhere Burns refers to this song as having been written before his twenty-third year (letter to Moore, August 1787). (It may be that the song existed in an early form before Burns wrote this version with its opening lines about having to leave his 'native shore'.)

Tune, 'Gilderoy':

Slow

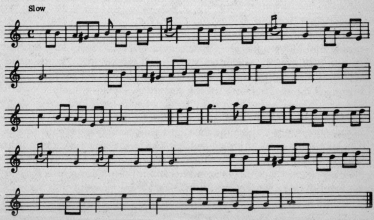

The Farewell (p. 126). Written in the early summer of 1786, possibly for a Masonic meeting on 24 June of St James's Lodge, Tarbolton, of which Burns had been depute master since July 1784. The song makes use throughout of the special language and terms of freemasonry, to which Burns was first introduced in 1781. (See William Harvey, 'Robert Burns as a Freemason', in *Robert Burns: Complete Works and Letters* (Masonic Edition), Glasgow [1928], v–xxxiv.) The tune to which 'The Farewell' is set was that of the then traditional Scottish parting-song (eventually to be replaced in public favour by Burns's highly popular song to the tune 'Auld Lang Syne'). Burns asked James Johnson to print 'The Farewell', with the accompanying air, as the final song in *The Scots Musical Museum*, and Johnson complied with his request (*SMM*, vol. vi, 1803, no. 600).

Tune, 'Goodnight and joy be wi' you a' ':

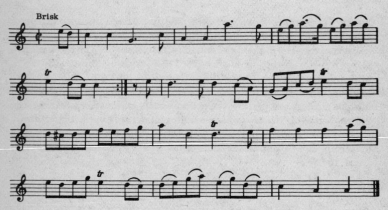

25. And YOU, farewell!: The master of the Lodge was Captain James Montgomerie, a younger brother of Colonel Hugh Montgomerie, afterwards Earl of Eglinton.

EPIGRAMS AND EPITAPHS (pp. 128–31).
Burns was a ready wit, with the ability to rhyme quickly and spontaneously. The brief selection of epigrams and epitaphs in the Kilmarnock edition is likely to have been included mainly to add to the length of the volume, although the poet must have felt more positively than this suggests about at least one epitaph, that 'For the Author's Father'.

Epitaph on a Henpecked Country Squire. A note in Burns's hand in a copy of the Kilmarnock *Poems* shows that 'Epitaph on a Henpecked Country Squire' and the two epigrams which follow it were written about Mr and Mrs William Campbell of Netherplace, a mansion near Mauchline. William Campbell died in 1786. The local talk was obviously unflattering to Campbell's widow, identified as Queen N[etherplace] in 'Another', l. 5.

On a Celebrated Ruling Elder. Dated April 1784 in the First Commonplace Book, where the subject is identified as 'Wm Hood, senr. in Tarbolton'.

On a Noisy Polemic. About James Humphrey, a mason in Mauchline. Burns uses 'polemic' in the sense 'argumentative person'. At this time 'bitch' (l. 3) was a term of contempt applied to either a man or a woman.

On Wee Johnie. Possibly about John Wilson, Tarbolton schoolmaster and apothecary, the object of Burns's satire in 'Death and Doctor Hornbook'; based on an English translation of a Latin epigram printed in *Nugae Venales*, 1663.

For the Author's Father. William Burnes died at Lochlea on 13 February 1784. This 'Epitaph on My Ever Honoured Father' is entered in the First Commonplace Book under April 1784. It is also engraved on the tombstone in Alloway Churchyard.

      8. 'For ev'n his failings lean'd to Virtue's side': The *Deserted Village*, l. 164.

For R. A. Esq. For Burns's 'lov'd . . . friend' Robert Aiken (see 'The Cotter's Saturday Night', l. 1, and note).

For G. H. Esq. For Gavin Hamilton. cf. 'A Dedication to G. H. Esq', and introductory note.

A Bard's Epitaph. Possibly written not long after the 'Epistle to a Young Friend', which is dated 15 May 1786. Burns describes himself as a man 'whose judgement clear, Can others teach the course to steer' (ll. 13–14).

He wrote several poems in a wry confessional vein, showing self-knowledge and also the ability to laugh at himself. A well known example is the 'Elegy on the Death of Robert Ruisseaux', with its revealing final stanza:

> Tho' he was bred to kintra wark,
> And counted was baith wight and stark,
> Yet that was never Robin's mark,
>   To mak a man;
> But tell him, he was learn'd and clark,
>   Ye roos'd him then!

Though sombre in comparison, 'A Bard's Epitaph' is in its own way no less characteristic, recalling in its concluding lines the practical advice offered in the 'Epistle to a Young Friend'.

Appendix A

Burns's Preface and Glossary
in *Poems, Chiefly in the Scottish Dialect*
(Kilmarnock, 1786)

PREFACE

The following trifles are not the production of the Poet, who, with all the advantages of learned art, and perhaps amid the elegancies and idlenesses of upper life, looks down for a rural theme, with an eye to Theocrites or Virgil. To the Author of this, these and other celebrated names their countrymen are, in their original languages, 'A fountain shut up, and a 'book sealed'. Unacquainted with the necessary requisites for commencing Poet by rule, he sings the sentiments and manners, he felt and saw in himself and his rustic compeers around him, in his and their native language. Though a Rhymer from his earliest years, at least from the earliest impulses of the softer passions, it was not till very lately, that the applause, perhaps the partiality, of Friendship, wakened his vanity so far as to make him think any thing of his was worth showing; and none of the following works were ever composed with a view to the press. To amuse himself with the little creations of his own fancy, amid the toil and fatigues of a labouring life; to transcribe the various feelings, the loves, the griefs, the hopes, the fears, in his own breast; to find some kind of counterpoise to the struggles of a world, always an alien scene, a task uncouth to the poetical mind; these were his motives for courting the Muses, and in these he found Poetry to be its own reward.

Now that he appears in the public character of an Author, he does it with fear and trembling. So dear is fame to the rhyming tribe, that even he, an obscure, nameless Bard, shrinks aghast, at the thought of being branded as 'An impertinent blockhead, obtruding his nonsense on the world; and because he can make a shift to jingle a few doggerel, Scotch rhymes together, looks upon himself as a Poet of no small consequence forsooth'.

It is an observation of that celebrated Poet,* whose divine Elegies do honor to our language, our nation, and our species, that 'Humility has depressed many a genius to a hermit, but never raised one to fame.' If any Critic catches at the word *genius*, the Author tells him, once for all, that he certainly looks upon himself as possest of some poetic abilities, otherwise his publishing in the manner he has done, would be a manoeuvre below the worst character,

---

* Shenstone

which, he hopes, his worst enemy will ever give him: but to the genius of a Ramsay, or the glorious dawnings of the poor, unfortunate Ferguson, he, with equal uaffected sincerity, declares, that, even in his highest pulse of vanity, he has not the most distant pretensions. These two justly admired Scotch Poets he has often had in his eye in the following pieces; but rather with a view to kindle at their flame, than for servile imitation.

To his Subscribers, the Author returns his most sincere thanks. Not the mercenary bow over a counter, but the heart-throbbing gratitude of the Bard, conscious how much he is indebted to Benevolence and Friendship, for gratifying him, if he deserves it, in that dearest wish of every poetic bosom – to be distinguished. He begs his readers, particularly the Learned and the Polite, who may honor him with a perusal, that they will make every allowance for Education and Circumstances of Life: but, if after a fair, candid, and impartial criticism, he shall stand convicted of Dulness and Nonsense, let him be done by, as he would in that case do by others – let him be condemned, without mercy, to contempt and oblivion.

GLOSSARY

Words that are universally known, and those that differ from the English only by the elision of letters by apostrophes, or by varying the termination of the verb, are not inserted. The terminations may be thus known; the participle present, instead of *ing*, ends, in the Scotch Dialect, in *an* or *in*; in *an*, particularly, when the verb is composed of the participle present, and any of the tenses of the auxiliary, to be. The past time and participle past are usually made by shortening the *ed* into *'t*.

A
ABACK, behind, away
Abiegh, at a distance
Ae, one
Agley, wide of the aim
Aiver, an old horse
Aizle, a red ember
Ane, one, an
Ase, ashes
Ava, at all, of all
Awn, the beard of oats, &c.

B

BAIRAN, baring
Banie, bony
Baws'nt, having a white stripe down the face
Ben, *but and ben*, the country kitchen and parlour
Bellys, bellows
Bee, *to let bee*, to leave in quiet
Biggin, a building
Bield, shelter
Blastet, worthless
Blather, the bladder
Blink, a glance, an amorous leer, a short space of time
Blype, a shred of cloth, &c.
Boost, behoved
Brash, a sudden illness
Brat, a worn shred of Cloth
Brainge, to draw unsteadily
Braxie, a morkin sheep
Brogue, an affront
Breef, an invulnerable charm
Breastet, sprung forward
Burnewin, *q.d.* burn the wind, a Blacksmith

C

CA', to call, to drive
Caup, a small, wooden dish with two lugs, or handles
Cape stane, cope stone
Cairds, tinkers
Cairn, a loose heap of stones
Chuffie, fat-faced
Collie, a general and sometimes a particular name for country curs
Cog, or coggie, a small wooden dish without handles
Cootie, a pretty large wooden dish
Crack, conversation, to converse
Crank, a harsh, grating sound
Crankous, fretting, peevish
Croon, a hollow, continued moan
Crowl, to creep
Crouchie, crook-backed
Cranreuch, the hoar frost
Curpan, the crupper
Cummock, a short staff

D

DAUD, the noise of one falling flat, a large piece of bread, &c.
Daut, to caress, to fondle
Daimen, now and then, seldom
Daurk, a day's labour
Deleeret, delirious
Dead-sweer, very loath, averse
Dowie, crazy and dull
Donsie, unlucky, dangerous
Doylte, stupified, hebetated
Dow, am able
Dought, was able
Doyte, to go drunkenly or stupidly
Drummock, meal and water mixed raw
Drunt, pet, pettish humour
Dush, to push as a bull, ram, &c.
Duds, rags of clothes

E

EERIE, frighted; particularly the dread of spirits
Eldritch, fearful, horrid, ghastly
Eild, old age
Eydent, constant, busy

F

FA', fall, lot
Fawsont, decent, orderly
Faem, foam
Fatt'rels, ribband ends, &c.
Ferlie, a wonder, to wonder; also a term of contempt
Fecht, to fight
Fetch, to stop suddenly in the draught, and then come on too hastily
Fier, sound, healthy
Fittie lan', the near horse of the hindmost pair in the plough
Flunkies, livery servants
Fley, to frighten
Fleesh, fleece
Flisk, to fret at the yoke
Flichter, to flutter
Forbears, ancestors
Forby, besides

Forjesket, jaded
Fow, full, drunk; a bushel, &c.
Freath, froath
Fuff, to blow intermittedly
Fyle, to dirty, to soil

G

GASH, wise, sagacious, talkative; to converse
Gate, or gaet, way, manner, practice
Gab, the mouth; to speak boldly
Gawsie, jolly, large
Geck, to toss the head in pride or wantonness
Gizz, a wig
Gilpey, a young girl
Glaizie, smooth, glittering
Glunch, a frown; to frown
Glint, to peep
Grushie, of thick, stout growth
Gruntle, the visage; a grunting noise
Grousome, loathsomely grim

H

HAL, or hald, hold, hiding place
Hash, a term of contempt
Haverel, a quarter-wit
Haurl, to drag, to peel
Hain, to save, to spare
Heugh, a crag, a coal-pit
Hecht, to forebode
Histie, dry, chapt, barren
Howe, hollow
Hoste or Hoast, to cough
Howk, to dig
Hoddan, the motion of a sage country farmer on an old cart horse
Houghmagandie, a species of gender composed of the masculine and
    feminine united
Hoy, to urge incessantly
Hoyte, a motion between a trot and a gallop
Hogshouther, to justle with the shoulder

I

ICKER, an ear of corn
Ier-oe, a great grand child
Ingine, genius
Ill-willie, malicious, unkind

J

JAUK, to dally at work
Jouk, to stoop
Jocteleg, a kind of knife
Jundie, to justle

K

KAE, a daw
Ket, a hairy, ragged fleece of wool
Kiutle, to cuddle, to caress, to fondle
Kiaugh, carking anxiety
Kirsen, to christen

L

LAGGEN, the angle at the bottom of a wooden dish
Laithfu', bashful
Leeze me, a term of congratulatory endearment
Leal, loyal, true
Loot, did let
Lowe, flame; to flame
Lunt, smoke; to smoke
Limmer, a woman of easy virtue
Link, to trip along
Lyart, grey
Luggie, a small, wooden dish with one handle

M

MANTEELE, a mantle
Melvie, to soil with meal
Mense, good breeding
Mell, to meddle with
Modewurk, a mole
Moop, to nibble as a sheep
Muslin kail, broth made up simply of water, barley and greens

N
NOWTE, black cattle
Nieve, the fist

O
OWRE, over
Outler, lying in the fields, not housed at night

P
PACK, intimate, familiar
Pang, to cram
Painch, the paunch
Paughty, proud, saucy
Pattle or pettle, the plough-staff
Peghan, the crop of fowls, the stomach
Penny-wheep, small beer
Pine, pain, care
Pirratch, or porritch, pottage
Pliskie, trick
Primsie, affectedly nice
Prief, proof

Q
QUAT, quit, did quit
Quaikin, quaking

R
RAMFEEZL'D, overspent
Raep or rape, a rope
Raucle, stout, clever
Raible, to repeat by rote
Ram-stam, thoughtless
Raught, did reach
Reestet, shrivelled
Reest, to be restive
Reck, to take heed
Rede, counsel, to counsel
Ripp, a handful of unthreshed corn, &c.
Rief, reaving
Risk, to make a noise like the breaking of small roots with the plough
Rowt, to bellow

Roupet, hoarse
Runkle, a wrinkle
Rockin, a meeting on a winter evening

S

SAIR, sore
Saunt, a saint
Scrimp, scant; to stint
Scriegh, to cry shrilly
Scrieve, to run smoothly and swiftly
Screed, to tear
Scawl, a Scold
Sconner, to loath
Sheen, bright
Shaw, a little wood; to show
Shaver, a humorous mischievous wag
Skirl, a shrill cry
Sklent, to slant, to fib
Skiegh, mettlesome, fiery, proud
Slype, to fall over like a wet furrow
Smeddum, powder of any kind
Smytrie, a numerous collection of small individuals
Snick-drawing, trick-contriving
Snash, abusive language
Sowther, to cement, to solder
Splore, a ramble
Spunkie, fiery; will o' wisp
Spairge, to spurt about like water or mire, to soil
Sprittie, rushy
Squatter, to flutter in water
Staggie, diminutive of Stag
Steeve, firm
Stank, a pool of standing water
Stroan, to pour out like a spout
Stegh, to cram the belly
Stibble-rig, the reaper who takes the lead
Sten, to rear as a horse
Swith, get away
Syne, since, ago, then

T

TAPETLESS, unthinking
Tawie, that handles quietly
Tawted, or tawtet, matted together
Taet, a small quantity
Tarrow, to murmur at one's allowance
Thowless, slack, pithless
Thack an' raep, all kinds of necessaries, particularly clothes
Thowe, thaw
Tirl, to knock gently, to uncover
Toyte, to walk like old age
Trashtrie, trash

W

WAUKET, thickened as fullers do cloth
Water-kelpies, a sort of mischievous spirits that are said to haunt fords, & c.
Water-brose, brose made simply of meal and water
Wauble, to swing
Wair, to lay out, to spend
Whaizle, to wheez
Whisk, to sweep
Wintle, a wavering, swinging motion
Wiel, a small whirlpool
Winze, an oath
Wonner, wonder, a term of contempt
Wooer-bab, the garter knotted below the knee with a couple of loops and ends
Wrack, to vex, to trouble

Y

YELL, dry, spoken of a cow
Ye, is frequently used for the singular
Young-guidman, a new married man.

Appendix B

A TITLE CHANGES HANDS

Poems, Chiefly in the Scottish Dialect was to remain the title of every edition of Burns's poetry with which he had any direct connection. Significantly, he kept as the basis of the 1787 Edinburgh collection all of the poems published at Kilmarnock (only epitaphs were excluded). The 1787 volume contained in addition a group of previously unpublished poems and songs, including:

> Death and Doctor Hornbook
> The Brigs of Ayr
> The Ordination
> The Calf
> Address to the Unco Guid
> Tam Samson's Elegy
> To a Haggis
> Address to Edinburgh
> John Barleycorn
> Behind yon hills where Stinchar flows
> Green Grow the Rashes
> The gloomy night is gath'ring fast.

Whereas Burns had retained complete authorial control over his first book, he sold the copyright of the Edinburgh edition – published like its predecessor by subscription, with the poet assuming financial responsibility – to William Creech, an Edinburgh bookseller-publisher. This put Creech in a position to issue new editions for his own profit. Accordingly, in 1793 an edition in two volumes appeared under the joint imprint of William Creech and Thomas Cadell (who as Creech's London agent had handled a London edition of the 1787 *Poems*). Its principal new poem was 'Tam o' Shanter'. This edition was reissued in 1794.

Appendix C

A FINDING-LIST OF POETIC MANUSCRIPTS

Listed below are the locations of the principal recorded manuscripts of individual poems included in the Kilmarnock edition in 1786. It will be noted that two or more separate manuscripts exist for a number of poems, while other poems are known only through print. On the important manuscript collections at Irvine and Kilmarnock, see above, p. xxxii (Note on the Text). In The Centenary Edition of Burns, 1896, Henley and Henderson refer in addition to manuscripts of 'To a Mouse' and 'Epistle to Davie'; the present whereabouts of these are not known. The Huntington Library, San Marino, California, has a copy of the 1793 edition of Burns's *Poems* with certain minor holograph corrections. The First Commonplace Book and Adam MS are privately owned.

The Twa Dogs Irvine Burns Club; Kilmarnock Monument Museum.
Scotch Drink Irvine; Kilmarnock.
The Author's Earnest Cry and Prayer Irvine; Kilmarnock.
The Holy Fair Irvine; Kilmarnock; British Library, Egerton MS 1656.
Address to the Deil Irvine; Kilmarnock.
The Death and Dying Words of Poor Mailie Kilmarnock; First Commonplace Book.
Poor Mailie's Elegy Kilmarnock.
To J. S**** Kilmarnock.
A Dream
The Vision Burns Cottage Museum, Alloway, Stair MS.
Halloween Burns Cottage Museum, Alloway; Kilmarnock.
The Auld Farmer's New-Year-Morning Salutation Kilmarnock.
The Cotter's Saturday Night Irvine; Kilmarnock; British Library, Egerton MS 1656.
To a Mouse
Epistle to Davie Kilmarnock; Adam MS.
The Lament
Despondency

Man Was Made to Mourn Kilmarnock; First Commonplace Book.

Winter Kilmarnock; First Commonplace Book.

A Prayer in the Prospect of Death First Commonplace Book.

To a Mountain-Daisy [See note in Kinsley, p. 1173].

To Ruin

Epistle to a Young Friend Kilmarnock; Edinburgh University Library Laing MS.

On a Scotch Bard Gone to the West Indies Adam MS; Huntington Library, San Marino, California.

A Dedication to G. H. Esq

To a Louse Bodleian Library, Oxford, MS Add. A. 111.

Epistle to J. L***k** First Commonplace Book.

To the same First Commonplace Book.

To W. S***n**

To J. R****

Song, 'It was upon a Lammas night'

Song, 'Now westlin winds' First Commonplace Book; British Library, Hastie MS.

Song, 'From thee, Eliza, I must go'

The Farewell

A Bard's Epitaph

Appendix D

THE KILMARNOCK EDITION: A NOTE ON SECONDHAND PRICES

The centenary of Burns's birth is usually seen as the point at which copies of his first published collection began to be sought after. Enterprising individuals had anticipated this market interest; one case is recorded of someone buying a copy from an Edinburgh bookseller in the early 1850s for a shilling. By the beginning of the twentieth century, Burns had a well established saleroom reputation. Naturally, a book limited to just over 600 copies, published not in London or New York, but in a Scottish country town, has often been described as 'rare', and *Poems, Chiefly in the Scottish Dialect* (1786) has consistently been much sought after by collectors. In mint condition, with the full original margins, it *is* a scarce book, but J. C. Ewing accurately noted in the *Burns Chronicle* in 1930, 'The first edition of the *Poems* has never been "rare", though booksellers and auctioneers have long declared it to be . . .' He quotes £2,450 from a sale at Sotheby's in 1929 as 'doubtless the highest price' paid by that date. *Book Auction Records* supply recent figures broadly in keeping with this. In 1974, a copy of the book was sold by Sotheby (New York) for $9,000. Christie auctioned a Kilmarnock edition, also in New York, for $8,000 in 1981. Maggs auctioned a copy in London for £3,800 in 1979. Outside the auction room, however, copies have been known to change hands for higher prices than these.

INDEX OF FIRST LINES